Manchester Medieval Sources Series

series advisers Rosemary Horrox and

CW00548805

This series aims to meet a growing need ⸱
history for translations of key sources that are directly usable in students own work.
It provides texts central to medieval studies courses and focuses upon the diverse
cultural and social as well as political conditions that affected the functioning of all
levels of medieval society. The basic premise of the series is that translations must be
accompanied by sufficient introductory and explanatory material, and each volume,
therefore, includes a comprehensive guide to the sources' interpretation, including
discussion of critical linguistic problems and an assessment of the most recent research
on the topics being covered.

JOAN OF ARC

MedievalSources*online*

Complementing the printed editions of the Medieval Sources series, Manchester University Press has developed a web-based learning resource which is now available on a yearly subscription basis.

Medieval Sources*online* brings quality history source material to the desktops of students and teachers and allows them open and unrestricted access throughout the entire college or university campus. Designed to be fully integrated with academic courses, this is a one-stop answer for many medieval history students, academics and researchers keeping thousands of pages of source material 'in print' over the Internet for research and teaching.

titles available now at Medieval Sources*online include*

John Edwards *The Jews in Western Europe, 1400–1600*

Paul Fouracre and Richard A. Gerberding *Late Merovingian France: History and hagiography 640–720*

Chris Given-Wilson *Chronicles of the Revolution 1397–1400: The reign of Richard II*

P. J. P. Goldberg *Women in England, c. 1275–1525*

Janet Hamilton and Bernard Hamilton *Christian dualist heresies in the Byzantine world c. 650–c. 1450*

Rosemary Horrox *The Black Death*

Graham A. Loud and Thomas Wiedemann *The history of the tyrants of Sicily by 'Hugo Falcandus', 1153–69*

Janet L. Nelson *The Annals of St-Bertin: Ninth-century histories, volume I*

Timothy Reuter *The Annals of Fulda: Ninth-century histories, volume II*

R. N. Swanson *Catholic England: Faith, religion and observance before the Reformation*

Jennifer Ward *Women of the English nobility and gentry, 1066–1500*

Visit the site at *www.medievalsources.co.uk* for further information and subscription prices.

JOAN OF ARC
La Pucelle

selected sources translated and annotated
by Craig Taylor

Manchester University Press
Manchester and New York

distributed exclusively in the USA by Palgrave

Published by Manchester University Press
Oxford Road, Manchester M13 9NR, UK
and Room 400, 175 Fifth Avenue, New York, NY 10010, USA
www.manchesteruniversitypress.co.uk

Distributed exclusively in the USA by
Palgrave, 175 Fifth Avenue, New York, NY 10010, USA

Distributed exclusively in Canada by
UBC Press, University of British Columbia, 2029 West Mall,
Vancouver, BC, Canada V6T 1Z2

British Library Cataloguing-in-Publication Data
A catalogue record for this book is available from the British Library

Library of Congress Cataloging-in-Publication Data applied for

ISBN 0 7190 6846 0 *hardback*
EAN 978 0 7190 6846 1

ISBN 0 7190 6847 9 *paperback*
EAN 978 0 7190 6847 8

First published 2006

15 14 13 12 11   10 9 8 7 6 5 4 3

Typeset in Monotype Bell
by Koinonia Ltd, Manchester
Printed in Great Britain
by Bell & Bain Ltd, Glasgow

CONTENTS

II: The trial of condemnation (February–May 1431)   137

III: Debating Joan of Arc (1431–1455)   225

PREFACE

This book emerged from conversations that took place with my colleagues at York regarding a document-based course ('Special Subject') in late medieval French history. My original intention was to develop a course that would examine either Valois royal ideology or French chivalry, my major research interests. But I had always enjoyed teaching Joan of Arc and realised how exciting it would be to enable students to explore a subject that touched upon all of the major themes of medieval history, from politics and warfare to religion, social history and gender. There would certainly be no shortage of sources, given that Joan of Arc is one of the best-documented figures of the middle ages. Such a course would explore the usual range of legal and administrative records of the period, together with Valois, Burgundian and English chronicles and writings which provide insight into both her life and contemporary reactions to her. The centrepiece would be the extraordinary testimony that she gave during the trial which condemned her to death at Rouen in 1431 and the statements provided two decades later by her friends and acquaintances during the Nullification trial that overturned the original verdict against her.

The problem was that this rich tapestry of primary sources remains largely inaccessible to modern audiences. Few of the texts had been translated properly into English and therefore my only choice was to do the work myself. Aided by a generous allocation of research leave from my department, extended by a grant from the Arts and Humanities Research Board, I set to the task. I quickly realised that the relevant sources are scattered across countless printed editions published in Europe and North America. The easy option would have been to rely upon the remarkable five-volume collection prepared by Jules Quicherat in the middle of the ninteenth century, but this is far from complete and has been overtaken by better editions, not least the new trial records prepared for the Société de l'Histoire de France by Pierre Tisset and Pierre Duparc.[1] I therefore identified the best editions for all of the sources, in the process recovering a number of documents that have fallen out of usage during the twentieth century and adding a few additional sources to the corpus. With the assistance of the Inter-Library Loan staff at my own university, together with trips to libraries in Paris, London, Oxford and Leeds, I slowly located a vast quantity of material, enough for four volumes the size of this book. Inevitably, therefore, I have had to omit material that merited a place in this book if there had been sufficient space.

---

1 P. Tisset and Y. Lanhers (eds), *Procès de condamnation de Jeanne d'Arc*, 3 vols, Paris, 1960-71, and P. Duparc (ed.), *Procès en nullité de la condamnation de Jeanne d'Arc*, 5 vols, Paris 1977–89.

Around one hundred and sixty witness statements were presented before the Nullification trial, but much of this material is repetitive and so I have made severe cuts, not least the testimony in 1450 and 1452. I have also left out the Seventy Articles, the first set of charges presented against Joan during the Rouen trial. This is an extremely valuable source, demonstrating the full range of attacks mounted upon Joan before the charges were whittled down to the final Twelve Articles. Experts will no doubt identify other sources that should have merited attention.

In preparing this book, I have discovered that there is room for far more research on Joan of Arc than I had ever expected, given the veritable mountain of books and articles published over the last two or three centuries. Exciting new scholarship has opened up important ways of interpreting the social and religious aspects of her life, but this has raced ahead of our knowledge and understanding of the primary texts themselves. Fundamental questions remain unanswered about many of the documents used to study Joan. On the one hand, the critical approaches employed with regard to the original trial records have not been applied to the wider corpus of documents, too often regarded as unproblematic and 'truthful' sources. More importantly, serious investigation of the Valois and Burgundian chronicles seems to have stopped generations ago and, as a result, we do not know the precise relationship between the accounts of the Pucelle presented in a variety of well-known and frequently cited texts. I intend to tackle these difficult problems in the future, abandoning the traditional, biographical approach to the story of Joan and instead exploring the ways in which her story was constructed and disseminated in different categories of sources. I take great pleasure in the thought that such a book would follow in the path set out by Charles Wayland Lightbody, a fellow graduate of Worcester College, Oxford, and the patron of a fund that supported me as a student.

I have chosen to present the documents in a chronological fashion rather than to organise them thematically. It is essential that the reader recognise the importance of the date at which a source was written in order to evaluate it properly. The most obvious example of this must be the eyewitness statements presented at the Nullification trial, remembering events that had taken place a quarter of a century earlier, no doubt influenced by the rumours and myths that were already building around Joan. In some cases, of course, it is extremely difficult to be certain about dating of a particular document and I have therefore had to impose my own judgement, though I have also identified other secondary sources that present contrary opinions.

I have generally kept the French spelling of names and titles except in cases such as Joan of Arc where there is a commonly accepted Anglicisation. Unlike most British or North American scholars, I have chosen to retain the French title for Joan of Arc, 'La Pucelle', rather than to translate this into the commonly used 'Maid' or 'Maiden'. My intention is to encourage modern readers to engage with the full range of meanings implicit in the term 'Pucelle' which was central to Joan's gender and status in contemporary society.² Some readers may also be confused about the fact that I refer to the son of King Charles VI as King Charles VII rather than the dauphin Charles. The title of dauphin was accorded to the heir apparent to the French throne from 1349 and was abandoned at the moment of accession to the throne, which took place at the death of the previous king and not at the royal coronation. Thus Charles VII was only dauphin from the death of his elder brother John on 5 April 1417 until the death of his father on 21 October 1422, even if Joan continued to use the title until his coronation on 17 July 1429, as witnesses at the Nullification trial later suggested [**80–82**].³

Finally it has become common in many modern books to render the testimony of both Joan of Arc and the witnesses at the Nullification trial (and indeed inquisitorial trials in general) in as vivid a manner as possible, particularly by use of the first person and the present tense. This is a particularly dangerous approach because it is liable to lull the reader into forgetting the exact nature of these records, that are not verbatim transcripts of the words of witnesses but rather carefully constructed and reshaped interpretations of what was said.⁴ I have therefore chosen to follow the original records as closely as possible, continuing to use the third person, and to present the statements in the past tenses, though I have had to iron out some inconsistencies in order to avoid confusion.

A number of individuals have provided invaluable advice and assistance throughout the preparation of this book. Christopher Allmand and Alan Lupack helped me to obtain copies of key books. Sarah Rees Jones and Natasha Glaisyer provided useful sounding boards when making difficult decisions about the organization and presentation of this book. Peter Ainsworth and Shelagh Sneddon provided assistance with particular translations. Angus Kennedy and Kenneth Varty kindly agreed to allow me to reproduce their translation of the *Ditié de Jehanne d'Arc.* Jeremy Goldberg, Katherine Lewis, Alastair Minnis and Cordelia Beattie gave me important advice and served as sounding-boards on the subject of gender. My undergraduate students on two Special Subject courses have provided a wonderful think-tank in which to test out ideas (not to mention a willing team of proofreaders!), as have audiences at a number of conferences and seminars. Malcolm Vale, Kathleen Daly, Gail Orgelfinger, Bonnie Wheeler and the members of the International Joan of Arc Society have all encouraged me in this endeavour and I hope that this book will be of use to them when teaching their own courses.

2 See pages 46 to 48 below.

3 This is not to deny, of course, that the coronation was a fundamentally important public ritual and a key element in the royal mythology, serving as a visible demonstration of God's support and approval for the new ruler: R. A. Jackson, *Vive le roi! A history of the French coronation from Charles V to Charles X*, Chapel Hill, 1984.

4 See pages 60 to 67 below.

I owe a particular debt of gratitude to my editor, Rosemary Horrox, who gave me detailed advice on my original proposal and has read the typescript on two separate occasions. Her comments and advice have improved this book and one can only wish that Thomas de Courcelles and Guillaume Manchon had had such assistance when preparing the record of Joan's trial at Rouen.

Finally my colleague and fiancée, Gabriella Corona, has not only spent many, many hours patiently talking over a host of questions throughout this project but also provided me with tremendous assistance in translating Latin and Italian documents.

Craig Taylor
York

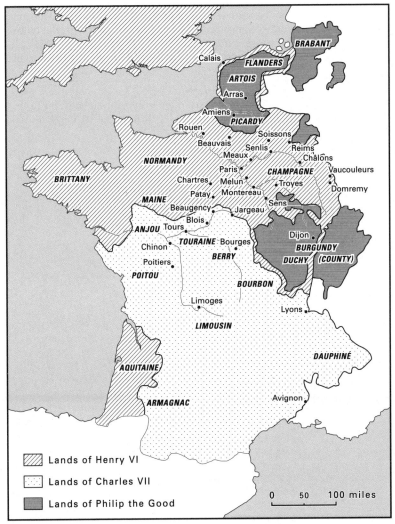

Calais

BRABANT

FLANDERS

ARTOIS

Arras

Amiens

PICARDY

Rouen

Soissons

Beauvais

Reims

Senlis

Châlons

NORMANDY

Meaux

Paris

CHAMPAGNE

Vaucouleurs

BRITTANY

Chartres

Melun

Troyes

Domremy

MAINE

Patay

Montereau

Beaugency

Jargeau

Sens

ANJOU

Blois

Dijon

Tours

Chinon

TOURAINE

Bourges

BURGUNDY

Poitiers

BERRY

DUCHY

(COUNTY)

POITOU

BOURBON

Limoges

Lyons

LIMOUSIN

DAUPHINÉ

AQUITAINE

ARMAGNAC

Avignon

///// Lands of Henry VI

⋰⋱ Lands of Charles VII

▤ Lands of Philip the Good

0   50   100 miles

Map of France in 1429

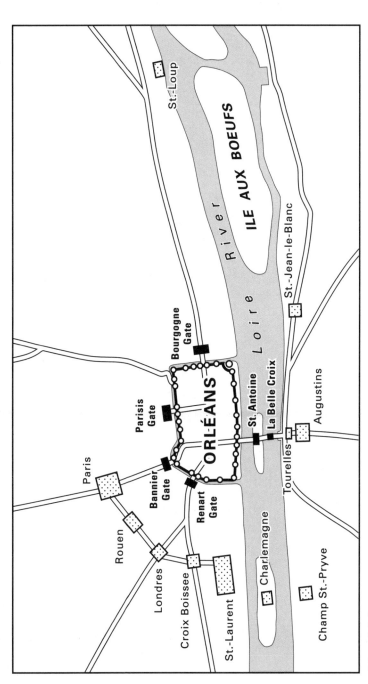

Map of Orléans

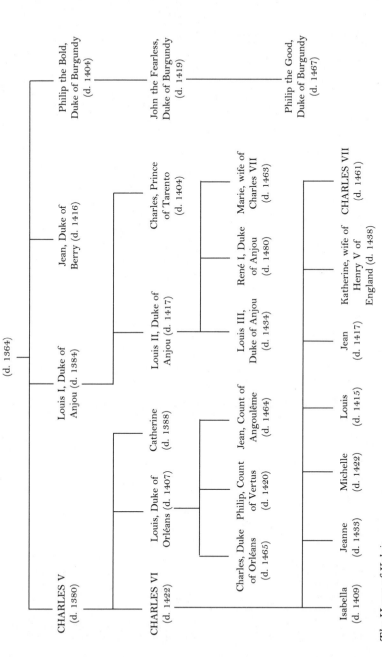

The House of Valois

CHRONOLOGICAL TABLE

24 October 1415	Henry V wins the battle of Agincourt
10 September 1419	Assassination of John the Fearless at Montereau
21 May 1420	Treaty of Troyes between Henry V and Charles VI
31 August 1422	Death of Henry V
21 October 1422	Death of Charles VI
c.1425	Joan first hears voices
13 May 1428	Joan's first meeting with Robert de Baudricourt
12 October 1428	Beginning of the siege of Orléans by the English
4 March 1429	Joan arrives at Chinon
March-April 1429	Joan questioned by the theologians at Poitiers
29 April 1429	Joan enters Orléans
8 May 1429	The English withdraw from the siege of Orléans
11-12 June 1429	Jargeau falls to French
17 June 1429	Beaugency falls to French
18 June 1429	Defeat of the English at the battle of Patay
17 July 1429	Charles VII crowned as king of France at Reims
15 August 1429	The aborted battle at Montépilloy between French and English armies
8 September 1429	Joan leads the unsuccessful assault on Paris
Late October 1429	The attack upon Saint-Pierre-le-Moûtier
24 November 1429	Joan lays siege to La Charité-sur-Loire
23 May 1430	Joan captured at Compiègne
23 December 1430	Joan arrives at Rouen
9 January 1431	Start of the heresy trial
19 May 1431	The University of Paris condemns Joan
24 May 1431	Joan is pushed into abjuring her crimes
28 May 1431	Joan is charged with relapsing into heresy
30 May 1431	Joan is burned at the stake
16 December 1431	Henry VI is crowned king of France in Paris
21 September 1435	Treaty of Arras between Charles VII and the Duke of Burgundy
13 April 1436	Paris recaptured by Charles VII
November 1440	Charles, Duke of Orléans released by the English
29 October 1449	Rouen recaptured by Charles VII
February 1450	Preliminary inquiry into the Rouen trial led by Guillaume Bouillé
May 1452	Canonical investigation into the Rouen trial led by Cardinal Guillaume d'Estouteville
7 November 1455	Opening of the Nullification trial
7 July 1456	The judges at the Nullification trial issue their sentence
1920	Joan is canonised

ABBREVIATIONS

Doncoeur (ed.), *L'enquête du Cardinal d'Estouteville en 1452*
P. Doncoeur and Y. Lanhers (eds), *La réhabilitation de Jeanne la Pucelle: l'enquête du Cardinal d'Estouteville en 1452. Documents et recherches relatifs à Jeanne la Pucelle*, 4, Melun, 1958.

Doncoeur (ed.), *L'enquête ordonnée par Charles VII en 1450*
P. Doncoeur and Y. Lanhers (eds), *La réhabilitation de Jeanne la Pucelle: l'enquête ordonnée par Charles VII en 1450 et le codicille de Guillaume Bouillé. Documents et recherches relatifs à Jeanne la Pucelle*, 3, Melun, 1956.

Doncoeur (ed.), *La minute française*
P. Doncoeur and Y. Lanhers (eds), *La minute française de l'interrogatoire de Jeanne la Pucelle, d'après le réquisitoire de Jean d'Estivet et les manuscrits d'Urfé et d'Orléans. Documents et recherches relatifs à Jeanne la Pucelle*, 1, Melun, 1952.

Doncoeur (ed.), *La rédaction épiscopale du procès de 1455–1456*
P. Doncoeur and Y. Lanhers (eds), *La réhabilitation de Jeanne la Pucelle: la rédaction épiscopale du procès de 1455–1456. Documents et recherches relatifs à Jeanne la Pucelle*, 5, Melun, 1958.

Doncoeur (ed.), *Instrument public des sentences*
P. Doncoeur and Y. Lanhers (eds), *Instrument public des sentences portées les 24 et 30 mai 1431 par Pierre Cauchon et Jean Le Maître contre Jeanne la Pucelle. Documents et recherches relatifs à Jeanne la Pucelle*, 2, Melun, 1954.

Duparc (ed.), *Procès en nullité*
P. Duparc (ed.), *Procès en nullité de la condamnation de Jeanne d'Arc*, 5 vols, Paris, 1977–89.

Fresh Verdicts on Joan of Arc
B. Wheeler and C. T. Wood (eds), *Fresh Verdicts on Joan of Arc*, New York, 1996.

Joan of Arc and Spirituality
A. Astell and B. Wheeler (eds), *Joan of Arc and Spirituality*, Basingstoke, 2003.

Quicherat (ed.), *Procès de condamnation*
J-E-J. Quicherat (ed.), *Procès de condamnation et de réhabilitation de Jeanne d'Arc dite la Pucelle*, 5 vols, Paris, 1841–9.

Tisset (ed.), *Procès de condamnation*
P. Tisset and Y. Lanhers (eds), *Procès de condamnation de Jeanne d'Arc*, 3 vols, Paris, 1960-71.

INTRODUCTION

The story of Joan of Arc has continued to elicit an extraordinary range of reactions throughout almost six centuries since her death. She has been presented as a saint but also a victim of the medieval Church, as a challenger to the social order but also a defender of the monarchy and nation, and as a role model and inspiration but also a fraud and even a madwoman.[1] Born around 6 January 1412, Joan was the youngest of the five children of a prosperous peasant named Jacques d'Arc and his wife, Isabelle Romée.[2] She claimed that, as a child, she was divinely inspired to offer her assistance in the face of the political and military crisis that threatened to overwhelm France.[3] As a mere teenager, she joined the reinforcements that King Charles VII (1422–61) dispatched to aid Orléans against a besieging army of Englishmen.[4] The situation was bleak for the inhabitants of the city when Joan arrived on Friday 29 April 1429, yet within just over a week the enemy had been forced to withdraw with their tails firmly between their legs [11, 35, 37, 81, 83–5, 90, 92, 95, 101, 105]. Over the following two months, the English garrisons were driven out of Jargeau, Meung-sur-Loire and Beaugency and their army

1 M. Winock, 'Joan of Arc', in P. Nora (ed.), *Realms of Memory: the construction of the French past. III: Symbols*, New York, 1996–8, pp. 433–80, and G. Krumeich, 'Joan of Arc between Right and Left', in R. Tombs (ed.), *Nationhood and Nationalism in France, from Boulangism to the Great War, 1889–1918*, London, 1991, pp. 63–73. Also see G. Krumeich, *Jeanne d'Arc in der Geschichte*, Sigmaringen, 1989.

2 For a more detailed overview of the life of Joan of Arc, see R. Pernoud and M-V. Clin, *Joan of Arc: her story*, revised and trans. J. Duquesnay Adams, New York, 1998, together with M. G. A. Vale, *Charles VII*, London, 1974, ch. 3. Joan's military career is analysed in K. DeVries, *Joan of Arc: a military leader*, Stroud, 1999.

3 I do not intend to debate whether Joan was truly inspired by a divine or supernatural power, or simply the victim of mental illness. It seems to me that this is less a historical question than a matter of personal opinion or faith. For contemporary reactions to her claims, see pages 9 to 39 below.

4 In theory, the city should have been immune from attack because its lord, Charles, Duke of Orléans, was then a prisoner in England after being captured at the battle of Agincourt in 1415. M. K. Jones, '"Gardez mon corps, sauvez ma terre". Immunity from war and the lands of a captive knight: the siege of Orléans (1428–1429) revisited', in M-J. Arn (ed.), *Charles d'Orléans in England (1415–1440)*, Cambridge, 2000, pp. 9–26.

suffered a humiliating defeat at the battle of Patay. The high point of
Joan's career ensued as she took part in the campaign that culminated
in Charles VII's coronation at Reims on 17 July 1429. The French
army then slowly moved towards Paris, where she was wounded in an
unsuccessful attack upon the capital on 8 September [**26, 35, 43, 45,
59, 67, 68**]. Before the attack could be resumed, Charles VII agreed a
truce and disbanded the army, leaving Joan politically isolated. Rather
than allow her to accompany the Duke of Alençon and his troops to
Normandy, Joan was sent with the Lord of Albret and a small army to
attack the mercenary captain Perrinet Gressart. They successfully
captured his stronghold at Saint-Pierre-le-Moûtier in early November
1429, but failed to take La Charité-sur-Loire because of the onset of
winter and a lack of supplies [**28, 101**]. The following spring, Joan
led a small band of men-at-arms that joined the defence against a
coordinated Anglo-Burgundian offensive along the river Oïse. Having
captured the Burgundian captain Franquet d'Arras at Lagny [**45**],
she arrived at Compiègne on 14 May and was herself taken prisoner
a week later by Jean Count of Luxembourg, a lieutenant of the Duke
of Burgundy [**40, 43, 67–8**]. Over the following year, she was
ransomed by her captors to their English allies who in turn handed
her over to the Church to be tried and finally executed for heresy at
Rouen on 30 May 1431. This slur against her reputation would
remain until her friends and acquaintances gave evidence before a
Nullification trial that eventually overturned the earlier judgement
against her on 7 July 1456.[5]

The fact that Joan's captors were Burgundian and that her judges
were French theologians and canon lawyers highlights the danger of
assuming that this was merely a war between France and England. It
is true that the two monarchies had been at war for centuries before
Henry V (1413–22) and his expeditionary force defeated the cream of
French knighthood at the battle of Agincourt. Two years later, he
returned to begin the full-scale conquest of Normandy.[6] Yet this
enormous military undertaking would not have been possible but for
the fact that France was racked by political divisions and tensions
which provided the invaders with a range of willing supporters and

---

5 See pages 41 to 45 below.

6 For Henry V's campaigns in France, see C. T. Allmand, *Henry V*, London, 1992.
For the wider context of the Hundred Years War and earlier conflicts, see M. G.
A. Vale, *The Origins of the Hundred Years War: the Angevin legacy, 1250–1340*,
Oxford, 1990 and C. T. Allmand, *The Hundred Years War: England and France at
war c.1300–c.1450*, Cambridge, 1988.

allies. Regions such as Aquitaine, Normandy and the Low Countries had consistently challenged the ambitions of the Valois kings of France to exercise full sovereignty over them.[7] More directly, King Charles VI (1380–1422) had suffered from repeated bouts of madness since 1392, creating a political vacuum and eventually civil war between the princes of the blood. On 23 November 1407, John the Fearless, Duke of Burgundy, ordered the murder of his rival, Louis, Duke of Orléans, triggering more than a decade of tensions and warfare between their supporters, known respectively as the Burgundians and the Armagnacs. It was this domestic strife that gave Henry V the opportunity to invade France, justifying his aggression by the claim to the French throne that he had inherited from his predecessor, Edward III (1327–77).[8] An even greater opportunity was presented to Henry when John the Fearless was murdered on 10 September 1419. This infamous crime was blamed upon the son and heir of Charles VI, the dauphin Charles, leader of the Armagnac faction.[9] Outraged at the murder of his father, the new Duke of Burgundy, Philip the Good, threw his support behind English proposals for a radical solution to the long-standing conflict between the two monarchies. Henry and Philip effectively forced the French king, Charles VI, to ratify the Treaty of Troyes on 21 May 1420, disinheriting his own son, the dauphin Charles, because of his crimes, and replacing him with Henry V as the new heir to the French throne [1].[10] The young English king never lived to see the two crowns united, but died on 31 August 1422, just months before his French counterpart. Nevertheless the Dual Monarchy created by the Treaty of Troyes became a reality in the hands of the ten-month-old Henry VI (1422–61), son of Henry V

7 P. S. Lewis, 'The centre, the periphery and power distribution in later medieval France', in *Essays in Later Medieval History*, London, 1985, pp. 151–65, and G. Small, 'The crown and the provinces in the fifteenth century', in D. Potter (ed.), *France in the Later Middle Ages*, Oxford, 2004, pp. 130–54.

8 C. D. Taylor, 'Edward III and the Plantagenet claim to the French throne', in J. S. Bothwell (ed.), *The Age of Edward III*, Woodbridge, 2001, pp. 155–69. French diplomats and writers were quick to observe that Henry V could not have inherited any such claim because his father Henry IV had usurped the English throne in 1399.

9 The origins of the civil war between the Armagnacs and the Burgundians is discussed in detail in R. C. Famiglietti, *Royal Intrigue: crisis at the court of Charles VI, 1392–1420*, New York, 1986.

10 M. H. Keen, 'Diplomacy', in *Henry V: the practice of kingship*, ed. G. L. Harriss, Oxford, 1985, pp. 181–99, and M. Warner, 'The Anglo-French Dual Monarchy and the house of Burgundy, 1420–1435: the survival of an alliance', *French History*, XI, 1997, pp. 103–30.

and his wife Katherine, daughter of Charles VI. Unsurprisingly, the dauphin Charles refused to accept his disinheritance, arguing that it was contrary to all divine, natural and human law. As a result, France was split between the two rival kings, Charles VII and Henry VI.[11] The territory north of the Loire was largely controlled by supporters of Henry VI and the Dual Monarchy, while the lands south of the Loire were held by Charles VII and his followers [2].

It was against this background that Joan presented herself as a champion of a France ruled solely by Charles VII. In her first letter to the English, she called upon Henry VI, the Duke of Bedford and their commanders to leave the kingdom of France, threatening to kill any Englishmen who remained behind [4]. When asked about this at the Rouen trial, she resolutely declared that 'before seven years are past, the English will lose a greater stake than they did at Orléans, for they will lose everything in France'. She was then asked if her voices only spoke in French and famously replied: 'Why should [St Margaret] speak English when she is not on the English side?' [38]. In her eyes, Charles VII was the only true king of France, chosen and supported by God who would grant him great military victories over his enemies.[12] When addressing the Duke of Burgundy, Joan simply declared that 'all who wage war against the holy kingdom of France, make war against King Jesus, King of Heaven', telling him to confine himself to waging war on Saracens because he would never win a battle against loyal Frenchmen [18].[13] Her entire mission was associated not just with the kingdom of France, but also with the King himself, and it was manifested in particular through powerful religious symbols that associated herself and Charles VII with the divine. Her banner displayed the royal symbol of the fleur-de-lys that also appeared on the coat of arms given to her family [37, 40].[14] The coronation of Charles VII was a fundamentally important aspect of her mission, serving as a public demonstration of God's special favour

---

11 Vale, *Charles VII*.

12 J. Strayer, 'France, the Holy Land, the chosen people and the most Christian king,' in *Medieval Statecraft and the Perspective of History*, Princeton, 1971, pp. 300–14. Also see N. Housley, 'Pro deo et patria mori: sanctified patriotism in Europe, 1400–1600', in P. Contamine (ed.), *War and Competition Between States*, Oxford, 2000, pp. 221–48, and *Religious Warfare in Europe, 1400–1536*, Oxford, 2002, pp. 56–8.

13 When the judges at Rouen asked her if God had been supporting the English when they were enjoying success earlier in the Hundred Years War, she declared that He had only been allowing the French to be beaten because of their sins [47].

14 W. M. Hinkle, *The Fleurs de Lis of the Kings of France, 1285–1488*, Carbondale, 1991.

and support for him.[15] Indeed, when pressed during the trial, she described another, even more visible, sign of God's support for Charles, in the story of an angel bringing him a crown [35–8, 40–3].

Of course, Joan's understanding of France, and therefore of national identity in general, was rather different from that of a modern person.[16] Her country was a vague and uncertain physical space, defined more by its association with a specific people than by its administrative or geographical boundaries. She consistently spoke of villages and towns, but gave little evidence of understanding the wider administrative or political geography of the country. She rarely spoke about regions or provinces such as the Lorraine or Burgundy, except when referring to their dukes or princes. The borders of her France were equally unclear to her. Throughout the Rouen trial, she consistently referred to her journey from Domremy *into* France, even though Domremy and the duchy of Bar were subject to the French Crown and hence part of the French kingdom [35, 37].[17] Moreover, Joan's view of her countrymen was defined more by her hostility to outsiders, and in particular the English, than by any particular national characteristics that united Frenchmen.

This view of a French people united together under their king against the foreign invaders was very much in line with the rhetoric and propaganda that had been developed by the Valois monarchy during the late middle ages. Throughout the Hundred Years War, writers had consistently emphasised the importance of French unity and of loyalty to the true king of France who enjoyed unique divine approval, calling upon those who were collaborating with the English to return to the fold. Such writers as Honoré Bouvet, Philippe de Mézières, Jean Gerson, Jean de Montreuil, Christine de Pizan and Alain Chartier employed a series of rhetorical devices and literary motifs to emphasise the importance of unity and loyalty to a French Crown that enjoyed special divine favour: they invoked a unique French history stretching back to a Trojan past; they emphasised God's favour to the

15 It has been suggested that the coronation of Charles VII was not part of Joan's original mission, but rather was added to the agenda after the siege of Orléans: C. T. Wood, 'Joan of Arc's mission and the lost record of her interrogation at Poitiers', in *Fresh Verdicts on Joan of Arc*, pp. 20–1.

16 For a general introduction to national identity in this period, see B. Guenée, *States and Rulers in Later Medieval Europe*, Oxford, 1985, ch. 3 and pp. 216–21.

17 Joan may have been using the word France in these situations to refer to the Île-de-France, the specific region around Paris that was directly controlled by the king, rather than the entire territory that was supposedly subject to the Crown.

kingdom and to the royal dynasty, asserting that France alone was
free of heresy because of the 'most Christian' king; and they described
the French as a chosen people who had replaced the Israelites in
God's favour.[18] Joan of Arc was herself woven into the fabric of this
rhetoric, for example through the comparisons with Old Testament
figures like Judith and Esther that not only emphasised God's ability
to work miracles through women, but also implicitly marked the
transferral of his love and support from the Israelites to the French
[7, 13, 20, 22, 103]. The Archbishop of Embrun, Jacques Gélu,
argued that in sending Joan, God had finally taken pity on the French
after they had been punished for their past misdeeds, just as he had
forgiven the Israelites and made them his (first) chosen people.[19]
Indeed the special Christian status of France even led supporters of
Charles VII to assert his credentials as the leader of a united Christian
crusade against the infidel: supported by the prophecy of a second
Charlemagne, both Joan of Arc and Christine de Pizan called for all
Christians to join together under the leadership of Charles VII and to
fight against the real enemy, the Saracens [4, 18, 20].[20]

Yet it is fundamental to recognise that, despite all the invocations and
the rhetoric, this notion of a France united under Charles VII was not
written in the heavens.[21] The country was racked by civil war and
Joan of Arc's call for national unity was in large part a partisan
assertion of the authority of the leader of one faction in the civil war
that divided France. The French allies of the English, in particular
the Burgundians, also presented themselves as the true defenders of
France and of peace. In their eyes, Charles VII and his supporters
were not 'true Frenchmen' but Armagnacs, and Joan was the 'whore
of the Armagnacs' [1, 59, 95]. Throughout the Rouen trial, the
notaries recorded Joan's references to 'her party', presumably refusing

18 See, for example, J. Krynen, *Idéal du prince et pouvoir royal en France à la fin du moyen
   âge (1380–1440): étude de la littérature politique du temps*, Paris, 1981, and '*Rex
   christianissimus*: a medieval theme at the roots of French absolutism', *History and
   Anthropology*, IV, 1989, pp. 79–96; C. Beaune, *The Birth of an Ideology: myths and
   symbols of nationhood in later medieval France*, Berkeley, 1992, esp. ch. 6.

19 Gélu's treatise appears in Quicherat (ed.), *Procès de condamnation*, III, pp. 393–410.

20 This had been a common argument throughout the Hundred Years War, building
   upon earlier crusading propaganda. Though this may have been a serious ambition
   at times, it could also provide a powerful weapon against an enemy that refused to
   make concessions in order to facilitate this higher goal.

21 The phrase is borrowed from the important prologue to Jean Juvénal des Ursins,
   Les écrits politiques de Jean Juvénal des Ursins, ed. P. S. Lewis, 3 vols, Paris, 1978–93,
   III, p. 5.

to use the terminology that she would have preferred, 'Frenchmen', just as they must have changed her identifications of 'the King' into 'her King'. Indeed, the English offered an alternative vision of France and its king, in the form of the Dual Monarchy, sustained and reinforced by the iconography of genealogies and coins, and by the propaganda of public speeches and rituals, all of which offered a different vision of France and the French king than that put forward by Joan and the supporters of Charles VII.[22] Thus in 1431, Nicolas Midi, fresh from his involvement in the trial of Joan of Arc, gave a speech on the occasion of Henry VI's entry into Paris for his coronation, declaring: 'This is the beginning of a great felicity for Christendom, for two kingdoms are now united that used to be divided and inimical, so that wars, conflicts, seditions, the ruin of many churches and the decline of worship were the results ... But henceforward, thanks to the union brought about by the grace of God, all those evils will cease; this is what we now hope for.'[23] As Midi suggested, the supporters of the Dual Monarchy, both English and French, painted their opponents as the enemies of peace: Henry was the rightful king of France, while Charles VII was an unlawful claimant, a rebel and an enemy of the peace that the Treaty of Troyes had offered to a war-ravaged France [1]. When Bedford issued a formal challenge to Charles on 7 August 1429, he refused to call his enemy dauphin or king, and predicted that God would support the English and their allies in any military encounter, not least because they alone truly wanted and promised peace for France [**24**]. The same ideas appeared in a tract written by Jean de Rinel in 1435, which argued that the Treaty of Troyes was a genuine attempt to end the ancient division between the two kingdoms as well as the civil war within France so that the people could live in peace, justice and tranquillity [**63**].

Joan herself appeared to despair of persuading the Burgundians and other collaborators of her vision of a France under Charles VII. Having urged the Duke of Burgundy and his followers to act as 'loyal

22 J. W. McKenna, 'Henry VI of England and the Dual Monarchy: aspects of royal political propaganda, 1422–1432', *Journal of the Warburg and Courtauld Institutes*, XXVIII, 1965, pp. 145–62, and L. R. Bryant, 'Configurations of the community in late medieval spectacles: Paris and London during the Dual Monarchy', in B. A. Hanawalt and K. L. Reyerson (eds), *City and Spectacle in Medieval Europe*, London, 1994, pp. 3–33.

23 H. Denifle and E. Chatelain (eds), *Chartularium Universitatis Parisiensis, IV: 1394–1452*, Paris, 1897, number 2399.

Frenchmen', she became increasingly disenchanted by their treachery, and eventually admitted that she had said that peace with Burgundy would only be found at a lance's point [18, 23, 31, 39]. It may well be that she became disillusioned by the Duke's unwillingness to listen to her pleas, but it is also possible that she herself was affected by the hostility created by decades of civil conflict and tension, that threatened her efforts to reunite France. She denied that her voices had told her to hate the Burgundians, or to be drawn on whether Charles VII had done well in killing the Duke of Burgundy at Montereau in 1419 [36, 48]. Nevertheless she did recount how the children of Domremy often returned with scratches and wounds after fights with their rivals from Maxey whom she described as Burgundians, and declared that she would willingly have allowed the one Burgundian from her village to be executed [36].[24] Perhaps these children merely used the allegiances of their parents as pretexts for childish squabbles, but the story does suggest that there were deep fault lines between Armagnacs and Burgundians. Domremy was located at the very eastern edge of the kingdom, on the borders of the duchies of Bar and of Lorraine, one of the few areas north of the Loire to remain loyal to Charles VII. The duchy of Bar had been held by René d'Anjou since he married the daughter of Charles, Duke of Lorraine, but this was contested by Antoine de Lorraine, Count of Vaudémont and Lord of Joinville, who repeatedly raided the region with the support of the Duke of Burgundy. Indeed, in July 1428, Joan and her family were forced to flee to the walled city of Neufchâteau, in order to seek protection from a raiding force led by the Burgundians Antoine de Vergy and Jean de Luxembourg.[25] It would hardly be surprising if she wrestled with the tension between her public calls for French unity and a resentment towards the Burgundians who had attacked her home and demonstrated very little loyalty to her King.

In short, Joan of Arc and the supporters of Charles VII offered an ideal of a country united under their God-given monarch, but their rhetoric contrasts strongly with the realities of a divided France. The Valois court itself was divided by political tensions that undermined such ideals, as different factions within the court of Charles VII

---

24 The solitary Burgundian in Domremy may well have been Gérardin d'Epinal, who testified during the Nullification trial that Joan had once called him a Burgundian: Duparc (ed.), *Procès en nullité*, I, pp. 278–80.

25 B. Schnerb, *Bulgnéville (1431). L'état bourguignon prend pied en Lorraine*, Paris, 1993, pp. 11–26.

jockeyed for position and favour.[26] Even the return of the Duke of Burgundy to the Valois side in 1435 did not put an end to the divisions within France.[27] Just five years later, the King had to deal with an aggressive conspiracy and revolt against his position, the Praguerie, which partially inspired Martin Le Franc to appeal yet again for French unity, using the example of Joan of Arc [66]. The reconquest of Normandy by 1450 and the expulsion of the English forces from Aquitaine by 1453 reinforced and gave some reality to the rhetoric of Charles VII, who could now entitle himself not only the 'very Christian King of France', but also the 'very victorious King'. Yet even at this moment, there was a sad footnote to this story of an emerging national unity crystallised around the figure of the King, the ideal championed by Joan. Once a loyal servant of Charles VII and the staunchest ally of Joan of Arc, the Duke of Alençon participated in the Praguerie and then began to conspire with the English in 1455 to assist them in invading France again. He was arrested just weeks after giving testimony at the Nullification trial [94].[28]

The supporters of Joan

Joan of Arc was a visionary and a holy woman who claimed to be guided by God through the medium of angels and saints. In this regard, she was not a unique figure, as she followed in the footsteps of a number of famous individuals who enjoyed great influence and spiritual authority in late medieval Europe. These included the Dominican tertiary Catherine of Siena (d. 1380), the Beguine nun Mechthild of Hackeborn (d. 1298/9), the anchoress Julian of Norwich (d. c.1416), the holy woman Bridget of Sweden (d. 1373) and Margery Kempe (d. c.1433).[29] Closer to home, there were a number of holy women and visionaries in France and the Low Countries who paved the way for Joan of Arc. Marguerite Porete (d. 1310) was a beguine from Hainault

26 Vale, *Charles VII.*

27 J. Dickinson, *The Congress of Arras, 1435: a study in medieval diplomacy,* Oxford 1955.

28 S. H. Cuttler, *The Law of Treason and Treason Trials in Later Medieval France,* Cambridge, 1981, pp. 195–212.

29 See R. Voaden and A. Minnis, *The Yale Guide to Medieval Holy Women in the Christian Tradition,* New Haven, forthcoming. Joan of Arc was a visionary rather than a mystic: a visionary received a spiritual or imaginary experience, literally seeing or feeling some revelation, whereas a mystic knew the presence of God inwardly through an intellectual rather than a sensory or symbolic experience.

whose book, *The Mirror of Simple Souls*, was condemned by twenty-one theologians and inspired the so-called heresy of the Free Spirit.[30] A widow from Reims named Ermine (d. 1396) saw visions that were both divine and demonic: sometimes the devil appeared to her as Sts Katherine, Agnes or Mary Magdalen.[31] Other individuals took a more overtly political role, particularly those women who claimed to be inspired by God to speak out against the crisis in the international Church caused by the transfer of the papacy to Avignon and the subsequent Great Schism. In 1384, Constance de Rabastens called upon the Count of Foix to support the Roman pope rather than his false rival from Avignon, and to lead King Charles VI of France on a crusade to recover the Holy Land.[32] The aristocratic Jeanne-Marie de Maillé (d. 1414) sought out the King to warn him of the election of a Franciscan pope who would end the Schism, while a peasant girl named Marie Robine, or Marie d'Avignon (d. 1399), also experienced visions about the Schism and travelled to the French court to counsel Charles VI.[33]

Yet Joan of Arc was a unique visionary, a young peasant girl who not only gained access to the King but also persuaded him to entrust her with such a prominent position in his army.[34] The first of these actions was accomplished with the assistance of Robert de Baudricourt, captain of the local town of Vaucouleurs. On two occasions Baudricourt refused to help her to travel across the war-ravaged countryside of France to reach Charles VII. Finally, in February 1429, he agreed to provide her with an escort to take her to the royal palace at Chinon. Travelling at night, the small party crossed Burgundian lands and arrived at their destination on 4 March 1429 [**77, 80**]. According to some Burgundian chroniclers, Baudricourt had instructed Joan on

---

30 R. Lerner, *The Heresy of the Free Spirit in the Later Middle Ages*, Berkeley, 1972, pp. 68–84, and Marguerite Porete, *The Mirror of Simple Souls*, trans. E. L. Babinsky, New York, 1993.

31 C. Arnaud-Gillet, *Entre Dieu et Satan: les visions d'Ermine de Reims (d. 1396) recueillies et transcrites par Jean Le Graveur*, Florence, 1997.

32 R. Blumenfeld-Kosinski, 'Constance de Rabastens: politics and visionary experience in the time of the Great Schism', *Mystics Quarterly*, XXV, 1999, pp. 147–68. No record of the date of Constance's death survives.

33 A. Vauchez, *Laity in the Middle Ages: religious beliefs and devotional practices*, ed. D. E. Bornstein and trans. M. J. Schneider, Notre Dame, 1993, pp. 205–15 and 255–64.

34 According to one of the supporters of Charles VII, Marie Robine had explicitly refused to take up arms but predicted the coming of the Pucelle to rescue the kingdom, though this does not appear among her recorded revelations and visions. See page 18 below.

how to act and to speak and was using her as the tool of a political
conspiracy that facilitated her access to the royal court [**66, 68, 103**].
These accounts smack of propaganda, using this story of a conspiracy
to demystify and undermine Joan's reputation, not least by strongly
hinting at sexual impropriety on her part. Nevertheless there may be
a kernel of truth in the observation that Joan needed important
sponsors to enable her to reach the King. Vale has suggested that the
key figures may have been René d'Anjou, his father-in-law Charles,
Duke of Lorraine, his sister Marie who was married to Charles VII,
and their mother, Yolande of Aragon.[35] Their faction at the royal court
had been implicated in the murder of the Duke of Burgundy in 1419
and was now fearful that its influence was crumbling as new men like
Georges de La Trémouïlle pushed for a reconciliation with the
Burgundians. Such individuals might well have welcomed the arrival of
Joan, especially when one immediate consequence was that
Trémouïlle's great rival, Arthur de Richemont, temporarily regained
limited royal favour. Certainly the military activities of Joan against the
Burgundians assisted both the Duke of Lorraine and René d'Anjou,
who disavowed his previous homage to the Duke of Bedford on 3
August 1429 and joined the miltary forces of Charles VII.[36]

Yet even if Joan won entry to the court through the assistance of
powerful patrons, this still does not explain why Charles VII would
have been willing to listen to her. It may well be that the King was
open to the possibility of divine assistance in this hour of extreme
military need. He was certainly willing to consider the potential merits
of other prophets and visionaries, such as the monk named Jehan de
Gand who predicted both the birth of Charles VII's son Louis and the
eventual defeat of the English, as well as Guillaume the Shepherd
(Berger) and Catherine de La Rochelle.[37] It is often assumed that the
King was riddled with doubt and needed reassurance that God
supported him. It is certainly possible that Charles' morale could have

---

35 Vale, *Charles VII*, pp. 49–51. Yolande had testified at the canonisation inquest in
    1414 into another female visionary, Jeanne-Marie de Maillé, who had gained access
    to Charles VI through the mediation of Yolande's husband, Louis II of Anjou:
    Vauchez, *Laity in the Middle Ages*, pp. 205–15.

36 Schnerb, *Bulgnéville*, p. 26.

37 P-A. Pidoux, *Un précurseur de la bienheureuse Jeanne d'Arc: le bienheureux Jehan de
    Gand, dit l'ermite de Saint-Claude, bénédictin. Sa vie et son culte*, Lille, 1911, and G.
    Gros, *Un siècle du passé de Saint-Claude*, Besançon, 1972. Also see H. Carey, *Courting
    Disaster: astrology at the English court and university in the later middle ages*, London,
    1992, and J. R. Veenstra, *Magic and Divination at the Courts of Burgundy and France:
    text and context of Laurens Pignon's 'Contre les devineurs'*, Leiden, 1998.

been affected by the lengthy war to win control of his inheritance, and some historians have also suggested that he may have been genuinely troubled by his involvement in the murder of the Duke of Burgundy at Montereau a decade earlier.[38] It seems far less likely that he felt demoralised by rumours that he was illegitimate, the son of an adulterous relationship between his mother, Queen Isabeau of Bavaria, and Louis, Duke of Orléans. The first suggestion of such an affair had appeared in *Le pastoralet*, a Burgundian pamphlet that was probably written between 1422 and 1425, but this claim does not appear to have been taken seriously at this time by either the French or the English. It was never referred to during the drafting of the Treaty of Troyes or in any of the pamphlets and tracts written either for or against it; moreover it only entered the political debate long after the death of Joan [**2, 63**].[39] As such, there is little reason to accept the famous picture of Charles as a man racked by doubts about his worthiness to inherit the throne until the arrival of Joan, as described in sources like the anonymous biography that was probably written around 1500, and the *Hardiesses des grand rois* by Pierre Sala (1516).

What sign could Joan have provided to reassure Charles and prove her own authenticity? Before her capture, some contemporary sources spoke vaguely about her meeting with the King [**8, 12, 21**]. During the Rouen trial, the judges repeatedly demanded that Joan explain how she had convinced him. Under this pressure, she finally explained that an angel had appeared at the court at Chinon and presented a crown to Charles. This was an extraordinary story, unconfirmed by any other contemporary source and which even Joan herself confessed to be untrue [**40–3**].[40] Yet earlier in the trial, Joan had hinted at a more palatable 'sign' when she reported 'that when she entered the room of her King, she recognised him among the others by the counsel of her voice that revealed this man to her' [**35**]. The Valois chronicler Jean Chartier subsequently expanded upon this story and during the Nullification trial Simon Charles reported that Joan had been able to recognise Charles VII despite his apparent attempts to hide among the courtiers, even though this witness had not been there at the time [**67, 96**]. Many scholars have argued that this story

---

38 B. Guenée, *Un meurtre, une société. L'assassinat du duc d'Orléans, 23 novembre 1407*, Paris, 1992, pp. 283–9.

39 Famiglietti, *Royal Intrigue*, pp. 41–5, and J. Blanchard (ed.), *Le pastoralet*, Paris, 1983.

40 K. Sullivan, *The Interrogation of Joan of Arc*, Minneapolis, 1999, pp. 61–81.

is quite plausible, particularly as deception and disguise were common themes in courtly games.[41] Yet it is somewhat suspicious that the story first appeared so long after the event, especially when it served as an extraordinarily powerful way of demonstrating that Joan was inspired by God, that Charles had a particular regal quality and enjoyed special divine favour, and that the two of them enjoyed a unique relationship. The same must be said of the testimony of her confessor, Brother Jean Pasquerel, who also was absent when Joan arrived at Chinon, but expanded upon earlier rumours that she had spoken in secret with the King by reporting that she told Charles that he was the true heir of France, revealing to him secrets that no one could know except God [**8, 12, 21–2, 95**].[42]

The claim that Joan provided Charles with a miraculous sign to prove her authenticity is undermined by the fact that he sent her to be examined at great length by a group of at least eighteen theologians and churchmen at Poitiers [**82, 91, 93-5, 100–1**].[43] The stories regarding Joan's first meeting with the King sidestep the difficult truth that she would have presented a grave dilemma for the King and his advisers. On the one hand, he risked derision if his armies were unsuccessful under her command, or perhaps worse if she were not just a fraud, but a pawn of the devil. On the other hand, to reject Joan would risk offending God if she had indeed been entrusted with a divine mission [**7**]. It is not surprising, therefore, that Charles turned to the Church to verify Joan's claims.

Medieval theologians did not have any doubt that both men and women could receive visions and prophecies from God, his angels or his saints. Indeed there were many examples of such figures who were accepted as authentic and thereby enjoyed great respect and influence. Nevertheless the Church did believe that it was essential to establish that the recipients were not being deceived by the devil. Visions depended upon the physical senses and therefore could easily be deceived or manipulated: Satan was more than capable of pretending to be an angel and fooling people into thinking that they had seen, spoken

41 J. Fraikin, 'Was Joan of Arc a "sign" of Charles VII's innocence?' in *Fresh Verdicts on Joan of Arc*, pp. 61–72.

42 The story of a saint winning over an important figure through secret words was a common topos in medieval hagiography.

43 R. G. Little, *The Parlement of Poitiers: war, government and politics in France, 1418–1436*, London, 1984, pp. 94–105, and D. Fraioli, *Joan of Arc: the early debate*, Woodbridge, 2000, pp. 5–23.

with, or even touched divine figures. Female visionaries were regarded as more susceptible to such deceptions than their male counterparts, not only because such men were more likely to be members of the Church, but also because of the misogynistic assumption that women, like Eve, were weak-minded and had an innate desire for attention. At the same time, of course, these holy women were effectively short-circuiting the established male hierarchies and participating in public life as prophets and channels to God, achieving status and authority that transcended their gender. It is therefore not surprising that the clerical authorities asserted their right to verify and control such visionaries, thereby protecting their own status as the primary intermediary to the divine.

The medieval Church had developed clear procedures for authenticating visions.[44] This process of *discretio spirituum*, or the discernment of spirits, had been explored in three tracts written by perhaps the most famous and influential French theologian of the fifteenth century, Jean Gerson (1363–1429).[45] His methods were summarised in the form of a small ditty: 'Ask who, what, why / To whom, what kind, from where.' He explained that this meant: 'Who is it to whom the revelation is made? What does the revelation itself mean and to what does it refer? Why is it said to have taken place? To whom was it shown for advice? What kind of life does the visionary lead? From where does the revelation originate?'[46] In other words, Gerson emphasised the importance of approaching the problem from two directions. Firstly it was necessary to test the visions and revelations, assessing whether they were orthodox and in accordance with the holy scriptures, and confirming that they aimed at good effects and results. Secondly, it was crucial to consider the quality of the individual claiming to receive these visions: was the person a virtuous,

44 R. Voaden, *God's Words, Women's Voices: the discernment of spirits in the writing of late-medieval visionaries*, Woodbridge, 1999, pp. 34–72.

45 D. Elliott, 'Seeing double: Jean Gerson, the discernment of spirits, and Joan of Arc', *American Historical Review*, CVII, 2001, pp. 26–54; D. Fraioli, 'Gerson judging women of spirit: from female mystics to Joan of Arc', and Y. Mazour-Matusevich, 'A reconsideration of Jean Gerson's attitude toward Joan of Arc in light of his views on popular devotion', in *Joan of Arc and Spirituality*, pp. 147–82.

46 *De probatione spirituum* (1415) in Jean Gerson, *Oeuvres complètes*, ed. P. Glorieux, 10 vols, Paris and Tournai, 1960–73, IX, p. 180. The other two tracts were *De distinctione verarum revelationum a falsis* (1400–1) and *De examinatione doctrinarum* (1423), in *Ibid*, III, pp. 36–56, and IX, pp. 458–75. *De distinctione* has been translated into English in Gerson, *Early Works*, trans. B. P. McGuire, New York, 1998, pp. 334–64.

selfless, humble and pious individual, worthy of such favour from God? Perhaps more importantly, were they willing to accept the authority of the clergy, and in particular the Church's unique status as the sole authority to verify whether such visions did indeed come from God? These questions provided the fundamental framework within which all contemporaries approached Joan's claims to divine inspiration, whether they were her enemies or her allies.

The records of Joan's questioning at Poitiers have disappeared, perhaps deliberately suppressed by the King or his supporters because it had thrown up testimony that later became embarrassing.[47] Nevertheless the *Conclusions of the Poitiers Investigation* do survive and demonstrate that the clerics had followed the principles of *discretio spirituum* when questioning Joan [**3**]. They believed that her mission to save France and to assist Charles VII was worthy and also argued that Joan was herself sufficiently virtuous to be chosen by God. Their lengthy investigation into her life had revealed only her goodness, humility, virginity, piety, honesty and simplicity. Yet they passed no comment on the actual mechanisms of her communication with God and her visions. Moreover the *Conclusions* did not give any indication that Joan proved her authenticity to Charles VII through a miracle or revelation, instead stating that she would give an unidentified sign in the future, during the siege of Orléans.[48] As a result, the *Conclusions* warned of the danger of dismissing Joan if she were inspired by the Holy Spirit, but could only offer conditional support for her in this regard, declaring that the real test of her veracity would be the fulfilment of her promise to provide an unidentified sign at Orléans.

These themes underpinned the defence of Joan offered by a series of polemical texts and chronicles by pro-Valois writers. The two most famous works were the anonymous theological tracts, *De mirabili victoria*

47 There is no evidence that these documents were deliberately lost, but it has been suggested that this may have happened because Joan had spoken about Antoine de Lorraine's raids on the duchy of Bar, which would have been somewhat embarrassing after he switched allegiance to Charles VII in 1443: S. Luce, *Jeanne d'Arc à Domremy: recherches critiques sur les origines de la mission de la Pucelle*, Paris, 1886, pp. 273–4. Another possibility is that Joan did not mention any plan to have Charles crowned at Reims at this early stage of her mission: C. T. Wood, 'Joan of Arc's mission and the lost record of her interrogation at Poitiers', in *Fresh Verdicts on Joan of Arc*, pp. 19–30. Of course, if the documents were in fact destroyed, which is unproven, it may simply be that the theologians at Poitiers had disagreed with one another about Joan or expressed real concerns about her that were masked in the narrower *Conclusions of the Poitiers Investigation* [**3**].

48 Seguin Seguin reported that Joan had said that she did not come to Poitiers to give signs [**100**].

and *De quadam puella*, often attributed to Jean Gerson himself. Like the *Conclusions*, these two tracts were somewhat tentative in their support for Joan, no doubt demonstrating that she continued to elicit some debate among the supporters of Charles VII [**7, 22**]. Other writers, including Jean Dupuy, Christine de Pizan, Alain Chartier, Jean Chartier and Martin Le Franc, were far more confident in their support for Joan [**6, 13, 20–1, 66–7**]. Indeed it is tempting to regard the written defences of Joan as forming a carefully interlaced and co-ordinated propaganda effort on behalf of the Pucelle, though there is very little evidence to suggest that this was the case, not least because so few of the writers were directly associated with the court of Charles VII. It would certainly be dangerous to assume that each writer had access to all previous texts and was therefore building upon those foundations. Nevertheless all of these writers shared certain key themes and approaches that ultimately derived from the theology of *discretio spirituum*.

Just as in the *Conclusions of the Poitiers investigation*, the first logical step was to demonstrate that Joan was a worthy enough individual to be selected by God for such an important mission.[49] Both the *De mirabili victoria* and Christine de Pizan's *Ditié de Jehanne d'Arc* invoked the authority of the Poitiers investigation itself to argue that Joan was just such an individual, while *De quadam puella* simply asserted that Joan was like an inexperienced and defenceless lamb away from the battlefield, demanding a life of chastity and devotion not only from herself but also her followers [**7, 20, 22**]. All three of these texts argued that God had deliberately selected a 'Pucelle', that is to say a young, female virgin, as his instrument, not just because of her clear virtue, but also because she was such a weak and unlikely individual as his weapon against his enemies, thereby emphasising the force of the miracle that was being enacted. Unlike the theologians at Poitiers, these writers did face up to the most significant piece of evidence against the supposed virtue of Joan, her decision to assume masculine roles and adopt male clothing, actions that were not only unconventional for women in general but also regarded as immoral and contrary to scriptural authority. Her defenders justified these actions by reference to historical precedent, particularly examples of heroic women from the Old Testament, and generally argued that it

---

49 The notion that Joan was an individual of outstanding moral worth was repeated consistently throughout the testimony at the Nullification trial, no doubt in part as a response to the mud that had been thrown at her during her trial at Rouen.

was necessary for her to wear male clothing because of the practical, utilitarian context of warfare.[50]

The defenders of Joan were rather more circumspect when it came to discussing the nature of her communication with the divine. For example, Alain Chartier stated that she heard voices from the clouds, while Christine de Pizan and *De quadam puella* merely stated that Joan had been sent by God, without exploring the precise details of that contact [20–2].[51] For these writers, like the judges at Poitiers, it was more relevant to talk about the goals to which Joan aspired under the influence of these voices: in their eyes, her mission to aid Charles VII and to drive the English out of France was so manifestly just that one could only approve of the Pucelle. Thus *De mirabili victoria* affirmed that Joan was the mouthpiece of divine revelation because the goal of her mission was to restore the King to his kingdom; the anonymous author urged his readers to consider the dire consequences that would ensue if the Valois party, which had right on its side, were to question or even reject her [7]. Christine de Pizan was even more clear about this in her *Ditié de Jehanne d'Arc*; Joan was presented as an the agent of God, sent to transform the fortunes of France and her King because of the special divine favour for the French royal line [20]. In short, the notion that Joan's mission was divinely inspired because of the justice of its goal served to legitimise the Pucelle and her visions, while also adding to the Valois propaganda that presented Charles VII as the lawful King of France.[52]

The *Conclusions of the Poitiers Investigation* had stated that the proof of Joan's divine mission would be a sign that she was going to perform in front of Orléans. *De mirabili victoria* made no mention of Orléans, perhaps suggesting that the text was written before Joan became involved in that siege. Yet the anonymous author did suggest that she had already carried out a miracle, implying that Joan's success at the Poitiers investigation could be compared with that of St Katherine of Alexandria who had miraculously converted a group of philosophers to Christianity [7, 12]. Joan's apparent involvement in the relief of Orléans on 8 May 1429 enabled later writers to be more direct. Christine de Pizan and Alain Chartier celebrated Joan's miraculous

---

50 See pages 50 to 57 below.

51 Similarly, most of the witnesses at the Nullification trial only spoke vaguely about her communication with God and her voices [77, 81, 88, 99–101].

52 For a more detailed discussion of this propaganda and rhetoric, see pages 4 to 6 above.

success at Orléans, together with her impact on a series of cities that surrendered to Charles VII on the way to the coronation: as Christine declared, God 'never performed so striking a miracle as He does for this woman' [20–1]. Similarly, Valois chroniclers and witnesses throughout the Nullification trial argued that the siege of Orléans could not have been broken without a miracle; they also reported a series of lesser military miracles that had occurred during the relief of the city, including Joan's crossing of the Loire and entry into Orléans without encountering English troops, as well as her recovery from severe injuries [81, 83, 90, 92, 94–5, 101, 105]. At the same time, stories began to emerge of miracles and signs that Joan had performed even before her arrival at Orléans. Jean Chartier and the anonymous *Journal du siège d'Orléans* recounted the famous tale of how Joan miraculously knew of the location of a sword hidden in the church of Sainte-Catherine-de-Fierbois. According to Chartier, Joan's defeats were caused by the fact that she accidentally broke this sword [37, 47, 67].[53]

These writers also reported on prophecies of the arrival of Joan that not only served to authorise her claims to be a visionary, but also emphasised the idea of divine support for Charles VII.[54] According to a witness at the Nullification trial, one of the theologians at Poitiers identified Joan with a prophecy of Marie d'Avignon concerning a virgin maiden who would rescue the kingdom by taking up the arms that Marie herself refused to wear [93 and also see 91].[55] This was apparently recast in a more popular form, judging by the testimony of witnesses at the Nullification trial. Durand Laxart and Catherine Le Royer claimed that Joan knew of a prophecy that effectively presented her as a figure like the Virgin Mary, who would redeem the sins of Eve [78–9].[56] It would appear that the supporters and advisers of Charles VII also drew upon a second set of prophecies that were

53 See page 51 below. One of the witnesses at the Nullification trial, Brother Seguin Seguin, even told the curious story of how some soldiers were miraculously frozen in place when preparing to ambush Joan on her way to Chinon [100].

54 J. Paul, 'Le prophétisme autour de Jeanne d'Arc et de sa mission', in G. L. Potesta (ed.), *Il profetismo gioachimita tra quattrocento e cinquecento. Atti del III congresso internazionale di studi gioachimiti, S. Giovanni in Fiore, 17–21 settembre 1989*, Genoa, 1991, pp. 157–82 and D. Fraioli, *Joan of Arc: the early debate*, pp. 55–68.

55 See footnote 34 above.

56 The Eve-like figure who destroyed France is generally assumed to be Isabeau of Bavaria, though care must be taken in accepting Burgundian propaganda about Charles VII's mother – especially when the version discussed at Poitiers did not involve an Eve to counterbalance the virgin.

commonly associated with the Venerable Bede and Merlin.[57] Thanks to the fourteenth-century English prophet John of Bridlington, Bede was credited with a rather impenetrable chronogram that circulated in Paris in 1429 and was interpreted by the French supporters of Joan as revealing the date of the arrival of a young girl who would carry a banner. More prominently, one of Merlin's prophecies in Geoffrey of Monmouth's *Historia Regum Britanniae* was subtly altered in order to predict that a virgin would ride on horseback, fight in armour and defeat the English archers; it was then used as an inspiration for a new verse prophecy in support of Joan, *Virgo puellares* [6, 81]. A more popular tradition grafted on to this prophecy a different statement, regarding a maiden who would come from an oak wood and work miracles; this claim was attributed to Merlin in Geoffrey of Monmouth. Joan seems to have been aware of this prediction during the Rouen trial, though she stated that she did not believe it [36, 78, 81].[58] These prophecies must have circulated widely, judging by their impact on both clerics and laymen throughout the Rouen and Nullification trials. They were cited by numerous chroniclers, such as Antonio Morosini, the author of *Sibylla Francica* and Mathieu Thomassin, and were most famously used in the *Ditié de Jeanne d'Arc* by Christine de Pizan [20]. Pizan cited the prophecies of Bede, Merlin and the Sibyl, without actually repeating their words, together with another popular prophecy that had appeared, for example, in the *Ballade du sacre de Reims* [19]. This was the famous second Charlemagne prophecy, that concerned Charles VII rather than Joan: it predicted that a French king named Charles would expel all his enemies from the kingdom of France and then become the emperor of all Christendom, restoring the Church and liberating the Holy Land.[59] The second Charlemagne prophecy was clearly an important weapon in support of Charles VII, and though Joan herself never cited it, she did associate herself with its crusading rhetoric. Her first letter to the English promised that, together, they could achieve 'the fairest deed that has ever been done

---

57 Bede (c.672–735) was an English historian and Benedictine monk; he was raised from age seven in the abbey of Saints Peter and Paul at Wearmouth-Jarrow, and lived there his whole life. Merlin was the fictional magician, prophet and adviser to King Arthur, created by Geoffrey of Monmouth in his *Historia Regum Britanniae* (c.1135).

58 Also cited by Pierre Miget, one of the clerics involved in the Rouen trial, at the Nullification trial in 1456, Duparc (ed.), *Procès en nullité*, I, p. 415.

59 M. Reeves, *The Influence of Prophecy in the Later Middle Ages. A study in Joachimism*, Oxford, 1969, particularly Part III, ch. 3.

for Christianity', while her letter to the Duke of Burgundy advised him to make peace with the King of France, Charles VII, and to fight only with the Saracens [4, 18; see also 30].

Yet despite the support offered to Joan by a succession of Valois writers, it would appear that her relationship with Charles VII was never entirely comfortable. The King gave public demonstrations of his support for Joan by allowing her to attend the coronation ceremony at Reims, by ennobling her and her family in December 1429 and by making her village of Domremy exempt from taxation. Yet in general, Charles VII was silent about Joan during this crucial period. One exception was the public letter that he sent to the inhabitants of Narbonne on 10 May 1429, in which Joan was presented as little more than a spectator to the great victory at Orléans [11]. When the armies of Charles VII and Bedford faced off at Montépilloy, Joan may have advocated a headlong charge at Bedford's lines, a wild and rash tactic that would undoubtedly have led to her defeat. Shortly afterwards, she was unsuccessful in the attack upon Paris, even if the real blame for that failure must fall upon Charles who pulled the rug out from underneath Joan and the army before the siege had effectively begun. Yet it is also conceivable that Charles was threatened by Joan, either worried by her mounting popularity or by whether she could be controlled if her loyalty lay first and foremost with God. Christine de Pizan was perhaps hinting at this in the *Ditié de Jeanne d'Arc*, when she emphasised that the King derived his authority from God and even offering a careful warning to Charles not to allow his success to go to his head if he wanted to have the great future that was promised to him [20].[60]

The real problem, though, was Charles' desire to make peace with the Duke of Burgundy, despite Joan's clear objections [18, 23, 31, 39]. Key advisers of the King, including Georges de La Trémouïlle, Raoul de Gaucourt and Regnault de Chartres, Archbishop of Reims, championed the idea that Charles should make peace with Burgundy and thereby deprive the English of their most important ally. Such a

60 It has recently been suggested that the poem was in fact written after the cracks in their relationship had become obvious, and should therefore be read as an even more direct attack on Charles: A. D. Lutkus and J. M. Walker, 'PR pas PC: Christine de Pizan's pro-Joan', in *Fresh Verdicts on Joan of Arc*, pp. 145–60. These ingenious arguments have been effectively scotched by A. J. Kennedy, 'La date du *Ditié de Jehanne d'Arc*: réponse à Anne D. Lutkus et Julia M. Walker', in E. Hicks (ed.), *Au champ des escriptures. IIIe colloque international sur Christine de Pizan*, Paris, 2000, pp. 759–70.

strategy was clearly opposed by the hawks who did not trust the Duke of Burgundy and perhaps feared for their own position at the court if the doves triumphed. In 1456, the Duke of Alençon testified that Joan had predicted that she would last for one year and no more, calling upon Charles VII to consider how best to employ her for that year [94]. It is hard to read this statement without feeling that the Duke was making an implicit comment on Charles' decision to negotiate with Burgundy rather than to fight. It certainly made Joan of Arc a major liability, as she continued to urge a military solution to the conflict and was directly involved in military actions against the Burgundians. The irony is that, from a purely objective perspective, the decision to exploit the developing rift between the Burgundians and the English would appear to have been the right course of action. The reconciliation between the French King and the Duke of Burgundy at Arras in 1435 was arguably the most important step towards the overall French victory in the Hundred Years War.

Many historians have even argued that the tensions which arose between Charles and Joan were so strong that the King actually betrayed the Pucelle.[61] There is little evidence to support the contention that Charles deliberately left her to be captured at Compiègne, any more than that she was betrayed by the captain of that city, Guillaume de Flavy.[62] It is equally unrealistic to imagine that Charles could either have rescued her from the clutches of her enemies or bought her freedom, even if Joan herself imagined that this would happen [35, 37]. Nevertheless a letter written by Regnault de Chartres, Archbishop of Reims, shortly after her capture does indicate the level of opposition to Joan within the royal court. He blamed Joan for her own capture, arguing that she had refused to listen to counsel, was haughty and proud, not least in wearing luxurious clothes, and ultimately did not do as God commanded.[63] Certainly there must be some truth to the contention that 'there were many fifteenth-century men – even among those who were on the side of Charles VII – who were not unduly disturbed by her fate'.[64]

61 G. du Fresne de Beaucourt, 'Jeanne d'Arc trahie par Charles VII', *Revue des questions historiques*, LXXI, 1867, pp. 286–91.

62 This widespread myth almost certainly derives from charges levelled against Flavy in the course of a legal case against him by the lawyer Rapioux: P. Champion, *Guillaume de Flavy, capitaine de Compiègne. Contribution à l'histoire de Jeanne d'Arc, et à l'étude de la vie militaire et privée au XVe siècle*, Paris, 1906.

63 Quicherat (ed.), *Procès de condamnation*, V, p. 168.

64 Vale, *Charles VII*, p. 47.

The enemies of Joan

Joan of Arc was captured by Burgundian troops outside Compiègne on 23 May 1430 [**40, 43, 67–8**]. On the day of her capture, the Duke sent out letters denouncing the mad belief of all those who had supported her.[65] Despite this rhetoric, he was in no great rush to hand her over to the English: negotiations dragged on until November of that year, as he and the Count of Luxembourg calmly ignored repeated letters from the Inquisitor of France and the University of Paris demanding that Joan be handed over so that she could be put on trial for heresy.[66] It has been suggested that the two princes were inclined to be merciful because of the mediation of their wives, Isabella of Portugal and Joan of Béthune, though there is no real evidence for such a romantic hypothesis. It is far more likely that the delays were caused by the difficult negotiations for the ransom of Joan, which promised much needed revenue for the Duke of Burgundy at a time when the continued siege of Compiègne was draining his resources.[67]

After the Duke finally ransomed Joan to the English in November, King Henry VI agreed that she should be handed over to the Church to be tried for heresy. Joan was brought to Rouen on 23 December 1430, just a few weeks after Henry VI had arrived in the administrative centre of the English government in Normandy.[68] Bishop Pierre Cauchon had led the negotiations for her ransom and now claimed the right to act as her judge because she had been captured within his diocese of Beauvais.[69] Cauchon had been in exile since the army of

65 Quicherat (ed.), *Procès de condamnation*, V, pp. 166–7; N. H. Nicolas and E. Tyrrell (eds), *The Chronicle of London from 1089 to 1483*, London, 1827, p. 170; A. H. Thomas and I. D. Thornley (eds), *The Great Chronicle of London*, London, 1938, p. 155.

66 Tisset (ed.), *Procès de condamnation*, I, pp. 4–11.

67 This must be seen against the background of the fracturing alliance with the English, triggered by differences over strategy, the Duke's demands for greater financial support, and concerns about the impact of Charles VII's new alliance with Austria upon the eastern side of the Burgundian lands. Warner, 'The Anglo-French Dual Monarchy and the house of Burgundy', pp. 103–30; W. Blockmans and W. Prevenier, *Promised Lands: the Low Countries under Burgundian rule, 1369–1530*, Philadelphia, 1999, pp. 72–102.

68 A. Curry, 'The "coronation expedition" and Henry VI's court in France, 1430 to 1432', in J. Stratford (ed.), *The Lancastrian Court: proceedings of the 2001 Harlaxton Symposium*, Donington, 2003, pp. 29–52.

69 Cauchon's authority in this matter was later challenged on the basis that Joan should have been judged by the bishop of the diocese in which she was born. Yet in contemporary canon law, heresy was generally regarded as being a continuous crime that inevitably occurred in the place in which the accused was arrested.

Charles VII captured Beauvais in August 1429 and so he had to secure permission to hold a trial in Rouen, the capital of the English territories in France.[70] He was joined by a second judge, a Dominican friar from the diocese of Rouen named Jean Le Maistre who took part as the representative of the Inquisitor of France, Jean Graverent, detained at Coutances by another trial.[71] Le Maistre initially protested that his commission as Vice-Inquisitor at Rouen did not give him the authority to take part in an action that concerned the diocese of Beauvais, but on 4 March 1431 Graverent issued a commission to enable Le Maistre to take part in the trial officially, which he did from 13 March onwards.

Over two-thirds of the churchmen involved in the trial were graduates of the University of Paris and both the faculties of Theology and Canon Law were later invited to give opinions on charges against Joan [53].[72] Cauchon himself had served as Rector of the University of Paris between 1397 and 1403. Six of his key assistants were professors from that university: Jean Beaupère (Rector from 1412 to 1413), Thomas de Courcelles (Rector from 1430 to 1432), Gérard Feuillet, Pierre Maurice (Rector in 1428), Nicolas Midi and Jacques de Touraine.[73] Even the public letters written on behalf of Bedford and Henry VI may have been influenced somewhat by the theological views of the University of Paris: Jean de Rinel, the royal notary and secretary who wrote Henry VI's letter at the end of the trial, as well as a further tract in 1435, was the nephew by marriage of Pierre Cauchon [33, 63].

The action against Joan of Arc at Rouen is perhaps the best recorded heresy trial of the middle ages. The judges ensured that a detailed record of the proceedings was compiled by the notaries Guillaume Manchon, Guillaume Colles and Nicolas Taquel. In addition, further

70 Cauchon was given permission by the chapter of Rouen on 28 December 1430, because there was no archbishop at that time. Jean de la Rochetaillé had been promoted to be a cardinal and transferred to the diocese of Besançon on 24 May 1426.

71 Pope Clement V (1305–24) had formally decreed that inquisitors were to assist bishops in the prosecution of heresy. For a short introduction to the Inquisition, see B. Hamilton, *The Medieval Inquisition*, New York, 1981.

72 C. R. de Beaurepaire, *Notes sur les juges et les assesseurs du procès de condamnation de Jeanne d'Arc*, Rouen, 1890, and Tisset (ed.), *Procès de condamnation*, II, pp. 383–425. Of the 131 clerics involved in the trial, just eight were English and of those, only two attended more than three sessions.

73 Cauchon's fellow judge, Jean Le Maistre, was also a Bachelor of Theology from the University of Paris.

insight into the 'trickery and falsification' that were employed at
Rouen is provided by the testimony of a host of clerics and laymen
during the Nullification trial in the 1450s [**34–56, 88–9, 98–9**].[74]
The first stage of the proceedings against Joan, known as the
Preparatory trial, began on 9 January 1431 with the appointment of
the officers to assist the judges, including Jean d'Estivet who was to
act as the Promoter, collecting the evidence against Joan and
effectively leading the prosecution. Cauchon and his colleagues then
reviewed the preliminary evidence against Joan of Arc between 13
January and 19 February, before citing Joan to appear before the
tribunal on 20 February. The official trial record does not give any
detail about this preliminary evidence, even though the rules of
inquisitorial procedure only allowed judges to bring charges against
an individual when there were clear grounds, and in particular a
widespread public belief (*fama publica*) that the accused was guilty – a
reasonable precaution, in order to avoid malicious prosecutions.[75] Why
did Cauchon not produce details of any evidence, particularly individuals to testify against Joan? It was later claimed that he had
commissioned agents to make inquiries about Joan in Lorraine, where
they questioned between twelve and fifteen witnesses at Domremy
and a further five or six in the neighbouring parishes but found no one
who would speak ill of the Pucelle.[76] Is it possible that the judges
simply could not find witnesses who were prepared to give evidence
against Joan, either out of loyalty to the Pucelle, or fear of the
consequences of speaking out against her? Certainly the subsequent
interrogations of Joan do suggest that the judges had access to some
preliminary information, because they were able to ask her very
leading questions about such matters as the Fairy Tree in her village
of Domremy [**36, 38, 47–8**], her stay at Neufchâteau [**35, 68**], her
trial at Toul for breach of promise of marriage [**41–2**], the sword of
Sainte-Catherine-de-Fierbois [**37, 67**] and her communications with

---

74 See pages 41 to 45 below. The phrase derives from R. Pernoud, *The Retrial of Joan
of Arc: the evidence at the trial for her rehabilitation*, trans. J. M. Cohen, London, 1955,
pp. 51–2.

75 The most useful study of the legal issues raised by the Rouen trial is Duparc (ed.),
Procès en nullité, V, pp. 3–128. Also see Tisset (ed.), *Procès de condamnation*. III, pp.
69–85, and H. A. Kelly, 'The right to remain silent: before and after Joan of Arc',
Speculum, LXVIII, 1993, pp. 992–1026, and 'Saint Joan and confession: internal and
external forum', in *Joan of Arc and Spirituality*, pp. 61–84.

76 The witnesses were Michel Lebuin and Nicolas Bailly, in Duparc (ed.), *Procès en
nullité*, I, pp. 292–4 and 301–3.

the Count of Armagnac [**25**].[77] The public statements of both the Rouen judges and the English would suggest that they did not regard it as necessary to prove *fama publica* by means of a *diffamatio*, a formal attack upon the reputation of the accused by honest people in order to justify a trial; they presented Joan as being so notorious that there would have been no need to bother with this [**33**]. Nevertheless the fact that they omitted any such evidence from the official record is extremely significant, because it meant that Joan was condemned solely on the basis of her own testimony. She was subjected to an intense barrage of questions that lasted for at least fifteen sessions, all without being given direct information regarding the (lack of) evidence and the charges against her [**34–48**].[78]

Joan was publicly questioned on six occasions from 21 February to 3 March, in front of a large audience made up of the judges and court officers, as well as additional theologians and canon lawyers whose role was to provide informal opinions on the trial and the accused [**34–9**]. Then on 10 March, the judges changed tack by arranging for Joan to be interrogated behind closed doors in nine sessions that lasted until 17 March, three times returning on the same day to resume the interrogations [**40–8**].[79] The sheer ordeal of defending herself against such a sustained attack would have been overwhelming for Joan, even without two further problems. Firstly, witnesses at the Nullification trial testified that one of Cauchon's assistants, Nicolas Loiseleur, entered her cell and pretended to be a priest and a supporter of Charles VII from her region; he not only gave her advice about the trial but also pretended to hear her confession [**98**]. Such tricks were not prohibited in such cases, and the result was presumably that Joan revealed secret information to her 'confessor' and a hidden audience that included Cauchon, the Earl of Warwick

77 One possible source for their information may have been the deposition that Catherine de La Rochelle gave in front of officials in Paris. Article fifty-six of the Seventy Articles stated: 'Joan has often boasted of having two counsellors, whom she calls her counsellors of the fountain, who came to her after she was captured, as has been proved by the confession of Catherine de La Rochelle before the official at Paris; this Catherine said that Joan would escape from her prison with the devil's aid if she were not well guarded.' (Tisset (ed.), *Procès de condamnation*, I, p. 264.)

78 It was normal procedure to reveal the charges at the start of an inquisitorial trial, but this may not have been essential, especially if the accused did not ask for it: nevertheless, without such charges, the defendant could refuse to cooperate with the trial.

79 Joan faced this barrage of question without the benefit of any legal counsel, though the official record does report that she refused assistance when it was offered on 27 March 1431.

and the notaries. Secondly, Joan was held under unusual conditions outside the court room. Under normal procedures, a female prisoner would have been held in an ecclesiastical prison, guarded by women and generally treated in a humane way. In Joan's case, the fiction that she was being detained by the judges was maintained by the fact that the two judges each held a key to her cell, along with Cardinal Beaufort. Yet in practice she was detained as a prisoner of war in the Crowned Tower at the fortress of Bouvreuil, under the guard of three English squires and a group of soldiers. Witnesses at the Nullification trial testified that Joan had been chained up and that she was terrified of being raped [55, 89, 97–9].

The primary goal of these lengthy interrogations was to generate evidence of Joan's guilt. Once this had been done, the Ordinary trial opened on 26 March 1431 and she was finally given the opportunity to hear the charges against her. As the Promoter in the trial, Jean d'Estivet's task was to prosecute Joan on behalf of the judges: he presented the case against her in the form of Seventy Articles that were read out on 27 and 28 March.[80] Usually such charges would be supported by the testimony of appropriate witnesses, but instead Estivet relied solely upon the words of Joan herself; at some later date, he translated extracts from the French record of the notaries (*Minute française*) into Latin and attached them to the list of Seventy Articles. On 5 April 1431, these charges were whittled down to a list of Twelve Articles, that were approved by the assembled clerics participating in the trial, as well as by the faculties of Theology and Law at the University of Paris [52–3]. A slightly revised version of the Twelve Articles was then read out to Joan on 23 May, and the following day she was taken to the churchyard of the abbey of Saint-Ouen in Rouen to hear a sermon from Guillaume Érard before receiving her final sentence: at the very last minute, she abjured, revoking her previous words and deeds, and so the judges condemned her to perpetual imprisonment [54, 98–9]. Yet, just two days later, she apparently resumed her male clothing and began to speak to her voices again, thereby providing the judges and the assessors with the grounds upon which to proceed against her as for relapse: on 30 May 1431, they passed a final sentence against her and handed her over to the lay authorities for execution [55–6].[81]

---

80 Tisset (ed.), *Procès de condamnation*, I, pp. 191–286.

81 On 7 July 1431, Cauchon held a posthumous inquiry at which some witnesses testified that Joan had denounced her voices at the very end (Tisset (ed.), *Procès de*

There can be little doubt that the English viewed the trial of Joan of Arc as an opportunity to discredit both her and Charles VII. This was certainly the thrust of a tract written by Jean de Rinel on the eve of the Congress of Arras, desperate to dissuade the Duke of Burgundy from any rapprochement with Charles [**63**]. During the Nullification inquiries, many witnesses were directly asked whether the English had a mortal hatred for Joan of Arc and had intended to defame Charles by incriminating her. Not surprisingly, many took the opportunity to argue that the English had sought to destroy Joan in order to embarrass and undermine the credibility and status of Charles VII. The most significant piece of evidence offered was the sermon that Guillaume Érard had given on 24 May 1431, shortly before Joan's abjuration: in 1450, Guillaume Manchon testified that Érard had said: 'Ah! Noble house of France which has always been the defender of the faith, have you been so abused that you would adhere to a heretic and schismatic?' Jean Massieu echoed this, reporting the words as: 'France, you, that have always been the most Christian country, are much abused. And Charles, the one who calls himself your king and governor, has subscribed as a heretic and schismatic, which he is, to the words and deeds of a worthless woman, defamed and completely full of dishonour.'[82] Though these statements were directly encouraged by the form of the question, they still sound plausible and even likely. Any successful attack upon the credibility of Joan was clearly a propaganda victory against Charles VII. The English were undoubtedly concerned in 1431 about the public impact of the coronation of Charles, as demonstrated by the haste with which they rushed Henry VI to Paris to be crowned as king of France; discrediting Joan would cast a shadow upon the consecration of Charles VII at Reims. Nevertheless it is intriguing that the English and their allies never referred directly to the heresy of Joan in their propaganda against Charles VII, and that there is no evidence that others highlighted this connection, at least in public. Indeed even the official record of the Rouen trial did not record the words of Érard's sermon at Rouen on the day of Joan's

---

condamnation, I, pp. 416–22); this claim was echoed in Henry VI's public letter on 28 June 1431 and, apparently, Jean Graverent's sermon in Paris [**57, 59**]. This claim was directly contradicted by the official trial record which showed that she was unrepentant at the end.

82 Doncoeur (ed.), *L'enquête ordonnée par Charles VII en 1450*, pp. 51–2 and 53–4. Similar testimony was offered by Isembart de La Pierre in 1452 and by Martin Ladvenu in 1456.

abjuration, thereby missing an obvious chance to make a connection between Charles VII and the Pucelle's heresy [**54**].

Some of the witnesses at the Nullification trial also suggested that the English had sought to destroy Joan of Arc in vengeance for her successes during the war. They were described as a superstitious people who feared that they would not win any further victories until she was dead.[83] There is limited evidence to support this claim, though it has to be recognised that the English and Burgundian authorities were hardly likely to admit that the Pucelle had had such a dramatic impact upon the morale of their troops. Historians often cite two writs issued by the English government on 3 May and 12 December 1430, that established penalties for those captains and soldiers who refused to cross into France or deserted from the army while fighting there. Yet even though these documents do demonstrate the significant loss of morale among the English forces at this dark hour in the war, they do not attribute it to Joan of Arc in any way whatsoever, despite the titles given to them by an eighteenth-century editor.[84] Four years later, John Duke of Bedford presented a report to the royal council in England in the summer of 1434. Citing the failure at Orléans as the decisive turning point in the war, he claimed that the actions of the Pucelle had sapped the courage of the English troops who feared that she was the disciple of the devil, a practitioner of false enchantments and of sorcery [**62**]. Yet it is important to note that Bedford's report was designed to exonerate himself from any blame for the failures in France: it was clearly immensely useful to be able to argue that English defeats should be blamed upon Joan of Arc. Moreover, his report contrasted with all the English and Burgundian letters and memoranda written before Joan's capture, including a report that Bedford himself sent to the royal council on 4 November 1430: none of these documents made any reference to Joan and her impact upon the course of military events.[85]

---

83 For example, the testimony of Jean Toutemouillé in 1450 and Thomas Marie in 1452, in Doncoeur (ed.), *L'enquête ordonnée par Charles VII en 1450*, pp. 39–43, and Duparc (ed.), *Procès en nullité*, I, pp. 238–40.

84 Rymer gave these documents the titles 'De proclamationibus contra capitaneos et soldarios tergiversantes, incantationibz Puellae terrificatos' and 'De fugitivis ab exercitu, quos terriculamenta Puellae animaverant, a[r]restandis', and they were reprinted under these headings in Quicherat (ed.), *Procès de condamnation*, V, pp. 162–4 and 192–4. Their actual titles in the Close Rolls are 'De proclamacionibus faciendis' and 'De certis personis arestandis'.

85 J. Stevenson (ed.), *Letters and Papers Illustrative of the Wars of the English in France During the Reign of Henry VI*, 2 vols in 3, London, 1861–64, II:i, pp. 156–64, and in general, pp. 95–181, as well as Champion, *Guillaume de Flavy*, pp. 142–60.

It may be more useful to see the trial of Joan of Arc as an expedient solution to the difficult situation in which the English found themselves once Joan had been captured. There could be no question of returning her to the French in return for a ransom, partly because they did not recognise her aristocratic status and hence entitlement to protection under the law of arms and chivalry, but also because of the real danger that she would pose in the future. On the other hand, they could not simply kill Joan and thereby risk creating a martyr who might be just as dangerous to them dead as alive.[86] The only possible solution was to entrust her to the Church to be tried on charges of heresy, hoping that a verdict against her would destroy her public reputation and also enable them to execute her in a legitimate and publicly acceptable fashion. Even this course of action was risky: the judges might fail to find sufficient evidence against Joan, which was why Henry VI reserved the right to resume control of her if she were exonerated by the trial [33]. Moreover, many would assume that the verdict against Joan had simply been manufactured and this in part explains the care with which the records of the investigation were compiled and later distributed, as well as the attempt to make the trial appear to be as open and fair as possible. Ultimately the only successful outcome would be if Joan were to die after publicly acknowledging her errors and thereby denying any divine mission to assist Charles VII. This was in fact achieved when she abjured on 24 May 1431, though there is some question about the precise wording of her public statement [55]. That she subsequently relapsed may have served English purposes in that it paved the way for her execution, but it also meant that she effectively retracted her abjuration, and again upheld the validity of her visions and of her religious beliefs. This volte-face would certainly explain the extraordinary posthumous inquiry that Cauchon held a week after her execution, at which a succession of witnesses testified that she had again abandoned her beliefs and admitted her errors just before her death. The same claim was made by Henry VI in his public letters, and was presumably voiced in public sermons across France, judging by the testimony of the Bourgeois of Paris [57, 59].

These public letters of Henry VI, dispatched to European princes and to the people of France, warned of the dangers posed by figures like Joan who seduced the people into heresy, taking advantage of their

---

86 At least one contemporary writer, Martin Le Franc, presented Joan as a Christ-like martyr [66].

readiness to believe in superstition and error [57].[87] It would be easy
to dismiss these claims as further propaganda, but it is important to
read these statements in light of the widespread threat that heresy
posed to secular authority. By definition, heretics were disobedient to
authority and thereby posed a threat to both the lay and ecclesiastical
establishments.[88] The Duke of Bedford made a direct link between
heresy and disobedience in his formal challenge to Charles VII on 7
August 1429; he attacked Joan for helping to drum up popular support
for Charles, and thereby encouraging the French people to break their
oaths to uphold the Treaty of Troyes [24]. Similarly, Henry VI
emphasised that Joan had seduced and deceived the simple people and
caused cruel murders, in the letter that he wrote to Pierre Cauchon on
3 January 1431 [33]. When Jean de Rinel wrote a tract to dissuade
the Burgundians from abandoning the Treaty of Troyes, he cited the
Pucelle as an 'uncontrolled woman, sorcerer, idolater and heretic', and
specifically charged her with attacking the Treaty of Troyes, and
encouraging the true and loyal subjects of Henry VI to abandon oaths
to maintain that agreement [63].

Modern scholars have tended to doubt whether the clerics involved in
the trial were genuinely concerned about heresy, not only because of
the testimony of the witnesses at the Nullification trial but also
because Joan was canonised five hundred years later. Yet it would be
dangerous, and even anachronistic, to assume that these churchmen
opposed Joan of Arc for purely political reasons. The University of
Paris had hardly been a tool of the English and the Burgundians since
they had captured the capital on 29 May 1418. The leaders of the
University generally sought to safeguard its privileges and to moderate
their political masters in the interests of peace. As a result, one
historian has characterised their vehement support for the trial of
Joan of Arc as 'a fanaticism more religious than political'.[89] This is
understandable given that heresy represented a severe threat both for

---

87 Tisset (ed.), *Procès de condamnation*, I, pp. 423–6.

88 The clerical attempts to link the Lollard heresy with a threat to secular authority
    are discussed in M. Aston, 'Lollardy and sedition, 1381–1431', in *Lollards and
    Reformers: images and literacy in late medieval religion*, London, 1984, pp. 1–47; S.
    Justice, *Writing and Rebellion: England in 1381*, Berkeley, 1994, pp. 67–101; P.
    Strohm, *England's Empty Throne: usurpation and the language of legitimation, 1399–
    1422*, New Haven, 1998, pp. 32–62.

89 J. Verger, 'The University of Paris at the end of the Hundred Years War', in J. W.
    Baldwin and R. Goldthwaithe (eds), *Universities in Politics: case studies from the late
    middle ages and early modern periods*, Baltimore, 1972, p. 55, and in general pp. 47–78.

the Church and the secular authorities in England, France and Bohemia in the middle of the fifteenth century. The later middle ages were a time of grave spiritual anxiety, not only because of the Black Death and wider developments within society, but also because of the disputed leadership of the Church during the Great Schism and the ensuing Conciliar Movement, as well as almost continual civil and international war. Such troubles provided fertile soil for unorthodox and extreme religious movements which the religious and secular authorities quickly identified as heretical.[90] Two of the English clerics who participated in the trial of Joan of Arc had had direct experience of the Lollard heresy that emerged in England and which had inspired a revolt against Henry V led by Sir John Oldcastle.[91] In Bohemia, the Emperor Sigismund launched five successive crusades against the Hussite heretics between 1420 and 1431; a contingent of three hundred and fifty men-at-arms led by Cardinal Beaufort was originally intended to join one of these crusades in the summer of 1429, but was instead diverted to reinforce the English army against Joan of Arc.

The Pucelle and her allies had certainly been aware of the danger of association with heretics and these religious extremists. Her confessor, Jean Pasquerel, sought to disassociate her from the Hussites in an open letter that he wrote on her behalf, attacking them for their crimes and errors [30, 65]. Yet the connections were clear to her enemies. In a public letter dated 7 August 1429, the Duke of Bedford associated Joan with 'an apostate and seditious mendicant friar' named Brother Richard [24]. Joan had met this Franciscan preacher in July 1429; he joined her at the coronation of Charles VII and heard her confession at Senlis in mid-August. Richard had been expelled from Paris in late April 1429 by the Faculty of Theology at the University, for preaching that the Antichrist had been born and that the end of times was about to arrive. In March of the following year he was imprisoned in the convent of the Franciscans at Poitiers and refused permission to preach by the vicars general of the Bishop and the Inquisitor; one of his associates, Piéronne the Breton, was burned at the stake in Paris on 3 September 1430 for claiming that God had appeared to her, and for taking communion repeatedly on a single day

---

90 M. D. Lambert, *Medieval Heresy: popular movements from the Gregorian reform to the Reformation*, 3rd edition, Oxford, 2002.

91 William of Alnwick, Bishop of Norwich, had condemned three Lollards to death after the arrest of sixty suspected heretics in 1428, while Robert Gilbert had served on the Oxford commission that had investigated Wyclif.

[**39, 59**].[92] Brother Richard may have also introduced Joan to Catherine de La Rochelle, who claimed to have received visions of a lady dressed in white; Catherine was arrested in Paris in December 1430, where she testified against Joan, but was released in June 1431 [**39, 59**]. Following the execution of Joan of Arc, the Dominican Inquisitor of France, Jean Graverent, gave a long sermon at Saint-Martin-des-Champs in Paris in which he denounced Joan as a heretic and claimed that Brother Richard had manipulated her, Catherine de La Rochelle and Piéronne the Breton. From the account of the sermon reported by a contemporary Parisian, it does not appear that Graverent was using this story for political ends, but rather as a genuine attempt to discourage his audience from being seduced by a heretical conspiracy that was insidious and had not been destroyed with the death of Joan [**59**].

In short, whatever efforts Joan made to dissociate herself from known heretics, it would hardly have been surprising if the churchmen involved in her trial were genuinely concerned about her religious orthodoxy. Though there were many examples of respected holy women in late medieval Europe, such individuals were initially regarded with suspicion by the Church. The Pucelle must have aroused more concern than most given her extraordinary actions, including evading the authority and control of the Church, presenting her divine mission in purely military terms and also choosing to wear male clothing.[93] In September 1429, an anonymous canon lawyer from the University of Paris wrote a tract against Joan entitled *De bono et malo spiritu* [**27**], a direct response to *De mirabili victoria* [**7**]. This attack upon the Pucelle was extremely learned and made detailed use of intellectual authorities that would have not been necessary in a work of public propaganda. The logical conclusion must be that the University was already debating the legitimacy of the Pucelle as her armies were attacking the capital, laying the ground for the case that would be mounted against her at Rouen in the spring of 1431.

92 On Joan's contact with Brother Richard, see E. Delaruelle, 'L'Antéchrist chez saint Vincent Ferrier, saint Bernardin de Sienne et autour de Jeanne d'Arc', in *La piété populaire au moyen âge*, Turin, 1975, pp. 329–54; S. Luce, 'Jeanne d'Arc et frère Richard', in *Jeanne d'Arc à Domremy: recherches critiques sur les origines de la mission de la Pucelle*, Paris, 1886, pp. ccxlv–cclxiii; J. de la Martinière, 'Frère Richard et Jeanne d'Arc à Orléans, mars–juillet 1430', *Moyen âge*, 3rd series, V, 1934, pp. 189–98.

93 For clerical concerns about female visionaries and mystics, see Voaden, *God's Words, Women's Voices*, and D. Elliott, *Proving Woman: female spirituality and inquisitional culture in the later middle ages*, Princeton, 2004.

The theology of *discretio spirituum* provided the framework for the attack upon Joan, just as it had shaped her defence by her Valois supporters. Long before the Rouen trial, Joan's enemies attacked the claims that she was good, humble, virginal, pious, honest and simple. According to Valois eye-witnesses, English soldiers and even Jean d'Estivet used terms of abuse to describe Joan that accused her of sexual immorality – an inevitable rebuttal to her claims to be the 'Pucelle' [81, 88, 95].[94] Indeed her claims to be an innocent virgin were also challenged in a more underhand manner during the Rouen trial, through hints and suggestions of sexual impropriety with soldiers at an inn at Neufchâteau, with Robert de Baudricourt, and with a young man from Toul who had taken her to court for breach of promise to marry. The lack of evidence to support such charges explains why they were not repeated in the Twelve Articles [35, 41].[95] Joan's enemies were able to make more capital out of her decision to cross-dress. This not only flouted the prohibition upon cross-dressing in the Bible and in canon law, but also suggested that she was involved in indecent behaviour.[96]

It is often assumed that Joan's resumption of male clothing was the sole reason for her execution. In fact, a marginal note in the manuscript of the record of the Rouen trial record says that when Joan admitted that she was speaking to her voices again on 28 May 1431, this was the 'responsio mortifera' – 'the fatal reply' [55]. Before the capture of Joan, her opponents were not in any position to comment directly on the orthodoxy of the manner in which she communicated with God. The Rouen trial finally gave Cauchon and his fellow theologians the opportunity to investigate the precise nature of her voices. Under extensive interrogation, she revealed that she spoke directly to three individuals: Michael the Archangel, St Margaret of Antioch and St Katherine of Alexandria [37, 39, 46].[97] Yet Joan did not actually identify these saints until the fourth public session of the

94 The extraordinary statement of Aimon, Lord of Macy, provides a different context with which to see these slurs [97].

95 Articles 8, 9 and 11 of 70 in Tisset (ed.), *Procès de condamnation*, I, pp. 200–1 and 204. The suggestion that the inn at Neufchâteau was a brothel was hinted at in the Burgundian chronicles of Enguerrand de Monstrelet [68] and Jean de Wavrin, and the idea of a sexually active Joan re-emerged centuries later, most notably in Voltaire's *La Pucelle d'Orléans*.

96 The important debate over Joan's cross-dressing is explored in greater detail below, pp. 50–7.

97 It is rarely noted that she also accepted that Gabriel was one of the voices when this was suggested to her by the judges [38–9, 52].

Rouen trial: during her earlier testimony, she only said that she had heard a voice from God at the age of thirteen; when asked directly about the identity of her voices, she denied that she was speaking with any saint [35–6]. Similarly, in the letters that she wrote before her capture she simply stated that she was communicating directly with God, without making any mention of intermediaries [4, 17, 25]. Was Joan deliberately trying to protect the secret of her voices? If so, was she doing this at their command or perhaps on the advice of her Valois supporters?[98] Is it possible that Joan was pressured, or even persuaded, by the judges at Rouen to identify the voices with these particular saints, and thereby channel her experiences into a form that suited the direction of their questioning?[99] These were appropriate choices. Both St Katherine and St Margaret were virgins who played a powerful, public role out of obedience to God, despite their age, gender and parents; St Katherine was investigated by fifty pagan philosophers because of her Christian beliefs, but miraculously converted them; St Michael was an angel who dressed in male clothing and was also linked to the Valois royal family.[100] There are other examples of the pressure during the trial forcing Joan to fabricate answers, not least of which is the unbelievable story of an angel appearing at Chinon, bringing a crown for Charles VII [35–8, 40–3].

From the perspective of the judges, the crucial issue was that Joan's testimony regarding her voices demonstrated that she was guilty of heresy. Firstly, they accused Joan of committing idolatry by venerating, embracing and kissing the saints when they came to her, and declared that she had been physically seduced by her false idols. She had experienced these saints in a physical form, despite the theological assumption that saints would not recover their bodies until the Resurrection. She had even been led to swear an oath, her vow of virginity, to the three saints when such a promise could only be made to God [37–9, 52–3].[101] Secondly, Joan had failed to secure any

98 Fraioli, *Joan of Arc: the early debate*, p. 197.

99 K. Sullivan, "'I do not name to you the voice of St. Michael": the identification of Joan of Arc's voices', in *Fresh Verdicts on Joan of Arc*, pp. 85–112.

100 G. Guéry, *La culte de Sainte Catherine d'Alexandrie*, Paris, 1912; E. Delaruelle, 'L'archange saint Michel dans la spiritualité de Jeanne d'Arc', in *La piété populaire au moyen âge*, Turin, 1975, pp. 389–400. It may not be appropriate to conflate the stories of St Margaret of Antioch and the St Margaret who was also known as St Pelagien.

101 S. Schibanoff, 'True lies: transvestism and idolatory in the trial of Joan of Arc', in *Fresh Verdicts on Joan of Arc*, pp. 31–60, and Sullivan, *The Interrogation of Joan of Arc*, pp. 36–8.

clerical advice about these voices. While the medieval Church accepted that both men and women could communicate directly with God and his angels or saints, it believed that learning and divine grace were necessary in order to determine whether such visions and mystical experiences were genuine, or frauds perpetrated by the devil. Holy women and visionaries were normally expected to take advice from a cleric, serving as their spiritual director.[102] Yet Joan testified that she had only spoken about the voices with Robert de Baudricourt and her King, and in general relied upon her own judgement in determining whether or not these were angels or saints, asserting that she recognised the angelic speech and language of St Michael [**37, 41**]. The judges were quick to point out the irony of the fact that Joan had not seen any need to seek confirmation of her own experiences, but then had sought to test Catherine de La Rochelle's claims to see visions [**39**].

Indeed, for the Rouen judges, this failure to accept the need for clerical approval for her actions and judgement was a clear manifestation of Joan's defiance of authority. They charged her with being a schismatic for failing to recognise the unity and authority of the Church militant on earth, united under the pope. All Christians were required to accept the necessity of belonging to the Church in order to attain eternal salvation, but the judges claimed that Joan had rejected these principles, claiming to speak directly to the Church triumphant in heaven [**36–7, 46–8, 51–2**]. It is far from certain that Joan was as dismissive of the Church on earth as the judges claimed. On 24 May 1431, Joan did in fact submit herself to the pope at Rome, and a number of witnesses at the Nullification trial stated that she had consistently upheld the authority of the papacy and the Church [**54, 89, 98–9**]. Moreover the attack that the judges levelled against her for failing to uphold the authority of Pope Martin V in response to a letter of Jean Count of Armagnac seems harsh [**25**]. Nevertheless, Joan did assert a direct relationship with God that effectively gave her the ability to bypass the Church. She warned Cauchon that he was in peril for daring to judge her [**36, 44**]. Furthermore, she was occasionally pushed into statements that sounded perilously close to claims that she was incapable of mortal sin, or at least that she could be certain of divine pardon for her sins [**36, 38–9, 52–3**].

Joan's enemies also tried to use her military achievements against her, denying that God would really condone such bloodshed and warfare, or even encourage the people of France to abandon their oaths to support the Treaty of Troyes. The tract *De quadam puella*, usually regarded as the work of a supporter of Joan, had questioned whether the offer of temporal happiness to a people (through military success) could be regarded as proof of divine favour [**22**]. The anonymous author of *De bono et malo spiritu* was even more direct, emphasising that Joan did not bring peace but rather war [**27**]. The same theme was prominent during the Rouen trial, when the clerics attacked Joan for being a warmonger. They argued that Joan's pretence to be inspired by God had encouraged violence and bloodshed which were 'contrary to holiness, and horrible and abominable to all minds' [**36, 48**].[103] Moreover, they held that Joan's decision to mount an attack upon Paris on 8 September 1429, the Feast of the Nativity of the Virgin, undermined all her claims to be virtuous and pious, and the defeat of the Valois forces demonstrated that God was on the side of the English and their allies [**35, 43, 45–6, 59**]. Similarly, her capture at Compiègne was presented as clear evidence that God's favour was with the supporters of Henry VI rather than those of Charles VII. As Pierre Cauchon declared at the very start of the trial, 'it has pleased Providence from above that a certain woman named Joan, commonly called the Pucelle, should be taken and apprehended by famous warriors within the boundaries and limits of our diocese and jurisdiction'.[104]

Yet if Joan was not in fact supported by God, from where did her military successes come? For her enemies, the most likely explanation was either that she was being aided by the devil, or that she was herself a supernatural being. *De quadam puella* admitted that the first question regarding Joan was whether she was in fact some being transmuted into human form, while the Bourgeois of Paris famously described her as 'a creature ... who was in the form of a woman that

---

103 The late medieval Church did accept that God could approve of warfare if fought for a just cause and with the right intention, which ultimately had to be the re-establishment of peace: J. Barnes, 'The just war', in N. Kretzmann, A. Kenny and J. Pinborg (eds), *The Cambridge History of Later Medieval Philosophy: from the rediscovery of Aristotle to the disintegration of scholasticism, 1100–1600*, Cambridge, 1982, pp. 771–84. It is unlikely that Joan was familiar with the complex theological debates surrounding this doctrine of the just war, but she consistently emphasised not just the legitimate grounds for the war but also her ultimate desire for peace, which would allow a united crusade against the real enemies of the Church [**4, 18**].

104 Tisset (ed.), *Procès de condamnation*, I, p. 1.

was named the Pucelle' [**22, 59**]. The churchmen from the University of Paris were more inclined to argue that Joan was in league with the devil, which in turn encouraged them to consider her to be a witch and a sorceress [**27, 54, 57, 59**]. Her trial took place at a pivotal moment in the development of clerical anxieties about witchcraft and sorcery, the beginning of the witch-hunts that marked the early modern period.[105] There was a rising paranoia among theologians who no longer imagined that sorcerers and witches were the innocent dupes of demons, but rather believed that such people were deliberately invoking and worshipping supernatural, diabolical powers.[106] There was an assumption that even popular magic depended upon the kind of complex rituals and invocations that had been employed in the demonic magic of necromancers. In short witches were guilty not merely of using sorcery and magic, but also of taking part in a wide conspiracy that involved the adoration, veneration and worship of demons, and even the rejection of the structures of the Church in favour of a completely different and rival structure. Thus before and after her capture, Joan's enemies claimed that she had been involved in superstitious and magical activities. During the Rouen trial she had to fend off a series of questions relating to witchcraft and magic, searching for evidence that she had encouraged people to worship, adore and idolise her. It is possible that Joan's enemies were picking up on wider rumours and stories that were circulating about her: the author of the *De mirabili victoria* felt the need to defend Joan against the potential charge that she had practised forbidden spells, superstitions or frauds, long before any surviving evidence that her enemies were making such claims [**7**].[107] The author of *De bono et malo spiritu*

105 M. D. Bailey, 'From sorcery to witchcraft: clerical conceptions of magic in the later middle ages', *Speculum*, LXXVI, 2001, pp. 960–90, and *Battling Demons: witchcraft, heresy and reform in the late middle ages*, Philadelphia, 2003; E. Peters, 'The medieval Church and state on superstition, magic and witchcraft: from Augustine to the sixteenth century', in B. Ankarloo and S. Clark (eds), *Witchcraft and Magic in Europe: the middle ages*, Philadelphia, 2002, pp. 173–245.

106 Throughout the later middle ages, such charges were extremely powerful political weapons: the Duke of Burgundy had justified the murder of Louis of Orléans in 1407 partially by charging him and his wife, Valentina Visconti, with plotting to use sorcery against King Charles VI (J. R. Veenstra, *Magic and Divination at the Courts of Burgundy and France: text and context of Laurens Pignon's 'Contre les devineurs' (1411)*, Leiden, 1998, pp. 81–5). Similar charges were levelled against both Joan of Navarre, second wife of Henry IV of England, and Eleanor Cobham, wife of the Duke of Gloucester, as well as against the Duke of Alençon and Gilles de Rais, companions of Joan of Arc.

107 Brother Richard tried to exorcise her at their first meeting at Troyes, until she promised him, presumably with some irony, that she would not fly away [**39**].

picked up on this, claiming that Joan had practised witchcraft, magic and heresy by dripping wax on to children in order to ensure that they would be good; he also reported that images of Joan were being venerated while she was still alive, despite the fact that no one should be treated as a saint while still living [27]. Both these charges were repeated in the Seventy Articles at Rouen, where the judges seem to have been well informed about very specific stories and examples of sorcery and witchcraft. The most famous example was the attempt to link her to the superstitious and even magical activities involving a tree in the village of Domremy known as the Tree of the Ladies, or the Tree of the Fairies. For the judges, such ritualistic actions and the involvement of the Fairies must have sounded suspiciously close to the involvement of witches in a diabolical sabbath [36, 38, 47–8, 74–6].[108] The judges also asked Joan about her knowledge of mandrake, a plant that was associated with the practice of magic, and her involvement in the resuscitation of a baby that had apparently died at Lagny [38–9]. Joan was questioned at length about whether she or her followers had tried to apply magic to rings, banners and standards, particularly through the use of the names 'Jhesus Maria': the implication was that Joan believed that these names had magical power or effects when she applied them to physical objects, including letters [37–8, 48, 52].[109] The judges also knew that Joan had found a special sword behind the altar at the church of Sainte-Catherine-de-Fierbois, and questioned Joan closely to discern whether she had employed magic in making this miraculous discovery.[110] Many of these charges were presented in the Seventy Articles, but all except the story of the Fairy Tree were dropped in the Twelve Articles that provided the formal grounds for Joan's condemnation [52].

In summary, there is no doubt that the judgement against the Pucelle removed a thorn from the English side and also served to undermine

108 Sullivan, *The Interrogation of Joan of Arc*, ch. 1. For the witches' sabbath, see M. D. Bailey, 'The medieval concept of the witches' Sabbath', *Exemplaria*, VIII, 1996, pp. 419–39; C. Ginzburg, *Ecstasies: deciphering the witches' sabbath*, London, 1990, and M. Ostorero, 'Folâtrer avec les démons'. *Sabbat et chasse aux sorciers à Vevey (1448)*, Lausanne, 1995.

109 There was a longstanding debate between the Franciscan Order, who encouraged popular reverence for the names of Jesus and Mary, and the Dominicans, who regarded it as a satanic cult of the Antichrist: Pope Martin V (1417–31) ruled that this devotion was acceptable if the name of Jesus was combined with a cross (J. Van Herwaarden, 'The appearance of Joan of Arc', in J. Van Herwaarden (ed.), *Joan of Arc: reality and myth*, Hilversum, 1994, pp. 63–4).

110 See page 18 above.

Charles VII. Nevertheless, this does not exclude the possibility that the clerics and their English allies were genuinely concerned about the threat posed by heresy and even witchcraft. Following the execution of Joan, there was a concerted campaign to disseminate the judgement that may have indirectly undermined Charles VII, but more obviously served to warn people about the dangers of heresy and witchcraft. This was the message of the letters written on behalf of Henry VI [57], as well as the public sermon delivered by the Inquisitor of France, Jean Graverent, at Saint-Martin-des-Champs in Paris on 4 July 1431; citing numerous details from the transcripts, he made it clear that his concerns went far beyond the particular case of Joan, not least by associating her with other heretics and thereby implying that this was a cancer that had not been completely extinguished [59]. Indeed at least twenty-four of the clerics who had taken part in the Rouen trial attended the Church Council at Basel (1431–49), where witchcraft was a topic of grave concern. There is no doubt that the case of Joan was considered there as part of a much wider problem. One of the Parisians, Nicolas Lami, spoke to a German theologian, Johannes Nider, who included Joan as an example of a sorceress in his famous treatise against demonology and witchcraft, *Formicarius* [65].[111]

Remembering Joan

The capture and death of Joan of Arc had little direct impact on English fortunes during the war, which had reached deadlock. She had played an important role in the victory at Orléans that was pivotal in preventing the English forces from crossing the Loire, and had also helped to inspire a new sense of self-belief in the men-at-arms. Moreover, her presence with the army may well have helped to persuade key towns to submit to the control of Charles VII.[112] Nevertheless most military historians are reluctant to argue that Joan played a crucial role in the process that culminated in the final defeat and expulsion of the English forces from France, over twenty years

111 The interest in Joan could be reflected by the fact that the only surviving copy of *De bono et malu spiritu* exists in a manuscript from Basel, where it was presumably brought by the delegation from the University of Paris [27].

112 K. DeVries, 'A woman as leader of men: Joan of Arc's military career', in *Fresh Verdicts on Joan of Arc*, pp. 3–18.

after her death.[113] Far more important were the final collapse of the Anglo-Burgundian alliance in 1435, and the radical reforms of the French army in the 1440s. Encouraged by two cardinals sent by Pope Eugenius IV and the Council of Basel, the French, Burgundians and English entered into lengthy diplomatic negotiations, which failed to secure an end to the conflict, but did result in the reconciliation of the Duke of Burgundy and the French King at Arras on 21 September 1435.[114] Deprived of their most important ally in France, the English military effort was all but doomed: diplomatic negotiations led to the marriage in 1444 of Henry VI and Margaret of Anjou, daughter of René of Anjou and niece by marriage of Charles VII, but even this personal union between the royal families failed to secure a permanent resolution to the war. During this period Charles had been reforming his army and, when the English broke the truce in March 1449, French military superiority led to the recovery of Normandy in less than a year. In 1451, Charles' forces invaded Aquitaine and quickly recovered most of the duchy; the defeat of the English under the command of John Talbot, Earl of Shrewsbury, at Castillon on 17 July 1453, effectively ended the Hundred Years War.

There is little doubt that the English and their allies initially made a sustained effort to publicise the judgement against Joan of Arc [**57, 59**]. Yet if the goal was to destroy her reputation, they were hardly successful. One Parisian, Clément de Fauquembergue, did accept the heresy trial without question, even invoking the authority of the trial record to support the judgement [**58**]. The so-called Bourgeois of Paris had also witnessed the Pucelle's attack upon the city and had access to extremely detailed information about the charges levelled against her at Rouen, but he did not automatically accept the judgement [**59**]. Even Burgundian sources such as the *Chronicle of the Cordeliers* and the chronicle of Enguerrand de Monstrelet were far more positive about Joan than one might expect. Monstrelet famously witnessed a meeting between the Duke of Burgundy and the Pucelle

---

113 C. T. Allmand, *The Hundred Years War*; A. Curry, *The Hundred Years War, 1337–1452*, 2nd edition, Basingstoke, 2003; M. G. A. Vale, 'France at the end of the Hundred Years War (c.1420–1461)', in C. T. Allmand (ed.), *The New Cambridge Medieval History, VII: c.1415–c.1500*, Cambridge, 1998, pp. 392–407. It is also crucial to consider the changing English reactions to the war: W. M. Ormrod, 'The domestic response to the Hundred Years War', in A. Curry and M. Hughes (ed.), *Arms, Armies and Fortifications in the Hundred Years War*, Woodbridge, 1994, pp. 83–101.

114 Warner, 'The Anglo-French Dual Monarchy and the house of Burgundy, pp. 103–30.

shortly after her capture, but judiciously avoided making any comment by claiming that he could not remember what was said; similarly, he made no comment on the Rouen trial [61, 68]. Even fifteenth-century English chroniclers were extremely quiet about Joan, generally saying little about her heresy or the trial at Rouen [32, 104].

Indeed the most remarkable postscript to the events at Rouen was the ease with which at least two women were able to claim to be Joan of Arc. It is tremendously difficult to establish exactly what happened from the confusing references scattered across a range of chronicles and sources. In 1436, a woman called Claude des Armoires, whose real name may have been Elisabeth of Görlitz, pretended to be the Pucelle, travelling around the German empire between Metz, Trier and Cologne where she was finally challenged by the Inquisitor [65]. Three years later, the false Joan reappeared in Orléans and then briefly allied with Gilles de Laval, Lord of Rais, one of the companions of Joan of Arc who would be arrested the following year and condemned to death for horrific crimes.[115] In 1440, the false Joan went to Paris, where she was brought before the Parlement, but it is unclear what happened to her. This is a remarkable story, not least because Claude des Armoires failed to act like the Pucelle in such obvious ways: she may have been married and had children, danced, feasted and drank, and spoke in vague parables. A few years later, another woman named Jeanne la Féronne briefly claimed to be Joan of Arc and was known as the Pucelle of Le Mans.[116]

During all these events, Charles VII and his advisers clearly decided that silence was the best course of action. The King made no public statement regarding Joan, while Jean Juvénal des Ursins shockingly ignored Joan when summarising the military events of the previous years in an account that he composed for diplomats taking part in the negotiations at Arras in 1435 [64].[117] It was not until twenty years later, during the reconquest of Normandy, that Charles was willing to open the events surrounding the Pucelle to public scrutiny. On 15 February 1450, he wrote to Guillaume Bouillé, asking him to

---

115 R. Hyatte (trans.), *Laughter for the Devil: the trials of Gilles de Rais, companion-in-arms of Joan of Arc*, London, 1984.

116 The surviving sources are far from clear about precisely what transpired, as demonstrated by D. A. Berents, 'The resurrection of Joan of Arc', in Van Herwaarden (ed.), *Joan of Arc: reality and myth*, pp. 75–95.

117 Only Jean Chartier was willing to include Joan in his continuation of the official chronicle written by the Monk of Saint-Denis [67].

undertake a preliminary investigation into the circumstances of the
Rouen trial [69]. Even then, the avowed objectives of this investigation were extremely narrow, and once it was complete, the
impetus for further progress only came from others, such as Joan's
family, Cardinal d'Estouteville and Guillaume Bouillé, and the Papacy
[70–2].

There were obvious practical reasons for the tentativeness of Charles
VII and his advisers. Firstly, any response to the judgement at Rouen
in May 1431 would depend upon access both to the records of the
original trial at Rouen and to the individuals who had participated in
it. Paris was not recaptured until April 1436, granting the King
access to many of those members of the University who had taken
part in the trial of Joan of Arc, while Rouen was not taken until 19
November 1449. Secondly, any attempt to overturn the verdict of the
Rouen trial, conducted by a bishop and a representative of the
Inquisitor of France, needed the assistance and authorization of the
Papacy. This created an extremely delicate situation for the French
Crown, especially after the Pragmatic Sanction of Bourges in 1438
had placed Charles VII at loggerheads with the Papacy over the
extent of its interference in the French Church. There was also the
possibility that the Pope might use the case of Joan of Arc to make
judgements on the legitimacy of Charles VII as King of France. More
fundamentally, there were clear risks in reopening the matter of Joan
of Arc. There is very little evidence that his enemies were attacking
Charles VII for his involvement with Joan and so dredging up the
past could only serve to remind people of the King's association with
a supposed heretic. Of course, such issues were less of a concern after
the English had been defeated and Charles VII had demonstrated the
justice of his claim to the throne in the most obvious and public
manner possible. Indeed, the re-examination of the Rouen trial offered
an opportunity to heal some of the wounds caused by Frenchmen
collaborating with the English. Throughout the Nullification trial,
the witnesses consistently avoided personal responsibility for any of
the actions of the Rouen trial, instead blaming the English for
exerting pressure to secure the death of Joan, and arguing that they
had been frightened into cooperating with such a manifestly unjust
action. In short, the primary goal of the Nullification trial may not
have been to restore the reputation of the Pucelle but to expunge the
legacy of collaboration with the English and to give added substance
to her dream of a united France. Certainly, Charles VII was deeply

reluctant to allow the emergence of any form of cult around Joan of Arc after the verdict of 1456.[118]

The inquiry led by Guillaume Bouillé opened on 4 and 5 March 1450 with the questioning of seven witnesses who had participated in the trial of Joan of Arc in 1431.[119] It may well be that his inquiry was stopped because of the war in Normandy or because of deteriorating relations with the Papacy: either way, he failed to collect any documents relating to the previous trial, as Charles had requested, or to talk to a number of obvious witnesses such as Jean Le Maistre, Guillaume Colles or Nicolas Taquel. The matter was put on hold until the arrival in France of Cardinal Guillaume d'Estouteville, Pope Nicholas V's emissary, in August 1451. The Cardinal favoured the resumption of inquiries into the Rouen trial: he presumably hoped that, if this pleased Charles VII, he might achieve his primary objectives of securing French support for a crusade against the Turks and of bringing an end to the legal limits on papal powers in France established by the Pragmatic Sanction of Bourges (1438). Yet the Cardinal was also a Norman, who had a personal desire to wipe away the stain on Joan's character: his father had been captured by the English when they seized Harfleur in 1415, his brother Louis had defended Mont-Saint-Michel and taken part in the recovery of Normandy in 1449 and 1450, and he himself was a cousin of Charles VII through his mother Marguerite of Harcourt. As a result, the Cardinal willingly chaired a preliminary and preparatory inquiry, in Rouen in May 1452, accompanied by Jean Bréhal, one of the two inquisitors of France; their objective was to collect evidence that the original trial had been irregular and unjust, and thereby justify a further judicial trial to render the judgement against Joan null and void. Five witnesses were interviewed on 2 and 3 May 1452, before the inquiry was effectively restarted, partly because the Cardinal was called away from Rouen but also to allow the questions being posed to the witnesses to be redrafted and expanded; the five witnesses were questioned again alongside another twelve individuals on 8 and 9 May. Their depositions, which provided the evidence justifying a full-scale trial, were presented to King Charles VII by Guillaume Bouillé and Jean Bréhal [70].

---

118 The Nullification trial may also have served as a response to the potential threat of false Joan of Arcs: see page 41 above.

119 This inquiry had no canonical authority and so these statements were not admitted as evidence during the Nullification trial.

Nevertheless it was not Pope Nicholas V but rather his successor, Calixtus III, who finally authorised a full-scale investigation into the trial of Joan of Arc. Immediately after he was elected, he issued a papal bull dated 11 June 1455, appointing three judges to respond to a petition from the family of Joan of Arc who had complained about the dishonour that they had suffered as a result of the infamy inflicted upon her [71–2]. The ensuing legal proceedings used to be known as the Rehabilitation trial, but this title is somewhat misleading. The aim was not to reform or overturn the earlier sentence, as would happen in an appeal court, but rather to demonstrate that it was entirely invalid and therefore to wipe it from the record and treat it as completely null and void. As a result, it is more appropriate to refer to the proceedings that opened on 7 November 1455 as a Nullification trial.

This Nullification trial followed completely different procedures from the original one at Rouen in 1431. Firstly, it was presented as an action by the family of Joan of Arc as plaintiffs against those responsible for the original trial at Rouen, that is to say the two judges, Pierre Cauchon and Jean Le Maistre, together with their Promoter, Jean d'Estivet; in practice, of course, this was a legal ploy because the defendants were dead by 1455 and so could never appear in court, and the individuals who had inherited their offices stead-fastedly refused to take any part in the new trial. Secondly, this new trial depended upon the testimony of a host of witnesses who had known Joan, or who had participated in the original trial, in stark contrast to the Rouen trial where no witnesses had been brought forward to support the charges against the Pucelle. These witnesses were questioned at Domremy, Vaucouleurs, Toul, Orléans, Paris, Rouen and Lyon between January and May 1456 [74–101]. In addition, the plaintiffs submitted a range of supporting documents at the conclusion of the trial in June 1456, including a collection of legal opinions in support of their case, written by a series of eminent theologians including Elie de Bourdeilles, Thomas Basin, Martin Berruyer, Jean Bochard, Jean de Montigny, Guillaume Bouillé, Robert Ciboule and Jean Bréhal.[120] Having reviewed all this evidence, the three judges pronounced their verdict in the form of a sentence of

---

120 The dossier also included *De mirabili victoria* [7] which was identified as the work of Jean Gerson These lengthy memoirs are edited in P. Lanery d'Arc (ed.), *Mémoires et consultations en faveur de Jeanne d'Arc, par les juges du procès de réhabilitation*, Paris, 1889, and Duparc (ed.), *Procès en nullité*, II.

nullification on 7 July 1456: they decreed that the Twelve Articles against Joan were falsely extracted from the trial record and were defamatory, and they proclaimed that the trial and sentences of condemnation at Rouen were null and void, and that neither Joan nor her family had incurred any stain of infamy as a result [**102**].

Yet it is important to recognise that there were important limits to the scope and to the verdict of the Nullification trial. The judges attacked the documents from the Rouen trial, but they did not blame any specific individuals, no doubt being concerned to heal the wounds that had divided France. In November 1449 Charles VII had granted letters of abolition to all the inhabitants of Normandy, protecting them against any legal repercussions for their actions during the English occupation. It is therefore not surprising that the Nullification judges did not condemn any of the clerics who had assisted in the original Rouen trial; indeed, the statements of those individuals who had participated in the original trial must be handled with some care, as they carefully sought to defend each other and to cast blame upon the English for treatment of Joan [**88–9, 98–9**]. At the same time, the Nullification judges did not pass any verdict on Joan's orthodoxy or sanctity: that would have to wait until nearly six hundred years later, when the Pucelle was finally canonised by the Catholic Church in 1920. Moreover, the results of the Nullification trial were not as widely publicised as the supporters of Joan might have hoped. The official sentence was not included in the official history of France, the *Grandes Chroniques*, as the d'Arc family had requested. The judges did order their sentence to be published in Rouen and had a cross erected in memory of Joan, but in practice there was an official effort to prevent a cult of Joan of Arc by expressly forbidding that 'images and epitaphs' should be set up at Rouen or elsewhere.

Yet the memory of Joan remained alive.[121] The clearest evidence of this comes from Orléans, the city that Joan had saved from the English. Even before the Nullification trial, Orléans had begun to stage an annual celebration to commemorate the relief of the city. The citizens not only provided a dinner for the officials involved in the Nullification trial, but also commissioned the *Journal du siège d'Orléans*. The city may also have had a special play, the *Mistère du siège d'Orléans*, performed at around the time of the Nullification trial [**105**]. Indeed, the tensions between Joan and Charles VII were

121 P. Lanéry d'Arc, *Le culte de Jeanne d'Arc au XVe siècle*, Orléans, 1887.

forgotten, it would seem, as a monument to the two individuals was also placed on the bridge to the fortress of the Tourelles.[122]

Gendering Joan

The accomplishments of Joan of Arc are remarkable, given that she had to overcome the significant cultural and social prejudices of a medieval society that valued men more highly than women. Indeed, her story sheds important light on contemporary ideas of gender, that is to say the perceptions and expectations of behaviour, familial roles, physical and mental abilities, and even sexual orientation that distinguished men and women. As a holy woman and a virgin, Joan asserted her right to self-determination and escaped the normal roles that would have been available to her as a female, particularly as daughter, wife and mother, not to mention the restrictions placed upon her by her social status as a peasant.[123] At the same time, though, Joan directly usurped male roles, both practically by acting as a warrior and symbolically by adopting male clothing.[124] As a result she acquired a level of power usually denied to women of all but the highest social status and directly challenged the assumption that 'all masculine duties are forbidden to women, for example, to preach, to teach, to bear arms, to absolve, to excommunicate' [27].[125]

At the centre of Joan's gendered identity was the title that she adopted, 'Pucelle'. There is very little evidence that either Joan or her contemporaries referred to her by the surname of her father, 'd'Arc'.[126]

122 V. L. Hamblin, '"En l'honneur de la Pucelle": ritualizing Joan the Maid in fifteenth-century Orléans', in *Joan of Arc and Spirituality*, pp. 209–26.

123 The social threat represented by Joan's humble origins may partly explain the extraordinary notion, first proposed in 1764, that she had in fact been of royal blood, the illegitimate daughter of Queen Isabeau and Louis, Duke of Orléans.

124 There is no evidence to suggest that Joan was deliberately aiming to access these roles for any other reason than to fulfil her divine mission.

125 There were other contemporary women who did exercise extraordinary levels of power, both through their status as holy women and visionaries or through high birth and marriage. For the latter, see for example, M. Sommé, *Isabella de Portugal, Duchesse de Bourgogne. Une femme au pouvoir au XVe siècle*, Villeneuve d'Ascq, 1998; G. and P. Contamine (eds), *Autour de Marguerite d'Ecosse: reines, princesses et dames du XVe siècle*, Paris, 1999; J. L. Laynesmith, *The Last Medieval Queens: English queenship, 1445–1503*, Oxford, 2004.

126 One explanation for the surname 'Arc' is that Joan's father Jacques carried a bow ('arc' in French), while others argue that Joan's father had a coat of arms with a

She may have used this name during the Rouen trial, and Pope
Calixtus III referred to Joan of Arc in his letter responding to the plea
of Joan's family for a re-examination of the Rouen trial of condemnation [34, 49, 71]. Yet even Calixtus recognised that Joan was more
commonly known as the Pucelle, the name that she used to refer to
herself in her letters [4, 9, 16–18, 23, 25b, 29].[127] At first sight, such
a name was an odd choice for a 'nom de guerre'. The word 'pucelle'
had first appeared in Old French in the eleventh century, when it
simply meant a 'young girl'. But a more nuanced meaning as 'young
female virgin' emerged from the twelfth century onwards, in both
Middle French and Anglo-Norman.[128] The terms 'pucelle' and 'vierge'
(virgin), or their Latin equivalents, 'puella' and 'virgo', were often
used in an interchangeable fashion.[129] Indeed supporters of Joan of
Arc were able to associate her with prophecies relating to virgins,
simply by replacing the term 'Virgo' with 'Puella'.[130] The same link
was indicated by Jean Pasquerel during his Nullification trial; he told
the story of a man who threatened Joan of Arc, promising that if he
spent a night with her, she would no longer be a 'pucelle' [95]. Jean
d'Aulon testified that the Queen of Sicily physically inspected Joan
and confirmed that she was a 'pucelle' [101]. The nearest English
translation of 'pucelle' would be 'maiden', a term used in late medieval
England to refer to a female who was passing through the transitional
period leading from childhood to full adulthood: she was on the cusp
of marriage, sex and motherhood but still untouched by these episodes,

---

gold 'arc' that gave them their surname. It seems more likely that the word 'Arc'
refers to a place, perhaps Arc (Art) sur Meurthe near Nancy or Arc-en-Barrois
near Chaumont. Joan's mother was known as Isabelle Romée because she had
presumably completed a pilgrimage.

127 It is unclear when Joan first used that name. According to her testimony at the
Rouen trial, her voices referred to her as 'Jeanne la Pucelle', but the villagers from
Domremy did not know her by this name [41, 74–6].

128 *Dictionnaire historique de la langue française*, Paris, 1992, II, p. 1666 and *Grand
Larousse de la langue française en sept volumes*, Paris, 1971, VI, 4765–6. Also see K.
M. Phillips, 'The Medieval Maiden: young womanhood in late medieval England',
PhD dissertation, University of York, 1997, pp. 22–3.

129 F. H. Stoertz, 'Young women in France and England, 1050–1300', *Journal of
Women's History*, XII, 2001, p. 23.

130 For example, the zodiac prophecies in S. Luce (ed.), *Chronique du Mont-Saint-
Michel (1343–1468)*, 2 vols, Paris, 1879–83, II, pp. 28–31. Note also the title of the
prophetic poem *Virgo puellares*, that sets these two terms alongside one another in
the first two words [6]. Similarly, in 1456, the *Registre Delphinal* of Mathieu
Thomassin compared the 'Pucelle Jehanne' with the 'pucelle Vierge Marie':
Quicherat (ed.), *Procès de condamnation*, IV, p. 310.

a youth who was required to hold on to her virginity until she was married.[131]

Thus the name 'Pucelle' celebrated Joan's youth and virginity, and in the process constructed a different, empowering identity for her, to stand against the more familiar roles of wife, mother or widow. It is perhaps not surprising then that her enemies attacked exactly this contention by suggesting that she was sexually active and even pro- miscuous.[132] Yet her virginity was confirmed on at least two occasions, firstly when she arrived at Chinon and secondly, during the Rouen trial, on the instructions of the Duchess of Bedford [**88–9, 95, 99, 101**]. Jean d'Aulon went further, claiming that he heard from Joan's female attendants that 'she never had the secret illness of women' [menstruation] and was thereby separated from the descendants of Eve [**101**]. Indeed Joan's virginity and lack of sexuality even became quasi-miraculous in the virtually hagiographic accounts offered by her military companions at the Nullification trial. They testified that they had lost all carnal desires around Joan, despite the fact that she was a beautiful woman, and also emphasised that she had refused to allow her soldiers to cavort with prostitutes and loose women [**77, 80–1, 90–2, 94, 101**].[133] At the same time, an array of clerical witnesses testified that the real sexual threat during the Rouen trial came from the guards, and even an unidentified English lord who had threatened to rape Joan [**98**].[134] The only source to question Joan's virginity with any conviction was a Middle English Continuation of the Prose *Brut*, written between 1464 and 1470: the chronicle told the entirely fictitious story of how Joan claimed to be pregnant after her arrest, thereby gaining a reprieve until this was revealed to be a lie, where- upon she was burned [**104**].

Virginity was important because it could be used to justify defiance of male authority. As the early Church Fathers had associated the Fall of

---

131 In late medieval England, girls might be betrothed while still children due to family, political or economic interests, though this did create some anxieties: K. M. Phillips, 'Maidenhood as the perfect age of a woman's life', in K. J. Lewis, N. Menuge and K. M. Phillips (eds), *Young Medieval Women*, Stroud, 1999, pp. 4–5.

132 See page 33 above.

133 Their testimony was somewhat contradicted by that of Aimon, Lord of Macy [**97**].

134 Also see the testimony of Martin Ladvenu in 1450 and 1456, Jean Toutmouillé in 1450, Isembart de La Pierre in 1452, in Doncoeur (ed.), *L'enquête ordonnée par Charles VII en 1450*, pp. 39–45, and Duparc (ed.), *Procès en nullité*, I, pp. 185–7 and 440–4.

Man with sexuality, virginity was naturally regarded as the praise-worthy ideal of Christian perfection. Female virginity could raise a woman to the status of a man, freed from the weaknesses of the flesh and its associated irrationality. Defending Joan of Arc, Martin Le Franc cited the authority of the Church Father, St Jerome, who had emphasised angelic and divine approval for virginity [**66**]; Jerome famously wrote: 'while a woman serves for birth and children, she is different from man as body is from soul. But when she wants to serve Christ more than the world, then she shall cease to be called a woman and shall be called man.'[135] More directly, Joan's identity as a 'pucelle' may have been influenced by the model of the Virgin Mary and the virgin martyrs, a select group of female saints such as Katherine and Margaret who were familiar figures to her.[136] The virgin martyrs may have served primarily as examples of ideal behaviour, examples of excellence and devotion, but that does not mean that they were understood by women in an uncomplicated way. Their stories could be read as social narratives, and the virgin martyrs may have served to provide a legitimising example for young maidens who wished to refuse to marry, and hence defy their parents by upholding the higher spiritual value of virginity.[137] Certainly during the Rouen trial, Joan testified that she had defied her parents, and therefore the command-ment to honour one's father and mother, by refusing to marry a young man from Toul; moreover, she had left home despite ominous warnings and threats from her father who had had dreams predicting that she would go off with men-at-arms [**41–2, 52**].

Yet Joan's defiance of her parents was based upon not just her virginity, but also her direct relationship with God and her status as a visionary. At the Rouen trial, Joan testified that she made the vow to remain a virgin when she first heard the voices, and she associated her decision not to marry the man from Toul with this promise that she made to God [**41**]. This began a pattern of defiance of male

135 St Jerome, *Commentarium in Epistolam ad Ephesios*, in R. Evans and L. Johnson (eds), *Feminist Readings in Middle English Literature: the Wife of Bath and all her sect*, London, 1994, p. 166. It is possible that Jerome should be understood as using 'man' in a gender-neutral sense.

136 For the influences that the Virgin Mary may have had upon Joan, see L. G. Edwards, 'Joan of Arc: gender and authority in the text of the *Trial of Condemnation*', in *Young Medieval Women*, pp. 138–9, and A. Astell, 'The Virgin Mary and the "voices" of Joan of Arc', in *Joan of Arc and Spirituality*, pp. 37–60.

137 Phillips, 'Maidenhood as the perfect age of a woman's life', and K. J. Lewis, 'Model girls? Virgin-martyrs and the training of young women in late medieval England', in *Young Medieval Women*, pp. 1–46.

authority that continued throughout her life: she persevered despite
Robert de Baudricourt's initial unwillingness to listen to her [35];
she was not afraid to voice her displeasure with the Duke of Burgundy,
and even hinted at her frustration with the policy of negotiation
adopted by Charles VII [23, 29, 31]. Most prominently, of course,
she was able to defy the powerful and frightening figures of Cauchon
and the clerics at Rouen. The judges treated Joan as their inferior,
weakened by ignorance, lack of education and her feminine emotion,
while she defied their authority in a manner that, in their eyes, was
highly inappropriate for her sex – even if it did echo the story of St
Katherine of Alexandria.[138] On two occasions, she even threatened
Cauchon by pointing out the risk that he was taking in daring to
judge her [36, 44]. She explained her self-confidence both by the
positive reassurances that her voices gave her, but also the fact that
she was more afraid of failing them by saying something that might
displease them, than of answering her interrogators [36, 42]. In
short, like other holy women and mystics, her direct connection to the
divine gave her power and authority, even if the judges at the Rouen
trial did expect her to recognise their authority and to accept the need
for her visions to be authenticated by the Church.[139]

Yet Joan did more than evade negative and limiting female roles: she
also accessed masculine roles that were normally closed off for
females, even holy women. The most obvious of these was her
function as a warrior, from the siege of Orléans to her capture at
Compiègne, even though different eye-witnesses presented different
interpretations of her precise strategic and tactical contributions [59,
67, 81, 90, 94, 101, 105].[140] At the same time, she challenged
contemporary gender roles by dressing in clothing that was normally
reserved for men. The only surviving picture of Joan of Arc produced
during her lifetime is a sketch that appears in the margin of the journal
of Clément de Fauquembergue; the Parisian had never actually seen
Joan in person and so naturally assumed that she had long hair and
wore a dress.[141] Yet in fact Joan wore male clothing throughout her
remarkable public career. It would seem that she first adopted this

138 Joan's ability to stand up to the scrutiny of the theologians at Poitiers was twice
    compared with the defiant actions of St Katherine of Alexandria, miraculously
    converting a group of philosophers to Christianity [7, 12].

139 See pages 34 to 35 above.

140 DeVries, *Joan of Arc: a military leader.*

141 During the Rouen trial, Joan mentioned that she had seen a picture of herself in
    full armour drawn by a Scotsman, but this has not survived [39].

garb after she had left her home in Domremy: some of the witnesses
at the Nullification trial said that she was wearing a red dress when
she arrived at Vaucouleurs but that Jean de Nouillonpont and the
people of the city gave her male clothing [77–80]. On the battlefield,
Joan had an expensive set of armour that Charles VII had given to her
[90, 94, 101]; she also owned a number of swords, including one
given to her by Robert de Baudricourt, the sword that she
'miraculously' recovered from the church of Sainte-Catherine-de-
Fierbois, another that she gave as a votive offering at the shrine of
Saint-Denis in September 1429, and a sword that she captured from
the Burgundian captain Franquet d'Arras [35, 37, 67, 78–80,
105].[142]

The decision to dress in male clothing was more than a matter of
mere convenience, given that Joan continued to cross-dress when she
was not on military campaign. In June 1429, she was given an
expensive robe by the city of Orléans, paid for by Duke Charles, and
the anonymous author of the *Chronicle of the Cordeliers* reported that
when Joan was not wearing armour, 'she maintained the condition
and dress of a knight, her shoes tied with laces to her feet, her hose
and her doublet shapely and a hat on her head; she wore very handsome attire of cloth of gold and silk, nicely trimmed with fur' [61].
Indeed, Joan deliberately continued to wear male clothing throughout
her trial at Rouen, in direct protest to and contradiction of the judges
who described her clothing as 'a short tunic, hood, doublet, breeches
and hose with multiple aiguillettes, the hair on her head cut in a circle
above her ears' [52]. Modern studies of the phenomenon of cross-
dressing have explained it with reference to material pressures, such
as poverty, but also by sexuality and emotional pressure. Susan Crane
has even suggested that we should not exclude the possibility that
Joan's decision to dress as a man may have reflected her own
sexuality, though there is no direct evidence for this.[143] Such ideas
would undoubtedly have been difficult for Joan to articulate, and it is

---

142 The sword from Sainte-Catherine-de-Fierbois is discussed by B. Wheeler, 'Joan of
   Arc's sword in the stone', in *Fresh Verdicts on Joan of Arc*, pp. xi–xvi, and also see
   G. Krumeich, 'Jeanne d'Arc et son épée', in J. Maurice and D. Couty (eds), *Images
   de Jeanne d'Arc. Actes de colloque de Rouen (25–27 mai 1999)*, Paris, 2000, pp. 67–75.

143 V. R. Hotchkiss, *Clothes Make the Man: female cross-dressing in medieval Europe*, New
   York, 1996, pp. 4–5; S. Crane, 'Clothing and gender definition: Joan of Arc',
   Journal of Medieval and Early Modern Studies, XXVI, 1996, pp. 297–320, and *The
   Performance of Self: ritual, clothing and identity during the Hundred Years War*,
   Philadelphia, 2002, pp. 73–106.

a significant problem that the only 'direct' record of her views on the issue, as opposed to statements attributed to her by other witnesses, comes in the unusual circumstances of the Rouen trial.

When questioned about her decision to wear male clothing during the trial, Joan did not initially appear to recognise that this was a serious or problematic issue, simply stating that it was necessary and convenient for her; on a number of occasions, she even said that she would be willing to wear women's clothing again if this were the price of being released [35–7, 39, 47, 49]. Yet as the trial moved forward and the judges continued to insist that she would not be allowed to attend mass unless she resumed female clothing, she shifted tack and asserted that her decision to dress as a man was not only pleasing to God, but also part of the mission that he had entrusted to her, just like her military activities: she therefore could not abandon her male clothes except at the command of God, any more than she could give up her virginity, or her wider mission. In short, Joan shifted ground from arguing that her cross-dressing was merely practical and utilitarian to presenting it as a crucial element of her divine mission, without explaining, or seeing the need to explain, what practical benefits this actually had for the accomplishment of that mission [36, 45, 47]. Only after her abjuration, when she resumed male clothing, did she add that she needed to dress as a man because she was surrounded by men; this was part of her wider anxiety at the fact that she was chained up in a secular prison with male guards, and also that she had not been allowed to hear mass [55].

Whatever the personal reasons for Joan to cross-dress, both her activities as a warrior and her male clothing gave her an air of maleness and masculinity, and enabled her to access the male hegemony and social constructs of gender. While the qualities of courage, strength and perseverance were not confined to men, she expressed them in a particular masculine context. Yet she did this without abandoning or suppressing her femininity: Joan herself was insistent that was female, as celebrated by her title of the 'Pucelle'. There was certainly no question that the male clothing served as a disguise that would fool people into thinking that she was a man, despite the famous statements of the Bourgeois of Paris, indicating some public confusion about her sex [59]. The judges at the Rouen trial were quite clear that her clothing did not mask 'that which nature has accorded to her as the distinctive mark of her sex', just as the military witnesses at the Nullification trial were quite direct about the female aspects of her appearance [52–3]. In short, Joan presented a blurring, or even a contamination, of the masculine and feminine, a strange combination that has led some scholars to argue that she became an androgyne, neither male nor female but rather transcending these states to achieve a superior, higher order that was unearthly like the angels.[144] Yet there is no evidence that she herself aspired to such a sexually transcendent or idealised status as an androgyne, or that any of her contemporaries viewed her in that fashion: Christine de Pizan may have ascribed masculine qualities to Joan, but clearly regarded her as a female, and indeed a credit to her sex [20]. Rather her male clothing and her assumption of masculine roles was a direct result and symbol of the authority that she claimed because of her identity as a holy woman.

Joan's decision to wear male clothing was also a dangerous strategy, given the theological and cultural opposition to female cross-dressing. According to the Old Testament, this was an abomination (Deuteronomy 22: 5) and St Paul stated in the New Testament that a woman should not cut her hair because it was her veil of modesty (1 Corinthians 11: 14–15).[145] Behind these scriptural authorities lay an assumption that cross-dressing not only encouraged women to usurp male roles such as teaching, preaching or fighting, but also that inappropriate clothing would lead to immorality, and in particular to fornication [7, 22, 27]. As a result, Joan's enemies charged that her decision to wear male clothing demonstrated that she did not possess the outstanding virtue expected and required of a holy woman and visionary [24, 33, 52–3, 57]. During her trial at Rouen, the judges cited her cross-dressing as the clearest proof that she was in breach of divine law, and guilty of scandalous and immoral behaviour, inspired either by the devil or by mortal figures such as Robert de Baudricourt or Jean de Nouillonpont. While her decision to continue to wear male clothing was a direct act of defiance against the authority of the judges, it also provided the most obvious grounds upon which to condemn her: when the theologians and lawyers of the University of Paris were shown the Twelve Articles, one of which concerned cross-

---

144 M. Warner, *Joan of Arc: the image of female heroism*, London, 1981, ch. 7. Edwards also uses the term 'androgyne' with less rigour and precision in L. G. Edwards, 'Joan of Arc: gender and authority in the text of the *Trial of Condemnation*', pp. 133–52.

145 These authorities were cited by her enemies, for example in the third charitable admonition delivered by Jean de Châtillon to Joan on 2 May 1431, but also by her supporters when rejecting the arguments: Tisset (ed.), *Procès de condamnation*, I, p. 339, and [7, 22, 66].

dressing, they agreed that Joan was guilty of blasphemy by attributing her actions to God's command and apostasy for cutting off her
hair, wearing male clothing and refusing to resume the clothes of a
woman in order to receive communion. They also charged her with
idolatry because, as the fifth article stated, her male clothing did not
leave 'anything on her body that proves or indicates the female sex,
excepting that which nature has accorded to her as the distinctive
mark of her sex' [52–3]. In other words, Joan was only partially
emulating a man and thereby creating a false image that failed to
mask her own sex completely. She did not make attempt to cover up
the fact that she was female and therefore was not following the licit
example of St Margaret also called Pelagien, who famously hid her
femininity by dressing as a monk and cropped her hair in order to
evade marriage and to protect her chastity.[146] When Joan abjured her
crimes on 24 May, she confessed that she had broken divine law, holy
scripture and canon law by wearing immodest male attire against the
decency of nature, and not only resumed female clothing, but also
allowed her hair to be shaved off in order to remove her masculine
hairstyle [54]. Yet days later, she resumed male clothing, a visible
sign that she had recanted after hearing her voices again, for which
she was condemned to death [55–6].

It is hardly surprising that Joan's enemies used her transvestism as a
weapon against her. More interesting is the reaction of her supporters
who clearly had to rationalise and assimilate her unconventional
assumption of masculine roles and clothing with her status as a holy
woman and visionary. Joan's military activities were somewhat difficult
to justify, given the clear gendering of such activities. In the *Book of
the City of Ladies*, Christine de Pizan argued that as a result of the
physical weakness of women, 'they are at least spared from committing
and being punished for the acts of appalling cruelty, the murders and
terrible violent deeds which men who are equipped with the necessary
strength have performed in the past and still do today'; when she
wrote the *Book of Deeds of Arms and of Chivalry* in 1410, she invoked
the example of the goddess Minerva, who made armour and organised
formations for battle, simply to demonstrate that a woman might
discuss military matters.[147] Amazons such as Penthesilea, or Camilla,

146 S. Schibanoff, 'True lies: transvestism and idolatry in the trial of Joan of Arc', in
     Fresh Verdicts on Joan of Arc, pp. 31–60.

147 Christine de Pizan, *The Book of the City of Ladies*, trans. R. Brown-Grant,
     Harmondsworth, 1999, p. 34, and *The Book of Deeds of Arms and of Chivalry*, trans.
     S. Willard, Philadelphia, 1999, pp. 11–13.

the warrior heroine of the *Aeneid*, may have served to counteract an automatic prejudice against women warriors; Joan was linked with these mythical figures by a number of her defenders [7, 13, 15, 103]. Nevertheless, the Amazon never became the dominant image for Joan, no doubt because her mission was fundamentally Christian, while they were pagans whose strength and ability was developed through training rather than through a divine gift.[148] Instead, Joan's actions as a warrior came to be defended more by reference to the precedent of women from the Old Testament, individuals who demonstrated the ability of the weak to overcome the strong with the assistance of God: Esther and her cousin Mordecai had prevented an attempt to kill the Jews in the Persian empire (Esther 6–7); Judith was a widow who defended God and her country by beheading the Assyrian general Holofernes (Judith 11–13); Deborah, a more military prototype, led the Israelites in a great victory on the plain of Esdraelon against the Canaanites (Judges 4–5) [7, 13, 20, 22, 59, 65–6, 103]. The point was that Joan possessed extraordinary military skills and abilities that far transcended her sex, which served as clear proof that God was working through her [81, 90, 94, 101].[149] At the same time, it was crucial that Joan never took any human life: while she might have threatened to kill the English and their allies in her public letters, she never said that she would take any direct part in this herself, and she later stated that she had never killed anyone and had preferred her standard to her sword [4, 37, 38].

Defending Joan's decision to wear male clothing was far more difficult.[150] It is clear that the matter was an immediate issue of concern after her arrival at Chinon in the spring of 1429 because during the Rouen trial she indicated that she was asked about her clothing at Poitiers [39]. Yet it is impossible to know how much

---

148 Virgil told the story of Camilla, a legendary Volscian girl who joined the army of Turnus and was killed in battle by the Etruscan Arruns. According to many legends, the Amazons were a race of female warriors who supposedly cauterised their right breast so as to enable them to throw javelins more easily. See D. Fraioli, 'Why Joan of Arc never became an Amazon', *Fresh Verdicts on Joan of Arc*, pp. 189–204.

149 Christine de Pizan could not resist making a direct comparison between Joan and male historical figures: the Pucelle exceeded Hector, Achilles, Joshua and Gideon in strength, and was braver than any man in history [20].

150 One of the theologians who provided a legal opinion at the Nullification trial, Robert Ciboule, claimed that Deborah had also worn male clothing and carried arms, citing the authority of Alexander of Hales: Duparc (ed.), *Procès en nullité*, II, p. 377.

anxiety her cross-dressing caused among those theologians and her later defenders. The attempt to link Joan with a prophecy of Marie d'Avignon may provide one small insight into the way in which this was justified: Marie had supposedly been too frightened to accept a suit of armour but instead predicted that the Pucelle would take up these arms and protect the kingdom.[151] The most likely manner in which they approached the subject of Joan's cross-dressing was demonstrated by Jacques Gélu, Archbishop of Embrun, who participated in the investigation and later argued that it was appropriate for Joan to wear male clothing while involved in warfare because of the contact with men.[152] The problem remained that Joan also wore such garb away from the battlefield. It is unclear whether the anonymous author of *De quadam puella* deliberately ignored this fact when he stated that Joan wore male clothing that invigorated her when taking part in battles but resumed female garb afterwards, when she again became innocent and naïve [**22**]. Similarly, most sympathetic chroniclers only mentioned Joan's cross-dressing in the context of war. The *Chronique de la Pucelle* argued that Joan wore male clothing in order to preserve her virginity by preventing the soldiers around her from having carnal thoughts, an argument that was contradicted by the statements of her military companions at the Nullification trial who claimed never to have lusted after her, even when they saw her naked.[153] Another related defence of Joan's cross-dressing, based upon the authority of St Thomas Aquinas, was that women could wear male clothing in a situation of necessity, such as to hide from the enemy, or because of lack of other clothing, or some similar situation; this argument was presented by the German cleric who wrote the *Sibylla francica* in the second half of 1429, and the theologians like Jean Bréhal who provided legal opinions for the Nullification trial.[154]

The notion that Joan was wearing male clothing because of necessity or for military reasons was contradicted by the plain fact that she continued to wear male clothing away from the battlefield, not to mention the reality that her 'disguise' was far from complete. As a

151 See page 18 above.

152 Quicherat (ed.), *Procès de condamnation*, III, pp. 393–410.

153 A. Vallet de Viriville (ed.), *Chronique de la Pucelle ou chronique de Cousinot, suivie de la Chronique Normande de P. Cochon*, Paris, 1859, reprinted Paris, 1994, pp. 276–7. Also see Perceval de Cagny, *Chronique des ducs d'Alençon*, ed. H. Moranvillé, Paris, 1902, p. 140.

154 *Sibylla Francica* in Quicherat (ed.), *Procès de condamnation*, III, pp. 440–1, and Nullification tracts in Duparc (ed.), *Procès en nullité*, II, pp. 40–600.

result, the witnesses at the Nullification trial adopted a different tack, ignoring her own explanations and instead arguing that Joan needed protection because of the ever-present threat of rape by her guards or an English lord.[155] These statements are plausible, especially in light of the rare honesty of Aimon, Lord of Macy, regarding the abuse that Joan suffered in jail. Male clothing might well have provided more protection, particularly because of the use of laces to tie together garments, though ultimately this would only have served as little more than symbolic protection for her against the guards; any safeguard that she enjoyed must have come from the official protection afforded to her by important figures like the Duchess of Bedford or the Earl of Warwick [97–9].

Whatever unease her male supporters may have felt about her cross-dressing, it was clear that they accepted her status as a holy woman, and did not feel that her encroachment upon masculine identity was unacceptable. It has been suggested that her transgressions might have appeared less dangerous because she was assuming masculine roles in order to perform masculine actions, and hence conforming with the existing gender hierarchy: she was trying to better herself by distancing herself from womankind.[156] Yet her disguise was only partial, and therefore far more threatening than if she were able to pass as a man; moreover, her decision to continue to wear male clothing away from the battlefield, when there was no clear necessity, must also have been problematic. That her supporters were willing to overlook such problems must be explained, in part, by the dire situation in which they found themselves, and by the other ways in which she proved herself, particularly her success at Orléans. Moreover it is important to note that Joan's transgressions were not direct protests against societal views of gender: she was not presenting a case for women in general to usurp male functions within society. When Joan came to the conclusion that Catherine de La Rochelle's visions were false, she told the woman to return to her husband, her housework and her children, implying that these were the 'normal' activities denied to herself as a holy woman [39]. During the Rouen trial, she indicated that she had been reluctant to listen to her voices

155 See page 26 above.

156 This argument was first put forward by V. Bullough, 'Transvestites in the middle ages', *American Journal of Sociology*, LXXIX, 1974, p. 1382. Hotchkiss has also suggested that medieval attitudes toward cross-dressing were perhaps not as uniformly hostile as one might expect, though her arguments have not received universal approval: Hotchkiss, *Clothes Make the Man.*

and to go on her mission, and that she wanted to return to a 'normal' life, refusing to say whether she wished that she were a man [**36**]. She even declared that she would take up women's clothing if the judges would then allow her to leave, adding that she would go to her mother's house, a domestic space far from the public arena in which she found herself [**49**]. Indeed it has been suggested that she may not have regarded her service to God and her virginity as a permanent state: she repeatedly said that she would continue to serve God for as long as he commanded, perhaps implying that at some future point her mission would end and she would be able to move forward with her life.[157]

Her supporters clearly sought to re-emphasise her feminine qualities and virtues both as a counterbalance to the masculine identity that she had assimilated, particularly by dressing as a man, but also to emphasise the magnitude of the miracle that enabled this woman to achieve all that had done.[158] The most obvious example of this was the image of the shepherdess that became such a familiar way of depicting the Pucelle, without any basis in reality. Yet the witnesses at the Nullification trial also presented a carefully constructed image of the Pucelle: she was pure and virginal, and men lost their carnal desires around her, just as she discouraged her soldiers from consorting with prostitutes and swearing [**77, 80–1, 90–2, 94, 101**]. She was merciful and had great pity even for her enemies: for example, Louis de Coutes described her comforting a dying English soldier, and Pasquerel reported her anguish at the death of the English commander Glasdale, who had previously screamed abuse at her [**90, 95, 101**]. Most importantly, many of the witnesses reported that Joan wanted more than anything to leave the hard and painful world of the soldier behind, and to return to an ordinary life that was no longer accessible for her. For example, the Count of Dunois told the touching story of how Joan revealed to the Archbishop of Reims that she prayed to God 'that I might retire, abandoning arms, and that I might go to serve my father and mother, looking after their sheep with my sister and my brothers, who would rejoice so much to see me'

---

157 Crane, 'Clothing and gender definition'.

158 This also responded to the attempt by the Rouen judges to present Joan as hostile to women, and as losing female traits: for example, when preparing the official record, Thomas de Courcelles altered statements from the *Minute française* in order to make it sound as if she resented, or was competitive towards, the other women of Domremy who sewed. He also removed Joan's request for a female servant at the very end of the trial [**35, 55**].

[81]. Whether or not such stories were true, they demonstrated that Joan herself affirmed the normal roles expected of a woman.

Recent scholarship has questioned the value of studying extraordinary individuals who are poor reflections of the normal realities of power and gender roles in a society.[159] Joan of Arc was certainly an exceptional person, who transcended societal biases against women and was able to participate in a range of activities that were closed off to most females in late medieval society. She was only able to do this through extremely unusual circumstances, adopting specific roles and even disguises that necessarily meant that she was not empowering women in general. This important point has been most clearly reflected in changing reactions to Christine de Pizan's *Ditié de Jehanne d'Arc* [20]. An equally extraordinary woman, Pizan had written a series of works in defence of women against the attack of misogynists. As a result some scholars have argued that her poem on Joan was the culmination of her wider defence of women: in Joan she found an example of female virtue, strength and leadership that was equal to any man, and the two women effectively gave authority and dignity to one another.[160] Yet it is now commonly accepted that Christine did not view Joan as a role model for women, but rather saw her as a unique agent and instrument of God, whose natural female weakness was crucial in emphasising that her masculine qualities and abilities were miraculous.[161] Nevertheless the story of Joan does shed important light upon the constraints imposed upon females in late medieval society. She continues to be seen as an inspirational figure, not only because of her success in a male-dominated culture, but also her remarkable personal courage and piety.[162]

159 See for example, the important remarks in M. C. Erler and M. Kowaleski, 'A new economy of power relations: female agency in the middle ages', in M. C. Erler and M. Kowaleski (eds), *Gendering the Master Narrative: women and power in the middle ages*, Ithaca, 2003, pp. 1–16.

160 A. P. Barr, 'Christine de Pisan's *Ditié de Jehanne d'Arc*: a feminist exemplum for the *Querelle de femmes*', *Fifteenth Century Studies*, XIV, 1988, pp. 1–12; E. J. Benkov, 'The coming to writing: *auctoritas* and authority in Christine de Pizan', *Le moyen français*, XXXV–XXXVI, 1994–5, pp. 33–48; C. McWebb, 'Joan of Arc and Christine de Pizan: the symbiosis of two warriors in the *Ditié de Jehanne d'Arc*', in *Fresh verdicts on Joan of Arc*, pp. 133–44.

161 R. Brown-Grant, '"Hee! Quel honneur au femenin sexe!" Female heroism in Christine de Pizan's *Ditié de Jehanne d'Arc*', *Journal of the Institute of Romance Studies*, V, 1997, pp. 123–33, and Fraioli, *Joan of Arc: the early debate*, pp. 103–25.

162 The spiritual inspiration offered by Joan is reflected in A. L. Barstow, 'She gets inside your head: Joan of Arc and contemporary women's spirituality', in *Joan of Arc and Spirituality*, pp. 283–93.

Reading Joan

Unlike most visionaries, holy women and saints of the late middle
ages, Joan of Arc did not write any tracts or books setting out her
religious beliefs, prophecies or revelations. There are eleven surviving
letters attributed to her, though these documents are more concerned
with the war. More importantly, the precise extent of her contribution to these documents is open to debate given the clear evidence
that they were written on her behalf [4, 9, 16–8, 23, 25, 28–31].[163]
Nevertheless the care that her enemies took in recording her testimony
during her trial for heresy in 1431 means that her voice echoes
throughout the records of that investigation [34–56]. Scholars
studying the life of Joan of Arc have made use of a wide range of
historical and literary sources. Yet unique light is shed on this story
by the two remarkable records of her trial for heresy at Rouen in 1431
[34–56] and the posthumous investigation that overturned and
nullified the verdict of that original trial, organised by her supporters
between 1450 and 1456 [71–102]. Indeed, two of the most popular
books of recent years have celebrated this fact in their titles, *Joan of
Arc in Her Own Words* and *Joan of Arc: by herself and her witnesses.*[164]

Yet recent scholars have emphasised the danger of assuming that
these legal records provide clear and straightforward access to the
'real' Joan of Arc.[165] Her testimony, and hence the representation of
her identity and beliefs, was actively shaped by the extreme pressures
and events surrounding her. Joan was being interrogated and therefore her statements were inevitably moulded by that context. She was
not allowed to speak freely during the trial, but was rather forced to
answer specific questions posed by the judges. The clerics who bom-
barded her with questions were determining which topics would be
discussed, setting the agenda and the tone for that conversation, and
inevitably influencing and shaping the manner in which she responded

163 For evidence regarding the composition of these letters, see documents **35**, **38** and
   91. For modern discussions of these issues, see J. M. van Winter and D. T.
   Enklaar (eds), *De brieven van Jeanne d'Arc*, Groningen-Jakarta, 1954, and Pernoud
   and Clin, *Joan of Arc: her story*, appendix I.

164 W. Trask (ed.), *Joan of Arc in Her Own Words*, New York, 1996, and R. Pernoud,
   Joan of Arc: by herself and her witnesses, trans. E. Hyams, London, 1964.

165 Sullivan, *The Interrogation of Joan of Arc*, pp. xi-xxv. These problems are not
   unique to Joan of Arc, but also arise for other medieval visionaries whose
   experiences were recorded by others, raising the problem of distinguishing
   between the relative contribution of the visionary and their scribes, editors or
   translators.

to their questions, causing her consciously or unconsciously to echo their choices of words and syntax. Their approach, and indeed their whole mode of thought, was the product of their scholastic and legal backgrounds, highly rational, logical, organised and apparently objective: these were the very principles upon which the interrogation was built, but this was not necessarily the way in which Joan approached or understood her religious experiences.

Indeed, it is crucial to recognise the extraordinary difficulty that Joan faced in standing up against this barrage, inevitably placed at a disadvantage by her limited educational background and lack of training in theology, by her social status and by her sex. Both Joan and various witnesses during the Nullification trial painted a picture of Joan's orthodox religious background, citing her knowledge of the Creed, the *Pater Noster* and the *Ave Maria*: she was no different from any other peasant girl in that she did not have the kind of theological training needed to stand up against the combined expertise of the judges and their colleagues from the University of Paris [34, 74–5]. Yet it would be equally wrong to imagine that she was defenceless, not least because of the confidence that her voices gave her. Despite the extreme pressure exerted by the judges at the start of each of the sessions, enjoining her to swear to tell the truth, she consistently upheld her right to withhold information that she did not deem to be relevant to the trial [34].[166] When the clerks tried to trap her by asking if she was in a state of grace, she gave the perfect answer by echoing a parish prayer: 'If I am not, may God put me there, and if I am, may God keep me there' [36].

It is also far from clear that the surviving documents provide an accurate record of what actually occurred during the interrogations and the trial in general. Great care was certainly taken to record what had occurred each day, not least because Joan's own testimony would provide the evidence with which to convict her. During the Nullification trial, the three notaries, Guillaume Manchon, Guillaume Colles and Nicolas Taquel, explained the procedures that they had adopted [98]. Manchon and Colles attended the interrogations of Joan and took notes of the testimony while Taquel merely listened to the exchanges. Then after dinner each day, the three men met to

166 S. Weiskopf, 'Readers of the lost Arc: secrecy, specularity and speculation in the trial of Joan of Arc', in *Fresh Verdicts on Joan of Arc*, pp. 113–32. On the legal validity of her position, see Kelly, 'The right to remain silent: before and after Joan of Arc'.

prepare a hasty summary of the proceedings in French, known as the *Minute française*. Where they were not sure of what Joan had said, they put the word 'Nota' in the margin of this French record, so that they could check it with her the following day. Occasional statements by Joan confirm that she was indeed informed about this record: she answered questions by referring the judges to the record of her testimony in the *Minute française*, asked that her responses be corrected, warned the notaries to take more care, and on one occasion, even asked for a copy of the record to be sent to Paris if she were to be tried there [**44, 46**]. Moreover at the end of the interrogations, the *Minute française* was read out to her and received her approval [**49**]. Yet this was far from a verbatim transcription of everything that was said at the Rouen trial, of the kind that a modern stenographer would produce. Rather this was a much more complex, subjective document, framed by conscious and unconscious decisions made by the notaries: they were making choices about what to write down during the sessions and about how to turn this into organised prose, conflating questions and answers, writing in an indirect, third-person style.[167]

During the Nullification trial it was also suggested that there was pressure on the notaries to alter the record in order to incriminate Joan, though it is unclear whether this materially affected the *Minute française*. Isembart de La Pierre testified in the preliminary inquiries that Joan's willingness to submit herself to the judgement of the Council of Basel was deliberately omitted from the trial record, though he was later much more vague about this, and the story was never confirmed by Guillaume Manchon. Nicolas Taquel reported in 1452 that the judges did not allow the notaries to write down materials that were irrelevant. Guillaume Manchon also claimed at the preliminary inquiries that the judges had pressed them to change the record, though he was somewhat evasive over this when questioned further. He also reported that two other writers were hidden behind a curtain where they copied down Joan's statements, carefully omitting anything that might justify her actions, but that he resisted the pressure to follow the account that they created of the trial [**98**].[168] Indeed, it is important to note that the complete record

---

167 This was normal practice, as explained by Bernard Gui in his *Manual* (c.1323–42), when he advised that inquisitorial records should aim to transcribe words that concerned the substance of the matter and best expressed the truth.

168 For Manchon's earlier testimony, see Doncoeur (ed.), *L'enquête ordonnée par Charles VII en 1450*, p. 50 and Duparc (ed.), *Procès en nullité*, I, pp. 183, 214–18.

of the interrogations was read out to Joan on 24 March 1431 and she apparently accepted that it was a faithful account of her words. Moreover both her family and the clerics at the Nullification trial agreed that the notaries had provided a fair account of what had been said.[169] Ultimately, the only clear example of fraud in the record, at least according to the Nullification judges, was the misrepresentation of Joan's views in the Twelve Articles: Manchon and the notaries claimed not to have any knowledge of how this document had been composed.

Another problem is created by the fact that no complete version of the original *Minute française* survives. The original text, inspected by the judges at the Nullification trial on 15 December 1455, has not survived, and there are now only two mutilated and muddled copies dating from the end of the fifteenth century.[170] As a result, scholars are forced to rely upon the Latin translation that was prepared by Guillaume Manchon and the Parisian Master Thomas de Courcelles, perhaps as early as the end of 1432.[171] This official transcript included both the Latin translation of the *Minute française* and an array of letters and documents relating to the trial, such as the public letter issued by Henry VI on 28 June 1431 [57].[172] Despite the official nature of this record, it clearly adds to the problems that modern scholars face. The text had been translated from French and therefore was subject to accidental or deliberate mistranslations.[173] Moreover, there are some key differences between this official version and the

---

169 Tisset (ed.), *Procès de condamnation*, I, p. 181, and Duparc (ed.), *Procès en nullité*, I, pp. 119–20, and III, p. 111.

170 A translation of one of these manuscripts, Bibliothèque Municipale d'Orléans, MS 518, appears in W. S. Scott, *The Trial of Joan of Arc: being the verbatim report of the proceedings from the Orleans manuscript*, London, 1956.

171 Various witnesses at the Nullification trial were vague about the date of production of the dossier, but an early date of composition is suggested by the facts that Cauchon is referred to as Bishop of Beauvais, when he became Bishop of Lisieux on 8 August 1432, and that Thomas Courcelles was almost certainly absent from Paris from October 1432 until 1435.

172 The original copy of this Latin trial record has disappeared but three of the five official copies that were signed and sealed by the judges and three notaries now survive, and have been used as the basis for modern editions: Tisset (ed.), *Procès de condamnation*. Immediately after the trial, the judges had issued an *Instrumentum sententiae*, containing a summary of the acts of the trial, the abjuration of Joan and the text of the two sentences delivered on 24 and 30 May: Doncoeur (ed.), *Instrument public des sentences*.

173 The most important of these mistranslations and alterations are noted in the footnotes below.

original *Minute française*. To cite two famous examples, the Latin record includes much longer versions of Joan's abjuration on 24 May 1431, and of the final sentence issued on 30 May 1431, than are contained in the original *Minute française* [**54, 56**].

In short, the records of Joan's trial, like all legal transcripts from lay and ecclesiastical courts in the middle ages, present severe problems for those who wish to use them as sources for (auto-)biographical studies. Is it possible to discern the 'real' Joan through such documents? Many literary scholars would prefer to distinguish between the true, historical Joan, and the constructed figure that is depicted in such sources. Yet is the Joan that appears in the transcript a character that was controlled, shaped and represented by the judges? Or should we imagine the historical Joan as a bold and confident figure, who gained control over the proceedings and the record, 'baiting her inquisitors to discern truth from fiction', and ultimately determining and shaping her own representation in these documents?[174] When the Joan of the trial record refuses to answer questions, commands the judges to move on from a topic, or otherwise challenges her interrogators, is this the voice of the 'real' Joan, a heroic figure showing fortitude and faith in the face of her persecution at the hands of Cauchon and the judges? Or is her defiance a construction by the authors of the record, deliberately attempting to underline her heresy by showing her actively disobeying clerical authority? This is the kind of conundrum that the Rouen trial record presents to the modern reader.

Far less attention has been paid by scholars to the problems involved in using the records of the Nullification trial. These documents offer the most important evidence on the life of Joan and the way that she was regarded by her contemporaries, not least because the majority of depositions were given by individuals who had personally witnessed the events in question. Yet before accepting these statements at face value, it is necessary to evaluate them with every bit as much care and attention as for the original trial of Joan of Arc. Just as in 1431, the testimony of most of the one hundred and twenty-five witnesses was strongly shaped and controlled by the inquisitorial format of the proceedings. In general these witnesses were asked to respond to specific questions which inevitably defined the scope of their testimony and shaped the responses that were provided. Unfortunately the lists

---

174 Weiskopf, 'Readers of the lost Arc', p. 117.

of questions posed to each set of witnesses do not always survive. Yet in 1452, witnesses were not invited to discuss Joan's voices, her revelations, her clothing or so-called crimes, and were only asked to comment on her piety in the context of the cruelty and injustices that she had suffered during the Rouen trial. At the main trial between 1455 and 1456, the articles of interrogation were drafted by the court officials in conjunction with the lawyers acting for the d'Arc family, and these were adapted for each set of witnesses. Again, these questions prescribed the boundaries for the testimony of the witnesses and, in many cases, clearly shaped the reply that they gave [**73**]. For example, it would appear that none of these questions invited the witnesses to discuss Joan's military failures after the coronation of Charles VII, and as a result, we have almost no evidence as to the ways in which those setbacks at Paris, La Charité-sur-Loire and Compiègne were interpreted by her closest allies and supporters.[175]

Given our clear understanding that the official record of the Rouen trial is incomplete and gives little insight into important events that occurred in the background, it is clearly a problem that modern scholars have no way of finding out what was taking place behind the scenes during the Nullification investigation itself. It is important to consider that many of these witnesses were far from impartial when giving testimony. When they were sworn in, they took oaths that their testimony would be free from passion, hatred, and not motivated by financial gain or fear. Yet most of the churchmen who did take part had not only collaborated with the English during the period of the Dual Monarchy, but had also played an active role in the original trial and execution of Joan of Arc. It is hardly surprising that such men would have wished to emphasise their loyalty to Charles VII and sought to escape blame for their actions by claiming that the English had physically threatened them.[176] Indeed it is hard to escape the conclusion that many of the clerics were actively seeking to protect one another: Guillaume Manchon supported Thomas de Courcelles' claim to have had very little to do with the trial, despite copious evidence to the contrary [**89, 98**]. Other witnesses may have recognised the opportunity to profit by the situation: the Count of Dunois

175 The one exception is the testimony of Jean d'Aulon who was questioned at Lyon, and who does not appear to have been responding to a specific set of questions [**101**].

176 Many of the senior clerics from the Rouen trial were not questioned during the Nullification inquiries, including Jean Le Maistre (d. 1455) and Raoul Roussel, the old treasurer of the chapter at Rouen and later Archbishop of Rouen (d. 1452).

had not demonstrated any great love for Joan during her military career, at least according to other witnesses at the Nullification trial, yet he would undoubtedly have recognised the benefit in supporting her, and by extension Charles VII [81, 101]. Of course, the simple fact that the new investigations were taking place twenty or thirty years after the events in question must cause us to have some concerns about the testimony provided by many individuals. Was it possible for people to remember every detail about such distant events? Certainly some found it extremely convenient to claim that they had forgotten what would have been particularly embarrassing and difficult matters, sometimes even changing their testimony from one inquiry to another. The Dominican Martin Ladvenu somehow forgot in 1450 that he had heard Joan's confession and given her communion on the day that she died, and attacked Cauchon for putting Joan of Arc in a lay prison; two years later, he could not remember who had been responsible for incarcerating her under these circumstances, but did remember that he had heard her confession; by 1456, he was able to provide a lively account of her final hours![177] Would it have been possible for the witnesses to recollect such events without being influenced by the subsequent events and thereby reflect what people believed about the Pucelle in the 1450s, rather than what had actually occurred? Certainly some witnesses provided a suspicious amount of information: Jean Lemaire only attended the Rouen trial for one day, but echoed a number of his friends in claiming that both Pierre Maurice, the Abbot of Fécamp, and Nicolas Loiseleur risked being killed by the English.[178]

The textual records of the Nullification trial also present problems for modern scholars, parallel to those for the original Rouen trial. Throughout the preliminary inquiries and the Nullification trial itself, the notaries, led in 1455 and 1456 by François Ferrebouc and Denis Lecomte, did not produce a verbatim account of what the witnesses actually said, but rather a précis of their testimony. The witnesses would undoubtedly have spoken in the vernacular, but their words were translated into Latin at an unidentified stage of the proceedings. Moreover, there is even debate among historians about which version of the trial record is the more accurate and faithful. Jules Quicherat

---

177 Doncoeur (ed.), *L'enquête ordonnée par Charles VII en 1450*, pp. 43–5; Duparc (ed.), *Procès en nullité*, I, pp. 188–90, 233–6 and 440–4. Also see Tisset (ed.), *Procès de condamnation*, I, pp. 416–18.

178 Duparc (ed.), *Procès en nullité*, I, p. 450.

and Paul Doncoeur criticised the official, notarial record of the Nullification trial which survives in three copies: they cited errors regarding dates and the first names of individuals, and therefore preferred an earlier draft of the trial record known as the Episcopal Redaction, drawn up by the three bishops who sat as judges in the trial. Yet Pierre Duparc has emphasised that this was very much a draft text that was incomplete, and also contained errors of dating and of names.[179] The only surviving record of the inquiry in 1450 is even more problematic, representing an unauthenticated copy which presumably drew upon an official instrument, but which cannot be checked or investigated.

In conclusion, the student of Joan of Arc follows in the footsteps of generations of scholars who have filled an entire library with their writings on the life and importance of the Pucelle. Yet new, critical approaches to the sources are opening up completely different ways of thinking about and understanding this important subject. On the one hand, we are forced to confront the limitations of the documents. It is impossible to assume that the trial records allow simple access to Joan of Arc or her contemporaries, which demonstrates how unwise it is take any of the sources relating to the Pucelle at face value without careful thought and consideration. On the other hand, a more sophisticated approach to these texts will enable us to reconstruct this story in a more historically valid manner, and also open up a range of additional issues that are only now being considered, particularly the construction of images of Joan, as well as wider perceptions of gender, heresy and witchcraft. Hopefully this sourcebook will contribute to these efforts, though I do advise serious scholars to remember the expression 'traduttore traditore' (translator, traitor) and to be inspired to return to the editions of these documents in their original languages.

---

179 Both versions of the Nullification trial record are presented in a slightly illogical order, ignoring chronology in favour of the complex order prescribed by contemporary legal practice, the *ordo judiciarius.*

I: THE LIFE OF JOAN OF ARC

1. The Treaty of Troyes (21 May 1420)

Source: P. Chaplais (ed.), *English Medieval Diplomatic Practice, Part I: documents and interpretations*, 2 vols, London, 1982, II, pp. 629–36.

Language: Latin

The treaty of Troyes was agreed by the Kings of England and France, Henry V and Charles VI, on 21 May 1420 in the cathedral of Saint-Pierre in Troyes. This extract comes from the English royal exemplar.

[Article 1] Firstly that through the bond of matrimony made for the good of peace between us and our most dear consort Katherine, daughter of the most serene [King] Charles, our very beloved father, and our most dear mother, Isabeau, his wife, [the King and Queen of France] have been made our father and mother, on account of which we shall hold them as our parents, and honour them as such, and as such and so worthy a prince and princess deserve, we shall venerate them before before all other temporal people of this world.[1]

[Article 2] Item, we will not disturb, distress nor obstruct our said beloved father, so that he will hold and possess the Crown and royal dignity of France, as much as he holds and possesses it at present, for as long as he lives, [along with] the rents, fruits and profits of the same, in order to sustain his estate and the charges of the kingdom. And our aforesaid, beloved mother shall also hold, as long as she lives, the estate and dignity of queen according to the custom of the realm, with a suitable and convenient part of the said rents and profits.

[Article 6] Item, it is agreed that immediately after the moment of the death of our beloved father [Charles VI] in France, and from that time onwards, the Crown and kingdom of France, with all of their rights and appurtenances, will remain and will belong to us, King Henry cited above, and our heirs in perpetuity.

---

1 Katherine (d. 1438) was the tenth child of King Charles VI of France, who ruled between 1380 and 1422, and his wife Isabeau of Bavaria. Katherine was also the elder sister of the dauphin Charles, who was disinherited by this Treaty but would subsequently rule France as Charles VII between 1422 and 1461.

[Article 7] Item, because our most beloved father [Charles VI] is afflicted with various infirmities so that he may not attend in person nor arrange for the business of the realm of France to be put in order, therefore during the whole life of our beloved father, the faculty and exercise of ruling and the disposition of the public business of the kingdom of France ... will remain and abide with us [Henry V] ...

[Article 12] Item, that we, King Henry cited above, will work and will do all that we can to place in the obedience of our father each and every one of the cities, towns, castles, places, regions and people within the kingdom of France of our father [that are] disobedient and rebellious, holding or belonging to the party commonly called of the dauphin or Armagnac ...²

[Article 29] Item, considering the horrendous and enormous crimes and wicked deeds perpetrated in this kingdom of France by Charles, who styles himself dauphin of Vienne, it is agreed that neither our beloved father, nor we, King Henry, nor our most beloved brother the Duke of Burgundy shall begin or make any treaty of peace or accord with this Charles, unless we do begin or act with the counsel and assent of each and every one of us, and of the three estates of both of our kingdoms.

2. La réponse d'un bon et loyal françois au peuple de France (1420?)

Source: N. Pons (ed.), 'L'honneur de la couronne de France': quatre libelles contre les Anglais (vers 1418–vers 1429), Paris, 1990, pp. 122–33.

Language: French

This anonymous pamphlet, 'The reply of a good and loyal Frenchman to the people of France', was almost certainly written at the same time as the Treaty of Troyes. The writer was evidently a supporter of the dauphin Charles and began by attacking the preliminary articles agreed by Henry V and the Duke of Burgundy at Arras on 2 December 1419, which were subsequently to be enacted as the Treaty of Troyes. The author carefully chose arguments that appealed to the heart, particularly through his repeated emphasis upon the fleurs-de-lys, that is to say the lilies that were the symbol of the French

---

2 'Armagnac' was a term first applied by the Parisians to the faction supporting the Duke of Orléans against the Duke of Burgundy in the summer of 1411, and reflected the strong influence of Count Bernard of Armagnac, son-in-law of the Duke of Berry, who was eventually put to death by the Burgundians on 12 July 1418. The dauphin Charles then became head of the anti-Burgundian party.

monarchy.[3] The pamphlet clearly served as part of the wider propaganda campaign to defend Charles in the wake of the murder of John the Fearless on 10 September 1419.[4] It circulated widely and was recorded in the register of the Parlement of Poitiers, as well as the archives of Bourges and Dijon.

Consider the lilies of the field,[5] you true Frenchmen of the realm. Consider the iniquity of the very evil treaty that the English, ancient enemies of the fleurs-de-lys, demanded in Latin, which has been accepted and sworn to by the Duke of Burgundy, as it appears in his letters patent, which begin 'Philip, Duke of Burgundy', given at Arras, the second day of December 1419. Consider that they all tend towards the total destruction and eradication of the fleurs-de-lys, and the subversion of the very noble and christian realm of France by its ancient and foreign mortal enemies, the English, who, says a historian named Pomponius, are a race so criminal and brutal that their animals are more good-natured than the men.[6]

[The author then attacked the circumstances of the negotiations, and in particular the fact that Charles VI was being forced to accept the terms of his mortal enemy.]

Consider the clear lie, when Henry in the first part of the treaty [article 1] says that he will take Katherine as his wife, without imposing anything on her parents, their friends or the subjects of the realm of France, as he steals the realm from the heirs who are rightful and legitimate, and transfers it to himself and his heirs who have no right there. [He claims] not to make any charge, but then requires oaths, fealties and obligations to serve and obey him and all his heirs, which he demands from all those of the realm, even prelates, under obscure words, when he speaks of both temporal and spiritual estates.

Consider what burdens on the conscience there could be and will be on all those of the realm of France forced to swear such oaths, against

---

3 The heraldic motif of the fleurs-de-lys was the most famous symbol of the French crown during the late middle ages. See W. M. Hinkle, *The Fleurs de Lis of the Kings of France, 1285–1488*, Carbondale, 1991.

4 B. Guenée, 'Les campagnes de lettres qui ont suivi le meurtre de Jean sans Peur, duc de Bourgogne (septembre 1419–février 1420)', *Annuaire-bulletin de la Société de l'Histoire de France*, 1993, pp. 45–65.

5 Matthew 6: 28 and Luke 12: 27.

6 There is only one passage in the work of Pomponius Mela that is close to the idea expressed here, but that concerns Gaul, where he says that one finds few evil animals there, but the people are proud, superstitious and barbaric, offering human sacrifices to God. Thus the author here transfers the remarks either deliberately, or by an error of memory, or because his source made an error.

the first and main loyalty that they owe to the Crown and the honour of the fleurs-de-lys, and what peace and concord will be by this disloyal and seditious treaty, for all the subjects of the Crown ...

Consider the second point of the treaty [article 2]. What honour does Henry wish to do to the King and Queen of France by taking them as his mother and father, when he drives out ... their son, the dauphin. Because as the wise and philosophical man says, the father and mother live in their son, and the honour of the son is the love of his father and mother. And it is here a marvellous and reverse adoption, because the father adopts the son, and the son [does not adopt] the father or mother.

Consider [article 7] ... Henry recognises and confesses that the King of France is held and hindered very seriously by an illness ... [and] requests that he himself be Regent, etc. I ask Henry what illness afflicts the King of France, and he cannot reply otherwise than an illness which affects wisdom and prudence. Thus I ask how a person who has no wisdom or prudence can freely dispose, according to law and reason, of anything civil or legitimate. And if he replies, as is true, that it cannot, and should not be done, how then can or could such a sick and weak King assent and validly accept such a great matter concerning all the French realm, which is the right of the Crown and the honour of the fleurs-de-lys, in perpetuity ...

[The author presented further articles against the proposed Treaty of Troyes, and then concluded.]

For the honour of the fleurs-de-lys, certain considerations follow, based in law, to oppose the damnable treaty that Henry seeks.

1. The honour of the fleurs-de-lys is the right of the Crown of France. It may not and ought not to be transported to strangers, especially those who are our ancient enemies, against the consent of those who ought reasonably to have a right or interest in this Crown and its conservation.

2. The honour of the fleurs-de-lys and the right of the Crown of France belongs clearly, according to the state of things in 1420, to Prince Charles, only son and heir to this Crown. As a result, neither the King, the Queen nor any other person can reasonably deprive him against his will, by marriage or another condition, under pretence of peace.

3. The honour of the fleurs-de-lys and of the Crown of France includes not only the King, Queen and their children, but all those of the royal house of France, present and to come, as nephews, cousins, nieces,

female cousins, and more generally all the three estates of the realm, according to diverse degrees and obligations.

4. The honour of the fleurs-de-lys and of the Crown of France ought to be upheld and kept by all those faithful and loyal to it, without granting consent to the opposite which might be or could be to the prejudice of it, its right and interest or lordship. Because to do otherwise would be against the law of God, natural, civil and canon law, and the good judgment of reason.

5. The honour of the fleurs-de-lys and of the Crown should not be obstructed by those who owe fealty and loyalty to the Crown on pain of treason, the crime of *lèse-majesté* and of rebellion.[7] Confederations made to the contrary, promises and oaths, are evil and unjust, and lead to eternal damnation.

6. The honour of the fleurs-de-lys and the right of the Crown ought to be kept by all those who are sworn and bound there, to sustain all bodily suffering that any loyal person might, before a breach of faith and loyalty, and this is according to the saying of Our Lord, 'Blessed are those who suffer persecution for justice'.[8]

7. The damnable treaty that Henry seeks under the pretence of a marriage with the daughter of the King of France, and of total peace between the realms of France and England, is full of tricks, frauds and deceptions, because, under the cover of marriage and peace, it tends towards countless perpetual divisions.

8. This treaty is very damnable, unjust and detestable, against the honour of God, and against faith and religion, because it tends to push out the right of another by tyrannical usurpation.

3. The conclusions of the Poitiers investigation (March–April 1429)

Source: Quicherat (ed.), *Procès de condamnation*, III, pp. 391–2.

Language: French

There is no surviving record of the investigation into Joan of Arc on behalf of Charles VII by the theologians at Poitiers. Nevertheless a document

---

7 On the concepts of treason and *lèse-majesté* in France, see S. H. Cuttler, *The Law of Treason and Treason Trials in Later Medieval France*, Cambridge, 1981.

8 Matthew 5: 10.

purporting to represent their conclusions was widely distributed, presumably as part of the propaganda effort in support of the Pucelle: copies survive in a Breton manuscript composed by a scribe named A. de Kaerrymell, the *Registre delphinal* of Mathieu Thomassin, the *Chronique de Tournai* and other chronicles from Scotland and various German towns.[9] In all of these cases, the chronicler or scribe added an introduction that attributed the document to the clerks or theologians assembled by Charles VII to question Joan.

Considering his own necessity and that of his kingdom, and considering the continual prayers of his poor people towards God, and all the others who love peace and justice, the King should not turn away from, or reject, the Pucelle, who says that she has been sent by God, but should give her help, even though her promises are human. Also [the King] should not believe in her too much and lightly, but, following the holy scripture, he must make her prove herself by two means: that is to say through human prudence, inquiring about her life, her morals and her intention, as St Paul the Apostle states: 'test the spirits, whether they are from God';[10] and through devout prayer, asking for a sign of some work or divine hope, by which it can be judged that she has come by the will of God. In the same way, God commanded Ahaz to ask for a sign, when God made a promise to him of victory, saying to him: 'Ask for a sign for yourself from your God';[11] Gideon did the same, who asked for a sign, and many others, etc.[12]

Since the arrival of this Pucelle, the King has observed and had the Pucelle investigated in these two ways: that is to say, testing through human prudence and by prayer, asking for a sign from God. As for the first, which is through human prudence, he has had this Pucelle put to the test regarding her life, her birth, her morals and her purpose, and has had her kept with him for the space of six weeks, to present her to all manner of people, be they clerics, churchmen, pious people, men-at-arms, women, widows and others. And she has conversed with all people publicly and privately: but no evil is to be found in her, only goodness, humility, virginity, devotion, honesty and simplicity; and many marvellous things are said to be true regarding her birth and life.

---

9 G. Léfèvre-Pontalis (ed.), *Les sources allemandes de l'histoire de Jeanne d'Arc: Eberhard Windecke*, Paris, 1903, pp. 32–5, and R. G. Little, *The Parlement of Poitiers: war, government and politics in France, 1418–1436*, London, 1984, pp. 108–13.

10 This quotation actually comes from 1 John 4: 1.

11 Isaiah 7: 11.

12 Judges 6: 11–23, 36–40.

As to the second manner of testing, the King has asked for a sign from her, to which she replies that she will show it before the city of Orléans, and nowhere else: for so she has been commanded by God.

The King, as far as it is possible for him, must not prevent [the Pucelle] from going to Orléans with his men-at-arms, given the testing that has been done of the said Pucelle, and that no evil is found in her, and considering her reply, which is to demonstrate a divine sign in front of Orléans; in light of her constancy and her perseverance in her purpose, and her insistent requests to go to Orléans, in order to show the sign of divine aid there, [the King] must have her taken there in good faith, hoping in God. For to doubt her, or to dismiss her, without [her showing any] appearance of evil, would be to repel the Holy Spirit, and would render one unworthy of the aid of God, as Gamaliel stated in a council of Jews, regarding the Apostles.[13]

4. Joan of Arc's letter to the English (22 March 1429)

Source: Tisset (ed.), *Procès de condamnation*, I, pp. 221–2.

Language: French

This unsigned letter was written around 22 March 1429 at Poitiers and sent from Blois between 24 and 27 April. This may have been the letter that Gobert Thibaut referred to in his testimony on 5 April 1456, when he described how Joan asked Master Jean Érault to write a letter for her to the English during her stay at Poitiers [91]. It evidently circulated widely: it was also reprinted in a range of French, Burgundian and German chronicles, and the judges at the Rouen trial questioned Joan about the letter and clearly had access to a copy [35, 38].[14]

+JESUS MARIA+

King of England, and you, Duke of Bedford, who call yourself Regent of the kingdom of France;[15] you, William de la Pole, Earl of Suffolk;

13 Acts 5: 34–9.

14 The letter was cited in full in the Seventy Articles presented against Joan on 27 March 1431: Tisset (ed.), *Procès de condamnation*, I, pp. 221–2. In the *Mistère du siège d'Orléans*, the commemorative play that was performed at Orléans, Joan dictated the letter to an anonymous cleric who actually pronounced the message to the audience. See the discussion of dissemination in Léfèvre-Pontalis (ed.), *Les sources allemandes de l'histoire de Jeanne d'Arc: Eberhard Windecke*, pp. 32–4, 50 and 139–43. Also see Little, *The Parlement of Poitiers*, p. 106.

15 John of Lancaster, Duke of Bedford (1389–1435), was a younger brother of Henry V and served as Regent of France on behalf of his nephew, Henry VI, from 1422. See 24, 62.

John Lord Talbot; and you, Thomas Lord Scales, who call yourselves lieutenants of the said Duke of Bedford, make satisfaction to the King of Heaven;[16] surrender to the Pucelle, who has been sent here by God, the King of Heaven, the keys of all the good towns [*bonnes villes*] that you have taken and violated in France.[17] She has come here from God to reclaim the blood royal. She is very ready to make peace, if you are willing to grant her satisfaction by means of rendering justice to France and paying for what you have held. And you too, archers, companions-at-arms, gentlemen and others who are before the town of Orléans, go back to your own country, by God. And if you do not do this, await news of the Pucelle who will come to see you shortly, to your very great harm. King of England, if you do not do this, I am commander of war, and in whatever place I come upon your men in France, I will make them leave, whether they wish to or not. And if they do not wish to obey, I will have them all killed; I have been sent here by God, the King of Heaven, to drive you out of all France, body for body.[18] And if they wish to obey, I will show them mercy. And do not believe otherwise, because you will never hold the kingdom of France from God, the King of Heaven, son of St Mary; for King Charles, the true heir, will hold it, because God, the King of Heaven, wishes it, and this was revealed to him by the Pucelle; she will enter Paris with a good company.[19] If you do not wish to believe the news from God and the Pucelle, then wherever we find you, we will strike there and raise a war cry greater than any that there has been in France for a thousand years, if you do not act reasonably. And believe firmly that the King of Heaven will send greater strength to the Pucelle, both to her and to her good men-at-arms, than you could

16 The letter refers to William de la Pole (1396–1450) as 'Count', the French form of 'earl'; he became Earl of Suffolk in 1415. He commanded the English forces at the siege of Orléans after the death of the Earl of Salisbury on 24 October 1428; he was subsequently captured at the siege of Jargeau in June 1429. John Talbot (c.1387–1453) was created a lord in 1421 and then became Earl of Shrewsbury in 1442. He led the defence of the fortress of Saint-Loup during the siege of Orléans and subsequently fought at Meung-sur-Loire and Beaugency, before being captured at Patay on 18 June 1429, along with Thomas Lord Scales.

17 The term '*bonnes villes*' was reserved for French towns which enjoyed particular privileges and liberties.

18 When questioned during the second public examination, Joan claimed that she had not called upon the English to 'Surrender to the Pucelle' but rather 'to the King', and that she had not used the words 'commander of war' or 'body for body'. See **35**.

19 The direct reference to the recapture of Paris, echoed in the letter of Guy Laval, is striking. When Joan was questioned by the judges at Rouen, she denied that her voices had commanded her to retake the capital [**15, 43, 46**].

overwhelm in all your assaults; and the one who has greater right from God in heaven will be revealed by this exchange of blows. You, Duke of Bedford, the Pucelle prays and requests that you do not bring destruction upon yourself. If you will grant satisfaction to her, you may still join her company, in which the French will do the fairest deed that has ever been done for Christianity.[20] And respond if you wish to make peace in the city of Orléans; and if you do not do this, you will be reminded shortly by your great injuries.

Written this Tuesday of Holy Week.

5. Fragment of a letter to Nicole de Giresme (April 1429?)

Source: Quicherat (ed.), *Procès de condamnation*, V, pp. 98–100.

Language: Latin

This fragment of an unsigned letter, missing any address, appears on the back of a copy of Joan's first letter to the English. It would appear to have been written by an anonymous knight of the Order of Saint John of Jerusalem to the Grand Prior, Nicole de Giresme, who led a contingent during the siege of Orléans. The author addressed his most 'Reverend father and revered preceptor' and praised the Pucelle as a divinely-inspired cure for the most Christian kingdom of France. He continued:

Let your most reverend power hear, I beg you, and your mind exult in the gift of so heavenly a girl [*puellari*], which the Almighty has consented to present in our times. A heavenly Pucelle has come, and [she must have been sent by God] because the Almighty Father himself has honoured the Virgin Mary above all others, with the intended result that he has drawn away every earthly desire from those who see that she is so beautiful, no matter who they might be, and [he has turned them away] from any kind of immoral life. Will not God, moreover, be said to have ordained the same about the virgin sent to us, Joan by name? Joan, I say, the Pucelle, clothed in the dress of a shepherdess, and yet manlike, has come by the command of Almighty God to the King through diverse and formidable routes, without violence, unwounded, unharmed, accompanied by other persons; she has come to the King, and it was ordained by the decision

---

20 This call upon the enemy to capitulate in order to facilitate a joint crusade against the enemies of Christendom was quite typical of military summonses. The normal aim was to present the enemy as opponents of both justice and the wider needs of Christians and the Church. See pages 19 to 20 above.

of the royal council that she should speak not to the King, but to many men and excellent clerics, doctors of theology, and to be examined diligently by others. But as it happened, that decision notwithstanding, the Pucelle went without delay to the Queen and asked [to see] the King, whom she was calling the dauphin. The King did not hold back, but immediately came to her ... [The letter stops.]

6. *Virgo puellares* (1429?)

Source: Quicherat (ed.), *Procès de condamnation*, IV, p. 305.

Language: French and Latin

This sixteen-line Latin poem survives in eleven manuscripts, including the *Scotichronicon* of Walter Bower, as well as three translations into the vernacular. The transcription by Mathieu Thomassin in his *Registre delphinal* in 1456 (which also included a copy of the *Ditié de Jehanne d'Arc* by Christine de Pizan [20]) is the most informative. Thomassin introduced the poem by reporting that it was composed by the advisers of Charles VII under the inspiration of a prophecy attributed to Merlin by Geoffrey of Monmouth. The poem itself is in Latin epic metre, perhaps echoing Virgil's *Fourth Eclogue* which also speaks of a golden age and a virgin, and was taken in medieval Europe to be a prophecy of Christianity.

Clerks and other men of understanding considered this matter [whether to place trust in Joan] and among the other writings was found a prophecy of Merlin, speaking in this manner: 'A virgin will descend on the back of the archer and will hide the virgin flower.'[21] From these verses, others were made of which the tenor follows here below:

The virgin, her maidenly [*puellares*] limbs clothed in male attire, at God's prompting, hurries to raise up the fallen lily-bearer and king, [and] to destroy the abominable enemies, especially those who are now at Orléans, outside the city, and beset it with a siege. And if men have a mind to commit themselves to war, and to follow her arms, which the kindly[22]

---

21 This is a paraphrase of a prophecy by Merlin reported in the *History of the Kings of Britain* by Geoffrey of Monmouth. In an earlier manuscript (Berne MS 25, which also contained the *Ditié de Jehanne d'Arc*), the Latin text of this vague prophecy was loosely translated into French as: 'There will be a virgin who will ride in arms against the backs of the English archers, and her sex and the flower of her virginity will keep secret.' Dunois later testified that, around 27 June 1429, he was sent a piece of paper containing this verse and another prophecy attributed to Merlin, that of a young girl coming from an Oak Wood. See pages 18 to 19 above as well as [81].

22 *Alma*: a term commonly associated with the Virgin Mary.

Pucelle [*Puella*] now prepares, she believes that the deceitful English will also succumb to death, when the French overthrow them with maidenly war [*marte puellari*]; and then there will be an end to fighting. Then the former treaties, then love and piety and the other laws will return; men will compete for peace, and all will favour their king of their own free will; and this king will also deal justice equitably to all of them, whom he will cherish in a beautiful peace. And now there will be no leopard-bearing enemy from the English,[23] who presumes to call himself king of the French.

7. *De mirabili victoria* (March–April 1429?)

Source: Duparc (ed.), *Procès en nullité*, II, pp. 34–9.

Language: Latin

This treatise, also known as *De puella Aurelianesis* circulated widely, reaching the abbey of St. Victor in Paris, Jean Dupuy in Rome [13], the author of *De bono et malo spiritu* [27], the Italian merchant Pancrazio Gustiniani, and the judges at the Nullification trial. Modern scholars are divided over whether it was written by Jean Gerson (1363–1429), one of the greatest French theologians of the fifteenth century. This attribution was attested by a letter that Gustiniani wrote on 20 November 1429, and by Jean Bréhal in his submission to the judges during the Nullification trial on 2 July 1456. Yet it has been observed that the polemical harangue of this text is quite different from other works by Gerson, and does not appear to have been written by a scholar of his calibre: it lacks polish and is somewhat careless in the handling of scriptural citations, and often approaches the key theological arguments, particularly regarding the discernment of spirits, in a different way from Gerson's known tracts.[24] The dating of the text is also uncertain. It must have been written before September 1429 when it was attacked by the author of *De bono et malo spiritu*, and the first printed edition in 1484 suggested that the treatise was written on 14 May 1429. Yet there is no further evidence to support that specific dating, and the silence regarding Joan's victory at Orléans on 8 May would suggest that the treatise predated that event. Is it

23 The term 'léopard' was used in medieval heraldry for a lion on a coat of arms who faced the observer, also known as 'lion passant guardant'. For the development of this symbol of the late medieval English crown, see S. Menache, *Vox Dei: communication in the middle ages*, Oxford, 1990, ch. 9.

24 This problem must be examined in conjunction with that of the authorship of *De quadam puella* [22]. Those who believe that this treatise was written by Gerson include D. G. Wayman, 'The Chancellor and Jeanne d'Arc', *Franciscan Studies*, XVII, 1957, pp. 273–305; D. Elliott, 'Seeing double: Jean Gerson, the discernment of spirits, and Joan of Arc', *American Historical Review*, CVII, 2001, pp. 26–54; B. P. McGuire, 'Jean Gerson, the Shulammite, and the Maid', in *Joan of Arc and Spirituality*, pp. 183–92. Critics include D. Fraioli, *Joan of Arc: the early debate*, Woodbridge, 2000, chs. 2 and 8.

possible that the miracle referred to within the text was either Joan's earlier journey to the court at Chinon, or her success in winning over the theologians at Poitiers?

[The treatise begins with a careful distinction between those essential truths which all Christians must hold, or else be charged with heresy, and other beliefs that are merely pious.]

About these [pious beliefs], it is popularly said: 'Whoever does not believe it, is not damned'. Three conditions are specially required for [such a] pious belief.

Firstly that they excite [one] to devotion and pious affections towards God and the divine; because they certainly rebound with praise for the divine power or clemency, in the miracles, and the cult of saints.

Another condition is that they are based upon some probable conjectures, or [come] from the common conviction, or from the testimony of the faithful who say that they have seen or heard [them].

A third condition may be added, weighed [carefully] by discreet men, versed in theology and good virtues: no falsity or error that manifestly leads to the detriment of the faith or of good morals, either directly or indirectly, openly or secretly, should be admitted or included in those truths which are said to concern the piety of the faith. To decide and to determine these things, judging and condemning them openly, just as in a lawsuit, is not permitted, especially when they are tolerated by the Church or by the prelates of the Church, in one or many provinces. Judgement and decision [on these matters] should be deferred to this same Church, to its prelates and to its doctors.

One could cite here, in particular, many subjects of pious belief, for example the Conception of the Blessed Virgin, the opinions discussed among theologians, and different questions relative to indulgences. Also in this regard the case of relics venerated in one place or another; even more, simultaneously in many, as has happened with the head of Saint-Denis, venerated at the same time in the church of Paris and in the abbey of Saint-Denis, near to Paris, which was recently in contention in the Parlement of Paris.[25]

It is concluded at last from these premises that it could be pious and salutary, of pious and devout belief and devotion to approve of the case of this Pucelle, considering the circumstances with their good outcome, looking at the final goal which is evidently very just, the

25 In 1406.

re-establishment of the King in his kingdom and the very just expulsion and defeat of his most stubborn enemies.

Moreover, it is also added that under observation, this Pucelle does not appear to have used spells prohibited by the Church, proscribed superstitions, or the deceits of fraudulent people in an open way; she is not seeking her own interest with any guile, since she exposes her own body to the supreme peril, in evidence of her faith.

Finally, if many people say many things and condemn her through their gossiping or inconstancy, or out of a devilish partiality or hatred, this sentence of Cato helps: 'it is not necessary to judge what everybody else says'.[26] But it is for us to judge what is believed and held, within the boundaries of modesty, reserved and detached from tumultuous discussions; because, as the Apostle said, a servant of the Lord must not quarrel [2 Timothy 2: 24]. 'We have no such custom' [1 Corinthians 11: 16], that is to say, quarrel. Therefore these opinions must be tolerated or referred to the decision of superiors, as has been said before. For, as is read in many sources, this was the course of action for previous canonisations of saints, which, strictly speaking, are not necessities of faith but of pious belief; they cannot be rejected, looked down upon or repudiated by anyone, and certainly less so than similar [cults] which are popular without canonisation.

The following circumstances may be added in favour of our cause.

Firstly that the council of the King and the men-at-arms could have been led to believe in the voice of this Pucelle in such a manner, and to obey her in such a way that, under her command and with one heart, they exposed themselves to the dangers of war, ignoring all fear of dishonour. What could have happened if, fighting under a young woman, they had been vanquished by such audacious enemies and they had been derided by all who heard this?

Also, the delight of the people after the event is apparent [and they have] so much pious belief, to the praise of God and to the confusion of the enemy.

Also, that the enemy, even their leaders, retire into hiding out of many fears and feel sluggish as if failing like a woman giving birth,

---

26 The full epigraph is 'When you live properly, do not worry about the words of evil men; it is not necessary to judge what everybody else says' (*Disticha Catonis*, III, 2). The *Distichs* were a very popular collection of sayings during the middle ages; they were attributed to Cato the Elder, and produced during the third century AD.

just like the invocation of the song by Mary, sister of Moses, with a dance played by drums: 'Let us sing to the Lord, for he has triumphed gloriously', adding 'Fear and dread shall fall upon them' [Exodus 15: 21, 16]. Let us see, recollect and sing together with devotion for our action.

Let us consider at the end the fact that this Pucelle and her military followers do not dismiss the path of human prudence; they act according to what is in them, so that it appears that they do not tempt God more than is necessary.[27] From this it follows that this Pucelle is not obstinate in her adhesion to her own leadership and also that she does not go beyond the instructions and inspirations that she attributes to God.

In addition, many circumstances of her life from her early childhood could be added, which have been investigated and researched for a long time by numerous people, of which nothing more will be inserted here.

Examples could be offered of Deborah and of St Katherine converting fifty doctors and rhetoricians no less miraculously, and many others also, such as Judith and Judas Maccabaeus; all of these cases always involve some aspect of natural order. And what men expect or have expected does not always follow from a first miracle. So, even though the Pucelle's waiting and ours were frustrated, which may God forbid, one should not conclude that what has been accomplished is the evil spirit's doing and not God's achievement. Our ingratitude, our blasphemies, other reasons could attract the divine anger, and, through a secret but just judgement of God, make it so that we would be frustrated in our hopes. May God turn away from us His anger and make everything turn out well.

Four civil and theological documents should be added.[28] The first concerns the King and princes of the blood; the second, the army of the King and the kingdom; the third concerns the ecclesiastics and the people; the fourth, the Pucelle herself. The goal of these documents is the same: to live well, in piety towards God, in justice towards the next man and in sobriety, which is in virtue and temperance towards oneself. And through the fourth document, the grace of God, manifested

27 From the Fourth Lateran Council (1215) onwards, theologians frequently expressed concern that warriors might be 'tempting' God by testing whether he would bring them victory in an ordeal, tournament, battle or military conflict.

28 It is not clear which documents are being cited here.

in this Pucelle, should not be received or taken, either for her or for other people, as the subject of vain curiosities, worldly complaints, the hatred of divisions, or inept boasting, but rather in mildness and eloquence, with the action of grace, and further with generosity in the contribution of possessions. Each person should himself work so that peace may return to his home and so that, freed from the hand of our enemy by a gracious God, we may serve Him in holiness and justice for all of our days, amen.[29] This has been done by the Lord.[30]

Here follow three truths in justification of the wearing of male clothing by the Pucelle, chosen while following her sheep.[31]

I. The old law [of the Old Testament], prohibiting the woman from using the clothing of a man and the man from the clothing of a woman [Deuteronomy 22: 5], is purely judicial and does not carry any obligation under the new law [of the New Testament]. [This is] because it is a constant and necessary truth for salvation that the judicial precepts of the ancient law [Old Testament] are quashed and, as such, do not bind the new one, unless they have been instituted again and confirmed by superiors.

II. This law [of the Old Testament] included a moral dimension that must remain in all law. It can be expressed as a prohibition on indecent clothing both for the man and for the woman, [as this is] contrary to the requirement of virtue. This should affect all circumstances bound by law, so that the wise person will judge when, where, to whom and how it is appropriate, and in this way the rest. This [law of the Old Testament] on these things is not confined to that one situation.

III. This law [of the Old Testament], whether judicial or moral, does not condemn the wearing of the clothing of a man and a warrior by our Pucelle, manly and a warrior, whom God in heaven has chosen

29 The words of Zachary as he celebrated the birth of his son John the Baptist, the herald of Christ, according to Luke 1: 74–5.

30 A song of victory over one's enemies from Psalm 117 (118): 23. The earliest printed editions of this treatise included a brief paragraph after this statement, indicating that the text was completed at Lyon on 14 May 1429 by the Chancellor [of the University of Paris], Jean Gerson.

31 Some scholars have argued that this section (the *Triplex veritas*) was not an original part of *De mirabili victoria*, but rather a separate text that was in circulation at this time. This is entirely possible but unproven, as is the additional claim that it may have been written by Jean the Celestine, Gerson's 'literary executor': McGuire, 'Jean Gerson, the Shulammite, and the Maid', p. 189.

through certain signs as his standard-bearer for those fighting the enemies of justice and to raise up his friends, so that he might overthrow by the hand of a woman, a young girl [*puellaris*] and a virgin, the powerful weapons of iniquity, with the help of the angels. By her virginity, she is loved and known, according to St Jerome; and this frequently appears in the histories of saints, such as Cecilia, visibly with a crown of roses and lilies. On the other hand, through this she is safeguarded from the [consequences of the] cutting of her hair, which the Apostle prohibits from being seen on a woman.[32]

Therefore may the inquitious talk be put to an end and cease. For, when divine virtue operates, it establishes the means according to its aim; hence, it is not safe to disparage or to find fault, out of rash bravado, with those things which are from God, according to the Apostle.

Finally many details and examples from sacred and secular history could be added; for example those of Camilla and the Amazons,[33] and moreover in cases either of necessity or evident utility, or where approved by custom, or by the authority and dispensation of superiors. But these are sufficient for brevity and for the truth. The party having just cause should be on close guard unless, through disbelief and ingratitude, or some injustices, they might render the divine help useless, that has begun so patiently and miraculously; just as [happened] for Moses and the sons of Israel, after having received such divine promises, as we read contained [in the scriptures]. For even if God does not change His advice, He does change his opinion according to what people deserve.[34]

8. Letter from the Lord of Rotselaer (22 April 1429)

Source: Quicherat (ed.), *Procès de condamnation*, IV, pp. 427–8.

Language: Latin

On 22 April 1429, the Lord of Rotselaer sent a letter to Brussels from Lyons, where he was the head of a delegation representing the Duke of Brabant, Philip of Saint-Pol, cousin of the Duke of Burgundy. This letter survives in

---

32 St. Paul stated that a woman should cover her head when praying and described her long hair as her veil of modesty, 1 Corinthians 11: 5–15.

33 See footnote 148, page 55 above.

34 The version of the text recorded in the Nullification trial record concludes with a statement that the treatise was composed by Jean Gerson, Chancellor of the University of Paris, in 1429.

the Rekenkamer in Brussels and was also quoted by Edmond de Dynther, *greffier* of the Chambre des Comptes of Brabant. It appears to confirm Joan's later statement at Rouen that she had predicted her injury at Orléans [**37**], though we are dependent upon Dynther's testimony regarding the date of the letter.

A certain Pucelle from Lorraine, seventeen years of age or thereabouts, is near the King and she told him that she would save the people of Orléans and chase the English from their siege, and that she would be wounded by an arrow during the combat near Orléans but would not die, and that the King himself would be crowned in the city of Reims next summer, and a variety of other matters which the King is keeping secret. This Pucelle every day rides on horseback, armed with a lance in battle, as all the other armed men guarding the King are accustomed to doing. And this King and his friends have placed great faith in the Pucelle.

9. Joan of Arc's ultimatum to the English (5 May 1429)

Source: Duparc (ed.), *Procès en nullité*, I, p. 393.

Language: Latin

The text of this letter derives from the Latin transcription of the testimony of Joan's confessor, Friar Jean Pasquerel, given at the Nullification trial on 4 May 1456 [**95**, and see also **81**].

You men of England, who have no right in this kingdom of France, the King of Heaven orders and commands you through me, Joan the Pucelle, to abandon your strongholds and go back to your own country. If not, I will make a war cry ('hahu') that will be remembered forever. And I am writing this to you for the third and final time; I will not write anything further.

Jesus Maria.

Joan the Pucelle.

[In postscript] I have sent my letters to you in an honest manner, but you are holding my messengers, or 'heralds' in French, as prisoners; for you have kept my herald, called Guyenne. If you are willing to send him back to me, I will return to you some of your men captured at the fortress of Saint-Loup, for they are not all dead.[35]

35 See **84**. An anonymous account of the siege of Orléans, written around 1467, but
    perhaps drawing upon a more contemporary source, stated: 'At nightfall, the Pucelle

10. *Ballade contre les Anglais* (May 1429?)

Source: P. Meyer, 'Ballade contre les Anglais, 1429', *Romania*, XXI, 1892, pp. 50–2.

Language: French

Like document **19** below, little is known about this anonymous ballad against the English that may have been written shortly after the end of the siege of Orléans. The only copy exists on the cover paper of a request by a watchmaker named Pierre Cudrifin for payment – a completely unrelated story.

Depart, English fools, depart! Your time here has come to an end. You must now drag home your banners that the good French have cut down to the ground by the will of [our] King Jesus, and Joan, the sweet Pucelle, which has confused you greatly [and] which is difficult for you to accept.

You were too arrogant in your ways, behaving in such a way far too long; in France, which you held on to foolishly, you found your grave. You came under false pretences, but, by just quarrel, you must now leave in disgrace, which is difficult for you to accept.

So imagine the state of those who supported you since your first endeavour.[36] I think they are all dead, or lost, for I do not see any who will, at present, support you, if they are not [already] troubled and facing strife, which is difficult for you to accept.

And as for your wages, they are at an end, [now that] you have a severe illness and a sickness,[37] and your throat is cut with a razor, which is difficult news for you to accept.

---

sent two heralds to the English army, and demanded that they release the herald who had carried her letters from Blois. Likewise the Bastard of Orléans instructed them that if they did not send him back, then he would kill by a brutal death all the Englishmen who were prisoners in Orléans, and also those among the lords of England who had been sent to negotiate for the ransom of others. For this reason the leaders of the army returned all the heralds and messengers to the Pucelle, instructing her, through them, that they would burn and set fire to her, and that she was just a trollop, and as such she should return to watching the cows.' (P. Charpentier and C. Cuissard (eds), *Journal du siège d'Orléans [et du voyage de Reims] 1428–29, augmenté de plusieurs documents, notamment des comptes de ville*, Orléans, 1896, p. 79.)

36 That is to say, the Burgundians.

37 The poem refers to the illness of 'la goute' and 'la gravelle'.

11. Letter from Charles VII to the inhabitants of Narbonne (10 May 1429)

Source: Quicherat (ed.), *Procès de condamnation*, V, pp. 101–4.

Language: French

On the evening of 9 May, Charles VII wrote a circular letter to the citizens of Narbonne that now survives in the municipal archives; copies were also sent to other major towns, including La Rochelle. He called upon them to give thanks to God for the success of the capture of the fortress of Saint-Loup, making no reference to Joan. During the evening, though, further messengers arrived that caused him to add two postscripts to the original letter.

Since these letters were written, a herald came to us here, around an hour after midnight, who reported upon his life that last Friday our men crossed the river by boat to Orléans, and they besieged the fortress at the end of the bridge [the Tourelles] from the side of the Sologne [the south side of the river, opposite to the city]. And that same day, they seized the house of the Augustins [an Augustinian convent]; and on that Saturday they also attacked the rest of that fortress, which was the boulevard [in front] of the bridge,[38] where there were a good six hundred English soldiers, under two banners and the standard of Glasdale.[39] And finally, through their great prowess and courage in arms, and always by means of the grace of Our Lord, they captured the whole of this fortress. And all of the English who were there were either killed or taken prisoner. And so, even more than before, you should praise and thank again our said Creator who, by His divine mercy, has not wished to forget us. And let us also honour the virtuous deeds and wondrous things that this herald, who was present, has reported to us, and the others too, regarding the Pucelle, who has always been present at the accomplishment of all of these deeds.

And once again, before the completion of these letters, two gentlemen have arrived before us, who have been involved in this matter, and who certify and confirm the same things but in greater detail than the

---

38 In modern French and English, the word 'boulevard' is most commonly used to refer to a large street, often lined with trees. Yet the term was originally used in the late middle ages to describe the raised mounds or bulwarks that were built as fortifications around a town or city.

39 William Glasdale, Bailly of Alençon for Henry VI, was captain of the towers and fortress of the bridge at Orléans after the death of the Earl of Salisbury at the end of October 1428. Glasdale died on the day of Joan's assault on the fortress of the Tourelles, 7 May 1429.

herald; and they have brought letters on this matter, in the hand of the Lord of Gaucourt.[40] Moreover we have this evening certain news that, after our men had taken and defeated the fortress at the end of the bridge last Saturday, at dawn on the following day the English who had remained ran away and cleared out so hastily that they left behind their bombards, cannons and artillery and the greater part of their food supplies and baggage.

Given at Chinon the 10th day of May [1429].

Signed: Charles; countersigned: Budé.

12. Letter from Pancrazio Giustiniani (10 May 1429)

Source: Antonio Morosini, *Chronique d'Antonio Morosini. Extraits relatifs à l'histoire de France*, ed. and trans. L. Dorez, 4 vols, Paris, 1898–1902, III, pp. 38–54.

Language: Italian

On 10 May 1429, an Italian merchant named Pancrazio Giustiniani wrote from Bruges to his father, Marco, in Venice. The letter arrived there on 18 June and was copied into the *Diario* of Antonio Morosini, who kept a record of all the news reported by his firm's overseas agents. Pancrazio offered an account of the relief of the siege of Orléans, making no reference to Joan's involvement in the enterprise until the very end; even then, he did not appear to know the Pucelle's true name.

For fifteen days or more before this news, there was endless discussion of many of the prophecies found at Paris, and of the other matters which also announced that the dauphin would prosper. And in truth, I agreed with an Italian on the state of things, and with many in making the most sharp jibes in the world, especially about a maiden [*una poncela*] shepherdess, born around Lorraine, who came a month and a half ago to the dauphin and who wished to speak with him alone and without any another person. And in short, she explained to him that God sent her to him, and said to him that he would surely enter into Paris from here on the [feast of] St John in the month of June [24 June]; that he would wage war against the English and would certainly win and enter into Paris and be crowned there; that afterwards, he would make an effort by means of his men to bring supplies

---

40 Raoul de Gaucourt had served as chamberlain to the Duke of Orléans before being captured at the siege of Harfleur by Henry V in 1415 and held prisoner for ten years. He was appointed Bailly of Orléans in 1428, and later testified at the Nullification trial on 25 February 1456.

to Orléans and to wage war against the English; and that surely he would be the victor, and would have the siege lifted amidst great confusion.[41] And moreover I can clearly explain to you that this person [Charles VII] received from her the revelation of great deeds, and I was kept in suspense by this woman like all of the others. And I find that I have letters from traders in merchandise who are in Burgundy, on 16 January,[42] who speak about these matters and about this young lady, and, on 28 [January], this news was repeated by another letter, saying that she said to men of high status that the siege would be lifted within a few days, etc.

For the moment, I have previously told you in every detail how these letters were written and what she was saying has been accomplished up to this day. And it is said that the one who wrote them is an Englishman named Lawrence [Trent],[43] whom Marino knows well, an honest and discreet person. Seeing what so many honourable and pious men were saying in their letters, he wrote about this matter: 'This has driven me mad.' Among other things he says that he had seen for the same reason that it was evident that many of the barons held her in esteem, and it appears that other commoners also do so, right up to now; and then he says that many of the men who wished to make fun of her are surely dead by a bad end. And yet, to conclude, they say what I am going to say. I have recounted it to you, but nothing may show it more clearly than her unquestionable victory in the debate with the masters of theology,[44] so much so that it seemed that she may be another St Katherine come down to earth, because for so many knights, hearing her speak and say so many marvellous and new things each day, it seems that this is a great wonder, after having heard her speak about so many notable matters ...

Moreover it was said that this lady [Joan] should accomplish two other great deeds and that afterwards she would die. May God bring aid to her, as all say, and may He not forget us and give us all long and good life with happiness! Amen.

41 This rather confused statement of the mission of Joan of Arc may testify to popular uncertainty about her goals, though it is worth noting that she herself did not make any mention of Reims in her first letter to the English [4].

42 The commentator upon this text, Germain Lefèvre-Pontalis, has argued that this date must in fact have been 16 April.

43 Lefèvre-Pontalis identifies this Englishman as Lawrence Trent and suggests that he may have been the author of the two letters of 16 and 28 April that had just been mentioned.

44 This is a reference to the investigation of Joan at Poitiers.

13. *Collectarium historiarum* of Jean Dupuy (May 1429?)

Source: A. Dondaine, 'Le témoignage de Jean Dupuy, O.P., sur Jeanne d'Arc. Note additionnelle à AFP XII (1942) 167–84', *Archivum fratrum praedicatorum*, XXXVIII, 1968, 34–41.

Language: Latin

In April 1429, a Dominican theologian and Inquisitor of Toulouse named Jean Dupuy, Bishop of Cahors, completed his *Collectarium historiarum*, an abridged history of the world. At the time he was resident at the court of Pope Martin V in Rome where he soon heard news of Joan of Arc; therefore he appended a new chapter on the Pucelle to his great work. Yet Dupuy left two large blank spaces in this text, perhaps intending to insert documents from the Poitiers investigation or extracts from *De mirabili victoria* [7], as was done in two subsequent copies.[45]

A certain Pucelle named Joan has entered into the kingdom of France. She only arrived when the kingdom was on the verge of complete ruin, and at the moment when the sceptre of this realm ought to have passed into a foreign hand. This young girl accomplishes actions which appear more divine than human. I would prefer to pass over in silence her bravery in war, rather than speak inexactly and insufficiently. Nevertheless, I am pleased to register here the means employed to confirm that confidence should be placed in her.

[There is a blank space of eleven lines in the (presumably original) Vatican manuscript of this text. It is unclear what was meant to fill this gap, but, in two other copies, the scribes have inserted a transcription of *De mirabili victoria* [7], up to the three proofs in favour of Joan's wearing of male clothes.]

In the second place, I wish to speak about the clothing of a man which Joan was attached to using, on which there are three points to note.

[There are another nine blank lines in the Vatican manuscript, which have been filled by the remaining text of *De mirabili victoria* in the two other copies. Dupuy then proceeded to recount in some detail the stories of Deborah, Judith, Esther and the Amazon Penthesilea.]

That our Pucelle equals, or even surpasses, all of these women is made evident by the extraordinary acts of bravery, of courage and of intrepidity of which I will only recount the beginning without going further, on the grounds cited above.

45 See A. Dondaine, 'Le frère prêcheur Jean Dupuy, évêque de Cahors et son témoignage sur Jeanne d'Arc', *Archivum fratrum praedicatorum*, XII, 1942, pp. 118–84; D. Fraioli, *Joan of Arc: the early debate*, ch. 9.

The town of Orléans was besieged by the enemies of the realm; the length of the siege had reduced it to such an extremity that the inhabitants could no longer hope for help except from God. It was then that this young girl, who had only watched over animals before, accompanied by a very great number of soldiers, attacked the besieging army, made up of a countless quantity of warriors, with such an impetuosity that in three days the whole of this army was captured or put to flight. To see the display of this army, the power of the combatants, the courage of the soldiers, the good leadership of the commanders, and the ardour of the young girl, it might have been thought that the forces gathered from all around could not have done in a month what the Pucelle accomplished in three days. Who else [can do this], except the one who can make many men fall under the hand of a few, and who can easily free them with many or with a few soldiers?[46] That is to say God, King of all kings, to whom I give thanks 'for having struck and humiliated the proud, and for having overcome our enemies by the force of your arms'![47]

If you wish to know the details, the Pucelle is seventeen years of age; her strength and her dexterity are such that, in enduring these tasks, she equals the most robust and well-trained men; there is not one man who could or pretends to equal her in activity. She does not seek any worldly benefit; she receives numerous gifts but she does not keep anything but rather distributes it. She replies simply, in a few words, showing herself to be very prudent with regard to her mission; her life is very decent, sober, without a shadow of superstition or of magic, although some people who are liars may accuse her of witchcraft.

That she is free from superstition and from magic can be demonstrated clearly by the three characteristics that distinguish the miracles accomplished by good people from the marvels that the evil people perform. Firstly, the energy of the power which acts in the good: this is the divine power, and it extends to those works which are not attained by the force of active nature, whatever that might be. Secondly, the usefulness of the marvels accomplished: the good do not

46 This echoes a passage from the Latin Vulgate Bible, I Maccabees 3: 18: 'It is an easy matter for many men to fall under the hands of a few, and there is no difference in the sight of the God of Heaven who can free them with many or with a few soldiers.'

47 This is a slight reworking of another passage from the Vulgate, Psalm 88: 11: 'You have humbled the proud one, as one that is slain: with your strong arm you have scattered your enemies.'

do these things except for useful purposes, the evil to destroy or for trivial reasons, for example to fly in the air, to restore lifeless limbs, and similar things ... The third difference, the end: the miracles of good people have as an end the affirmation of the faith and good morals, those of the evil to ruin them.

But consider that the Pucelle confesses herself every day before hearing mass; that she receives communion extremely devoutly once a week; that if her acts exceed the strength of her sex, they tend to a useful and just end, that is to say the pacification of the kingdom of France; that this pacification leads to the recovery of the faith that would not have fallen [into decline] as it has if the kingdom had not disappeared into the whirlpool of such wars, judging by the support once given by France to the faith. As a result, one would be forced to conclude that the works of the Pucelle come from God, and are not the effect of magic, even though the people mentioned before, who are liars, say this.

What more to add? One day, the Pucelle asked the King to give her a present. Her request was granted. She then asked for the kingdom of France itself as a gift. The King, astonished, gave it to her after some hesitation, and the young girl accepted it. She even wished that the act might be solemnly drawn up and read by the King's four secretaries. After the charter had been drafted and recited in a loud voice, the King was somewhat astonished, when the young girl, pointing to him, said to the audience: 'Here is the poorest knight in his kingdom'.

And shortly afterwards, in the presence of the same notaries, disposing of the command of the kingdom of France, she returned it into the hands of God Almighty. Then, after a few moments, acting in the name of God, she invested King Charles with the kingdom of France. And she wished that all of this might be drafted in writing in a solemn act.

14. A report on Joan from Brittany (4 June 1429)

Source: Morosini, *Chronique d'Antonio Morosini,* pp. 88–97.

Language: Italian

This anonymous letter from Brittany was included in a letter sent by Pancrazio Giustiniani at Bruges on 9 July 1429 to his father, Marco, in Venice.

This Pucelle is eighteen years of age or thereabouts; [she was born] in the region of Lorraine, on the border of France, and she was a shepherdess, the daughter of a villager. At the beginning of March,

leaving her flock, she prayed to God and her parents and two gentlemen who agreed without contradiction [to follow her] and said to
them that she was leading them by divine inspiration, etc.

Having come into the presence of the noble prince, the dauphin
Charles, son of the King of France who recently died, she informed
him by Jesus our redeemer that he should be pleased [that she came]
for three goals, which would follow, so she said, if he had complete
confidence in her, gave up the life [that he followed], mended his
ways and controlled himself like her, moved by the grace of God, by
whose command she had been stirred to act.

First she had come to raise the siege of the English at Orléans, and in
the second place, to crown him without obstacle and make him king of
all of France and its possessions, and in the third place to make peace
between him and the English, and then to have the good Duke of
Orléans freed from his prison in England ...[48]

15. Letter from Guy and André de Laval to their mother
   (8 June 1429)

Source: Quicherat (ed.), *Procès de condamnation*, V, pp. 105–11.

Language: French

This letter was written by Guy and André to their mother Jeanne de Laval
and their grandmother Anne de Laval, who had been driven from their castle
at Laval and were sheltering at Vitré in Brittany. Guy was created Count at
the coronation of Charles VII on 17 July 1429. His brother André later
became Admiral and Marshal of France, and is often referred to as the
Marshal of Loheac; his son was Gilles de Laval, Baron of Rais, infamously
executed for sorcery on 26 October 1440. Their grandmother had been
married to Bertrand du Guesclin and they were also the cousins of Georges
de La Trémouïlle.

And on the Monday, I left with the King to come to Selles en Berry,
four leagues from Saint-Agnan. And the King made the Pucelle come
before him, who had been at Selles before. Some say that I was
favoured because I saw her: the Pucelle gave a very warm welcome to
my brother and myself, fully armoured except for her head and
holding the lance in her hand. Afterwards, when we had gone to

---

48 Charles Duke of Orléans was a prisoner in England after being captured at the
   battle of Agincourt in 1415.

Selles, I went to see her at her lodging. She had wine brought and said to me that she would soon make me drink it in Paris. It all seemed entirely divine, her deeds, and to see and to hear her. She left Selles that Monday at Vespers to go to Romorantin, three leagues away, scouting ahead and approaching the location, with the Marshal of Boussac, a great number of men-at-arms and the common people.[49] And I saw her completely covered by plate armour except for her head,[50] a small axe in her hand, mounted on horseback, a great black charger, which reared up fiercely at the entrance of her lodging and would not allow her to mount. Then she said, 'Take him to the cross', which was in front of the church down the street. There she mounted without him moving, as if he had been tied. She then turned towards the church door, which was very close, and said in a quiet female voice: 'You priests and churchmen, lead a procession and prayers to God.' And then she returned the way she had come, saying: 'Carry it ahead, carry it ahead,' [speaking of] the unfurled standard which a gracious page carried; she had her small axe in her hand and her brother [Pierre] who had come eight days before, also left with her completely covered in plate armour ...

The Pucelle said to me in her lodgings, as I had gone to see her there, that three days before my arrival, she had sent to you, my grandmother, a very small gold ring, but that this was a very small thing and that she would willingly have sent you something better considering your recommendation.[51]

16. Joan of Arc's letter to the city of Tournai (25 June 1429)

Source: Quicherat (ed.), *Procès de condamnation*, V, pp. 123–5.

Language: French

This letter was delivered to Tournai on 6 July by Thierry de Maubray who brought 'news of our lord the King and of his victories and the recovery of his kingdom, along with letters of the Pucelle and of her confessor'. Joan's

---

49 The Marshal of Boussac was Jean de Brosse (d. 1433), also known as the Marshal of Saint-Sévère.

50 The reference to Joan as 'armée tout en blanc' does not mean that she was dressed in white, as is often assumed, but rather wearing plate armour.

51 It is unclear what this recommendation might have entailed, though Guy also referred to another letter that his mother had sent to their cousin, La Trémouïlle, as a result of which 'the King has made a point of keeping me with him'.

letter was copied and transmitted to the thirty-six 'Banners' or sections of the city.

Jhesus Maria.

Gentle, loyal Frenchmen of the town of Tournai, the Pucelle informs you of the news from here that in eight days, she has chased the English out of all the places that they held on the river Loire by assault and other means. Many of them are dead or captured, and they have been beaten in battle. And believe that the Earl of Suffolk, la Pole his brother, Lord Talbot, Lord Scales, and my lord John Fastolf, with many knights and captains have been captured, and the brother of the Earl of Suffolk and Glasdale are dead.[52] And now you good, loyal Frenchmen, I pray and call upon you to be ready to come to the consecration of the gentle King Charles at Reims, where we shall shortly be; and come before us when you hear that we are approaching. May God watch over you and grant you grace to uphold the just cause of the kingdom of France.

Written at Gien, the 25th day of June [1429].

To the loyal Frenchmen of the town of Tournai.

17. Joan of Arc's letter to the city of Troyes (4 July 1429)

Source: Quicherat (ed.), *Procès de condamnation*, IV, pp. 284–8.

Language: French

This letter was written to the citizens of Troyes as the royal army approached the city, which submitted to Charles VII within the week. The original does not survive but it was transcribed in the register of municipal documents of Reims compiled by Jean Rogier (d. 1637).

Jesus Maria.

Very dear and good friends, if this [title] applies to you, lords, townsmen and inhabitants of the town of Troyes, Joan the Pucelle commands and informs you in the name of the King of Heaven, her rightful and sovereign Lord, in whose royal service she is each day, that you should render true obedience and recognition to the gentle King of

---

52 Sir William Glasdale was killed at Orléans on 7 May. Sir John de la Pole and his brother, William de la Pole, Earl of Suffolk, were captured at Jargeau on 12 June 1429, while their brother Alexander died there. Thomas de Scales, seventh Lord Scales, was taken prisoner at Orléans and then at Patay on 18 June, as was John Lord Talbot; Sir John Fastolf evaded capture.

France; he will soon be in Reims and Paris, whoever may come against him, and in his good towns [*bonnes villes*] of this holy kingdom, with the aid of King Jesus. Loyal Frenchmen, come before King Charles and if you act in this way, you will not be at fault, and need not fear for your lives or your property. And if you do not do this, I promise you and certify upon your lives that we will enter, with God's help, all the towns that should belong to the holy kingdom, and establish a good, firm peace there, whoever comes against us. I commend you to God; may He watch over you if it pleases Him. Reply soon.

Written before the city of Troyes, at St. Phal, on Tuesday 4 July [1429].

18. Joan of Arc's letter to the Duke of Burgundy (17 July 1429)

Source: Quicherat (ed.), *Procès de condamnation*, V, pp. 126–7.

Language: French

This letter, which survives in the original, was sent to the Duke of Burgundy while Joan was in Reims for the coronation of Charles VII. Burgundy was one of the six secular peers of the kingdom, who were expected to attend such a function, along with the six spiritual peers.

Jhesus Maria.

Great and mighty prince, Duke of Burgundy, Joan the Pucelle calls upon you by the King of Heaven, my rightful and sovereign Lord, that the King of France and you make a firm and lasting peace, pardoning each other with a sincere heart, as faithful Christians should do. And if you want to make war, wage it against the Saracens. Prince of Burgundy, I pray, beg, and very humbly request, rather than demand, that you no longer wage war in the holy kingdom of France, and swiftly and in a short time withdraw your people who are in some places and fortresses in this holy kingdom. And as for the gentle King of France, he is ready to make peace with you, saving his honour, if you do not keep it [i.e. the peace]. And I would have you know, by the King of Heaven, my rightful and sovereign Lord, for your good, for your honour and upon your life, that you will not win any battle against loyal Frenchmen, and that all those who wage war against the holy kingdom of France, wage war against King Jesus, King of Heaven and of all the world, my rightful and sovereign Lord. I pray and beseech with clasped hands that you do not make any battle or wage war against us – not you, your people nor your subjects. And be assured that, however many soldiers you bring against us, they will never win, and there will be great sorrow for the great battle and the blood that will be spilled there among those who come against us. And three weeks ago I wrote to you and sent letters by a herald, that you should be at the consecration which today, Sunday the seventeenth day of this present month of July, is taking place in the city of Reims:[53] I have not had any reply to this, nor have we heard any word from the herald.[54] I commend you to God, and may He watch over you if it pleases Him. And I pray God that He will make a firm peace.

Written in the aforesaid place of Reims, the 17th day of July [1429].

19. *Ballade du sacre de Reims* (July 1429?)

Source: P. Champion, 'Notes sur Jeanne d'Arc', *Le moyen âge*, 2nd series, XIII, 1909, pp. 370–7.

Language: French

This cryptic ballad of the coronation at Reims blends a range of prophetic traditions to support Charles VII and the royal family [the beautiful garden of the noble fleurs-de-lys] against the English and those false hearts who supported them. The only copy survives in a manuscript dating from 1472, that also contains poetry by François Villon and is now in the royal library in Stockholm. The title (*Ballade du sacre de Reims*) associates it with the coronation of Charles VII, although there is no internal evidence to support or contradict this claim. It certainly echoes key themes that appear in Christine de Pizan's *Ditié de Jehanne d'Arc* [20].

Here comes the noble Flying Stag [*Cerf Vollant*],[55] Asnel, emerging from the celebrated fountain,[56] who comes to reign, with strength and

---

53 The term 'consecration' was commonly used in French to refer to the royal coronation, which culminated in the placing of the crown upon the head of the king, after the recipient had been anointed or consecrated, like a priest, with an oil from the Holy Ampulla: R. A. Jackson, *Vive le roi! A history of the French coronation from Charles V to Charles X*, Chapel Hill, 1984.

54 This earlier letter to the Duke of Burgundy does not survive.

55 The flying stag is a clearly a reference to Charles VII. This animal had widespread allegorical significance, particularly as the symbol of the longevity of a dynasty, and became a symbol of the French monarchy in the second half of the fourteenth century. Both Charles V and the Duke of Berry commissioned statues of stags, and writers such as Eustache Deschamps and Philippe de Mézières referred to the king as the 'Cerf Vollant' and presented the allegory of this animal driving marauders out of the 'forest' of his kingdom.

56 It is unclear from where the references to Asnel and the fountain derive, though this may be an allusion to stories and prophecies surrounding Merlin.

might, in the forest of his noble domain; here comes the second Charlemagne, true successor of the arms of Clovis and arising from the pure roots of the beautiful garden of the noble fleurs-de-lys![57]

Sibyl,[58] daughter of the noble King Priam, one thing is most certain about the noble stag: it was already foretold to the Romans, that there would be much pain in his time [i.e. the stag's], and for him too. This was not an idle promise, because false hearts have destroyed the surroundings in the forest of those close relatives of the beautiful garden of the noble fleurs-de-lys.[59]

Many cruel beasts, while ravaging, have dishonoured the sovereign of the flowers [Charles VII] so many times through ardent ambition, compelling all to hold him [the sovereign] as a stranger: but since God desires Reason to retrieve him [Charles VII], he saw the good will of his friends who were on this side of the Seine in the beautiful garden of the noble fleurs-de-lys.

Bodies corrupted by the deeds of the False-Seeming One [the devil], divided, red and full of vain order,[60] hearts fled over the troubled sea, big and swollen from the blood of human life, depart from Aquitaine![61] You will be destroyed, as false and evil, by the sowing of the very noble grain, in the beautiful garden of the noble fleurs-de-lys.

O stag, native of the noble and of valiant blood, true light of all just men, who comes to give his friends assurance! Truly it is not in vain; soon we will see the week, the day, the month, in word and in deed,

---

57 The so-called 'second Charlemagne' prophecy that a French king would emulate the achievements of his most illustrious forbear by surpassing all monarchs and becoming emperor was widely known at the start of the fifteenth century. See M. Reeves, *The Influence of Prophecy in the Later Middle Ages: a study in Joachimism*, Oxford, 1969, particularly Part III, ch. 3.

58 The daughter of King Priam of Troy was Cassandra, who shared the gift of prophecy with her twin brother Helenus. This reference to such a famous sibyl, or inspired visionary, reinforces the prophetic dimensions of the poem.

59 The beautiful garden of the fleurs-de-lys is clearly an allegorical representation of the French royal family, so that their close relatives in the forest outside must be the wider aristocracy.

60 It is unclear what this phrase means, and it may be that the text in the surviving manuscript has been corrupted.

61 The Hundred Years War (1337–1453) was largely the result of the tensions created by the possession of the duchy of Aquitaine in the south-west of France by the kings of England. The reference clearly indicates that the 'bodies' being asked to leave are the English.

that we have daily pleasure in the beautiful garden of the noble fleurs-de-lys.

All loyal hearts will say aloud, Our Lady, Montjoye, Saint-Denis![62] Long live the righteous stag, white and mighty in the beautiful garden of the noble fleurs-de-lys!

20. *Ditié de Jehanne d'Arc* by Christine de Pizan (31 July 1429)

Source: Christine de Pizan, *Le ditié de Jehanne d'Arc*, ed. and trans. A. J. Kennedy and K. Varty, Oxford, 1977.[63]

Language: French

Christine de Pizan (1364?–1430?) is one of the most famous late medieval French writers.[64] After an illustrious career, she retired in 1418 to the abbey of Poissy, outside Paris, and only broke her silence to compose the *Ditié de Jehanne d'Arc*. This famous work has variously been interpreted as a commemoration of recent events, a prayer of thanks to and praise for God, and a celebration of the proof that Joan offered of Christine's consistent defence of women against misogyny.[65] According to the surviving copies of the poem, it was completed on 31 July 1429, though it has recently been suggested that Christine actually wrote the poem later in 1429 or early in 1430, and deliberately pretended that it had been written at the high point of Joan's career in order to present an ironic attack upon the King for his supposed betrayal of the Pucelle. It should be noted, though, that Christine had never faked the dating of a text before, and it is far from clear what her objectives might have been in staging such an assault upon Charles VII.[66] It is therefore more reasonable to accept the textual evidence for the dating, and therefore to assume that the poem reflects Christine's genuine hopes and

---

62 These were battle-cries of the French Crown.

63 My thanks to Angus Kennedy and Kenneth Varty for their permission to reproduce their translation of this text.

64 C. C. Willard, *Christine de Pisan: her life and works*, New York, 1984, and E. J. Richards, 'Christine de Pizan (c.1365–c.1431)', in D. Sinnreich-Levi and I. S. Laurie (eds), *Literature of the French and Occitan Middle Ages: eleventh to fifteenth centuries*, Farmington Hill, 1999, pp. 86–101.

65 The secondary literature is enormous, but good starting points are provided by R. Brown-Grant, '"Hee! Quel honneur au femenin sexe!" Female heroism in Christine de Pizan's *Ditié de Jehanne d'Arc*', *Journal of the Institute of Romance Studies*, V, 1997, pp. 123–33, and D. Fraioli, *Joan of Arc: the early debate*, ch. 7.

66 A. D. Lutkus and J. M. Walker, 'PR pas PC: Christine de Pizan's pro-Joan', in *Fresh Verdicts on Joan of Arc*, pp. 145–60, and A. J. Kennedy, 'La date du *Ditié de Jehanne d'Arc*: réponse à Anne D. Lutkus et Julia M. Walker', in E. Hicks (ed.), *Au champ des escriptures. IIIe colloque international sur Christine de Pizan*, Paris, 2000, pp. 759–70.

fears at this crucial moment in the campaign to recover France, and in the developing relationship between Charles VII and Joan of Arc.

1. I, Christine, who have wept for eleven years in a walled abbey where I have lived ever since Charles (how strange this is!) the King's son – dare I say it? – fled in haste from Paris, I who have lived enclosed there on account of the treachery,[67] now, for the first time, begin to laugh;

2. I begin to laugh heartily for joy at the departure of the wintry season, during which I was wont to live confined to a dreary cage. But now I shall change my language from one of tears to one of song, because I have found the good season once again ...

3. In 1429 the sun began to shine again. It brings back the good, new season which had not really been seen for a long time – and because of that many people had lived out their lives in sorrow; I myself am one of them. But I no longer grieve over anything, now that I can see what I desire.

4. But since the time when I came to stay where I am the situation has completely changed, great sorrow has given way to new joy and, thanks be to God, the lovely season called Spring, which I have longed for and in which everything is renewed, has brought greenness out of barren winter.

5. The reason is that the rejected child of the rightful King of France, who has long suffered many a great misfortune and who now approaches, rose up as if towards prime,[68] coming as a crowned king in might and majesty, wearing spurs of gold.

6. Now let us greet our King! Welcome to him on his return! Overjoyed at the sight of his noble array, let us all, both great and small, step forward to greet him joyously – and let no one hold back – praising God, who has kept him safe, and shouting 'Noël!' in a loud voice.

7. But now I wish to relate how God, to whom I pray for guidance lest I omit anything, accomplished all this through His grace. May it

67 On 29 May 1418, the Burgundians entered the city of Paris with the aid of 'traitors' such as Perrinet Leclerc. Around two thousand of the supporters of the dauphin were killed, though the future Charles VII himself escaped.

68 i.e. 'like one rising up to go to prime'.

be told everywhere, for it is worthy of being remembered, and may it be written down – no matter whom it may displease – in many a chronicle and history-book!

8. Now hear, throughout the whole world, of something which is more wonderful than anything else! See if God, in whom all grace abounds, does not in the end support what is right. This is a fact worthy of note, given the matter in hand! And let it be of profit to the disillusioned, whom Fortune has cast down!

9. And note how, when someone finds himself quite unjustly attacked and hated on all sides, there is no need for such a person to feel dismayed by misfortune. See how Fortune, who has harmed many a one, is so inconstant, for God, who opposes all wrong deeds, raises up those in whom hope dwells.

10. Did anyone, then, see anything quite so extraordinary come to pass (something that is well worth noting and remembering in every region), namely, that France (about whom it was said she had been cast down) should see her fortunes change, by divine command, from evil to such great good,

11. as the result, indeed, of such a miracle that, if the matter were not so well-known and crystal-clear in every aspect, nobody would ever believe it? It is a fact well worth remembering that God should nevertheless have wished (and this is the truth!) to bestow such great blessings on France, through a young virgin.

12. And what honour for the French Crown, this proof of divine intervention! For all the blessings which God bestows upon it demonstrate how much He favours it and that He finds more faith in the royal house than anywhere else; as far as it is concerned, I read (and there is nothing new in this) that the lilies of France [*fleurs de lix*] never erred in matters of faith.

13. And you Charles, King of France, seventh of that noble name, who have been involved in such a great war before things turned out at all well for you, now, thanks be to God, see your honour exalted by the Pucelle who has laid low your enemies beneath your standard (and this is new!)

14. in a short time; for it was believed quite impossible that you should ever recover your country which you were on the point of

losing. Now it is manifestly yours for, no matter who may have done you harm, you have recovered it! And all this has been brought about by the intelligence of the Pucelle who, God be thanked, has played her part in this matter!

15. And I firmly believe that God would never have bestowed such grace upon you if it were not ordained by Him that you should, in the course of time, accomplish and bring to completion some great and solemn task; I believe too that He has destined you to be the author of very great deeds.

16. For there will be a King of France called Charles, son of Charles, who will be supreme ruler over all kings.[69] Prophecies have given him the name of 'The Flying Stag' [Cerf Vollant],[70] and many a deed will be accomplished by this conqueror (God has called him to this task) and in the end he will be emperor.

17. All this is to the profit of your soul. I pray to God that you may be the person I have described, and that He grant you long life, to nobody's harm, so that you may yet see your children grown up, I pray too that all joy come to France because of you and them! But, as you serve God always, may you never wage war to the death there again!

18. I hope that you will be good and upright, and a lover of justice and that you will surpass all others, provided your deeds are not tarnished by pride, that you will be gentle and well-disposed towards your people, that you will always love God who elected you as His servant (and you have a first manifestation of this), on condition that you do your duty.

19. And how will you ever be able to thank God enough, serve and fear him in all your deeds (for He has led you from such great adversity to peace and raised up the whole of France from such ruin) when His most holy Providence made you worthy of such signal honour?

69 A reference to the 'second Charlemagne' prophecy that a French king would follow in the footsteps of Charlemagne and become emperor.

70 Writers such as Jean Froissart, Eustache Deschamps and Philippe de Mézières had previously identified the 'Cerf Vollant' with Charles VI, but now Christine de Pizan, like the anonymous author of [19], links the symbol directly with Charles VII.

20. May you be praised for this, great God! We are duty-bound to thank you, who decreed time and place for these blessings to come about. With hands clasped, both great and small, we all thank you, heavenly Lord, who has guided us through the great tempest into peace.

21. And you, blessed Pucelle, are you to be forgotten, given that God honoured you so much that you untied the rope which held France so tightly bound? Could one ever praise you enough for having bestowed peace on this land humiliated by war?

22. Blessed be He who created you, Joan, who were born at a propitious hour! Pucelle sent from God, into whom the Holy Spirit poured His great grace, in whom there was and is an abundance of noble gifts, never did Providence refuse you any request. Who can ever begin to repay you?

23. And what more can be said of any other person or of the great deeds of the past? Moses, upon whom God in His bounty bestowed many a blessing and virtue, miraculously and indefatigably led God's people out of Egypt. In the same way, blessed Pucelle, you have led us out of evil!

24. When we take your person into account, you who are a young maiden, to whom God gives the strength and power to be the champion who casts the rebels down and feeds France with the sweet, nourishing milk of peace, here indeed is something quite extraordinary!

25. For if God performed such a great number of miracles through Joshua who conquered many a place and cast down many an enemy, he, Joshua, was a strong and powerful man.[71] But, after all, a woman – a simple shepherdess – braver than any man ever was in Rome! As far as God is concerned, this was easily accomplished.

26. But as for us, we never heard tell of such an extraordinary marvel, for the prowess of all the great men of the past cannot be compared to this woman's whose concern it is to cast out our enemies. This is God's doing: it is He who guides her and who has given her a heart greater than that of any man.

---

71 Joshua was Moses' successor as leader of the Israelites, his main achievement being the conquest of the land of Canaan. The most celebrated miracle associated with him is the halting of the sun which allowed him to complete his victory over the Amorites (Joshua 10: 12–14).

27. Much is made of Gideon, who was a simple workman, and it was God, so the story tells, who made him fight; nobody could stand firm before him and he conquered everything.[72] But whatever guidance God gave [him], it is clear that He never performed so striking a miracle as He does for this woman.

28. I have heard of Esther, Judith and Deborah,[73] who were women of great worth, through whom God delivered His people from oppression, and I have heard of many other worthy women as well, champions every one: through them He performed many miracles, but He has accomplished more through this Pucelle.

29. She was miraculously sent by divine command and conducted by the angel of the Lord to the King, in order to help him. Her achievement is no illusion for she was carefully put to the test in council (in short, a thing is proved by its effect)

30. and well examined before people were prepared to believe her; before it became common knowledge that God had sent her to the King, she was brought before clerks and wise men so that they could find out if she was telling the truth. But it was found in histories that she was destined to accomplish her mission;

31. for more than five hundred years ago, Merlin, the Sibyl and Bede foresaw her coming, entered her in their writings as someone who would put an end to France's troubles, made prophecies about her, saying that she would carry the banner in the French wars and describing all that she would achieve.[74]

32. And, in truth, the beauty of her life proves that she has been blessed with God's grace – and for that reason her actions are more readily accepted as genuine. For whatever she does, she always has her eyes fixed on God, to whom she prays and whom she invokes and serves in word and deed; nowhere does her devotion ever falter.

33. Oh, how clear this was at the siege of Orléans where her power

---

72 Like Joan, Gideon was entrusted with a divinely-ordained mission to deliver his country from oppression. On his conquest of the Midianites, see Judges 6–8.

73 Esther's defeat of Haman's Plot against the Jews is related in Esther 6–7; Judith's victory over Holofernes is in Judith, 8–16; Deborah's overthrow of Sisera at the Battle of Kishon is in Judges 4–5.

74 Pizan invokes three famous prophetic figures to authorise Joan. See pages 19 to 20 above.

was first made manifest! It is my belief that no miracle was ever more evident, for God so came to the help of His people that our enemies were unable to help each other any more than would dead dogs. It was there that they were captured and put to death.

34. Oh! What honour for the female sex! It is perfectly obvious that God has special regard for it [the female sex] when all these wretched people who destroyed the whole kingdom – now recovered and made safe by a woman, something that five thousand men could not have done – and the traitors have been exterminated. Before the event they would scarcely have believed this possible.

35. A little girl of sixteen (isn't this something quite beyond nature?) who does not even notice the weight of the arms she bears – indeed her whole upbringing seems to have prepared her for this, so strong and resolute is she! And her enemies flee before her, not one of them can stand up to her. She does all this in full view of everyone,

36. and drives her enemies out of France, recapturing castles and towns. Never did anyone see greater strength, even in hundreds or thousands of men! And she is the supreme captain of our brave and able men. Neither Hector nor Achilles had such strength! This is God's doing: it is He who leads her.

37. And you trusty men-at-arms who carry out the task and prove yourselves to be good and loyal, one must certainly make mention of you (you will be praised in every nation!) and not fail to speak above all else of you and your valour,

38. you who, in pain and suffering, expose life and limb in defence of what is right and dare to risk confronting every danger. Be constant, for this, I promise, will win you glory and praise in heaven. For whoever fights for justice wins a place in heaven – this I do venture to say.

39. And so, you English, draw in your horns for you will never capture any good game! Don't attempt any foolish enterprise in France! You have been checkmated. A short time ago, when you looked so fierce, you had no inkling that this would be so; but you were not yet treading the path upon which God casts down the proud.

40. You thought that you had already conquered France and that she must remain yours. Things have turned out otherwise, you treacherous lot! Go and beat your drums elsewhere, unless you want to taste

death, like your companions, whom wolves may well devour, for their
bodies lie dead amidst the ploughed fields!

41. And know that she will cast down the English for good, for this
is God's will: He hears the prayer of the good whom they wanted to
harm! The blood of those who are dead and have no hope of being
brought back to life again cries out against them. God will tolerate
this no longer – He has decided, rather, to condemn them as evil.

42. She will restore harmony in Christendom and the Church. She
will destroy the unbelievers that people talk about, and the heretics
and their vile ways, for this is confirmed by prophecy, which predicts
it.[75] Nor will she have mercy on any place which treats faith in God
with disrespect.

43. She will destroy the Saracens, by conquering the Holy Land.[76]
She will lead Charles there, whom God preserve! Before he dies he
will make such a journey. He is the one who is to conquer it. It is
there that she is to end her days and that both of them are to win glory.
It is there that the whole enterprise will be brought to completion.

44. Therefore, in preference to all the brave men of times past, this
woman must wear the crown, for her deeds show clearly enough
already that God bestows more courage upon her than upon all those
men about whom people speak. And she has not yet accomplished her
whole mission! I believe that God bestows her here below so that
peace may be brought about through her deeds.

45. And yet destroying the English race is not her main concern for
her aspirations lie more elsewhere: it is her concern to ensure the
survival of the Faith. As for the English, whether it be a matter for
joy or sorrow, they are done for. In days to come scorn will be heaped
on them. They have been cast down!

46. And all you base rebels who have joined them, you can see now
that it would have been better for you to have gone forwards rather

---

75 The 'second Charlemagne' prophecy postulated that the French king would
   become emperor and thereby assume the duty of protecting the Church against its
   enemies. Contemporary readers of the poem would no doubt have remembered the
   threat posed by the Turks who had defeated an expeditionary force composed
   mainly of French troops at Nicopolis in 1396, as well as by the Hussites in
   Bohemia.

76 See **4, 18**.

than backwards as you did, thereby becoming the serfs of the English.[77] Beware that more does not befall you (for you have been tolerated long enough!), and remember what the outcome will be!

47. Oh, all you blind people, can't you detect God's hand in this? If you can't, you are truly stupid for how else could the Pucelle who strikes you all down dead have been sent to us? And you don't have sufficient strength! Do you want to fight against God?

48. Has she not led the King with her own hand to his coronation? No greater deed was performed at Acre; for there were certainly plenty of opponents.[78] But in spite of everyone, he was most nobly received and truly anointed, and there he heard mass.

49. It was exactly on the 17th day of July 1429 that Charles was, without any doubt, safely crowned at Reims, amidst great triumph and splendour and surrounded by many men-at-arms and barons; and he stayed there for approximately five days[79]

50. with the little Pucelle. As he returns through his country, neither city nor castle nor small town can hold out against them. Whether he be loved or hated, whether they be dismayed or reassured, the inhabitants surrender. Few need to be attacked, so fearful are they of his power.

51. It is true that some, in their folly, think they can resist, but this serves little purpose, for, in the end, whoever does offer opposition must pay God for his mistake. It is quite pointless. Whether they want to or not, they must surrender. No matter how strong the resistance offered, it collapses beneath the Pucelle's assault,

52. even though huge forces were gathered together, in order to launch a surprise attack and bar his return; but there is no need for a doctor's attentions now, for all his opponents have been captured and killed, one by one, and dispatched, so I've been told, to heaven or hell.

---

77 This was no doubt a reference to the Burgundians, Gascons and other Frenchmen who supported Henry VI against Charles VII.

78 The capture of Acre in 1191 during the Third Crusade led by Philip Augustus and Richard Lion-Heart.

79 Charles and Joan arrived at Reims on 16 July and left on 21 July 1429.

53. I don't know if Paris will hold out (for they have not reached there yet) or if the Pucelle will delay. But if it decides to see her as an enemy, I fear that she will subject it to a fierce attack, as she has done elsewhere. If they offer resistance for an hour, or even half an hour, it's my belief that things will go badly for them,

54. for [the King] will enter Paris, no matter who may grumble about it! The Pucelle has given her word that he will. Paris, do you think Burgundy will prevent him from entering? By no means, for he does not see himself as an enemy.[80] Nobody has the power to prevent him, and you will be overcome, you and your presumption![81]

55. Oh Paris, how could you be so ill-advised? Foolish inhabitants, you are lacking in trust! Do you prefer to be laid waste, Paris, rather than make peace with your prince? If you are not careful your great opposition will destroy you. It would be far better for you if you were to humbly beg for mercy. You are quite miscalculating!

56. It is the evil inhabitants I'm referring to, for there are many good people there, I have no doubt about that; but, take my word for it, these good people, who are no doubt much displeased to see their prince rejected in this way, do not dare speak out. They will not merit the punishment which will fall upon Paris and cost many a person his life.

57. And as for you, all you rebel towns, all of you who have renounced your lord, all of you men and women who have transferred your allegiance to another, may everything now be peacefully settled, with you beseeching his pardon! For if force is used against you, the gift [i.e. of forgiveness] will come too late.

58. And so as to avoid killing and wounding anyone [the King] delays for as long as he can, for the spilling of blood grieves him. But, in the end, if someone does not want to hand over, with good grace, what is rightly his, he is perfectly justified if he does recover it by force and bloodshed.

---

80 It is unclear whether it is Charles VII or the Duke of Burgundy who 'does not see himself as an enemy', but this is clear allusion to the diplomatic negotiations taking place between the two men on the eve of the attack upon Paris.

81 Neither Joan's nor Christine's optimism turned out to be well-founded: the attack on Paris on 8 September 1429 failed, and Charles VII was not to enter Paris until 12 November 1437, having reconciled himself with the Duke of Burgundy by the Treaty of Arras on 21 September 1435.

59. Alas! He is so magnanimous that he wishes to pardon each and everyone. And it is the Pucelle, the faithful servant of God, who makes him do this. Now as loyal Frenchmen submit your hearts and yourselves to him! And when you hear him speak, you will not be reproached by anyone.

60. And I pray to God that He will prevail upon you to act in this way, so that the cruel storm of these wars may be erased from memory and that you may live your lives in peace, always loyal to your supreme ruler, so that you may never offend him and that he may be a good overlord to you. Amen.

61. This poem was completed by Christine in the above mentioned year, 1429, on the last day of July. But I believe that some people will be displeased by its contents, for a person whose head is bowed and whose eyes are heavy cannot look at the light.

Here ends a very beautiful poem composed by Christine.

21. *Epistola de puella* by Alain Chartier (July 1429)

Source: Alain Chartier, *Les oeuvres latines*, ed. P. Bourgain-Hemeryck, Paris, 1977, pp. 326–9.

Language: Latin

Alain Chartier (c.1390–1430) was a notary and secretary of Charles VII who served as an ambassador to Germany and Italy; he was the author of a number of famous works of literature including the *Quadrilogue invectif* (1422) and the unfinished *Livre de l'esperance* (1428–30). His letter regarding the Pucelle is one of his very last works and survives in four manuscripts; it is also known as the *Epistola ad imperatorem*. It was written at Bourges in late July 1429, and addressed to an anonymous foreign prince, perhaps the Duke of Milan. The ambassador named Conrad in the letter may have been a Milanese envoy Corrado de Carreto who had taken part, like Chartier, in complex diplomatic exchanges between 1425 and 1428.

Most honourable prince, your ambassador Conrad Bituris met with me yesterday, and stated that he was sent to France by you in order to obtain a report, either from the Abbot of Saint Anthony, or from the Archbishop of Reims,[82] of what is said about the Pucelle. But, having met with neither of them, he eagerly asked me whether I

---

82 The Archbishop of Reims was Regnault de Chartres (d. 1445), who first entered that city in 1429 in the company of Charles VII and Joan of Arc.

might prepare this letter for you, if I wanted to do such a friendly action for you. But moved by your splendour and greatness, I did this of my own will, lest your messenger return empty-handed and without those things which you wish to know.

Firstly, I believe that you will want to know to whom the Pucelle belongs. If you asked about her nation [*nacionem*], she belongs to the kingdom; if [you asked] about her homeland [*patriam*], [she belongs] to the city of Vaucouleurs, that is to say by the river Meuse, born from parents who dedicated themselves to farming and sheep.[83] Having reached the age of puberty, she was placed in charge of the sheep. Indeed when she reached the age of twelve, she was admonished again and again by a voice coming from the clouds that she should go to the King and succour the falling kingdom. But since the English were besieging the mighty fortifications and fortresses of Orléans with a powerful army, she was not so much warned by the oracle of the gods above, as threatened with a very harsh punishment unless she went swiftly to the King. As she asked how she could act, or what it would be fitting to do, the answer was: 'After abandoning your female clothing, wear those of a man; and ask the captain of Vaucouleurs for men to accompany you and guide you to the King. Then you may proceed, and after you have spoken with the King, ensure that the siege of Orléans is lifted. From there lead the King to Reims to be crowned, [and] return to Paris with the crowned one and give the kingdom back to him.'[84]

The Pucelle did not delay. She went to the captain, received the companions, wore a manly garment, and mounted a horse, which she had not done before. She journeyed on across the countryside, by towns, hostile cities, and through the enemy's arrows. Eventually she safely arrived where the King was, having led her companions unharmed. But the King, having heard of the arrival of the Pucelle, and having realised why she had come, first decided to take the advice of the council; he neither dismissed her nor accepted her until he could establish how he could prove whether she was good or bad, real or fake, peaceful or dishonest. Therefore, the Pucelle was examined in

83 Chartier clearly regarded Joan as a subject of the French Crown, but makes an important distinction between the kingdom and nation, and her homeland or region [*patria*] which he identifies as Vaucouleurs, the administrative centre of Domremy.

84 This statement demonstrates that the letter must have been written before the unsuccessful assault on Paris on 8 September 1429.

front of very learned men as if in a contest, and thereupon, having been questioned again and again about many things, both human and divine, she always answered in an honourable and praiseworthy way, so that she appeared to have studied at university rather than cared for sheep in the fields. [This was] certainly a very wonderful spectacle: the woman with the men, the unlearned one with the learned ones; one against many; the most junior person discussing the highest matters. And indeed when the King realised what words she used and how she persevered, he commanded that she be summoned in front him, and listened carefully to her speech. [Even though] there is nobody who knows what she said, it is nevertheless very obvious that the King was indeed filled with no small joy, as if restored by hope.

After these things, the Pucelle, burning to fulfil the divine precepts, asked immediately to be given an army with which she could succour Orléans, which was already in danger. Lest she might act rashly, this was initially refused but afterwards granted to her. Having received [the army], she headed to Orléans with a great quantity of food supplies. They were not detected by any enemies when they passed under their fortresses;[85] for the enemies, as if turned from enemies into friends, men into women, or tied by the hands, allowed the supplies to be carried into the city peacefully. When the supplies had been brought into the city, she entered those fortresses. The manner in which she captured them, in such a short time, was miraculous, especially that one constructed almost in the middle of a bridge [the Tourelles] that was so sturdy, equipped with everything and fortified, that one would not believe that it could be taken even if every people and nation were to attack. She attacked one fortress, then a second and a third, which, since they were surrounded by rivers, full of soldiers and huge garrisons, had appeared impossible to subdue by any means. The she-warrior destroyed the conquered fortresses like a tempest but then, having heard that the English were approaching with an military force, led the army and the battle line toward these enemies, attacking with a brave spirit, not at all dissuaded by the fact that the enemy were by far superior in number. The English could not sustain the Pucelle's assault, so that, like lambs to the slaughter, they were all defeated and finally killed. After this she announced that they were not to delay, that the time had come to take the crown of the kingdom and to go to Reims. These things were seen by many as

85 Chartier is presumably referring to the fortresses of Saint-Loup, the Augustinians and the Tourelles, that he mentions subsequently.

not only difficult but impossible, because it was necessary to go through cities and places in enemy hands. But those very cities surrendered voluntarily to the King. Then they arrived at Reims and the King, led by the Pucelle, was crowned.

So that I do not go on at length, but try to summarise many things into a few, there is no mortal man who, even if he thinks that she is not to be admired, would not wonder at these sayings, and indeed at these facts – at the strength and the greatness of these countless, marvellous deeds she performed in such a short period of time. But why wonder? For what is necessary for leaders in battle that the Pucelle does not have? Perhaps military skill? She has an admirable one. Or a strong spirit? She has the highest one and surpasses all. Or attentiveness? She beats the others. Or justice? Or strength? Or good fortune? She is adorned with these things too above everyone.[86] And in fact she herself leads the army into battle against the enemy, she arranges the camps, she urges to war and to battle, bravely demonstrates military skills, which [were] long ago the skills of a leader. And when the sign has been given [to her], she quickly takes the spear, and seizing it she shakes it, brandishes it against the enemy, and spurring on her horse, she charges into the line with great force.

This is the one who came not so much from a place on earth, but was rather sent from heaven. She seems to sustain falling France on her head and shoulders; she led the King ashore to harbour, as he struggled in the vast sea with tempests and hurricanes. She raised his spirit to hope for better times. Suppressing English ferocity, she stirred the French courage, saved the French from ruin and ignited the French flame. O unique virgin, worthy of all glory and praise, worthy of divine honours, you, pride of the kingdom, you lamp, you light, you pride not only of the French, but also of all Christians. May Troy remember and rejoice in Hector, may Greece exult in Alexander and Africa in Hannibal, may Italy take pride in Caesar and all the Roman leaders. Even if France has had many [such men] from ancient times, nevertheless, an eager girl has dared to raise herself and to contend with other nations for military praise, and indeed, to place herself ahead of them, if she could.

---

86 Chartier echoed criticisms of the French King Jean II for lacking a series of key skills and qualities and thereby contributing to the disastrous defeat by the English at the battle of Poitiers in 1356: A. Vernet, 'La *Tragicum argumentum de miserabili statu regni Francie* de François de Monte-Belluna (1357)', *Annuaire-bulletin de la Société de l'Histoire de France*, 1962–63, p. 136.

This is what I have gathered so far about the Pucelle. If I have recounted
it more briefly than you might have wished, bear in mind that if I had
gone into more detail, I would have written a book, not a letter.

22. *De quadam puella* (Summer 1429?)

Source: Quicherat (ed.), *Procès de condamnation*, III, pp. 411–21.

Language: Latin

Unfortunately there is no clear evidence to indicate when this important
treatise was written. The references to military successes suggest that it was
composed during the summer of 1429, though it is curious that there is no
direct mention of the victories at Orléans, Jargeau and Patay. The author was
clearly a learned theologian who carefully presented arguments for and
against Joan in a typically scholastic fashion. In 1484 the treatise was
included in the first printed edition of the writings of Jean Gerson, but a
second edition printed in Strasbourg in 1514 attributed it to a Dutch student
and follower of Gerson named Heinrich van Gorcum (1386–1431). Perhaps
unsurprisingly, many modern scholars do not accept that Gerson wrote this
treatise, and prefer to believe that his views on Joan of Arc are better
represented by *De mirabili victoria* [7]. Certainly *De quadam puella* is
extremely cautious about the Pucelle, and seems ultimately to oppose her,
given the effective victory of the negative arguments presented in the second
half of the treatise.[87]

To the glory of the blessed Trinity and ever-glorious Virgin Mother
of God and also to that of the whole court of heaven.

'Then the Lord took me away as I followed the flock, and said to me:
"Go prophesy to my people Israel"' [Amos 7: 15].[88] The people of the
kingdom of France can, without disagreement, be called spiritually
the people of Israel; [they] have always flourished, out of faith in God
and the observance of Christian religion. A very young person, the
daughter of a shepherd, who herself followed a flock of sheep, it is
said, has come to see the son of King [Charles VI]. She has declared
that she had been sent by God so that, through her, this kingdom
might be brought to obey him. So that her claim would not be
considered rash, she has also made use of supernatural signs, such as
revealing secret thoughts and foreseeing what was about to occur. In
addition it is reported that she has had her hair cut in the style of a

87 See page 78 above.

88 These words of the prophet Amos to Amaziah were particularly appropriate for a
   discussion of Joan of Arc, given the allusion to Amos' earlier role as a shepherd.

man and that, when she wants to go to war, she puts on male clothing and arms, and climbs on to a horse; and while she is on the horse, carrying a standard, she immediately becomes marvellously energised, as if she were the leader of an army, used to marshalling it with skill. Then the soldiers are all affected by her sprit, while on the opposite side, her adversaries are filled with fear and [act] as if they had lost their strength. But when she dismounts from her horse, reassuming her normal nature, she is the most straightforward and inexperienced person with regard to secular matters, just like an innocent lamb. It is also reported that she lives in chastity, sobriety and moderation, devoted to God, prohibiting murder, robbery and any other violence by all those who wish to prove their obedience. Because of this, and similar reasons, cities, towns and castles submit themselves to the son of King [Charles VI], pledging their faith.

Given these facts, some questions emerge and learned minds are prompted to declare:

Should one believe that she is truly a young girl, human and natural, or was she changed into a similar, fantastical likeness [of a person]?

When she acts, can these things be done by her in a human fashion, or through her by some superior cause?

If [it is] through a superior cause, [is this] for good, and therefore by a good spirit, or for bad, through an evil spirit?

Can one trust her words and approve her actions as if they are divine, or should one consider them as deceitful and illusory?

[The author argued that it was necessary to set out both sides of the case, exploring her words and actions both in private and in public. He began by presenting six arguments or propositions in support of the Pucelle].

Propositions in support of the Pucelle.

I. It must be simply affirmed that this is a true Pucelle and a genuine person of human nature.

This proposition is revealed by the fact that the rule of the philosophers is that action demonstrates form; and indeed our Saviour bears witness that knowledge is to be accepted through actions. Therefore, since this young female is continually found to conform with other men in human actions, [that is to say] speaking, desiring food, eating, drinking, staying awake, sleeping and other similar things, who would dare say that she is not truly a person of human nature, with whom others communicate in similar token of human nature?

II. The time of prophecy was ordained before the coming of Christ, continuing into the dawn of the Church, alongside the accomplishment of miracles.

[The anonymous author then argued that even the prophets who lived during the time of the early Church had to employ miracles in order to persuade people to believe their words].

III. In our time today, it is not considered unworthy that certain people are stirred to inspire by prophecy and moved to work miracles ...

IV. It is consonant with the holy scriptures that God may present the joy of salvation to peoples and to kingdoms by means of the weaker sex and innocent youths.

This proposition is evident because, according to the Apostle's testimony, 'God has chosen the weak things in the world to put to shame the things which are mighty [I Corinthians 1: 27].'[89] Hence, from there, proceeding by way of example, one may read of Deborah [Judges 4–5], Esther [the book of Esther] and Judith [Judith], who obtained salvation for the people of God, and Daniel who was stirred to free Susannah during his boyhood [Daniel 13].[90] Similarly, David, in his youth, felled Goliath [I Samuel 17]; and this was very fitting, because the abundance of divine piety became more evident through this, and this man did not ascribe his actions to his own strength, but rather attributed them to the God of grace. In similar fashion, the redemption of all of humanity proceeded from a humble Virgin.

V. The holy scriptures do not bear witness to men of depraved lives being sent by God in such a form or manner as the common account that sings the praises of this Pucelle.

[The author accepted that there were examples in the Bible of evil men successfully making prophecies].

But it is quite different with this Pucelle, who has command of the use of supernatural gifts that reveal what is hidden and foretell the future that will follow from her service; moreover she prohibits, as has already been said, murders and other injuries, and encourages virtues

89 The Latin Vulgate actually reads 'infirma mundi elegit Deus ut confundat fortia'.

90 The story of Daniel clearing Susannah from a charge of adultery was included in the Vulgate Bible, but is now usually treated as an apocryphal piece because it is only found in the Greek translations of the Book of Daniel.

and other honest works in which God is glorified. Therefore, just as Joseph was sent into Egypt by the spirit of God, ahead of his father and brothers, [as was] Moses for the liberation of the people of Israel, and Gideon and the women named above, likewise it is consistent that this young female should be counted among the good people sent specifically by God, especially as she does not seek reward and she works for the good of peace with complete devotion. This is certainly not the act of an evil spirit, an agent of dissension rather than of peace.

VI. Following on as a sort of corollary from the previous propositions, this girl is a true person with a human nature specially sent to her by God, whose works do not follow the manner of men but are divine, and whose faith is clearly displayed.

This proposition is revealed when replying to the previous questions. For the first proposition demonstrates that she is a real human being. And because, even nowadays, God does not cease to make special provision through supernatural signs, it is not inconsistent for Him to employ an innocent Pucelle, following on from the fourth proposition. And as she possesses this enduring gift for a godly purpose, and [acts] by the means of virtue and honesty, as the fifth proposition asserts, it would therefore seem that this sixth proposition must be conceded. And it should not be surprising that there is greater insight [to be won] through the condition of a knight than the usual status of a woman, because even David, wishing to consult the Lord, put on the ephod [a priestly garment] and took the psalterium [harp]. And Moses worked miracles while he was carrying his rod, because, according to Gregory, 'the Holy Spirit frequently adapts itself inwardly to the external conditions'.

So a supporter of this position could take the opportunity to defend her cause by means of the previous [propositions], proceeding even further towards a stronger declaration. But because others may be found who are more inclined towards the opposite side, it remains to bring forward certain evidence from the holy scripture which they may be able to use as a buttress to support their position, considering the propositions written below.

Propositions against the Pucelle

I. Many false prophets have come, claiming to have been sent from God by divine inspiration.

Here is a proposition of our Saviour, who said that 'in the very end of days', namely of the law of the gospel, 'many will say that they come in my name and many will be deceived by them'.[91] From there too, the Apostle declares that '[the angel of] Satan himself is transformed into an angel of light' [2 Corinthians 11: 14]. And this is no marvel, because that ruler of all sons of pride strives ceaselessly to usurp the excellence of the divine, and to this end, he looks after false prophets that have been sent in the Lord's name in order to deceive.

II. False prophets frequently predict concealed thoughts and the result of events that are part of the immediate future.

This proposition is usually accepted by the doctors; their reason is that the higher a virtue, the further it reaches. On the other hand, it is agreed that the intelligence of demons is much higher than the intelligence of man, and so those things that are hidden and in our future are unknown to us, but are known by an evil spirit.

III. It is not easy to distinguish a true from a false prophet by means of external appearances and signs.

This proposition is evident because it is not necessary that a prophet lead a virtuous life or be in a state of grace, and demons can predict for a prophet things that are hidden from us and [are in] the future; in this way, as in many other things, they are just like true prophets. If they foretell falsely now and then, they know how to cover up by giving another interpretation, or by alleging that real prophets sometimes predict things that do not happen. This may be read in the case of the prophets Isaiah and Jonah. Because of this, even the Apostle says, 'do not believe every spirit, but test whether they are from God' [1 John 4: 1], insinuating that it is difficult to make a distinction between good and bad prophets.

IV. Now, at the time of grace [the Christian era], it appears to be unlikely that God would send a spiritual mission [to secure] the good fortune of temporal happiness.

This proposition can be drawn from those things that Augustine frequently mentions. For the profits of this present life are granted in equal measure to the good and to the bad, to the just and to the unjust, especially at this time of grace. Good people do not pin their love on the transitory profits in which the wicked abound so very

---

91 This quotation is close to Mark 13: 6 and, particularly, to Matthew 24: 5.

much; for at the same time that they are awaiting the good that is reserved in the future life for friends [of God], His enemies are collecting transitory profits in abundance during this life. Therefore it would seem far from likely that a mission would be established to secure happiness for the present and to predict what is assigned little weight. Yet at the time of the Old Testament, those people were serving God in proportion to these temporal profits, and one reads that now and then, such a mission did occur.

V. This Pucelle commits two actions which are defined as forbidden in the holy scriptures.

This proposition is evident because the law of Deuteronomy 22 prohibits a woman from wearing the clothes of a man, and the Apostle forbids a woman from cutting her hair as a man does [I Corinthians 11: 14–15]. Yet the Pucelle is reported [to do] the opposite. And at first sight, it would seem that this Pucelle is inclined towards a certain indecency of youths, riding on horseback while dressed in the clothes of a man; and, as God prizes modesty, it would seem that she detracts from the fulfilment of her divine mission, if she hides her femininity under the guise of a man. Neither does such a guise seem to be in harmony with a confidential mission, so far as such a mission acts more through the spirit to sanctify the soul inwardly, according to *Wisdom* VII: 'The wisdom of God passes into holy souls; it establishes the friends of God and the prophets.'[92] On account of this, if the mission of this young girl is prophetic, she should be a person of excellent saintliness and [have] a divine soul inside her; and it would seem indecent that such a person should transform themselves into a secular man-at-arms. For one does not read anything like this regarding Esther and Judith, who dressed themselves with particular care, as women were permitted, and so were more pleasing by this when they began to act.

VI. It cannot be adequately proven that the Pucelle has been specially sent by God, that God works through her, and that trust should be placed in her.

This proposition is evident as the corollary of what has gone before. For if many false prophets have come resembling true ones, if there may not be a special mission [to secure] the good fortune of temporal happiness during the time of grace, if her course of action conflicts

92 The quotation is close to Wisdom 7: 27.

with the divine mandate, how can one assert that a girl of this kind
has been chosen by God to do that which is publicly reported?

From these points, it is also certain that the partisans of this position
could give some colour to their case by attacking the other position,
above all by considering the previous propositions and investigating
them more closely. For that reason, these points have been collected
here and arranged together, and are presented to those who may see
the cause of this present case or a similar one in the future, so that
they may be able to reply in some way to those putting forward
similar questions. Forever to the glory of God, who reigns forever
[and] who is blessed. Amen.

23. Joan of Arc's letter to Reims (5 August 1429)

Source: Quicherat (ed.), *Procès de condamnation*, V, pp. 139–40.

Language: French

This was the first of three letters that Joan sent to Reims, all of which
survive in original copies. It was written against the backdrop of diplomatic
negotiations between her King and the Duke of Burgundy, that threatened to
undercut Joan's military mission, and in particular the attack on Paris.
Georges de La Trémouïlle had travelled to the Burgundian court at Dijon on
30 June, and in response David de Brimeu had led an embassy to Reims while
the King was there for the coronation, bearing a letter to Queen Marie of
Anjou and her mother Yolande, expressing optimism that the King would
conclude a treaty. On 16 August, Regnault de Chartres, Archbishop of Reims,
led an embassy to Duke Philip, offering to make reparation for the murder at
Montereau, in return for Burgundy's neutrality; the Duke agreed to take part
in a peace conference proposed by Amadeus VIII of Savoy. Shortly afterwards, Charles VII issued the truce at Compiègne on 28 August 1429,
suspending hostilities against the Burgundians everywhere except Paris for
four months, until 25 December. Following the abortive attack on Paris, the
truce was extended to cover that city by a letter issued at Senlis on 18
September.

My dear and good friends, kind and loyal Frenchmen of the city of
Reims, Joan the Pucelle sends you her news, and prays and requests
that you do not have any doubt about the merit of her cause that she
is waging for the blood royal. And I promise you and certify that I
will never abandon you so long as I live. And it is true that the King
has made truces with the Duke of Burgundy for fifteen days, by which
he [Burgundy] must peacefully return the city of Paris at the end of

fifteen days. Nevertheless, do not be surprised if I do not enter it so quickly. No matter how many truces are made like this, I am not at all happy, and I do not know if I will keep them. But if I do, it will only be to protect the honour of the King, and also so that they do not take advantage of the blood royal, because I will keep together and maintain the army of the King so as to be prepared at the end of those fifteen days, if they do not make peace. For this reason, my very dear and perfect friends, I pray that you do not suffer uneasiness so long as I am alive, but I do request that you keep good watch and defend the good city [bonne ville] of the King, and let me know if there are any traitors who wish to harm you, and as soon as I can I will drive them out. And let me know your news. I commend you to God, that He may protect you.

Written this Friday, 5th day of August, near Provins, in a camp in the fields on the road to Paris.

24. The Duke of Bedford's challenge to Charles VII (7 August 1429)

Source: Enguerran[d] de Monstrelet, *La chronique d'Enguerran[d] de Monstrelet en deux livres avec pièces justicatives (1400–44)*, ed. L. Douët d'Arcq, 6 vols, Paris, 1857–62, IV, 340–4.

Language: French

While Charles VII and Joan of Arc were travelling to Reims for the coronation, the dukes of Bedford and Burgundy were meeting in Paris, to marshal their defences. On 7 August, Bedford issued a formal and traditional challenge to Charles and his forces to meet them upon the battlefield; it was ostensibly designed to goad the enemy into battle, but it also served a wider propaganda purpose, highlighted by the fact that Bedford chose to write the letter at Montereau, scene of Charles VII's most infamous action: the murder of the previous Duke of Burgundy almost ten years earlier, on 10 September 1419. On 15 August 1429 the two armies met at Montépilloy, outside Senlis, but neither side was willing to take the offensive and the English retreated towards Paris.

We, John of Lancaster, Regent of France and Duke of Bedford, make known to you, Charles of Valois, who are accustomed to name yourself dauphin of Vienne, and now without cause entitle yourself King, that because you have wrongfully made new attempts against the Crown and lordship of the most high and excellent prince, my sovereign lord Henry, by the grace of God natural and rightful King of the kingdoms of France and England, by leading the simple people to believe that you are coming to give them peace and security, which is not the fact, nor can it be done by the means that you have pursued and are now following. And you are seducing and abusing ignorant people, and you are aided by superstitious and damnable persons, such as a woman of disorderly and infamous life, dressed in man's clothes, and of immoral conduct, together with an apostate and seditious mendicant friar, as we have been informed.[93] Both of them are, according to holy scripture, abominable to God. And you have also occupied, by force of arms, the county of Champagne and other regions, cities, towns, and castles belonging to my lord the King, and you have constrained and induced the subjects living there to disloyalty and perjury, making them break and violate the final peace for the kingdoms of France and England, solemnly sworn by the then kings of France and England who were then alive, and the great lords, peers, prelates, and three estates of this kingdom.[94]

To guard and to defend the true right of my lord the King, and to drive out you and your force from his lands and his lordships, by the aid of the omnipotent [God], we have set out and taken the field in person, with the power that God has given to us. And, as you may have heard, we have pursued you, and are pursuing you from place to place in the hope of finding and meeting you, which we have not yet done, because of the warnings that you have obtained and are receiving. We desire an end to the war with all our heart, and so we summon and require that, if you are the kind of prince who seeks honour and has compassion for the poor people, who have been so long and so very inhumanely treated, oppressed and stifled because of you, so that there might be an end to their afflictions and suffering, without continuing the war longer, meet us in the field in the country of Brie, where we both are. [Or meet us] in the Île de France, which is very close to each of us, or in any convenient or reasonable place in the countryside, within a short and appropriate time, depending upon how close each of us are now and [therefore] what is possible and feasible. Appear on this day and this place, in person, bringing the deformed woman and the apostate cited before, and all the perjurers

93 The friar in question was Brother Richard. See pages 31 to 32 above.

94 The Treaty of Troyes [1], that was ratified by the Estates General in Paris on 10 December 1420, and which the politically important swore to uphold at public ceremonies across English-controlled France.

and other force that you wish and can muster. God willing, we will meet you in person in the name of my lord the King.

And then, if you wish to propose anything, or to put anything forward regarding the good of peace, we will hear it, and we will do every thing that a good catholic prince should and could do. And we are, and we will always be, inclined and willing [to follow] all worthy paths to peace, that are not false, treacherous, duplicitous, debased or perjured such as at Montereau-faut-Yonne, when, through your fault and connivance, that most horrible, detestable and cruel murder was committed, against every law and the honour of chivalry, against the person of our late very dear and very well beloved father, Duke John of Burgundy, may God pardon him.[95] Because of the peace that you broke, violated and betrayed, all the nobles and other subjects of this realm and elsewhere have remained and still stay free and exempt from you and your lordship, and from whatever estate you may have or may attain, and they have been absolved and acquitted from all oaths of fealty and of subjection, as your letters patent, signed in your hand and by your seal, can clearly reveal. Nevertheless, if we cannot profit from the good of peace because of the iniquity and malice of men, each of us can certainly guard and defend with a sword his cause and his quarrel, if God, who is the only judge, and to whom my lord has to answer, and to no other, will give grace to him. We therefore most humbly beseech God, as the one who knows and understands the true right and legitimate cause of my lord, to dispose in this matter as He pleases. And in such a way, the people of the kingdom may enjoy a long peace and respite, free from such pressures and oppressions, as all Christian kings and princes who govern should seek and request.

So we are letting you know hastily and without any more delay, [so that you will] not spend time [merely] writing arguments, which we do not want you to do. Because if by your lack of action, more great evils, harms, continuations of war, pillaging, ransoms, murders of people and depopulation of the countryside should occur, we take God as our witness and we protest before Him and men, that we are in no way the cause, and that we have done and are doing our duty. And we have proposed and are willing to accept, according to reason and honour, either peace, or a battle [to prove who is] the right prince –

---

95 Bedford's first wife, Anne (d. 1432), was the daughter of John, Duke of Burgundy and sister of Philip the Good.

powerful and great opponents can do nothing more than this. In witness of this, we have sealed these present [documents] with our seal.

Given at Montereau-faut-Yonne, the 7th day of August, the year of grace 1429.

Signed by my lord the Regent of France, the Duke of Bedford.

25. Joan of Arc's letter to the Count of Armagnac (22 August 1429)

Source: Tisset (ed.), *Procès de condamnation*, I, pp. 225–6.

Language: French

In 1417, the Council of Constance apparently ended the Great Schism by electing Pope Martin V (d. 1431). Yet one rival pope, Benedict XIII (d. 1423), defied the authority of the Council that tried to depose him on 26 July 1417; his successor, Clement VIII, did not accept the superior authority of Martin V and resign until 26 July 1429. Throughout this period, one of their most important supporters was Jean IV Count of Armagnac (1418–50) who was declared to be schismatic, but finally pardoned by Martin V on 4 March 1430. Nevertheless, the Count wrote to Joan of Arc shortly afterwards, apparently asking for her advice on this matter but clearly hoping to secure her support for a new candidate for the papacy, his own protégé, Jean Carrier, who called himself Benedict XIV. She replied in an unsigned letter written on 22 August 1429 at Compiègne. During the Rouen trial, these letters were used as evidence that Joan was also a schismatic: 'she not only cast doubt upon which was [the true pope], when there was only one true and authentic pope, but also ... preferring her own word to the authority of the whole Church, she affirmed that within a fixed interval, she would inform him which pope he should believe in; which she would discover by God's counsel, as her letter declares at greater length'.[96]

(a) The letter of the Count of Armagnac to Joan

My very dear lady, I commend myself humbly to you and pray to you before God, considering the division which there is at present in the holy universal Church regarding the matter of the popes, for there are three men contending for the papacy: one dwells at Rome and calls himself Martin V, whom all the Christian kings obey; another dwells at Peñiscola, in the kingdom of Valencia, and calls himself Clement

96 This was the charge in article 30 of the Seventy Articles presented against Joan on 27 March 1431, immediately after the letters had been read to the court, Tisset (ed.), *Procès de condamnation*, I, pp. 225–6. Joan briefly referred to the letters in **38**.

[VIII];[97] no one knows where the third lives unless it is the Cardinal of St. Etienne, and those few men with him, and he calls himself Benedict XIV. The first, who is called Pope Martin, was elected at Constance by the consent of all the Christian nations; the one who is called Clement was elected at Peñiscola after the death of Benedict XIII by three of his cardinals; the third, who is named Pope Benedict XIV, was secretly elected at Peñiscola, also by the Cardinal of St. Etienne. I beseech you to beg Our Lord Jesus Christ that, in His infinite mercy, He might wish to declare to us through you which of the three men is the true pope, and which He would have us obey in future – the one called Martin, or the one called Clement, or the one called Benedict – and in whom we should believe, in secret and in hiding, or publicly and in the open. For we are all ready to do the will and pleasure of Our Lord Jesus Christ.

Wholly yours, the Count of Armagnac.

(b) The letter from Joan to the Count of Armagnac

Jhesus Maria.

Count of Armagnac, my very dear and good friend, Joan the Pucelle informs you that your message has reached me, which says that you have sent to me to discover which of the three popes mentioned in your memoir you should believe. On this matter I cannot honestly tell you the truth at the moment, or until I may be in Paris or elsewhere, at rest, because I am at the present time too occupied with the business of war. But when you know that I am in Paris, send me a message and I will let you know in all truth whom you should believe, all that I will have learned by the counsel of my rightful and sovereign Lord, the King of all the world, and what you should do, to the best of my abilities.

I commend you to God; may God protect you.

Written at Compiègne, the 22nd day of August [1429].

97 Clement VIII's real name was Gilles Munoz (d. 1447).

26. The *Journal* of Clément de Fauquembergue
   (8 September 1429)

Source: Clément de Fauquembergue, *Journal de Clément de Fauquembergue, greffier du Parlement du Paris, 1417–1435*, ed. A. Tuetey and H. Lacaille, 3 vols, Paris, 1903–15, II, pp. 322–4.

Language: French

Clément de Fauquembergue succeeded Nicolas de Baye as the *greffier* or clerk of the Parlement of Paris.[98] During his tenure of office from 1417 to 1435, he compiled a journal of events relating to the Parlement and to Paris in general. This included brief reports of the most of the key events relating to Joan of Arc, together with a famous sketch of the Pucelle drawn in the margin next to his account of the end of the siege of Orléans written on 10 May 1429. He was an eyewitness to the Valois attack upon Paris in September 1429.

On Thursday, the 8th day of September [1429], the feast of the Nativity of the Mother of God, the men-at-arms of my lord Charles of Valois [Charles VII] assembled in great number near the wall of Paris, toward the Saint-Honoré Gate, hoping to put a strain upon and to damage the city and inhabitants of Paris, more by the upheaval of the people than by power or force of arms. At about two o'clock in the afternoon, they began to make a show of attacking the city of Paris. And very quickly many of them were on the Place aux Pourceaux and thereabouts, near to the said Gate, carrying long bundles of sticks and faggots and they descended and went into the first ditches, which did not contain any water, and they threw the bundles of sticks and faggots into the other ditch close to the walls, which held much water.

And at that hour there were confused and dishonest men inside Paris, who raised a cry in all parts of the city on both sides of the bridges, crying that all was lost, and that the enemy had entered inside Paris, and that everyone should withdraw and make every effort to save himself. And at that cry, at the same hour as the approach of the enemy, all the people left the sermons in the churches of Paris, and they were greatly afraid, and many withdrew into their houses and shut their eyes. But, because there was no other commotion among

98 Unlike the English Parliament, the Parlement of Paris was not a representative assembly but purely a legal body, the supreme appeal court and chamber for registering and disseminating royal legislation. R. C. Famiglietti, 'The role of the Parlement of Paris in the ratification and registration of royal acts during the reign of Charles VI', *Journal of Medieval History*, IX, 1983, pp. 217–25, and J. H. Shennan, *The Parlement of Paris*, London, 1968.

the inhabitants of Paris, those who had been assigned remained at the guard and defence of the gates and of the walls of this city. And many other inhabitants came to their aid, and they provided a very stout and strong resistance against the men of my lord Charles of Valois, who held on inside the first ditch, and outside on the Place aux Pourceaux and thereabouts, until ten or eleven o'clock that night when they withdrew from harm. And there was much death and distress among them from arrows and cannons. And among them a woman known as the Pucelle was wounded in the leg by an arrow; she led the army with the other captains of my lord Charles of Valois, who expected to harm Paris more through this commotion than by assault or force of arms, because if they had had four times as many men with them, they would not have taken the city of Paris by assault or siege while there were supplies inside the city, which was then well provided for a long time. And the inhabitants were closely united with the men-at-arms of the city in resisting this assault and enterprise, and especially because it had been said and was said publicly of Paris that my lord Charles of Valois, son of King Charles VI, recently deceased, may God pardon him, had abandoned the city of Paris and its inhabitants, great and small, of all estates, men and women, to his men.

27. *De bono et malo spiritu* (September 1429)

Source: N. Valois, 'Un nouveau temoignage sur Jeanne d'Arc: la réponse d'un clerc parisien à l'apologie de la Pucelle par Jean Gerson (1429)', *Annuaire-bulletin de la Société de l'Histoire de France*, XLIII, 1906, pp. 175–9.

Language: Latin

This reply to the *De mirabili victoria* [7] was written by an anonymous member of the University of Paris between the attack upon the city on 8 September 1429, referred to within the text, and 22 September when the University of Paris paid for a copy of it. The only surviving copy exists in a manuscript that was almost certainly circulated at the Council of Basel in 1435, and which also includes *De mirabili victoria*.[99]

Regarding the preceding, I mean to deduce from canon law a small number of issues, in praise of all-mighty God, and in exaltation of the holy catholic faith.

---

99 G. Peyronnet, 'Gerson, Charles VII et Jeanne d'Arc: la propagande au service de la guerre', *Revue d'histoire ecclésiastique*, LXXXIV, 1989, pp. 358–9; D. Fraioli, *Joan of Arc: the early debate*, pp. 159–72.

And first, we have a duty to adhere firmly to the catholic faith, following the chapter *Firmiter* of the title *De Summa Trinitate*,[100] without giving in any manner our approval to superstitious innovations, seeing that they engender discords, as one reads in the chapter *Cum consuetudinis* of the title *De consuetudine*.[101]

Item, to give his support so easily to a young girl that was not known, without the support of a miracle or on the testimony of the holy scriptures, is to undermine this truth and this unchanging force of the catholic faith: wise men and canonists would not have any doubt about this. The proof is in the chapter *Cum ex injuncto* of the title *De hæreticis*.[102]

Item, if those who approve of the matter of this Pucelle say that she has been sent by God in an invisible, and in some sense inspired way, and that such an invisible mission is much more worthy than a visible mission, just as a divine mission is more worthy than a human mission, it is reasonable to reply to them that as this entirely inner mission escapes observation, it is not enough that someone claims purely and simply to be sent from God – this is the claim of all heretics – but it is necessary that he proves this invisible mission to us through a miraculous work or by a precise testimony drawn from the holy scripture.' All this is demonstrated in the chapter cited above, *Cum ex injuncto.*

Item, as this Pucelle has not proved in any of these ways that she has been sent from God, there is no room to believe in her on her word, but there is room to proceed against her as if suspected of heresy.

Added to this, if she has really been sent from God, she would not take clothing prohibited by God and forbidden for women by canon law under penalty of anathema, according to the chapter *Si qua mulier*, distinction 30e.[103]

Moreover, in the case where those who let themselves be deceived by this Pucelle attempt to excuse and to justify her clothing in consideration of the matter for which she was supposedly sent, such niceties are useless; these are rather those excuses of which the Psalmist speaks, that one searches for to excuse sins (Psalm 140: 4), and they

---

100 Decretals of Gregory IX: X.1.1.1.

101 X.1.4.9.

102 X.5.7.12.

103 *Decretum* of Gratian, 1st part, D. 30.

accuse more than they excuse, as it says in chapter *Quanto* of the title *De consuetudine*.[104] In this case, one might do lots of evil things under the appearance of good. And yet it is necessary to refrain not only from evil, but from all appearance of evil, as one reads in the chapter *Cum ab omni* of the title *De vita et honestate clericorum*.[105]

Item, if a women could put on male clothing as she liked with impunity, women would have unrestrained opportunities to fornicate and to practice manly acts which are legally forbidden for them according to doctrine, etc., [as this is] against the canonical teaching contained in the chapter *Nova quædam* of the title *De pænitentiis et remissionibus*.[106]

Item, in general, all masculine duties are forbidden to women, for example, to preach, to teach, to bear arms, to absolve, to excommunicate, etc., as one sees in that chapter *Nova quædam* and in the Digest, in the [second] law of the title *De regulis juris*.[107]

Item, the aforesaid master who compiled the treatise in question in favour of this Pucelle praised her strongly, and rashly (saving the respect which is owed to him), and he seems to have paid little attention to the saying of Cato: 'Be sparing with your praise, for one day the person whom you will frequently test, [will reveal whether he is a friend]'.[108]

Item, if he had properly considered the rule of law *Qui scandalizaverit*, under the title *De regulis juris*, he would not tolerate the fact that, on the pretext of winning the realm, the truth of the faith might be violated in any respect, even if he might regard it as a scandal that the realm was transferred to the English, considering that in such a case 'it would be better to allow a scandal to be born than to brush aside the truth', as one reads in the chapter *Qui scandalizaverit* of the title *De regulis juris in antiquis*.[109] And, as St Augustine says, it is not necessary to commit evil because that is the result of [doing] good.

Item, after the works, the 'fruits' of this Pucelle,[110] we can honestly, piously and duly judge whether she comes from God or from the Enemy

104 X.1.4.4.

105 X.3.1.10.

106 X.5.38.10.

107 *Digest*, 50.17.

108 Cato the Elder, *Disticha Catonis*, 4.28, 228 and 229. The author of *De mirabili victoria* [7] had also cited from the Distichs of Cato the Elder.

109 X.5.41.3.

110 This argument, drawing upon Matthew 7: 20, was in fact used by Jacques Gélu rather than the author of *De mirabili victoria*.

of the faith, following the chapter *Estote misericordes* under the title *De regulis juris*,[111] seeing that she has stirred up a more intense war among the princes and the Christian people than there was before. Nevertheless Our Lord, Jesus Christ, 'this peace-loving King, has prescribed, in His pious mercy, that His subjects might be discreet, peaceable and modest', as one reads in the preamble of Pope Gregory:[112] this Pucelle has notoriously done the opposite, by herself or by her own men.

Item, if she had been sent from God, she would not have got men to kill one another on the chief feasts of the holy Virgin, Mother of God, the day of the Assumption and the day of the Nativity – which she did: insults that the Enemy of humanity has inflicted on the Creator and on His very glorious Mother through this woman. And, although some massacres resulted, thanks to God they were not such as this Enemy wished for.

Item, if she had been guided by the Holy Spirit, she would never have lied in her predictions. But among her principal lies, there was this one: she predicted that there would a great war between the King and some princes before the King came to Reims. There has been nothing of the sort. Thus, she was not guided by the Spirit of truth, from which all truth originates, but by the Devil, father of lies, whose plans she endeavours to accomplish, according to what is written in chapter *Quæritur* of the Decretal, § *Non enim*, cause 22, second question.[113]

Item, she should never allow children to make offerings to her, on their knees, burning candles: this is what happened, it is said, in many notable towns in the obedience of our enemies, and she accepts these candles as a sort of offering. This is a type of idolatry, and in this she appears to have usurped the honour and respect which are only due to the Creator: the true crime of idolatry, the most serious of all, as one sees in the chapter *Idolatria* of the cause 28, first question,[114] and in the chapter *De homine* of the title *De celebratione missarum*.[115]

Moreover, if all of these things were passed over in silence, it would result in serious risks, divisions, scandals and very great dangers for the faith, all the more so since in many of the regions, portraits and

---

111 X.5.41.2.

112 These were the first words of the Bull that Pope Gregory IX promulgated on 5 September 1234, which served as a preamble to his Decretals.

113 *Decretum* of Gratian, 2nd part, cause 22, q. 2, c. 22.

114 X.3.41.7.

115 X.2.20.52.

statues of this Pucelle have already been raised and worshipped, all as if she had already been beatified:[116] so that a great error threatens us unless a remedy is found as quickly as possible. It is certain that no one should be venerated as a saint during their life, nor even after their death unless they have been authorised and canonised by the Church, as one reads in the chapter *Venerabili* of the title *De testibus*, and throughout the title *De reliquiis et veneratione sanctorum.*[117] It may now be seen that the position of this Pucelle may not be tolerated without undermining the faith.

Item, this would be to scoff at the faith, which ought not to be done, because: 'Fame, faith and the eye do not suffer tricks'.[118]

Item, in terms of piety and devotion compatible with the catholic faith, the matter of this Pucelle should not be defended, if one considers that which is truly obvious. Because she provokes the superstitions already mentioned among the simple people, which do not do honour but rather offend the Creator, and which constitute a danger for souls by aiming to overturn the Christian faith. This is what has been demonstrated above.

Item, according to what is reported, she seems to make use of spells. Thus, for example, when the children of which it has been spoken offered to her the wax candles in question, with the veneration that I have said, she shook down on to their heads three drops of wax from each burning candle, predicting to them that because of the virtue of such an act, good would come to them.[119] Thus, [this is] idolatry in

116 Article 52 of the Seventy Articles stated that 'Joan has so misled the catholic people by her inventions that many adored her as a saint ... they set up her images on the altars of saints, wear medals of lead or other metal in her likeness, like those made for the anniversaries of saints canonised by the Church; and they preach in public that she is sent from God, an angel rather than a woman': Tisset (ed.), *Procès de condamnation*, I, p. 261.

117 The first of these Decretals of Gregory XI (X.2.20.52) concerned the necessity of examining witnesses in canonisation processes with care, and the second (X.3.45) discussed the papal prerogative in canonisation and the display of relics.

118 This proverb, more commonly known in its French form than the Latin version given in this text, had been cited in the *De mirabili victoria* [7].

119 This claim was repeated in the Seventy Articles at the Rouen Trial on 28 March 1431: 'At Saint-Denis in France the said Joan offered and deposited in the church in a high place the armour in which she had been wounded in the assault on Paris, so that it might be honoured by the people as relics. And, in the same town, she had waxen candles lit, from which she poured melted wax on the heads of little children, foretelling their fortune, and making by these enchantments many divinations about them.' (Article 59: Tisset (ed.), *Procès de condamnation*, I, p. 271).

the matter of the offering and, in the matter of allowing this wax to drip, sorcery compounded by heresy. As a result, it behoves the Inquisitor for the faith, because of his office, to inquire about the crime of heresy and to impose punishments according to what is noted by the doctors in the chapter *Accusatus*, § *Sane*, at the note *Nisi hæresim saperent*, under the title *De hæreticis* of the *Sextus*, book V.[120]

Finally, it follows from what has been said that all of this manifestly contains error and heresy, causing, directly and indirectly, openly and notoriously, harm to the orthodox faith. This is why it is in the interest of all faithful Christians, but above all it behoves the University, my mother, the Bishop and the Inquisitor to fight, for the honour of God, such superstitions and this without further ado and with speed.[121] 'Fight against it at the beginning. It is late in the day to make up medicine.'[122] See the chapter *Ad hæc* of the title *De rescriptis*: 'It is necessary to cut off the gangrenous flesh and to drive out the scabby ewes from the fold', from the chapter *Resecandæ* of cause 24, third question.[123]

And these words are enough for the present.

28. Joan of Arc's letter to Riom (9 November 1429)

Source: Quicherat (ed.), *Procès de condamnation*, V, pp. 147–8.

Language: French

This letter in French was sent from Moulins to the people of Riom. The original survives in the Archives Communales of Riom and is signed by Joan herself – the first of three surviving examples of her signature. Jules Quicherat claimed to have seen a black hair caught in the wax of the seal, though there is no way to prove that this belonged to Joan.

Dear and good friends, you well know how the town of Saint-Pierre-le-Moûtier was taken by assault, and with the help of God I intend to

---

120 VI.5.2.8.

121 It is unclear who this bishop might be, though it is possible that the anonymous author is already imagining that Pierre Cauchon would lead the effort against Joan.

122 The remainder of the sentence is 'when delay has given the disease time to get a hold on you' (Ovid, *Remedia amoris*, lines 91–2).

123 Gratian's *Decretum*: 2nd part, cause 24, q.3, c.16.

clear out the other places which are hostile to the king.[124] But because such a great outlay of gunpowder, arrows and other military supplies has been made before that town, and because I and my men are poorly prepared to lay siege to La Charité, where we will be going shortly, I pray that you, for as much as you love the good and honour of the king and also that of all the others here, will wish to send aid immediately for the siege, [that is to say] gunpowder, saltpetre, sulphur, arrows, heavy crossbows and other military supplies.[125] And do this so that this [siege] may not be prolonged for lack of gunpowder and other military supplies, and so that no one may say that you were negligent or unwilling. Dear and good friends, may Our Lord [God] protect you.

Written at Moulins the 9th day of November.

Joan

29. Joan of Arc's letter to Reims (16 March 1430)

Source: Quicherat (ed.), *Procès de condamnation*, V, pp. 159–60.

Language: French

This is the second surviving letter that Joan sent to Reims.

Very dear and good friends, whom I greatly desire to see, Joan the Pucelle has received your letters mentioning that you fear being besieged. Please know that you will not have to [fear this], if I can intercept them soon. And if it should so happen that I do not encounter them coming to you, shut your gates, because I will be with you shortly. And if they are there, I will make them put on their spurs in such haste that they will not know where to put them, and I will relieve you there so quickly that it will seem almost immediate. I will not write anything more to you for the moment, except that you should always be good and loyal. I pray to God that He may protect you.

Written at Sully[-sur-Loire], the 16th day of March.

---

124 The siege of the town of Saint-Pierre-le-Moûtier, that belonged to the mercenary captain, Perrinet Gressart, took place in late October or early November 1429.

125 The siege of La Charité-sur-Loire by Joan and the royal forces began on 24 November and lasted for almost a month; they were finally forced to withdraw, abandoning most of their artillery.

I would send you some additional news at which you would be very joyful, but I fear that the letters might be seized along the way and that the news would be seen.[126]

Joan

30. Jean Pasquerel's letter on behalf of Joan to the Hussites (23 March 1430)

Source: Quicherat (ed.), *Procès de condamnation*, V, pp. 156–9.

Language: Latin

This letter purports to be from Joan of Arc and the general tone and content of this letter is certainly consistent with her characteristic views. Nevertheless, it is not clear whether it was actually her work or that of her confessor, Jean Pasquerel, who signed the letter. It was written in Latin, and most of the specific wording is not in her style. The recipients, the Hussites, were a heretical movement in Bohemia who had just waged a particularly vicious campaign that had devastated significant areas in Hungary, Silesia, Lusatia, Meissen and Saxony.

Jesus Maria.

For some time now rumour and public comment has reported to me, Joan the Pucelle, that from true Christians you have become heretics. Like the Saracens you have blighted the true religion and worship, embracing a disgraceful and criminal superstition; in wishing to protect and propagate it, there is not a disgraceful deed or belief that you do not dare. You blight the sacraments of the Church, you tear up the articles of the faith, you destroy the churches, you break and burn the statues which have been erected as memorials, you massacre Christians simply because they protect the true faith.

What is this frenzy? What rage or madness consumes you? This faith, which God Almighty, the Son, and the Holy Spirit have revealed, established, elevated to power and glorified a thousandfold through miracles is the faith that you persecute and which you wish to overthrow and destroy. You are blind, but not because you lack eyes or foresight. Do you believe that you will remain unpunished for it? Or are you unaware that God opposes your criminal efforts and will not

---

126 Joan also implied that there had been a risk of her letters being intercepted when she said that 'sometimes she put the cross as a sign that the person of her party to whom she was writing should not do what she had written to him' [**38**].

permit you to remain in darkness and error? The more that you indulge yourselves in crime and sacrilege, the more He will prepare great punishments and torment for you.

As far as I am concerned, to tell you frankly, if I was not occupied with these English wars, I would have come to see you a long time ago. But if I do not learn that you have reformed yourselves, I might leave the English and set off against you, so that, by the sword if I cannot do it any other way, I may eliminate your mad and obscene superstition and remove either your heresy or your lives. But if you would prefer instead to return to the catholic faith and to the original light, send me your ambassadors and I will tell them what you must do. If you do not wish to do so and if you obstinately kick against the spur,[127] remember what injuries and crimes you have perpetrated and await me, who will inflict a similar fate on you with the aid of divine and human forces.

Given at Sully[-sur-Loire], the 23rd of March to the heretics of Bohemia.

Pasquerel.

31. Joan of Arc's letter to Reims (28 March 1430)

Source: Quicherat (ed.), *Procès de condamnation*, V, pp. 161–2.

Language: French

This is the last letter sent by Joan, addressed 'to my very dear and good friends, the churchmen, magistrates, burghers, inhabitants and residents of the good town of Reims'. It was sent from Sully-sur-Loire, and survives in the original, signed copy.

Very dear and good friends, may it please you to know that I have received your letters, which make mention of how word had been brought to the King that there are many evil people in the good city of Reims. If you wish to know the real truth, it was reported to him that there are many who are part of an alliance to betray the city and let the Burgundians inside. And since then, the King has learned otherwise, because you have sent him an assurance, and he is therefore very pleased with you. And believe that you are much in his favour, and if you have to fight he will aid you in the event of a siege.

127 This phrase echoes Acts 26:14.

And he well knows that you have suffered much from the hardships
that these treasonous Burgundians, the enemy, have done to you. So
he will deliver you, God willing, very soon – that is to say as soon as
possible.[128] I beg and call upon you, very dear friends, to defend carefully your good city for the King and to keep good watch. You will
soon receive my good news more directly. I will not write anything
more for the present, except that all of Brittany is now French and
that the Duke must send three[129] thousand soldiers to the King, paid
for six[130] months' service. I commend you to God that He may protect
you.

Written at Sully[-sur-Loire] on the 28th day of March.

Joan.

32. The *Chronicles of London* (c.1430?)

Source: C. L. Kingsford, *The Chronicles of London*, Oxford, 1905, pp. 96–7.

Language: Middle English

It is extremely difficult to establish the precise relationship between, not to
mention the dates of, the many copies of the vernacular chronicles of London
that were produced in the fifteenth century. This makes it challenging to use
this important evidence for reactions in England, and in particular among the
citizens of London, to the news of the capture of Joan of Arc. Nevertheless,
most of the surviving manuscripts present a variant of the following
narrative, which does not provide any account of the Rouen trial. The
chroniclers usually provided the brief reference to Joan in the context of a
detailed account of the punishment of Lollard heretics in England and the
news of the coronation of Henry VI in France, both of which must have
served to emphasise the importance of the English Crown in overcoming the
threat posed by Joan and other enemies of the Church.[131]

In this same year, upon St Leonard's day, was King Henry VI, not
fully eight years of age, crowned at Westminster [6 November 1429];
at whose coronation were made thirty-five knights; and on St George's

---

128 A truce with Burgundy was in effect at that time, and remained in effect until April.

129 This number is not clear and has been variously interpreted as a three and as a
four.

130 This number may be a two, a four or a six.

131 M-R. McLaren, *The London Chronicles of the Fifteenth Century: a revolution in
English writing. With an annotated edition of Bradford, West Yorkshire Archives MS
32D86/42*, Woodbridge, 2002, pp. 85–91. Also see **104**.

day next following [23 April], he passed over the sea to Calais; and the 23rd day of May towards night, before the town of Compiègne, there was a woman taken armed in the field with many other worthy captains, the which was called Pucelle de Dieu, a false witch, for through her power the dauphin and all our adversaries trusted wholly to have reconquered all France, and never to have been beaten whenever she was there, for they held her among them for a prophetess and a worthy goddess.

33. Letter from Henry VI to Pierre Cauchon (3 January 1431)

Source: Tisset (ed.), *Procès de condamnation*, I, pp. 14–15.

Language: French

Henry, by the grace of God King of France and of England, to all those who shall see these present letters, greeting.

It is notorious and well known how for some time a woman who calls herself Joan the Pucelle has put off the habit and dress of the female sex, which is contrary to divine law, abominable to God, condemned and prohibited by every law; she has dressed and armed herself in the state and habit of a man, has committed and caused cruel murders and, it is said, has given the simple people to believe, through seduction and deceit, that she was sent from God, and that she had knowledge of His divine secrets, together with many other very dangerous dogmatic theories, most prejudicial and scandalous to our holy catholic faith. While pursuing these abuses, and exercising hostilities against us and our people, she was captured in arms before Compiègne by some of our loyal subjects, and has since been brought as a prisoner before us. And because she has been reputed, charged and defamed by many people for superstitions, false dogmas and other crimes of divine treason, we have been most urgently required by our well beloved and loyal counsellor the Bishop of Beauvais, the ecclesiastical and ordinary judge of the said Joan, because she was taken and apprehended within the boundaries and limits of his diocese, and we have similarly been exhorted by our very dear and well-loved daughter the University of Paris, to surrender, present and deliver this Joan to the said reverend father in God, so that he may question and examine her and proceed against her according to the ordinances and dispositions of canon and divine laws, when the proper assembly can be called together. Therefore, for the respect and honour of God's name, for the protection and exaltation of His holy Church and catholic faith, we devoutly desire, as a true and humble son of the Church, to obey the requests and demands of the said reverend father in God and the exhortations of the doctors and masters of our daughter, the University of Paris: and we command and grant, whenever the reverend father shall think fit, that this Joan shall be surrendered and delivered by our men and officers in whose hands she now is, so that the reverend father in God may question, examine, and proceed against her according to God, reason, divine law and the holy canons.

So we command our men and officers who guard this Joan to surrender and deliver her to the reverend father in God without contradiction or refusal, whenever he shall require, and we further command all our men of law, officers and subjects, English or French, not to occasion any hindrance or difficulty by their actions or in any other manner to the reverend father, or to any who are or shall be appointed to assist, participate in or hear the said trial.[132] But if [the guards] are so required by the said reverend father in God, they shall give him protection, aid, defence, guard and comfort, under pain of grave punishment. Nevertheless it is our intention to retake and regain possession of this Joan if it comes to pass that she is not convicted or found guilty of the said crimes, or those of them concerning or touching our faith.

In witness of this, we have affixed our signet seal in the absence of the great seal, to these present [letters].

Given at Rouen, 3rd January, in the year of grace 1431, and the ninth of our reign.

Signed: By the King, on the advice of his Great Council.

Jean de Rinel.[133]

---

132 These instructions foreshadow the arrangements during the trial where Joan was not kept in an ecclesiastical prison, but rather treated as a prisoner of war under the guard of English soldiers, except when escorted by Jean Massieu to the sessions of the court.

133 Jean de Rinel was a royal notary and secretary, and also the nephew by marriage of Pierre Cauchon [63].

II: THE TRIAL OF CONDEMNATION (FEBRUARY–MAY 1431)

34. First public examination (Wednesday 21 February 1431)

Source: Tisset (ed.), *Procès de condamnation*, I, pp. 35–42.

Language: Latin

The first public examination began at eight o'clock in the morning in the royal chapel at the castle of Rouen, with Cauchon and forty-two clerics present, together with the notaries. The usher, Jean Massieu, reported that Joan had asked for the judges to 'invite ecclesiastics of the French side, equal in number to those of the English party, to join you' and had also begged to hear mass. When Joan was brought into the room, the judges explained that she was being investigated because of the 'common report and public rumours' of her actions against the orthodox faith.

[We] immediately exhorted and charitably asked Joan, then seated before us, in order to accelerate the present matter and the discharge of her own conscience, to speak the whole truth on what she might be asked in matters of faith without looking for any subterfuges or ruses which might hinder the confession of the same truth.

Moreover, by virtue of our office, we lawfully required the same Joan to swear an oath in due form, while touching the holy gospels, to speak the truth as might be appropriate on those points on which she would be questioned.

Joan replied in this manner: 'I do not know what you want to question me about. Perhaps you might ask me such things as I will not say to you.'

At which we said to her: 'You will swear to speak the truth about what you are asked concerning the matter of faith and about what you know.'

She replied once again that she would willingly swear with regard to what concerned her father and her mother and what she had done after she had taken the road to France. But as for the revelations that had been sent to her by God, she had never told or revealed them to anyone except only to Charles, who, she said, was her King, and she would not reveal them even if her head should be cut off, because she would not reveal to anyone what she knew from her visions or her secret counsel; and within the following eight days, she would know for sure whether she ought to reveal these things.

Once again, and on many occasions, we, the aforementioned Bishop [Pierre Cauchon], admonished and asked Joan to take the oath to speak the truth regarding those things which concerned our faith. Joan, on her knees and with her two hands placed upon the book, in this instance a missal, swore to speak the truth about what she was asked and what she knew concerning the matter of faith, without mentioning the previous condition that she would not say nor divulge to anyone the revelations that had been made to her.[1]

Item, having taken the oath in this way, Joan was questioned by us about her name and her surname. To which she replied that in her country she was called Jeannette and that after she came into France she was called Joan [Jeanne]. But as for her surname, she said that she did not know anything of this.

Then questioned about the place of her origin, she replied that she was born in the village of Domremy which is joined with the village of Greux, and it is in Greux that the principal church is found.[2]

Item, questioned about the name of her father and mother, she replied that her father was called Jacques d'Arc and her mother, Isabelle.[3]

Asked in what place she was baptised, she replied [that it was] in the church of Domremy.

Asked who were her godfathers and godmothers, she said that one of her godmothers was called Agnès, another Jeanne, another Sibille [Isabelle?]; one of her godfathers was called Jean Lingué, another Jean Barrey; she had many other godmothers, according to what she heard from her mother.[4]

Asked which priest baptised her, she replied that it was my lord Jean

---

1 The Latin trial record differs from the testimony in the *Minute française*, which only stated that Joan would tell the truth in all matters concerning the faith, 'but that, regarding the aforesaid revelations, she would not tell them to anyone.'

2 Domremy as situated in the valley of the Meuse, in the duchy of Bar, right on the frontier with the Empire. From a religious perspective, it was annexed to Greux whose church was dedicated to Saint Maurice; the church in Domremy was dedicated to Saint Rémi after whom the village was named.

3 Joan's father Jacques (or Jacquot) was born around 1375 at Ceffonds in the diocese of Troyes. Her mother Isabelle (or Isabeau) was known as 'Romée'.

4 Many of these godparents were identified during the Nullification trial.

Minet, or so she believed.[5] Asked if he is still alive, she replied yes, or so she believed.

Item, asked how old she was, she replied that, as far as she knew, she was around nineteen years old. She also said that her mother taught her the *Pater Noster*, the *Ave Maria* and the *Credo*; and that she did not derive her knowledge from anyone other than her mother.

Item, asked by us to say her *Pater*, she replied that if we would hear her in confession then she would say it willingly to us. And as we asked her this again repeatedly, she replied that she would not say the *Pater*, etc., if we would not hear her in confession. We then said to her that we would willingly assign one or two notable men of the French language,[6] to whom she might say the *Pater*, etc. To which Joan replied that she would not speak to them if they would not hear her in confession.

After this had taken place, we, the aforementioned Bishop [Cauchon], prohibited Joan from leaving the prison assigned to her in the castle of Rouen without our permission, under penalty of being convicted of the crime of heresy.[7] But she replied that she did not accept this injunction, adding that if she escaped, no one could blame her for having broken or violated her oath because she had never given her oath to anyone. Then she complained about being held in chains and in bonds of iron. We then said to her that she had tried to escape from other prisons on many occasions and that is was for this that an order had been given to bind her with chains of iron so that she might be more safely and securely guarded. To which she replied: 'It is true that elsewhere I wished to escape and would still do so, as is lawful for all people who are incarcerated or imprisoned'.

We then committed the safeguard of Joan to the nobleman John Grey, esquire of the body of our lord the King, and with him Jean Berwoit [or Barow] and William Talbot, enjoining them to guard her well and faithfully, without allowing anyone to speak to her without our permission. They solemnly swore this, touching the holy gospels.

5 This individual is unknown: the parish priest during Joan's youth was Guillaume Fronté or Frontey.

6 The *Minute française* simply stated 'one or two notable people from this company'.

7 The Latin trial record inverts the order of the *Minute française*, where the debate about Joan's imprisonment took place before the discussion of her place of birth and upbringing.

35. Second public examination (Thursday 22 February 1431)

Source: Tisset (ed.), *Procès de condamnation*, I, pp. 44–54.

Language: Latin

The official record listed forty-eight clerics who joined Cauchon for the second public examination in the great hall at the castle of Rouen. Before Joan entered the room, Jean Le Maistre, Cauchon's fellow judge and the Inquisitor for the trial, tried to escape involvement in the trial by announcing that he could not take part in the proceedings until the Inquisitor of France, Jean Graverent, had extended his commission to include this case.

Then after Joan had appeared before us in that place, we required and exhorted her, under the penalties of law, to take the oath that she had sworn the day before, promising simply and absolutely to speak the truth on the questions that would be put to her in the matter for which she had been accused and defamed. To which she replied that she had taken the oath yesterday and that this should be sufficient.

We again required her to swear; for no one, even a prince, could refuse to take this oath when required in a matter of faith. She again replied: 'I have taken this oath for you yesterday; that should be quite enough for you. You place too great a burden on me.' Finally she swore to speak the truth on those things which concerned the faith.

After this, the distinguished professor of sacred theology, Master Jean Beaupère, at our order and command, questioned Joan on those things which follow.

And first he exhorted her to speak the truth about what he would ask her, as she had sworn. She replied: 'You may well ask me such a thing about which I will answer truthfully and another on which I will not reply to you.' And she added: 'If you were well informed about me, you ought to wish that I were out of your hands. I have not done anything except by revelation.'

Asked then about her age when she left her father's house, she said that she did not know [and could not] testify about her age.

Asked if in her youth she had learned a craft, she said yes, to sew linen and to spin; and she did not fear any woman in Rouen [when it came to] sewing and spinning.[8] Then she confessed that, out of fear of the

---

8 The Latin record distorts the original *Minute française* which merely reported Joan as saying: 'her mother taught her to sew; and that she did not believe that there was any woman in Rouen who could teach her anything of this.'

Burgundians, she left her father's house and went to Neufchâteau, in Lorraine, to the home of a woman named La Rousse, where she stayed for about fifteen days. She added, too, that as long as she was in the house of her father, she attended to the ordinary domestic tasks of the home and did not go to the fields with the sheep and the other animals.[9]

Item, asked if she confessed her sins each year, she replied yes, and to the priest of her own parish,[10] and with his permission when he was busy, she confessed to another priest. Sometimes also, two or three times as far as she remembered, she confessed to mendicant friars: this was at the town of Neufchâteau. And she received the sacrament of the Eucharist at Easter.

Asked if she received this sacrament of the Eucharist at other feasts than Easter, she told the interrogator to move on. Then she confessed that when she was aged thirteen, she had a voice from God to help her to guide herself. And the first time she was greatly afraid. And this voice came around noon, in summer, in the garden of her father, and Joan had not fasted on the preceding day. She heard the voice on the right-hand side, towards the church, and she rarely heard it without a light. This light came from the same side that she heard the voice, but generally there was a great light there. And when Joan came to France, she often heard this voice.

Asked how she saw the light which she said was there, since this light was to the side, she gave no reply, but moved on to another matter. She said, in addition, that if she was in a wood, she clearly heard the voices coming to her. She also said that it seemed to her that it was a worthy [*digna*] voice and she believed that this voice had been sent from God, and that, after she had heard this voice three times, she

---

9 The *Minute française* merely recorded that 'she went to Neufchâteau with a woman named La Rousse, where she stayed for a fortnight. In this house she did the household tasks, and did not go into the fields to keep the sheep or other animals.' The purpose of this line of questioning was revealed in Article 8 of the Seventy Articles, read before Joan on 27 March 1431: 'Joan, when she was about [fifteen], of her own will and without the leave of her said father and mother, went to the town of Neufchâteau in Lorraine and there for some time served in the house of a woman, an innkeeper named La Rousse, where many young unguarded women stayed, and the lodgers were for the most part soldiers. Thus, dwelling at this inn, she would sometimes stay with the said women, sometimes would drive the sheep to the fields, and occasionally lead the horses to drink, or to the meadow, or pasture; and there she learned to ride and became acquainted with the profession of arms.' (Tisset (ed.), *Procès de condamnation*, I, p. 200). This charge was not repeated in the Twelve Articles.

10 Guillaume Fronté, or Frontey, of Neufchâteau.

knew that this was the voice of an angel. She said also that this voice had always protected her well and that she understood this voice clearly.

Asked about the instruction that this voice gave to her for the salvation of her soul, she said that it taught her to conduct herself well, to go to church often, and that it was necessary that she should travel to France. Joan added that her interrogator would not learn from her, on this occasion, in what form that voice had appeared to her. Furthermore, she confessed that this voice told her two or three times a week that it was necessary that she, Joan, should leave and come into France; and [she confessed that] her father did not know anything about her departure. She also said that the voice told her that she should come into France and that she could no longer stay where she was, and that it said to her that she would raise the siege positioned around Orléans. She said moreover that the voice had told her that she, Joan, should go to find Robert de Baudricourt in the town of Vaucouleurs, of which he was captain, and that he would provide her with men to travel with her.[11] Joan then replied that she was a poor girl who did not know how to ride on horseback or to lead in war. She also said that she went to find her uncle and that she told him that she wanted to stay with him for a short length of time; and she stayed there for about eight days.[12] She then said to her uncle that it was necessary that she go to Vaucouleurs and her uncle took her there.

Item, she said that when she reached the town of Vaucouleurs, she recognised Robert de Baudricourt, even though she had never seen him before; and she recognised Robert by means of her voice, for the voice told her that this was he. And Joan said to Robert that she had to travel to France. But Robert twice refused and dismissed her; at the third time, he accepted her and gave some men to her. And the voice had also told her that it would happen in this way.

Item, she confessed that the Duke of Lorraine ordered that she be brought to him;[13] she went there and said to him that she wished to go to France. And the Duke questioned her about the recovery of his health but she said to him that she knew nothing about that. And she

---

11 Vaucouleurs was the last scrap of territory that Charles VII possessed on the eastern borders of his kingdom.

12 The uncle was in fact her first cousin by marriage, Durand Laxart or Lassois, labourer at Burey-le-Petit (now Burey-en-Vaux), eleven kilometres south of Vaucouleurs. Laxart testified at the Nullification trial [78].

13 Charles II, Duke of Lorraine (1390–1431), whose residence was at Nancy.

said little about her journey to the Duke, but she did tell him to give his son and some men to her, to escort her into France, and that she would pray to God for his health.[14] Joan had travelled under a safe-conduct to the Duke from where she returned to the town of Vaucouleurs.

Item, she confessed that on her departure from the town of Vau-couleurs, she was dressed in the clothing of a man, carrying a sword that Robert de Baudricourt had given to her, without any other arms;[15] accompanied by a knight, a squire and four servants, she went as far as the town of Saint-Urbain and there she spent the night in the abbey.[16]

Item, she said that on her journey she passed through the town of Auxerre where she heard mass in the great church [cathedral]; and from that time she frequently heard her voices, including the one mentioned already.

Item, called upon to say on whose advice she took the clothing of a man, she refused to answer many times. Finally she said that she would charge no one with this; and she changed [her testimony] many times.

Item, she said that Robert de Baudricourt made those who were escort-ing her swear to guide her well and safely. And Robert said to Joan when she was departing: 'Go, depart and let what may happen, happen.'

Item, this Joan then said that she knew very well that God loved the Duke of Orléans and also that she had had more revelations concern-ing him than any man alive, except the one whom she called her King [Charles VII].[17] In addition, she said that it was necessary that she changed her clothing for that of a man. Item, she also believed that her adviser counselled her well.

Item, she said that she sent letters to the English who were before Orléans, telling them that they should depart, as was recorded in the

14 The son in question is undoubtedly René d'Anjou, son-in-law and heir of Charles II, Duke of Lorraine; his parents were Louis II of Anjou and Yolande of Aragon, and his sister, Marie of Anjou, was married to Charles VII.

15 See **77–79**.

16 Her companions were the squire Jean de Nouillonpont, also known as Jean de Metz [**77**], and his servant Jean de Honnecourt; Bertrand de Poulengy [**80**] and his servant Julien; Colet de Vienne, a royal messenger, and his servant, Richard the archer. They stayed at the abbey of Saint-Urbain in Champagne around 25 February 1429.

17 Charles, Duke of Orléans (1394–1465), had been taken prisoner by the English at the battle of Agincourt in 1415.

copy of the letters which had been read to her in this town of Rouen, excepting however two or three words which appeared in that copy, for example, where this copy gives 'Surrender to the Pucelle', it should read 'Surrender to the King.' These words also appear there: 'body for body' and 'commander of war', which were not in the original letters.[18]

Joan then said that she went without hindrance to the man whom she calls her King and when she had arrived at the town of Sainte-Catherine-de-Fierbois she sent first to the man that she called her King, and then she went to Chinon where he was to be found.[19] She arrived there around midday and found lodgings in an inn and, after dinner, she went to the one whom she called King, who was at the castle.

Item, she said that when she entered the room of her King, she recognised him among the others by the counsel of her voice that revealed this man to her. And she said to her King that she wanted to go to wage war against the English.

Asked if there had been any light in the place where the voice revealed her King to her, she answered: 'Move on.'

Asked if she did not see any angel above her King, she answered: 'Spare me that. Move on.' She said that before her King put her to work, he had numerous apparitions and beautiful revelations.

Asked about the revelations and apparitions that her King had, she answered: 'I will not tell you. Still this is not a reply to you, but send to the King and he will tell you.'

Item, this Joan said that the voice had promised her that, soon after she came to the King, he would receive her.[20] She also said that those of her party knew well that the voice had been sent to Joan from God, and that they perceived and knew this voice; she asserted that she certainly knew this. In addition she said that her King and many others heard and perceived the voices which came to her, and that Charles de Bourbon was present with two or three others.[21]

18 This is a reference to Joan's letter to the English dated 22 March 1429, which was later cited in full during the reading of the Seventy Articles [4].

19 The *Minute française* does not mention her stay at Sainte-Catherine-de-Fierbois at the start of March. She arrived at Chinon on 6 March 1429.

20 In fact Joan had to wait two days to meet the Dauphin.

21 Charles de Bourbon was the Count of Clermont. He was the son and heir of Jean Duke of Bourbon, who had been captured at Agincourt but did not die until 1433 in England.

Item, Joan said that there was not a day when she did not hear this voice and also that she had much need of it. She also said that she never asked the voice for any other final reward than the salvation of her soul. Moreover Joan confessed that the voice told her that she should remain at the town of Saint-Denis in France; and she, Joan, wished to remain there but, against her will, the lords took her away.[22] However if she had not been wounded, she would not have left. And she was wounded in the trenches before Paris, where she had arrived after coming from the town of Saint-Denis; but in five days she was healed. Further she confessed that she had started a skirmish before the town of Paris.[23]

And when she was asked if it was not a feast day then, she answered that she certainly knew that it was a feast day.

Asked if this had been done well, she replied: 'Pass on.'[24]

36. Third public examination (Saturday 24 February 1431)

Source: Tisset (ed.), *Procès de condamnation*, I, pp. 57–68.

Language: Latin

According to the official record, the third public examination in the great hall at the castle of Rouen was attended by Cauchon and sixty-two clerics. Before the interrogation began, the judges again implored Joan to swear an oath to answer truthfully, but she repeatedly refused because she defended her right not to answer certain questions, especially regarding her revelations.

Then at our order she was questioned by the distinguished doctor, Master Jean Beaupère, named above, who first asked her at what hour she had eaten or drunk last. She answered that she had neither eaten nor drunk since yesterday afternoon.

---

22 Joan was based in Saint-Denis from 9 to 13 September 1429.

23 The assault on the Saint-Honoré Gate to the Saint-Denis Gate took place on 8 September 1429, the feast of the Nativity of the Virgin; Joan was hit in the leg by a crossbow bolt.

24 Contemporary legal thought held that feast days were ordained for the service of the Lord, and so armies were supposed to abstain from fighting except in cases of self-defence: John of Legnano, *Tractatus de bello, de represaliis et de duello*, ed. T. E. Holland and trans. J. L. Brierly, Oxford, 1917, p. 126; Honoré Bonet [now correctly identified as Bouvet], *The Tree of Battles*, ed. G. W. Coopland, Cambridge, MA, 1949, p. 155.

Item, asked at what time she had heard the voice that came to her, she answered: 'I heard it yesterday and today.'

Item, asked at what time yesterday she had heard the voice, she replied that she had heard it three times during the day, once in the morning, once at vespers and the third time when the *Ave Maria* was rung in the evening. And very often she heard it more frequently than she said.

Asked what she was doing yesterday in the morning when the voice came to her, she answered that she was sleeping and the voice woke her.

Asked if the voice woke her by touching her arms, she replied that the voice woke her without touching her.

Asked if this voice was in her room, she replied that not, as far as she knew, but it was in the castle.

Asked if she thanked the voice and if she knelt down, she answered that she thanked it while sitting on her bed, and she put her hands together; and this happened after she had asked for help. The voice told Joan to answer boldly.

Item, asked about what the voice said to her when she was awakened, she replied that she herself asked the voice for counsel on what she ought to reply, saying to the voice that she would seek advice regarding this from God. And the voice told her that she should answer boldly and that God would help her.

Asked if the voice spoke any words to her before she called upon it, she answered that the voice said certain words to her but she did not understand it all. Nevertheless after she was woken from her sleep, the voice told her to answer boldly.

Item, she said to us, the Bishop [Cauchon]: 'You say that you are my judge; take care what you are doing because, in truth, I have been sent by God and you put yourself in great danger.'

Asked if the voice did not sometimes change its advice, she replied that she never found it [give] two contrary words. She also said that she heard it tell her to answer boldly that night.

Asked if the voice forbade her from answering questions put to her, she said: 'I will not answer you about that. And I have revelations concerning the King which I will not tell you.'

Asked if the voice forbade her from divulging her revelations, she answered: 'I do not have advice on that. Give me a delay of a fortnight and I will answer you on this.'[25] And as she had again asked for a delay in order to reply, she said: 'If the voice prohibited me, what then would you wish to say?'

Asked again if that was forbidden to her, she replied: 'Believe that it is not men who have forbidden me.' Item, she said that she would not answer that day and she did not know whether she ought to say it or not until this had been revealed to her. Item, she said that she firmly believed – as firmly as she believed in the Christian faith and that God redeemed us from the pains of hell – that this voice came from God and by His command.

Asked if this voice, which she said appeared to her, was an angel, or if it came immediately from God, or if it was the voice of a male or female saint, she answered: 'This voice comes from God; and I believe that I am not telling you clearly what I know, and I am much more afraid of failing them by saying something that may displease these voices than I am of answering you. And as for this question, I ask you that I may have a delay.'

Asked if she believed that it was displeasing to God that the truth be spoken, she replied: 'The voices told me to say certain things to the King and not to you.' Item, she said that the voice told her many things for the good of the King that night which she wished that the King knew at that moment; and she would not drink wine until Easter: for, as she said, he would be more happy at dinner.[26]

Asked if she could act towards the voices in such a way that they would wish to obey her and carry news to her King, she replied that she did not know whether the voice would obey her, unless this were the will of God and God consented. And if it pleased God, she said, He could certainly send revelations to the King. 'And I would be very pleased by that.'

Asked why this voice no longer spoke now with her King, as it was doing when Joan was in his presence, she answered that she did not know if this was the will of God. And she added that, if it was not for the will of God, she would not know to do anything.

25 This paragraph and those immediately before and after do not appear in the *Minute française*, raising the possibility that the request for a delay of a fortnight was added later, when the Latin trial record was prepared.

26 Joan was undoubtedly echoing a contemporary proverb, though the precise meaning is not clear.

Asked if her counsel revealed to her that she would escape from prison, she answered: 'Must I tell you that?'

Asked if the voice had not given her counsel and advice that night about what she should reply, she answered that if the voice revealed such things to her, she did not understand them.

Asked if on the two last days that she heard the voices, any light had appeared there, she replied that the light came at the name of the voice.[27]

Asked if she noticed anything else with the voices, she answered: 'I will not tell you everything; I do not have permission and my oath does not touch that. The voice is good and worthy and I am not bound to answer this.'

Item, she asked that the points on which she was not answering now should be given to her in writing.

Then she was asked if the voice from which she asked counsel had sight and eyes; she replied: 'You will not have that yet.' And she said that a saying among little children is that sometimes men are hanged for having told the truth.[28]

Asked if she knew whether she was in the grace of God, she answered: 'If I am not, may God put me there, and if I am, may God keep me there.[29] I would be the saddest person in the world if I knew that I was not in the grace of God.' Then she said that, if she were in sin, she believed that the voice would not come to her; and she wished that everyone might hear the voice as well as her. Item, she said that she thought that she was thirteen years of age or thereabouts when the first voice came to her.

Asked if in her youth she went to run around in the fields with the other children, she answered that she certainly went there sometimes but she did not know at what age.

Asked if the people of Domremy supported the Burgundians or the other party, she replied that she only knew one Burgundian there,

---

27 The *Minute française* stated that: 'She replied that light came before the voices'.

28 Joan was again using a proverb. The judges later referred back to this statement at the end of the questioning in **47**.

29 This was a common prayer. L. Carolus-Barré, '"Jeanne, êtes-vous en état de grace?" et les prières du prône au XVe siècle', in *Bulletin de la Société des Antiquaires de France*, 1958, pp. 204–8.

whose head she would have wished to be cut off, that is, if this had pleased God.[30]

Asked if [those of] the village of Maxey were Burgundians or enemies of the Burgundians, she answered they were Burgundians.[31]

Asked if the voice told her in her youth to hate the Burgundians, she answered that since she knew that the voices were for the King of France, she did not like the Burgundians. Item, she said that the Burgundians would have war if they did not do as they should; and she knew it from her voice.

Asked if she received a revelation from the voice in her youth that the English should come to France, she replied that the English were already in France when the voices began to come to her.

Asked if she was ever with the little children who fought for the party that she supported, she answered not as far as she remembered, but she certainly saw some [of them] from the village of Domremy who had fought against those of Maxey, returning sometimes wounded and bleeding.

Asked if in her youth she herself had any great desire to pursue the Burgundians, she answered that she had a great wish and desire for her King to have his kingdom.

Asked if she had greatly wanted to be a man when she had to come to France, she replied that she had answered this elsewhere.[32]

Asked if she did not take the animals to the fields, she said that she had answered this elsewhere and that after she was older and had attained the age of reason, she did not generally look after the animals but she certainly helped to lead them to the meadows and, for fear of the men-at-arms, to a castle called the Île.[33] But she does not recall if she tended them when she was young or not.

Item, she was questioned about a tree to be found near her village. To which she answered that there was a certain tree fairly near to

---

30 On 30 January 1456, one of the villagers from Domremy named Gérardin d'Epinal testified that he had been a Burgundian: Duparc (ed.), *Procès en nullité*, I, pp. 278–80.

31 The neighbouring village of Maxey was down the river Meuse from Domremy; it was located in the Barrois, just outside the sphere of influence of Charles VII.

32 There is no sign of this previous statement, and so Joan may be referring to an answer which the notaries had not recorded.

33 The castle of the Île of Domremy was built upon a meadow in front of the village on an island at the edge of the river.

Domremy called the Arbre des Dames [Tree of the Ladies], known as the Arbre des Fées [Tree of the Fairies] by others, and nearby was a spring. And she heard it said that those sick with fever drank of this spring and went there to find its water to restore their health. And she had seen this herself, but she did not know if they were cured in this way or not. Item, she said that she heard that the sick, when they could get up, went to the tree to walk around it. And it was a great tree, a beech, from where the [greenery for the feast of 1st day of] May comes, 'le beau mai' as they say in French; it was reputed to belong to my lord Pierre de Bourlémont, knight.[34]

Item, she said that sometimes she went to run around with the other young girls and made crowns of flowers for the image of Our Lady of Domremy. And often she heard it said by the old people, that were not from her family, that the Fairy Ladies lived there. She heard it said by a woman named Jeanne, wife of Mayor Aubery of this village and godmother to the one who was speaking, Joan [of Arc], that she had seen the Fairy Ladies; but she herself did not know if this was true or not. Item, she said that she never saw the Fairies at the tree, that she knew; but if she saw them elsewhere, she did not know if she had seen them or not. Item, she said that she saw the young girls putting garlands on the branches of the tree and she herself sometimes hung these with them; and sometimes they took them away, and sometimes they left them there. Item, she said that since she knew that she had to come to France, she took little part in their games and frolics, the least that she could. And she did not know whether she herself had danced near to the tree since she had developed judgement, but she certainly danced there sometimes with the children and she sang there more often that she danced.

Item, she said that there was a wood there which was called the Oak Wood, in French the 'Bois chesnu', which can be seen from her father's door and is not more than half a league away. Item, she did not know and had never heard that the Fairy Ladies had lived there but she heard it said by her brother that in the country around it was said that she herself, Joan, received her task from the Tree of the Fairy Ladies. But she said that she had not done this and she denied

---

34 The Bourlémont family held lordships in Champagne and the duchies of Bar and Lorraine, and owned a castle on the bank of the Meuse, upstream from Domremy; the line was extinguished on 4 April 1412 with the death of Pierre de Bourlémont. The connection between this family and the Tree of the Fairies was repeated by the witnesses from Domremy at the Nullification trial [74–6].

it to him. Item, she also said that when she came to her King, certain people asked her if there was a wood known as the 'Bois chesnu' [Oak wood] in her region, because there were prophecies saying that from the surroundings of this wood would come a young girl [*puella* in the Latin record, *pucelle* in the *Minute française*] who would do wonderful things. But Joan said that she put no faith in that.[35]

Asked if she wanted to have a woman's dress, she replied: 'Give me one; I will take it and depart: otherwise I will not have it. And I am content with this since it pleases God that I wear it.'

37. Fourth public examination (Tuesday 27 February 1431)

Source: Tisset (ed.), *Procès de condamnation*, I, pp. 69–79.

Language: Latin

According to the official record, the fourth public examination in the great hall at the castle of Rouen was attended by Cauchon and fifty-four clerics. Before the interrogation began, the judges again called upon Joan to swear an oath to answer truthfully but she would only agree to speak the truth concerning her trial and not on everything that she knew.

Then at our order, the aforementioned Master Jean Beaupère began to question her. And first he asked her how she had been since the previous Saturday. And she answered: 'You certainly see how I have been. I have been as well as possible.'

Asked if she would fast every day of Lent, she replied by asking: 'Is that for your trial?' And as it was said to her that this was connected with the trial, she answered: 'Yes, truly. I have always fasted during Lent.'

Asked whether since Saturday she had heard the voice which came to her, she replied: 'Yes, truly, I have heard it many times.'

Asked if on Saturday she had heard it in this room where she was being questioned, she answered: 'That is not for your trial.' And then she said that she had heard it here.

Asked what her voice had said to her on Saturday, she replied: 'I did

35 This is a reference to a prophecy attributed to Merlin in Geoffrey of Monmouth's *History of the Kings of Britain*, which stated that 'Ex nemore canuto puella eliminabitur ut medelae curam adhibeat': this was popularly taken to refer to Joan, 'ex nemore canuto' being interpreted as 'from the Oak Wood' of Domremy. See pages 18 to 19 above.

not understand the voice well and I did not understand anything I could repeat to you, until I had returned to my room.'

Asked what the voice said to her in her room when she went back, she answered: 'It told me to answer you boldly.' And she said that she asked for counsel from the voice on what was being asked of her. She then declared that she would willingly say what she had permission from the Lord to reveal; but with regard to the revelations concerning the King of France, she would not say this without the permission of her voice.

Asked if the voice forbade her from saying everything, she replied that she did not entirely understand it.

Asked what the voice said to her on the last occasion, she answered that she asked for counsel on certain things about which she had been questioned.

Asked if the voice had given her counsel on anything, she answered that she received advice on some points, and she might certainly be asked to reply on other things but she would not reply without permission. And if she replied without permission, perhaps she would not have the voices as guarantor, in French 'en garant';[36] but when she did have permission from the Lord, she would not be afraid to speak because she would have a good guarantor.

Asked if it was the voice of an angel that spoke to her or if it was the voice of a saint, male or female, or directly from God, she replied that this was the voice of St Katherine and St Margaret. And their figures were crowned with beautiful crowns, very opulent and very precious. She said: 'And I have the permission of the Lord for this. But if you doubt this, send to Poitiers where I was questioned not long ago.'[37]

Asked how she knew that it was these two saints, and whether she clearly knew one from the other, she answered that she knew well that it was them, and she certainly recognised one from the other.

Asked in what way she recognised one from the other, she replied that she recognised them by the greeting that they gave to her. She also said that a good seven years had passed since they undertook to guide her. She also said that she recognised the saints because they named themselves to her.

36 The archaic term 'en garant' carried both legal and chivalric overtones.
37 In March–April 1429.

Asked if these saints were dressed in the same material, she answered: 'I will not tell you another thing now and I do not have permission to reveal it to you. If you do not believe me, send to Poitiers.' She also said that these were revelations for the King of France and not for those who questioned her.

Asked if the saints were the same age, she replied that she did not have permission to say.

Asked if the saints spoke at the same time or the one after the other, she answered: 'I do not have permission to tell you; nevertheless I have always had counsel from both of them.'

Asked which one of them appeared to her first, she replied: 'I did not recognise them that quickly; and I certainly knew this in the past, but I have forgotten; and if I had permission, I would tell this to you willingly. And it is recorded in the register at Poitiers.' Item, she also said that she had received comfort from St Michael.

Asked which of the apparitions came to her first, she answered that it was St Michael who came first.

Asked if a long time had passed since she heard the voice of St Michael for the first time, she replied: 'I do not speak to you of the voice of St Michael, but I am speaking of a great comfort.'

Asked which was the first voice which came to her when she was aged thirteen or thereabouts, she answered that it was St Michael whom she saw before her eyes; and he was not alone, but well accompanied by angels from heaven. She also said that she only came to France by the command of God.

Asked if she saw St Michael and the angels corporeally and really, she replied: 'I saw them with the eyes of my body, just as well as I see you; and when they left me, I wept, and I certainly would have wished that they had taken me with them.'

Asked about the figure of St Michael, she answered 'There is no reply on this for you yet, and I still do not have permission to say it.'

Asked what St Michael said to her the first time, she replied: 'You will still not have any reply today.'[38] Item, she said that the voices told her to answer boldly. Item, she said that she had indeed once told her

38 The surviving manuscripts of the *Minute française* provide no further information about this session: manuscript O stops at this point and does not resume until near the end of the fifth public examination, while manuscript U does not begin until part way through the sixth public examination.

King everything that had been revealed to her because this concerned him. Nevertheless she said that she still did not have permission to reveal what St Michael said to her. She then said that she certainly wished that her interrogator had a copy of the book which was at Poitiers, provided that God would be happy with this.[39]

Asked if the voices forbade her from speaking about her revelations without their permission, she answered: 'I will still not reply to you about that; and I will willingly answer about that for which I have permission. But if the voices have forbidden this, I have not understood clearly.'

Asked what sign indicated that this revelation came from God and that these were St Katherine and St Margaret who spoke with her, she replied: 'I have said to you enough that it is St Katherine and St Margaret; believe me if you wish.'

Asked if it was forbidden for her to say, she answered: 'I have not clearly understood whether this was prohibited or not.'

Asked how she knew how to distinguish between replying to certain points and not to others, she answered that on some points she had asked for permission and on some points she had it. Then she said that she would prefer to be torn apart by horses than to have come to France without the permission of God.

Asked if he ordered her to wear the clothing of a man, she answered that the clothing was such a small matter, the least thing; and she did not take male clothing on the advice of any man of this world; and she did not take this outfit, or do anything, except by the command of God and the angels.

Asked if it seemed to her that the command for her to take up male clothing was lawful, she replied: 'Everything I have done is by the command of the Lord; and if He had ordered me to take up a different outfit, I would have done it, because this would have been done by the command of God.'

Asked if this was done on the order of Robert de Baudricourt, she answered no.

Asked if she believed that she had done well in taking male clothing, she replied that everything that she had done by the command of the Lord, she believed had been done well and she expected a good guarantor and aid for it.

39 The records of the inquiry at Poitiers have not survived. See page 15 above.

Asked if in this particular case, in taking male clothing, she believed that she had done well, she answered that there was nothing in the world that she had done that was not by the command of God.

Asked if there was a light when she saw this voice which came to her, she replied that there was much light on all sides and that this was very appropriate. She also said to the interrogator that all the light was not coming to her alone.

Asked if there was an angel above the head of her King when she saw him for the first time, she answered: 'By the Blessed Mary! If there was, I do not know and did not see it.'

Asked if there was a light, she replied: 'There were more than three hundred knights and fifty torches, without counting the spiritual light. And I rarely have revelations without there being light.'

Asked how her King gave credence to her words, she answered that he himself had [received] good signs,[40] and by means of the clerics.

Asked what revelations her King had, she replied: 'You will still not have them from me this year.' Item, she said that for three weeks she was questioned by the clerks at Chinon and Poitiers, and her King had a sign regarding her deeds before believing in her. And the clerks of her party were of the opinion that there was nothing but good in her actions, as it seemed to them.

Asked if she was at Sainte-Catherine-de-Fierbois, she answered yes, and that she heard three masses in one day there, and then she went to Chinon. Item, she said that she sent letters to her King in which it was stated that she was sending them to find out if she should enter the town where her King was, that she had certainly travelled for a hundred and fifty leagues to come to help him, and that she had much good news for him. And it seemed to her that in these same letters, it was indicated that she would certainly recognise her King among all the others. Item, she said that she had a sword which she took to Vaucouleurs. She also said that when she was at Tours or at Chinon, she sent to find a sword which was to be found in the church of Sainte-Catherine-de-Fierbois, behind the altar; immediately afterwards it was found all rusted over.[41]

---

40 This statement should be read against the various stories of signs from God that encouraged Charles to put faith in Joan. See pages 12 to 13 above.

41 This story was also recounted by Jean Chartier [**67**].

Asked how she knew that this sword was there, she replied that this
sword was in the earth, rusted, bearing five engraved crosses; and she
knew that the sword was there through her voices and she had never
seen the man who went to find this sword. And she wrote to the
clergy of this place [to ask if] it might please them for her to have
this sword, and they sent it to her. It was not deep under the ground
behind the altar; yet she did not know exactly if it was in front of the
altar or behind it, but she thought that it was written at that time that
the sword was behind the altar. She also said that immediately after
the sword was found, the churchmen of that place rubbed it and the
rust immediately fell off without effort. And it was an armourer of
Tours who went to find it, and the churchmen of that place gave a
scabbard to Joan, as did the men of Tours along with them; and they
made two scabbards, one of crimson velvet, in French 'de velois
vermeil', and the other of gold leaf. And she had another made of very
strong leather. But she said that when she was captured she did not
have this sword. She also said that she carried this sword continually
from when she received it up until she left Saint-Denis after the assault
on Paris.

Asked what benediction she made, or had made, over this sword, she
answered that she never blessed it herself, nor did she have it blessed,
and she would not have known what to do. Item, she said that she
certainly loved this sword because it had been found in the church of
St Katherine whom she loved greatly.

Asked if she was at Coulange-la-Vineuse, she replied that she did not
know.[42]

Asked if she ever put her sword on an altar, she answered that, as far
as she knew, it was not placed in this way in order that the sword
might be more fortunate.

Asked if she ever prayed for her sword to have better fortune, she
replied: 'It is well to know that I would have wished that my armour
might be very fortunate.'

Asked if she had her sword when she was captured, she answered no,
but she had a sword that had been taken from a Burgundian.

Asked where the sword was left and in what town, she replied that
she offered a sword and armour at the abbey of Saint-Denis, but this

42 The town of Coulanges-la-Vineuse near Auxerre surrendered to Joan in June 1429
   according to the *Geste des nobles français*.

was not that sword. Item, she said that she had this sword at Lagny, and after Lagny, she carried the sword of the aforementioned Burgundian right up to Compiègne, because this was a good sword for war, and good for giving hard clouts and strong blows.[43] But she said that it was not relevant to the trial to say where she had left it, and she would not reply on this for the time being. She then said that her brothers had her possessions, horses and sword, as far as she knew, and other things which were worth more than 12,000 écus.

Asked if she had a standard or banner when she went to Orléans, and of what colour, she answered that she had a standard with a field that was sown with lilies, and the world was depicted there, and two angels at the sides; and it was white in colour, of white linen or boucassin,[44] and on it were written the names Jhesus Maria, it seemed to her, and it was fringed with silk.

Asked if these names Jhesus Maria were written above, below or at the side, she replied at the side, or so it seemed to her.[45]

Asked about which she preferred, either her standard or the sword, she answered that she liked her standard four times as much as her sword.

Asked who had her make this painting on the standard, she replied: 'I have told you often that I have done nothing except by the command of God.' She also said that she herself carried the standard when she was attacking the enemy, in order to avoid killing anyone; and she said that she never killed anyone.

Asked what company her King gave her when he set her to work, she answered that he gave her ten or twelve thousand men, and that she went first to Orléans, to the fortress of Saint-Loup and then to the fortress of the bridge [the Tourelles].

Asked at which fortress she found herself when she had her men withdraw, she replied that she did not remember. She also said that

---

43 In April and May 1430.

44 Boucassin was a kind of white cloth that was used primarily for the lining of garments.

45 The judges were no doubt mindful of the contemporary debate between the Franciscans, who encouraged reverence for the names of Jesus and Mary, and the Dominicans who urged the papacy to forbid it as a satanic cult of the Antichrist: Pope Martin V had ruled that this devotion was acceptable if the name of Jesus was combined with a cross. J. Van Herwaarden, 'The appearance of Joan of Arc', in J. Van Herwaarden (ed.), *Joan of Arc: reality and myth*, Hilversum, 1994, pp. 63–4.

she was very sure, thanks to a revelation made to her, that she would secure the lifting of the siege of Orléans, and thus she had said this to the King before going there.

Asked if, when the attack was to be made, she did not tell her men that she would receive arrows, crossbolts and stones from engines or from cannons, she answered no. There were indeed a hundred wounded or more; but she certainly told her men not to be afraid and that they would raise the siege. She also said that at the assault made upon the fortress of the bridge [the Tourelles], she was wounded in the neck by an arrow or crossbolt, but she received great comfort from St Katherine and was healed in a fortnight. But she did not stop riding on horseback or carrying out her tasks because of this.

Asked if she knew beforehand that she would be wounded, she replied that she knew it well and had said this to her King, but that, notwithstanding this, she would not abandon the carrying out of her work.[46] And this was revealed to her by the voices of the two saints, that is to say the Blessed Katherine and the Blessed Margaret. She than said that she was the first to lean her ladder against the top of the ramparts of the fortress of the bridge [the Tourelles], and as she was lifting the ladder, she was wounded in the neck by the crossbolt, as she said.

Asked why she had not agreed to the treaty with the captain of Jargeau, she answered that the lords of her party replied to the English that they would not have the delay of a fortnight that they asked for, but that they should leave immediately, these men and their horses.[47] She also said that for her own part, she told the people of Jargeau to leave with [just] their doublets or tunics, and their lives safe, if they wished; otherwise they would be taken by assault.

Asked if she then deliberated with her counsel, that is to say with her voices, to find out if she should grant the delay or not, she replied that she did not remember.

46 See **8, 95**.

47 Jargeau was captured on 11 to 12 June 1429 and its captain was Sir Henry Biset, who died there.

38. Fifth public examination (Thursday 1 March 1431)

Source: Tisset (ed.), *Procès de condamnation*, I, pp. 81–90.

Language: Latin

According to the official record, the fifth public examination took place in the great hall at the castle of Rouen and was attended by Cauchon and fifty-seven clerics.

In their presence we summoned and required the said Joan to make and swear simply and absolutely to speak the truth about what was asked of her. She replied that she was ready to swear to speak the truth on all that she knew concerning the trial, as she had already said. Item, she said that she certainly knew things that did not concern the trial and there was no need to tell them. Then she said again: 'Everything that I truly know to relate to the trial, I will gladly tell.'

Item, again summoned and required as before to swear, she answered: 'What I know how to answer in truth, I will willingly say if it concerns the trial.' And she swore in this manner, touching the holy gospels. Then she said: 'I will willingly tell the truth about what I know that concerns the trial; and I will say everything just as I would speak if I were in front of the pope of Rome.'

Asked about what she said concerning our lord the pope and whom she believed to be the true pope, she replied by asking if there were two of them.

Asked if she had not had letters from the Count of Armagnac, asking which of the three sovereign pontiffs he should obey, she answered that the said Count did write letters to her on this matter, to which she replied, among other things, that she would give him an answer when she was in Paris, or left alone elsewhere. And she was about to mount her horse when she gave this answer.

And as for the copy of the letters of this Count and of Joan that we then had read to the audience, this same Joan was questioned as to whether this was her reply that was reproduced in the above copy. She replied that she thought that she had made this reply in part but not all of it.[48]

Asked if she had said that she knew what this Count should think

48 See **25**. The Latin trial record did not reproduce these letters at this point, but instead offered a cross-reference to the subsequent Seventy Articles where the correspondence was transcribed in full.

about this by means of the counsel of the King of Kings, she answered that she knew nothing about this.

Asked if she had any doubts about whom the Count should obey, she replied that she did not know how to instruct him about which person he should obey, because the Count asked to know whom God wanted him to obey. But as for herself, Joan held and believed that we should obey our lord the pope who was at Rome. She also said that she had said other things to the messenger of the Count that were not contained in this copy of the letter; and if the messenger had not left straight away, he would have been thrown into the water, but not however by her. Item, she said that regarding how the Count asked to know whom God wanted him to obey, she replied that she did not know; but she commanded him to do several things which were not put into writing. And as for herself, she believed in our lord the pope who is in Rome.

Asked why she had written that she would give an answer on that somewhere else, since she believed in the pope at Rome, she answered that the reply given by her was on another matter than the issue of the three sovereign pontiffs.

Asked if she had said that she would have counsel on the matter of the three sovereign pontiffs, she replied that she neither wrote, nor had anything written, concerning the three sovereign pontiffs. And she swore by her oath that she never wrote, nor had anything written.

Asked if she was in the habit of putting in her letters these names, 'Jhesus Maria', with a cross, she answered that in some she did put them and in others she did not; and sometimes she put the cross as a sign that the person of her party to whom she was writing should not do what she had written to him.

Then the letters that Joan herself sent to our lord the King [Henry VI], to my lord the Duke of Bedford and to others, were read to Joan.[49]

She was then asked if she recognised these letters. She replied yes, excepting three words: that is to say where it was written 'surrender to the Pucelle', it should read 'surrender to the King'; secondly, where it said 'commander of war'; and thirdly where it stated 'body for body', which were not in the letters that she had sent. She also said that no

---

49 See **4, 35**. The Latin trial record again offered a cross-reference to the Seventy Articles where this document was transcribed.

lord ever dictated these letters, but that she herself dictated them before they were sent; nevertheless they were indeed shown to certain men among her party.

Item, she said that before seven years were past, the English would lose a greater prize than they did before Orléans, and that they would lose everything in France. She added that the English would suffer a greater loss than they had ever had in France, and that this would be a great victory that God would send to the French.

Asked how she knew this, she answered: 'I know this for sure by revelation that has been made to me, and that this will happen within seven years; and I am greatly irritated that it has been delayed in this way.' She also said that she knew this by revelation, just as well as she knew that we were then in front of her.

Asked when it would happen, she replied that she did not know either the day or the hour.

Asked in what year it would happen, she answered: 'You will not have that yet: nevertheless I heartily wish that it may be before the feast of the Blessed St John [24 June].'

Asked if she had said that it would happen before the feast of St Martin in winter [11 November], she replied that she had said that before the feast of St Martin in winter many things would be seen and that it might be that it was the English who would be struck down.

Asked about what she said to John Grey, her guard, about this feast of St Martin, she answered: 'I have told you.'

Asked through whom she knew that this would happen, she replied that she knew it through Sts Katherine and Margaret.

Asked if St Gabriel was with St Michael when he came to her, she answered that she did not remember it.

Asked if she had spoken with Sts Katherine and Margaret since the previous Tuesday, she replied yes, but that she did not know at what time.

Asked on what day, she answered the day before and that day, and that there was not a day when she did not hear them.

Asked if she always saw them in the same clothing, she replied that she always saw them in the same form and their figures were very richly crowned. She did not speak about other clothing. Item, she said that she did not know anything about their robes.

Asked how she knew that the apparition was a man or a woman, she answered that she knew it for certain and recognised them by their voices, and that they revealed it to her; she did not know anything except by revelation and the command of God.

Asked what she saw of their figure, she replied that she saw their face.

Asked if the saints who appeared to her had hair, she answered: 'It is good to know.'

Asked if there was anything between their crowns and their hair, she replied no.

Asked if their hair was long and hanging down, she answered: 'I do not know anything [about this].'[50] She also said that she did not know if they had anything like arms, or if they had other kinds of members. Item, she said that they spoke very well and marvellously, and she understood them very well.

Asked how they spoke since they did not have any members, she replied: 'I leave that to God.' Item, she said that the voice was gentle, soft and low, and spoke the French language.

Asked if St Margaret did not speak the English language, she answered: 'Why should she speak English when she is not on the English side?'

Asked if on the crowned heads there were not rings of gold or other substances, she replied: 'I do not know anything.'

Asked if she herself did not have some rings, she answered, speaking to us, the Bishop [Cauchon]: 'You have one of mine; give it back to me.' Item, she said that the Burgundians had another ring. And she asked that, if we had this ring, we might show it to her.

Asked who gave the ring to her which the Burgundians had, she replied that it was her father or her mother, and it seemed to her that the names Jhesus Maria were written on it – she did not know who had them written; she did not think that there was a stone in it, as it seemed to her. And this ring was given to her at Domremy. Item, she said that her brother gave her the other ring which we had and she charged us to give it to the Church. Item, she said that she never cured anyone with any of her rings.

50 Intriguingly St Katherine's hair was sometimes depicted in devotional books as being short, in the masculine fashion, though this was not the norm in sculptures, altar paintings and other contexts: K. A. Winstead, 'St Katherine's hair', in J. Jenkins and K. J. Lewis (eds), *St Katherine of Alexandria: texts and contexts in western medieval Europe*, Turnhout, 2003, pp. 171–99.

Asked if Sts Katherine and Margaret spoke with her under the tree of which mention was made above, she answered: 'I do not know anything.'

Asked if the saints spoke with her at the spring which is near to the tree, she replied yes, and that she heard them there. But she did not know what they said to her there.

Asked about what these same saints promised her, there or elsewhere, she answered that they did not make any promises to her, except by the permission of God.

Asked what promises they made to her, she replied: 'That is not part of your trial.' And, among other things, they told her that her King would be restored in his kingdom, whether his enemies wished it or not. She also said that they promised to lead this Joan to heaven and so she asked it of them.

Asked if she had [received] any other promise, she answered that there was another promise, but that she would not say it and that it did not concern the trial. And she said that within three months she would reveal the other promise.

Asked if the voices had told her that within three months, she would be delivered from prison, she replied: 'That is not in part of your trial. Nevertheless, I do not know when I will be freed.' And she said that those who wished to remove her from this world, could well leave it before her.

Asked if her counsel had not told her that she would be delivered out of her present prison, she answered: 'Speak to me in three months' time; I will reply then.' She added: 'Ask those present, on their oath, if this concerns the trial.'

Asked afterwards, when those present had deliberated and all declared that this did concern the trial, she said: 'I have always told you clearly that you cannot know everything. One day I must be freed. And I need permission to say this to you; that is why I ask for a delay.'

Asked if the voices forbade her to speak the truth, she answered: 'Do you want me to tell what concerns the King of France? There are many things that do not concern the trial.' She also said that she knew for certain her King would win the kingdom of France, and she knew this just as well as she knew that we were in front of her in judgement. She added that she would have been dead if this had not been the revelation that comforted her each day.

Asked what she did with her mandrake, she replied that she did not have a mandrake and had never had one; but she had heard it said that there was one of them near to her village, and she never saw any. She also said that she had heard it said that this was a dangerous and evil thing to keep; but she did not know what purpose it served.[51]

Asked in what place the mandrake of which she had heard speak was found, she answered that she had heard it said that it was in the earth, near to the tree which had been spoken of before; but she did not know the spot. She also said that she had heard it said that a hazel tree grew over the mandrake.

Asked what she had heard about the use of the mandrake, she replied that she had heard that it attracted money, but she did not believe any of it. And she said that her voices never told her anything about this.

Asked how St Michael looked when he appeared, she answered that she did not see his crown, and she knew nothing about her clothing.

Asked if he was naked,[52] she replied: 'Do you think God does not have the means to clothe him?'

Asked if he had hair, she answered: 'Why would it have been cut off?' She added that she had not seen the Blessed Michael since she left the castle of Crotoy, and she did not see him very often. And finally she said that she did not know whether he had hair.[53]

Asked whether he had a set of scales, she answered: 'I do not know anything of this.'[54] Item, she said that she was filled with great joy when she saw him and it seemed to her that, when she saw him, she was not in a state of mortal sin. Item, she said Sts Katherine and Margaret had her confess willingly from time to time, in turn. Item, she did not know if she herself was in mortal sin.

Asked if, she believed herself to be in mortal sin when she confessed, she answered that she did not know whether she was in mortal sin and she did not believe that she had done such deeds. She said: 'And

51 Mandrake was characterised by an enormous root thought to be shaped like a human body, and was considered a magical plant with numerous uses, mainly harmful.

52 The only surviving manuscript of the *Minute française* to include materials from this session, manuscript O, restarts at this point.

53 Joan was brought to Crotoy in Ponthieu in November 1430 when the Burgundians delivered her to the English, and then departed for Rouen on 20 December. This discussion of St Michael's hair does not appear in the *Minute française*.

54 St Michael was often represented with a set of scales in his hands to weigh souls.

may it please God that I will never be [in mortal sin], and may it also please Him that I may never commit, nor have committed, deeds by which my soul may be burdened.'

Asked what sign she gave to her King that she came from God, she replied: 'I have always answered that you will not drag that from my mouth. Go and ask him.'

Asked if she did not swear to reveal what was asked of her concerning the trial, she answered: 'I have said to you not long ago that I will not tell you what could concern or what deals with our King. And as for what is about him, I will not tell you.'[55]

Asked if she did not know the sign that she gave to the King, she replied: 'You will not learn it from me.'

Then, because it was said to her that this concerned the trial, she answered: 'I will not tell you anything about that which I have promised to keep most secret.' And she also said: 'I have promised this in such a place that I could not tell you without perjury.'

Asked to whom she promised this, she replied that she promised Sts Katherine and Margaret, and this was shown to the King. Item, she said that she promised this to the two saints without them asking her. And Joan herself did so at her own volition because too many people might have asked this of her if she had not made this promise to the saints.

Asked if there was anyone other than her in her presence when she showed the sign to her King, she answered that she thought that there was no one, although many people were fairly near.

Asked if she saw the crown on the head of her King when she showed him the sign, she answered: 'I cannot tell you without perjury.'

Asked if her King had a crown when he was at Reims, she replied that, as far as she knew, her King took the crown that he found at Reims with pleasure, but a very rich one was brought to him afterwards.[56] And he did this to hasten [the ceremony], at the request of the people of Reims, to avoid the burden of the men-at-arms;[57] and

55 According to the *Minute française*, Joan ended on a more positive note by promising to tell everything that was relevant to the trial.

56 The normal regalia was housed at the abbey of Saint-Denis, which remained in enemy hands until Charles VII and the royal army approached Paris two months after his coronation.

57 In other words the expense and disruption caused to the city by the visiting troops.

if he had waited, he would have had a crown a thousand times richer.

Asked if she saw this crown which was more sumptuous, she answered: 'I cannot tell you without committing perjury. And if I have not seen it, I have heard it said that it is so rich and opulent.'

39. Sixth public examination (Saturday 3 March 1431)

Source: Tisset (ed.), *Procès de condamnation*, I, pp. 91–109.

Language: Latin

According to the official record, the sixth public examination in the great hall at the castle of Rouen was attended by Cauchon and forty clerics. According to the *Minute française*, the questioning was again undertaken by Jean Beaupère.

In their presence, we required Joan to swear simply and absolutely to speak the truth about that which would be asked of her. She answered: 'I am ready to swear as I have already done.' And she swore in this way, while touching the holy gospels.

Then, because she had said that St Michael had wings, and with this she had not spoken of the bodies and members of Sts Katherine and Margaret, she was asked what she wanted to say on this subject.[58] To which she replied: 'I have told you what I know, and I will not answer anything more to you.' She also said that she had seen St Michael and the saintly women so clearly that she knew for sure that they were saints in heaven.

Asked if she saw anything of them besides the face, she answered: 'I have told you all that I know about that: and I would rather have you cut my throat than tell you everything that I know.' Item, she said that she would willingly tell everything she knew concerning the trial.

Asked if she believed that St Michael and St Gabriel have natural heads, she replied: 'I saw them with my eyes and I believe it is them as firmly as [I believe in] God.'[59]

---

58 The matter of St Michael having wings had not appeared previously in either the *Minute française* or the *Procès*, suggesting that this topic had been omitted by the notaries.

59 The *Minute française* includes an additional question and response omitted in the official Latin record: 'Asked whether she believed that God made them with heads as she saw them, she answered: 'I saw them with my own eyes. I will not say anything else to you.'

Asked if she believed that God created them in the fashion and form that she saw them, she answered yes.

Asked if she believed that God created them in that fashion and form from the beginning, she replied: 'You will not have anything more from me than I have told you, for the present.'

Asked if she had known by revelation that she would escape, she answered: 'That does not concern your trial. Do you want me to speak against myself?'

Asked if her voices told her anything about this, she replied: 'That is not in your trial; I refer myself to God. And if everything concerned you, I would tell you everything.' She added that, by her faith, she did not know at what hour or day she would escape.

Asked if the voices had told her anything in general about this, she answered: 'Yes, indeed; they told me that I will be freed, though I do not know the day or the hour, and that I must put on a brave face.'

Asked if, when she came to her King for the first time, he asked her if it was a revelation that had made her change her clothing, she replied: 'I have answered that for you; nevertheless I do not recall if I was asked this. And it is written at Poitiers.'

Asked if she remembered whether the masters who examined her under the other authority, some for a month and others for three weeks, had questioned her about her change of clothing, she answered: 'I do not recall. But they asked me where I had taken this male outfit; and I told them that I had taken it at Vaucouleurs.'

Asked if these masters questioned her as to whether it was by her voices that she had taken this clothing, she replied: 'I do not recall.'

Asked if her Queen [Marie d'Anjou, wife of Charles VII] did not question her on the subject of the change of clothing when she paid her a visit for the first time, she answered: 'I do not remember.'

Asked if her King, Queen and others of her party did not sometimes ask her to set aside the clothing of a man, she replied: 'That is not part of your trial.'

Asked if she was not asked this at the castle of Beaurevoir, she answered: 'Yes, truly. And I replied that I would not set it aside without the permission of God.'[60]

60 The Latin text does not include the following from the *Minute française*: 'Item, she said that the young lady of Luxembourg asked my lord of Luxembourg that she

Item, she said that the unmarried lady of Luxembourg and the lady of Beaurevoir offered her a woman's dress, or the cloth to make one, asking Joan to wear such an outfit.[61] And she replied that she did not have the permission of God, and that it was not yet time.

Asked if my lord Jean de Pressy and others at Arras offered her a woman's dress, she answered that he and many others often asked her to take an outfit of that sort.[62]

Asked if she believed that she would have been delinquent or in mortal sin for taking a woman's dress, she replied that she did better to obey and to serve her sovereign Lord, that is to say God. Item, she said that if she had had to take this woman's clothing, she would rather have done it at the request of the two ladies than of any other ladies that were in France, save her Queen.

Asked if, when God revealed to her that she should change her outfit for the clothing of a man, it was by the voice of St Michael, or by the voice of St Katherine or St Margaret, she answered: 'You will have nothing more now.'

Asked if, when her King set her to work and she had her standard made, the other men-at-arms did not have pennons made in the manner and following the example of her pennon, she replied: 'It is well known that lords use their own arms.' Item, she also said that some of her companions-in-arms did have pennons made at their pleasure, and others did not.

Asked of what material they had them made, whether this was of linen or of woollen cloth, she answered that it was of white satin, and on some there were fleurs-de-lys. And Joan only had two or three lances in her company, but her companions-in-arms sometimes had

---

not be handed over to the English': this statement was instead bizarrely inserted under article 16 of the Seventy Articles presented by Estivet. This also marks the point where the incomplete manuscript of the *Minute française*, manuscript U, begins.

61 The unmarried lady (*damoiselle*) of Luxembourg was Jeanne, Countess of Ligny and of Saint-Pol after the death of her great-nephew in 1420; she was the godmother of Charles VII and supported the Valois party, but was living with her nephew Jean Count of Luxembourg when Joan of Arc was being held at Beaurevoir; the lady of Luxembourg was the count's wife, Jeanne de Béthune.

62 Joan was taken to Arras at the very end of September 1430, after her detention at Beaurevoir. Jean de Pressy was a knight, Lord of Mesnil and a councillor and chamberlain to the Duke of Burgundy; he also served as a member of the Great Council of Henry VI in France.

pennons made resembling hers and they did this only to distinguish their men from others.

Asked if the pennons were very often renewed, she replied: 'I do not know. When the lances were broken, new ones were made.'

Asked if she had sometimes said that the pennons made to resemble hers were more fortunate, she answered that sometimes she certainly did say to her men: 'Drive boldly into the English', and she herself would go there.

Asked if she had told them to bear the pennons boldly and that they would have good fortune, she replied that she had indeed told them what happened and what would happen again.

Asked if she put, or had holy water put on the pennons when they were first taken up, she answered: 'I do not know anything about that. And if it was done, it was not by my command.'

Asked if she did not see them sprinkled with holy water, she replied: 'That is not part of your trial. And if I had seen it done, I am not now advised to answer.'

Asked if her companions-in-arms did not have the names 'Jhesus Maria' written on their pennons, she answered: 'By my faith, I do not know anything of this.'

Asked if she went around an altar or a church with pieces of cloth to be made into pennons, or had others go around in a kind of procession, she replied no and that she had never seen it done.

Asked what it was she wore at the back of her helmet when she was before the town of Jargeau, and if it was something round, she answered: 'By my faith, there was nothing.'[63]

Asked if she had ever known Brother Richard, she replied: 'I had never seen him when I came before the town of Troyes.'[64]

Asked how Brother Richard acted towards her, she answered that the people of Troyes, so she thought, sent him to her, saying that they questioned whether Joan was not a thing sent from God; and when this same Brother approached her, he made the sign of the cross and threw holy water. She then said to him: 'Approach boldly, I shall not fly away.'

---

63 On 11 June 1429.

64 Joan came to Troyes in July 1429. For Brother Richard, see page 31 above.

Asked if she herself had seen, or had any images or paintings made of herself and in her likeness, she replied that at Arras she saw a painting in the hands of a Scotsman; this depicted her fully armed, presenting letters to her King, on bended knee.[65] And she said that she had never seen or had any other image or painting made of her.

Asked if in the house of her host in Orléans there was a tableau of three women painted with the inscription 'Justice, peace, union', she answered that she knew nothing of that.[66]

Asked if she knew that those of her party had had a service, a mass and prayers offered in her honour, she replied that she knew nothing of it; and if they had had any service, it was not by her command; on the other hand, if they prayed for her it seemed to her that they were not doing wrong.

Asked if those of her party firmly believed that she was sent by God, she answered: 'I do not know whether they believe it, and I refer you to their opinions; but if they do not believe it, I am still sent by God.'

Asked if she believed that they were right in thinking that she was sent by God, she replied: 'If they believe that I am sent by God, they are not deceived in this.'

Asked if she did not know the opinions of those of her party when they kissed her feet, her hands and her garments, she answered that many came to see her willingly, but they kissed her hands as little as she could help; but the poor people gladly came to her because she did not do them any injury, but rather helped them by her power.

Asked what reverence the burghers of Troyes paid to her at the entry into the town, she replied that they paid no reverence to her. She added that she thought that Brother Richard entered the town of Troyes with her and her men, but she did not remember if she saw him entering.

Asked if Brother Richard gave a sermon at the arrival of Joan into the town, she answered that she did not stop there for long and did not sleep in the town; and as for the sermon, she did not know anything.[67]

Asked if she remained for a long time at Reims, she replied that as far

---

65 The *Minute français* reported that this took place at Reims.

66 Joan's host in Orléans between 29 April and 8 May 1429 was the Treasurer of the city, Jacques Boucher, whose daughter Charlotte testified during the Nullification trial [86].

67 Joan entered Troyes on 11 July 1429.

as she believed, she and her men stayed there for five or six days.[68]

Asked if she lifted any child to the baptismal font [acted as god-mother] there, she answered that at Troyes she lifted one; but she did not recall that she lifted any at Reims or at Château-Thierry, though she lifted two at Saint-Denis in France. And she gladly gave the name of Charles to the boys, in honour of her King, and the name of Joan to the girls; and sometimes she named them as the mothers wished.

Asked if the women of the town did not touch their rings to the ring that Joan wore on her finger, she replied: 'Many women touched my hands and my rings, but I do not know their thought or intention.'

Asked who were the men of her company who caught butterflies in her standard in front of Château-Thierry,[69] she answered that this was never done by their party, but it was those of the other party who invented it.

Asked what she did at Reims with the gloves with which her King was crowned, she replied that the gloves were distributed as gifts to the knights and nobles who were present;[70] and there was one of them who had lost his gloves, but she did not say that she would find them. She also said that her standard was in the church of Reims; and it seemed to her that it was fairly near to the altar when the King was crowned, and she herself held it for a short time. But she did not know whether Brother Richard bore it.

Asked if, when she was going through the country, she often received the sacrament of the Eucharist and of penance when she was in the towns [bonnes villes], she answered yes, from time to time.

Asked if she received these sacraments in male clothing, she answered yes, but she did not remember receiving them in armour.

Asked why she took the hackney of the Bishop of Senlis, she replied that this hackney was bought for two hundred saluts.[71] She did not know whether he received them or not, but there was an arrangement

68 Joan stayed at Reims from 16 to 21 July 1429.

69 It is not clear what the judges were imagining by this curious question. Joan was there on 7 August 1429.

70 Gloves were often distributed to participants in public events including royal feasts and dubbing ceremonies, as well as episcopal elections and entries into cities.

71 A hackney was a horse of middle size and quality, used for ordinary riding. The Bishop of Senlis was Jean Fouquerel, who fled from the city in August 1429 because of the advancing Valois army. A 'salut d'or' was a coin struck during by the administration of Henry VI in France.

and he was paid; she herself wrote to this Bishop that he could take it back if he wanted, and that she did not want it, because it was useless for heavy work.

Asked what was the age of the child that she restored to life at Lagny,[72] she answered that the child was three days old and it was brought before an image of Our Lady at Lagny [at the altar of Notre-Dame-de-Lagny in the church of Saint-Pierre], and Joan was told that the young girls of the town were in front of this image, and she might wish to pray that God and Our Lady would give life to the baby. Then she went and prayed with the other young girls, and at last life appeared in the child who yawned three times and was then baptised. It died immediately and was buried in consecrated ground. For three days, it was said, there was no sign of life in the child and he was as black as Joan's tunic, but when he yawned, the colour began to return to him. And Joan was with the young girls, praying on their knees, before Our Lady.

Asked if it was said in the town that she had brought about this resuscitation,[73] and that it was due to her prayers, she replied that she did not inquire about this.

Asked if she had known or seen Catherine de La Rochelle, she answered yes, at Jargeau and at Montfaucon in the duchy of Berry.[74]

Asked if Catherine showed her a lady wearing a dress whom she said appeared to her sometimes, she replied no.

Asked what this Catherine said to her, she answered that Catherine told her that a white lady dressed in cloth of gold came to this Catherine, telling her that she should go through the towns [bonnes villes] and that her King would give heralds and trumpets to her to proclaim that whoever had gold, silver or hidden treasure should immediately bring it; and that those who had these things hidden and would not bring them, would be easily discovered by this Catherine, and that she would certainly know how to find these treasures, and that she would pay for Joan's men-at-arms in this way. At this Joan

---

72 The Latin translation deliberately implies that Joan herself was instrumental in curing him: the original *Minute française* merely said: 'Asked what was the age of the child at Lagny that she went to see ...' Joan was in Lagny between April and May 1430.

73 The original *Minute française* says: 'Asked it if were not said by the town that she had brought this about'.

74 See pages 31 to 32 above.

replied to Catherine that she should return to her husband, do her housework and look after her children. And to be certain regarding Catherine, Joan spoke to St Katherine or St Margaret who said to her that this was just madness and that this was all nothing. And she wrote to [tell] her King what he ought to do in this matter, and when she came to him, she told him that this was folly and that there was nothing to the case of this Catherine. Nevertheless Brother Richard wanted to set this Catherine to work, and Brother Richard and this Catherine were thus annoyed with Joan.

Asked if she spoke with this Catherine about the project to go to La Charité-sur-Loire, she replied that the said Catherine advised her not to go there and that it was too cold, and she said to Joan that she would not go.[75] Item, the same Joan said to Catherine, who wished to go to the Duke of Burgundy in order to make peace, that it seemed to her that peace would not be found except at the end of a lance. Item, she said that she asked this Catherine if the white lady who appeared to her came every night, saying that for this reason, she would sleep with her in the same bed. And in fact Joan slept there and watched until midnight and saw nothing; then she went to sleep. And when the morning came, she asked Catherine if the white lady had come to her. Catherine replied to her yes, while Joan was sleeping, and that she had not been able to wake her. Then Joan asked if this lady would come another night, and Catherine answered yes. Joan then slept for the day so that she could stay awake the whole of the following night. And that night she went to bed with Catherine and watched all the night; but she saw nothing, although she often asked Catherine whether this lady would come or not, and Catherine answered: 'Yes, shortly.'

Then when Joan was asked about what she did in the ditches of La Charité, she answered that she had an assault made there, but she did not sprinkle holy water or have it sprinkled.

Asked why she did not enter this town of La Charité since she had a command from God, she replied: 'Who told you that I had this command from God?'

Asked if she had counsel from her voice, she answered that she herself wanted to come to France,[76] but the men-at-arms told her that it was better to go first before the town of La Charité.

75 Joan laid siege to La Charité-sur-Loire, held by Perrinet Gressart, in November 1429.

76 After the siege of Saint-Pierre-le-Moûtier between October and November 1429.

Asked if she remained in the tower of Beaurevoir for a long time, she replied that she was there for four months or thereabouts [from August until November 1430]. And she said that when she knew that the English were to come and take her, she was very angry; though the voices often forbade her to jump from the tower, at last, out of fear of the English, she jumped and commended herself to God and to Our Lady, and she was injured. And after she had jumped, the voice of St Katherine told her to put a good face on it,[77] and that the people at Compiègne would have aid. Item, she said that she always prayed with her counsel for the people of Compiègne.[78]

Asked what she said when she had jumped, she answered that some people said that she had died, and as soon as it appeared to the Burgundians that she was alive, they told her that she had jumped.

Asked if she said at that time that she would rather die than be in the hands of the English, she replied that she would rather render her soul to God than be in their hands.

Asked if she was then very angry and blasphemed the name of God, she answered that she never blasphemed the saints, and that she was never accustomed to swear.

Asked if she had renounced God in the matter of Soissons and of the captain who had surrendered the town, in saying that if she held this captain, she would have him cut into four pieces, she replied that she never renounced any saint, and that those who said or reported this, had misunderstood.[79]

40. First private examination (Saturday 10 March 1431)

Source: Tisset (ed.), *Procès de condamnation*, I, pp. 110–18.

Language: Latin

Cauchon consulted with his fellow clerics between 4 and 9 March, and then decided to change tack by conducting private interrogations of Joan in her cell in the castle of Rouen. He was assisted at the first private examination by

77 The *Minute française adds:* 'and that she would be healed'.

78 The town of Compiègne was relieved from the Burgundian siege on 15 October 1430.

79 In May 1430, Guichard Bournel, a Picard squire and captain of Soissons, refused to hand the town over to Joan and her companions; instead he delivered it to the troops of the Duke of Burgundy in July in return for 4000 saluts d'or from the king of England.

Jean de La Fontaine, Nicolas Midi, Gérard Feuillet, Jean Secard and Jean Massieu. They began the proceedings by again calling upon Joan to swear to tell the truth.

Then Joan was questioned by Master Jean de La Fontaine, specially charged and deputed by us for the purpose. And he asked her, by the oath that she had sworn, from where she had set off the last time that she went to Compiègne. She answered that she had left from the town of Crépy-en-Valois.[80]

Asked if she spent a long time in Compiègne before making a sally, she replied that she came at a time [that was kept] secret in the morning and entered into the town without her enemies knowing anything, so she thought, and on the same day, towards evening, she made the sally in which she was taken.[81]

Asked if, when she was attacking, the bells were rung, she answered that if they were rung, it was not done at her command nor did she know it; and she did not think so, nor did she remember if she had said that they might be rung.

Asked if she made this sally at the command of her voice, she replied that in the previous week of Easter, when she found herself in the ditches of Melun, she was told by her voices, namely by Sts Katherine and Margaret, that she would be captured before the feast of St John [24 June], and that it was necessary that this happen in this way, and that she should not be astounded but should accept it gladly, and God would aid her.

Asked if it was not said to her by her voices after [being at] this place of Melun that she would be taken, she answered yes, several times and nearly every day. And she asked her voices that she might die soon after being taken, without the long torment of prison. And these voices told her that she should accept it all gladly and that it was necessary that it should happen this way; but they did not tell her the hour. And if she had known the hour, she would not have gone there. She had often begged these voices in order to find out the hour of her capture, but they did not tell it to her.

Asked if she would have gone if her voices had ordered her to sally out of Compiègne, letting her know that she would be taken, she

80 Joan left Crépy-en-Valois late in the evening of 22 May 1430 and arrived at Compiègne shortly before dawn.
81 Joan was captured on 23 May 1430.

replied that if she had known the hour and that she was to be taken, she would not have gone willingly; nevertheless she would have followed the command of the voices, whatever it would bring for her.

Asked if, when she made this sortie from Compiègne, she had had any voice or revelation to go out and make this raid, she answered that she did not know about her capture that day and that she did not have another command to go out, but it had always been said to her that it was necessary that she should be a prisoner.

Asked if she crossed over the bridge of Compiègne when she made this sortie, she replied that she went over the bridge and the boulevard,[82] and was accompanied by the men of her party, against the men of Lord Jean de Luxembourg and drove them back two times as far as the camp or lodgings of the Burgundians, and on the third time, right up to the middle of the road. Then the English who were there cut off Joan and her men from the road. And while retreating, she was captured in the fields on the side towards Picardy, near to the boulevard. And between the place where she was captured and Compiègne there was the river in the middle and the boulevard with its ditch; there was nothing more in between.

Asked if the world and two angels, etc., were painted on the banner which she carried, she answered yes and that she only ever had the one.

Asked what it signified, to paint God there holding the world, accompanied by two angels, she replied that Sts Katherine and Margaret told her that she should take the banner and carry it boldly, and that she might have the King of Heaven painted there. And she told this to her King, very much against her will; and she did not know anything more about its significance.

Asked if she had a coat of arms, she answered that she never did, but her King gave arms to her brothers, namely a shield of azure on which were two fleurs-de-lys of gold and a sword in the middle;[83] and in that town [Rouen?] she described these arms to a painter who asked her what arms she bore. Item, she said that this was given by the King to her brothers, not by her request and without revelation.

---

82 The boulevard was a fortification with a drawbridge that defended the head of the bridge.

83 Charles VII had ennobled Joan of Arc and her family by letters published in December 1429.

Asked if she had a horse when she was captured, either a charger or a hackney, she replied that she was then on horseback, on a demi-charger.[84]

Asked who had given her this horse, she answered that her King, or the men of her King, gave it to her out of the King's money; and she had five chargers paid for by her King, not counting her hackneys which numbered more than seven.

Asked if she ever had other riches than these horses from her King, she replied that she asked for nothing from her King except good arms, good horses and the money to pay the men of her household.

Asked if she had a treasury, she answered that it was worth ten or twelve thousand écus, but this was not a great treasury to conduct the war and this was very little indeed; and she thought that it was her brothers who had this. And she said that what she had was properly her King's [property].

Asked about the sign that she gave to her King when she went to him, she replied that it was as worthy, honourable, clearly credible, good and powerful as there was in this world.

Asked why she did not wish to tell or show this sign, since she wanted to see the sign of Catherine de La Rochelle, she answered that she would not have asked to know the sign of Catherine if it had been shown just as well as her sign was in front of the notable churchmen and others, archbishops and bishops, namely before the Archbishop of Reims and others whose names she did not know,[85] Charles de Bourbon,[86] my lord of La Trémouïlle,[87] the Duke of Alençon,[88] and many other knights were there who saw and heard it as distinctly as she, Joan, saw the men who spoke to her and who were in front of her. And moreover she already knew through Sts Katherine and Margaret that in this regard, Catherine was entirely worthless.

Asked if this sign of Joan still survived, she replied that it certainly did and that it would last for a thousand years and more. Item, she

---

84 In the *Minute française*, Joan went on to say that she was captured while on this demi-charger. A charger was commonly used on the battlefield and a hackney or palfrey was employed for normal service.

85 The Archbishop of Reims was Regnault de Chartres who became Chancellor of the King of France in 1424 and died in 1445.

86 Charles de Bourbon, then Count of Clermont (1401–56).

87 Georges lord of La Trémouïlle (1382–1446).

88 Jean Duke of Alençon (1407–76). See **94**.

said that the sign was in the treasury of the King.

Asked if it was of gold [or] silver, a precious stone, or a crown, she answered: 'I will not tell you anything more and no man could describe a thing so rich as this sign; but the sign that you need is for God to deliver me from your hands and that is the most certain sign that He knows to send to you.' Item, she then said that when she had to leave to go to her King, it was said to her by her voices: 'Go boldly: when you are before the King, he will have a good sign to receive you and to believe in you.'

Asked what reverence she showed to the sign when it came to her King and whether it came from God, she replied that she gave thanks to God for the fact that He had delivered her from the pain that the clerks of that party were causing who argued against her; and many times she knelt down. Item, she said that an angel from God and not from anyone else, gave the sign to her King, and she thanked God a number of times for this. She also said that the clerks stopped arguing with her when they had this sign.

Asked if the churchmen of her party saw this sign, she answered that when her King and those who were with him saw this sign, and the angel himself who gave it, she asked her King if he was happy, and he replied yes. And then she left and went to a nearby chapel and she then heard that after her departure more than three hundred people saw this sign. She added that for love of her and so that the men would stop questioning her, God had allowed the men of her party who wished to see this sign, to view it.

Asked if her King and she paid reverence to the angel when he brought this sign, she replied that she did pay reverence, kneeling down and uncovering her head.

41. Second private examination (Monday 12 March 1431)

Source: Tisset (ed.), *Procès de condamnation*, I, pp. 121–6.

Language: Latin

On Monday 12 March, Cauchon received the letter of commission (4 March 1431) which authorised Jean Le Maistre to act on behalf of the Inquisitor of France, Jean Graverent. Joan was then interrogated in her prison cell by Cauchon, Jean de La Fontaine, Nicolas Midi, Gérard Feuillet, Thomas Fiefvet, Pasquier de Vaux and Nicolas de Hubent. The proceedings began with the standard request that Joan swear to speak truthfully.

Then questioned at our order by Master Jean de La Fontaine, firstly about whether the angel that brought the sign to her King, of which mention was made above, did not speak, she answered yes, and that he told her King to set Joan to work and the country would be relieved.

Asked if the angel that brought the sign to her King was the same angel that had first appeared to her, she replied that it was always one and the same and that he never failed her.

Asked if this angel did not fail her by not bringing good fortune in that she was captured, she answered that she believed that since this pleased God, it was better for her to be taken prisoner.

Asked if this angel did not fail her by not bringing her grace, she replied: 'How would he fail me, when he comforts me every day?' And she understood, as she said, that this comfort came from Sts Katherine and Margaret.

Asked if she called these Sts Katherine and Margaret, or if they came without being called, she answered that they often came without being called and sometimes, if they did not come, she would certainly ask God to send them.

Asked if sometimes the saints did not come when she called them, she replied that she had never needed them without having them.

Asked if St Denis ever appeared to her, she answered no, not as far she knew.[89]

Asked if she spoke to God when she promised Him to keep her virginity, she replied that it should be quite enough to promise it to those who were sent by him, namely Sts Katherine and Margaret.

Asked about what moved her to have a man in the town of Toul cited in a case of marriage, she answered: 'I did not have him cited, but it was he who cited me; and there I swore before the judge to tell the truth.' And finally, she said that she had not made any promise to this man. Item, she said that the first time that she heard her voice, she made a vow to keep her virginity as long as it would please God and she was then thirteen years old, or thereabouts. Item, she said that her voices assured her that she would win her trial in the town of Toul.

Asked if she spoke to her parish priest or any other churchman about these visions which she claimed to have, she replied no, excepting

---

89 St Denis was the patron saint of the kings of France: C. Beaune, *The Birth of an Ideology: myths and symbols of nationhood in later medieval France*, Berkeley, 1992, ch. 1.

only to Robert de Baudricourt and to her King. She added that her voices did not compel her to conceal them, but she was very afraid of revealing them out of fear that the Burgundians would hinder her journey; and in particular, she greatly feared that her father would prevent her from making her journey.

Asked if she believed that she had done well in leaving without the permission of her father and mother, when she should honour her father and mother, she answered that in all other things she certainly obeyed them, excepting this departure; but afterwards she wrote to them and they pardoned her.

Asked if she thought she was sinning when she left her father and mother, she replied that since God commanded it, it was necessary to do so. She also said that since God commanded it, if she had had a hundred fathers and mothers, or had been the daughter of the King, nevertheless she would have left.

Asked if she asked her voices whether she should tell her father and mother about her departure, she answered that as for her father and mother, the voices would have been very happy for her to tell them, were it not for the trouble that they would have caused if she had told them about her departure; and as for her, she would not have told them about this for anything. Item, she said the voices left it to her to tell her father and mother or to be silent.

Asked if she paid reverence to St Michael and to the angels when she saw them, she replied yes, and she kissed the ground on which they had stood after their departure.

Asked if these angels remained with her for a long time, she answered that they often came among Christians and were not seen, and she often saw them among Christians.

Asked if she had had letters from St Michael or from her voices, she replied: 'I do not have permission to tell you and I will gladly tell you what I know in a week from now.'

Asked if her voices did not call her 'daughter of God', 'daughter of the Church', 'daughter with a great heart', she answered that before the raising of the siege of Orléans and every day since, when they spoke with her, they often called her 'Joan the Pucelle, daughter of God'.

Asked since she called herself daughter of God, why she would not say the *Pater Noster* willingly, she replied that she would willingly say it, and that recently when she refused to say it, she did this with the intention that we, the aforesaid Bishop [Cauchon], should hear her in confession.[90]

42. Third private examination (Monday 12 March 1431)

Source: Tisset (ed.), *Procès de condamnation*, I, pp. 126–9.
Language: Latin

Cauchon and the same six clerics gathered again in Joan's cell that afternoon.

Joan was questioned by the said La Fontaine at our command, and firstly concerning the dreams that her father was said to have had about her before she left his house. To this she replied that when she was in the house of her father and mother, it was often said to her by her mother that her father said that he dreamed that his daughter Joan would leave with men-at-arms; and her father and mother took great care to watch over her, and they kept her in great subjection: and she was obedient in all things except for the trial which she faced in the town of Toul on the matter of marriage. Item, she said that she heard it said to her mother that her father told her brothers: 'Truly if I thought that what I have dreamed about my daughter would happen, I would want you to drown her, and if you would not do it, I would drown her myself.' And her father and mother almost lost their senses when she left to go to the stronghold of Vaucouleurs.

Asked if these thoughts and dreams came to her father after she had her visions, she answered yes, more than two years after she had her voices.

Asked if it was at the request of Robert de Baudricourt or herself that she first took up male clothing, she replied that it was of her own accord and not at the request of any living man.

Asked if the voice commanded her to wear the clothing of a man, she answered: 'Everything that I have done well, I have done by the command of my voices; and as for the clothing, I will answer that another time; I am not now advised, but tomorrow I will answer that.'

Asked if she thought that she was doing wrong in taking male clothing, she replied no; and even now, if she were back with those of her own party in this male clothing, it seemed to her that this would be of great benefit for France to do as she did at first, before her capture.

90 See the end of **34**.

Asked how she would have delivered the Duke of Orléans, she answered that she would have captured enough Englishmen on this side of the sea to have him again [through an exchange of prisoners]; and if she did not have enough on this side, she would have crossed the sea to go in force to find him in England.

Asked if Sts Margaret and Katherine had told her absolutely and without condition that she would take enough men to have the Duke of Orléans, who was in England, or otherwise that she would cross the sea to find him,[91] she replied yes: and she said this to her King and that he let her have her way with the lords of England who were then prisoners. She also said that if she had gone on without hindrance for three years she would have delivered this Duke. Item, she said that there was a shorter time limit to do it than three years and longer than one year, but she did not remember it.

Asked what was the sign that she gave to her King, she answered that she would take counsel from St Katherine on this.

43. Fourth private examination (Tuesday 13 March 1431)

Source: Tisset (ed.), *Procès de condamnation*, I, pp. 133–42.

Language: Latin

Pierre Cauchon, Jean Le Maistre, Jean de La Fontaine, Nicolas Midi, Gérard Feuillet, Nicolas de Hubent and Isembart de La Pierre gathered in Joan's cell for the fourth private examination. Le Maistre formally appointed officers to represent him in the trial, generally choosing the same individuals who were already fulfilling those functions on behalf of Cauchon, and then the two judges began the interrogation of Joan.

And first at our command Joan was asked what was the sign that she gave her to her King, to which she replied: 'Would you be happy if I perjured myself?'

Item, asked if she had sworn and promised St Katherine not to reveal this sign, she answered: 'I have promised and sworn not to reveal this sign of my own accord because I was under so much pressure to say it.' And then she herself promised that she would not speak any more about it to anyone. Item, she said that this sign was that an angel

---

91 The *Minute française* added: 'and bring him back within three years'. The Duke had originally been captured at the battle of Agincourt in 1415 and was not freed until 1440, partly through the mediation of the Duke of Burgundy.

assured her King by bringing him the crown and saying to him that he would have the whole kingdom of France in its entirety with God's help and Joan's efforts, and that he should put Joan to work, that is to say, that he should give her men-at-arms, or else he would not be crowned and consecrated so quickly.

Asked if she had spoken with St Katherine since the previous day, she replied that she had heard her since the previous day; however she was told many times to answer the judges boldly on what they should ask her regarding the trial.

Asked about the manner in which the angel brought the crown and whether he placed it on the head of her King, she answered that the crown was given to an archbishop, namely the Archbishop of Reims, so it seemed to her, in the presence of her King: and the Archbishop received it and gave it to her King; and Joan was present. And this crown had been put into the King's treasury.

Asked to where the crown was brought, she replied that it was in the chamber of her King in the castle of Chinon.

Asked about the day and the hour, she answered that she knew nothing of the day, and as for the hour, it was late; beyond that she could not recall the hour. And it was in the month of April or March, or so she thought. And she said that in the next month of April or in the present month of March two years would have passed; and it was after Easter.

Asked if on the same day that she saw the sign, her King saw it too, she replied yes and that the King himself had it.

Asked what the crown was made of, she answered that it should be known that it was of pure gold; and this was such a rich and precious crown that she did not know how to count or value the riches that were found in it; and this crown signified that her King would hold the kingdom of France.

Asked if there were precious stones, she replied: 'I have told you what I know of it.'

Asked if she held or kissed the crown, she answered no.

Asked if the angel who brought this crown came from on high, or if he came on the ground,[92] she replied that when the angel came before

92 The Latin trial record omits Joan's reply and the following question from the *Minute française*: 'she answered: "He came from on high. And listen: he came by the command of Our Lord. And he entered by the door of the room." Asked if the angel walked on the ground and then entered through the door of the room ...'

her King, he paid reverence to him, bowing before him and pronouncing the words that she herself, Joan, previously said regarding
the sign. And with this the angel recalled to the memory of this same
King the sweet patience that he showed in the great tribulations
which had come to him. And from the door the angel walked and
went across the ground coming towards her King.

Asked what space there was from the door to the place where her
King then was, she answered that, as far as she believed, there was
certainly a space the length of a lance; and the angel departed whence
he had come. Item, she said that when the angel came, she
accompanied him and went with him by the stairs to the chamber of
her King; and the angel went in first, and then Joan herself; and Joan
said to her King: 'Sire, here is your sign; take it.'

Asked about the place where the angel appeared to her, she replied: 'I
was nearly always praying that God might send the sign to the King,
and I was in my lodging, in the house of a good woman near the castle
of Chinon, when the angel came; and then he and I went together to the
King; and the angel was well accompanied by other angels that were
with him, that no one saw.' And she also said that if it not been for
love of her and to relieve her from the trouble caused by the men who
argued against her, she was sure that many who saw the angel would
not have seen him.

Asked if all those who were there with the King saw the angel, she
answered that as far as she believed, the Archbishop of Reims, the
lords of Alençon, of La Trémouïlle and Charles de Bourbon saw him.[93]
And as for the crown, many churchmen and others saw it who did not
see the angel.

Asked of what appearance and size the said angel was, she replied that
she did not have permission to say that, and that she would answer
the following day.

Asked if all the angels who accompanied this angel were of the same
appearance, she answered that some of them certainly resembled him,
and others did not, as far as she saw them; and some of them had
wings and some were also crowned; and in their company were Sts
Katherine and Margaret who were with this angel and also the other
angels until the chamber of the King.

Asked how the angel left her, she replied that he left her in a little

93 See the earlier testimony at the end of the first private examination [40].

chapel and she was very angry at his departure;[94] she also cried and would gladly have gone with him, that is to say that her soul would have gone.

Asked if she remained happy at the departure of the angel,[95] she answered that he did not leave her in fear or scared, but she was angry at his departure.

Asked if it was for any merit of hers that God sent His angel to her, she replied that the angel came for a great matter and this was in the hope that her King would believe the sign, that men would stop arguing with this Joan and opposing her, and to give help to the good people of the town of Orléans, as well as for the merits of her King and of the good Duke of Orléans.

Asked why he had come to her rather than to another, she answered that it pleased God to act in this way through a simple young girl [a *pucelle* according to the *Minute française*] to drive back the enemies of the King.

Asked if she had been told where the angel had taken the crown, she replied that the crown was brought from God, and there was no gold-smith on earth who would know how to make it so rich and beautiful; and as for where the angel had taken the crown, Joan submitted her-self to God and did not know otherwise where it was taken.

Asked if this crown had a pleasant odour and if it was shiny, she answered that she did not remember and would think it over. But afterwards she said that it smelt good and would smell good, as long as it was well guarded, as was appropriate; and it was in the form of a crown.

Asked if the angel had written letters to her, she replied no.

Asked what sign her King, the people who were with him, and she herself had to believe that it was an angel who had brought this crown, she answered that her King believed it through the instruction and teaching of the churchmen who were there and by the sign of the crown.

Asked how the churchmen knew that this was an angel, she replied that they knew it by their learning and because they were clerks.

---

94 During the first private examination [40], Joan had mentioned that she withdrew to a small chapel after leaving the King.

95 The *Minute française* adds: 'or were you scared and in great fear'.

Asked about a married priest and a lost cup, which it was said that she had found, she answered that she did not know anything about this and that she had never heard talk of it.

Asked if when she went before Paris, she had gone there through a revelation from her voices, she answered no, but that she went there at the request of the gentlemen who wanted to launch a skirmish [*escarmouche*] or an armed attack, and she certainly had the intention of going beyond and crossing the ditches of Paris.

Asked if she also had a revelation to go before the town of La Charité, she replied no, but that she went at the request of the men-at-arms, as she said previously.

Asked if she had any revelation to go to Pont-l'Évêque,[96] she answered that after she had the revelation in the ditches at Melun that she would be captured,[97] she usually deferred to the captains on the matter of war, and yet she did not tell them that she had had a revelation that she would be captured.

Asked if it was well done to attack the town of Paris on the day of the Nativity of Our Lady, which was a feast day, she replied that it was good to observe the feast of Our Lady, and it seemed to her in her conscience that it would be good to keep the feast of Our Lady from beginning to end.

Asked if she had not said in front of the town of Paris: 'Surrender this town to Jesus', she answered no, but that she said 'Surrender it to the King of France.'

44. Fifth private examination (Wednesday 14 March 1431)

Source: Tisset (ed.), *Procès de condamnation*, I, pp. 143–9.

Language: Latin

On the morning of 14 March, Jean Le Maistre appointed Nicolas Taquel as his notary for the trial. Then Jean de La Fontaine, Nicolas Midi, Gérard Feuillet, Nicolas de Hubent and Isembart de La Pierre questioned Joan in her prison cell.

96 Pont-l'Évêque was occupied by the English in April 1430. On 14 May 1430, Joan and some of the captains sallied out of Compiègne to help Choisy against the Burgundians, but English troops from Pont-l'Évêque and the garrison from Noyon stopped them.

97 Joan was at Melun for Easter week in the middle of April 1430.

And first [she was asked] why she leapt from from the tower of Beaurevoir. She replied that she had heard it said that all the people of Compiègne up to the age of seven years were to be put to the sword, and that she would rather die than live after such a destruction of good people; and this was one of the reasons for her leap. The other was that she knew that she had been sold to the English, and that she would have much preferred to die than to be in the hands of the English, her enemies.

Asked if this leap was made by the counsel of her voices, she answered that St Katherine told her almost every day not to leap and that God would help her, and the people of Compiègne too. And Joan said to St Katherine that since God would aid the people of Compiègne, she wanted to be there. Then St Katherine said to her, 'Do not be mistaken, you must accept this thankfully; you will not be delivered until you have seen the King of the English.' And Joan replied: 'Truly I do not wish to see him, and I would rather die than be put into the hands of the English.'

Asked if she said to Sts Katherine and Margaret words of this sort, 'Will God let these good people of Compiègne die so wretchedly?', she answered that she did not say the words 'so wretchedly', but she spoke in this way: 'How will God let these good people of Compiègne die who have been, and are, so loyal to their lord?' Item, she said that after she had fallen from the tower, for two or three days she did not wish to eat and she was so injured by this fall that she could neither eat nor drink. And yet she was comforted by St Katherine who told her that she should confess and ask for pardon from God for having leaped,[98] and that, without fail, the people of Compiègne would have help before the feast of St Martin in the winter [11 November]. Then she started to recuperate and began to eat, and she was soon healed.

Asked if when she leaped, she expected to kill herself, she replied no, but, as she leaped, she commended herself to God. And she expected to escape from being delivered to the English by means of this leap.

Asked if when she recovered her speech she denied God and His saints because, it was said, this had been established by the inquiry,

98 Suicide was regarded as a mortal sin (i.e. a sin that destroys sanctifying grace and causes the supernatural death of the soul, meaning that the individual will go to hell) by the authority of holy scripture and the Church.

she answered that she did not remember that she had ever denied God or His saints, either there or anywhere else.[99]

Asked if she wished to submit this matter to the inquiry that had been or was being made, she replied: 'I submit to God and to none other, and to a good confession.'

Asked if her voices asked her for time to answer, she replied that St Katherine sometimes answered her, and sometimes Joan failed to understand because of the disturbance in the prison and the noise made by her guards. And when she made a request to St Katherine, then St Katherine and St Margaret made the request to God and then, at God's command, they gave an answer to Joan.

Asked if when the saints came to her there was a light with them, and if she did not see the light when she heard the voice in the castle, not knowing whether it was in her room, she replied that there was not a day when they did not come to her in the castle, and they did not come without light. And as for the time about which she was being questioned, she did not remember whether she saw a light or whether she saw St Katherine either. Item, she said that she asked three things of her voices: one was her deliverance; the second was that God should aid the French and carefully defend the towns in their obedience; and the third was the salvation of her soul.

Item, she asked that if it was the case that she was to be taken to Paris, she might have a copy of their questions and her replies, so that she might give them to the people at Paris and be able to say to them: 'Here is how I have been questioned at Rouen, with my replies'; in this way, she would not be tormented any more with so many questions.

Item, because she had said that I, the aforenamed Bishop [Cauchon], was exposing myself to great danger by putting her on trial, she was asked what this was and in what peril or danger I was putting both myself and others.[100] She answered that she had said to me, the aforesaid Bishop, 'You say that you are my judge; I do not know if you are this, but be well advised that you do not judge poorly, because you would put yourself in great danger. And I warn you so that if God punishes you, I am doing my duty in telling you this.'

---

99 The *Minute française* added: 'and she did not confess it because she did not have any memory that she had said or done this'.

100 Joan had made this veiled threat to Cauchon at the start of the third public examination [**36**].

Asked what was this peril or danger, she replied that St Katherine told her that she would have help; and she did not know whether this meant being freed from prison or that, during her trial, some disturbance would arise that would allow her to be delivered.[101] And she believed that it would be one or the other. And more often the voices told her that she would be delivered by a great victory, then saying to her: 'Accept everything thankfully, and do not worry about your martyrdom; in the end you will come to the kingdom of heaven.' And the voices told her this simply and definitely, that is to say without faltering. And she called this martyrdom on account of the pain and adversity which she suffered in prison; and she did not know whether she would suffer greater pain, but on this she committed herself to God.

Asked if, since her voices had told her that at the end she would go to heaven, she felt assured of being saved and that she would not be damned in hell, she answered that she firmly believed what her voices told her, namely that she would be saved, as firmly as if she were already there.

Asked if after this revelation she believed that she could not commit a mortal sin, she replied: 'I do not know anything of this; but I submit to God entirely.'

And, as it was said to her that this answer was of great weight, she answered that she too held it to be a great treasure.[102]

45. Sixth private examination (Wednesday 14 March 1431)

Source: Tisset (ed.), *Procès de condamnation*, I, pp. 149–54.

Language: Latin

Later that afternoon, Jean de La Fontaine, Nicolas Midi, Gérard Feuillet, Isembart de La Pierre and Jean Manchon continued the interrogation of Joan in her prison cell.

Joan said first regarding the preceding article concerning the certainty of her salvation, upon which she had been questioned that morning, that she understood what she had said: provided that she kept the

---

101 Either Joan was deliberately avoiding the question, or the notary has missed out a discussion of the 'peril'.

102 The *Minute française* inverts the order of these two questions and answers.

oath and promise that she had made to God, that is that she should carefully protect her virginity both of body and of soul.[103]

Asked if she needed to confess, since she had a revelation from her voices that she would be saved, she answered that she did not know that she had committed mortal sin, but if she were in mortal sin, she thought that Sts Katherine and Margaret would abandon her at once. And replying to the question, she believed that one cannot do too much to cleanse one's conscience.

Asked if since she was in this prison she had denied or cursed God, she replied no, and that sometimes when she said in French, 'Bon gré Dieu', 'Saint Jehan' or 'Nostre Dame,' those who could have reported the words, misunderstood them.

Asked if it was a mortal sin to take a man for ransom and to have him put to death while a prisoner, she answered that she had not done that.

And because she was told about Franquet d'Arras whom she had had put to death at Lagny,[104] she answered that she had consented to his being killed, if he deserved it, because he confessed himself a murderer, thief and traitor. And she said that his trial lasted for a fortnight and that he was judged by the Bailly of Senlis and legal officers of Lagny. She also said that she asked to have Franquet in order to [exchange him for] a man of Paris, the landlord of the Bear Inn;[105] and when she learned that this man was dead and the bailly said to her that she intended to do a great injustice in freeing this Franquet, then she said to the bailly, 'Since the man I wished to have is dead, do to this man what justice requires of you.'[106]

103 The *Minute française* merely stated: 'As for this article, provided that she kept the vow and promise that she made to Our Lord, that is to say that she should carefully protect her virginity both of body and of soul.'

104 Franquet d'Arras was a Burgundian mercenary captain who was defeated and captured by Joan near Lagny-sur-Marne in May 1430. Only the official Latin record of the Rouen trial accused Joan of wrongdoing in this matter. The original *Minute française* merely stated: 'about a man named Franquet Darras who was put to death at Lagny'.

105 The landlord of the Bear Inn at the Baudoyer gate in Paris was Jacquet Guillaume.

106 The Burgundian chronicler, Enguerrand de Monstrelet, reported the story in this way: 'At the beginning of the month of May [1430], a valiant man-at-arms named Franquet of Arras ... had made an sortie with about three hundred combatants toward Lagny-sur-Marne, but on his return was met by Joan the Pucelle and four hundred French. ... in the end, the Burgundians, after doing great harm to the enemy's cavalry, were overcome, and the better part of them put to the sword. The Pucelle even caused Franquet to be beheaded, whose death was exceedingly lamented by his party, for he was a man of most valiant conduct.' (Enguerran[d]

Asked if she gave money, or had money given, to the man who captured this Franquet, she replied that she was not the master of the mint or the Treasurer of France to give out money.

And when she was reminded that she had attacked Paris on a feast day, that she had taken the horse of the Lord Bishop of Senlis, that she had thrown herself from the tower of Beaurevoir, that she wore male clothing and that she had consented to the death of Franquet d'Arras, she was asked whether she did not believe that she had committed any mortal sin. On the first point regarding the attack on Paris, she answered that in this matter she did not think that she was in state of mortal sin and that if she were, it was for God to know and for the priest to hear in confession.[107]

And secondly, concerning the horse, she replied that she firmly believed she did not sin against God in this, because this horse was valued at the sum of two hundred gold saluts for which the Bishop received an assignation [promise of payment]; and the horse was also sent back to the Lord of La Trémouïlle to return it to the Bishop of Senlis; this horse was of no use to her for riding. Moreover she did not take it from the Bishop. She also said that in any case, she did not wish to keep it, because she heard it said that the Bishop was displeased that his horse had been taken, and also because this horse was useless for men-at-arms. Finally, in conclusion, Joan did not know whether the Bishop was paid the money due to him or whether his horse was returned to him; and she thought not.

And thirdly, regarding the fall from the top of the tower of Beaurevoir, she answered: 'I did this not out of despair, but in the hope of saving my body and of going to aid many good people who needed help.[108] And after the leap, I confessed myself and asked pardon of the Lord.' And also she was pardoned by the Lord and she believed that it was not right to make this leap; this was wrong. Item, she said that she knew that she had been pardoned by a revelation from St Katherine after she confessed; and it was at the advice of St Katherine that she made confession.

Asked if she was given a major penance for this, she replied that she

---

107 The *Minute française*: 'this was for God to know, and for confession to God and to a priest'.

108 Despair was regarded as mortal sin.

suffered a large part of her penance in the injury that she did to herself in falling.

Asked if she believed that the misdeed that she committed in leaping was a mortal sin, she answered that she knew nothing about this and submitted herself to God.

And fourthly, that she wore the clothing of a man, she replied: 'Since I do this by the command of God and in His service, I do not think that I am doing wrong; and this clothing will be set aside immediately when God chooses to command it.'

46. Seventh private examination (Thursday 15 March 1431)

Source: Tisset (ed.), *Procès de condamnation*, I, pp. 154–64.

Language: Latin

Joan was questioned in her prison cell by Jean de La Fontaine with the assistance of Nicolas Midi, Gérard Feuillet, Nicolas de Hubent and Isembart de La Pierre.

With charitable exhortations, Joan was warned and required, that if she had done anything against the faith, she should be willing to accept the decision of our holy mother the Church, to which she should submit herself. She answered that her replies should be seen and examined by the clerks, and then she might be told if there were anything which was contrary to the Christian faith; she certainly knew to say what this would be, and then said that she would find out about this from her counsel. Moreover, if there were anything evil advanced against the Christian faith [and] that God prescribed she would not wish to uphold it, and would certainly be fierce against it.

Item, the distinction between the Church triumphant and the Church militant was explained to her, what each of them were, and she was required to submit herself at that time to the verdict of the Church on whatever she said or did, whether it was good or evil. She replied: 'I will not give another reply to you now.'

Item, Joan was required, under the oath that she had sworn, to say how she meant to escape from the castle of Beaulieu between two pieces of wood.[109] She answered that she was never a prisoner in any

---

109 Beaulieu-les-Fontaines in Vermandois near Compiègne was the castle of Jean de Luxembourg where Joan was taken between May and July 1430, shortly after her capture.

place from which she would not gladly escape; and, finding herself in this castle, she would have shut her guards in the tower if it had not been [for] the porter who saw her and blocked her path. Item, she said regarding this that it seemed to her that God was not pleased that she should escape at that time, and that it was necessary for her to see the King of England, as her voices had told her, just as it was written above.

Asked if she had permission from God or from her voices to leave [prison] whenever she wished, she replied: 'I have often asked for it but I do not have it yet.'

Asked if she would now leave if she saw the door open, she answered that she would go if she saw the door open and God had commanded it. And she firmly believed that if she saw the door open and that her guards and the other Englishmen did not make any resistance, she would take this as her permission and believe that God was helping her. But she would not go without permission unless she herself attempted to leave by force, to see whether God approved; and she cited the widely used proverb in French: 'God helps those who help themselves.' And she said this so that if she escaped it would not be said that she had departed without permission.

Since she had asked to hear mass, she was asked whether it did not seem to her more respectable to wear female clothing; and she was asked which she would like better, to take the clothing of a woman and to hear mass, or to remain in male clothing and not to hear mass. She replied: 'Promise me that I will hear mass if I am in the clothing of a woman, and I will give you my answer.'

Then the interrogator said to her: 'I myself guarantee that you will hear mass if you are in the clothing of a woman.' She answered: 'And what do you say if I have promised and sworn to our King not to set aside this clothing? Nevertheless I reply to you: have a long dress reaching down to the ground made for me, without a train, and give it to me to go to mass; and then, on my return, I will put on again my present clothing.'

Asked again if she would wear the clothing of a woman to go to hear mass, she replied: 'I will take counsel on this and then I will answer you.' And then she requested for the honour of God and of Blessed Mary that she be allowed to hear mass in this good town [*bona villa* in Latin, or *bonne ville*].

And at this the interrogator told her to put on the clothing of a woman, simply and absolutely [i.e. without condition]. She answered: 'Give me a dress like that of the daughter of a burgher, that is to say a long *houppelande* [a loose-fitting greatcoat], and I will wear it to go and hear mass.'[110] She added that she again begged most insistently that she be allowed to hear mass in the outfit that she wore, without changing it.

Asked if she wished to submit to and accept the decision of the Church on what she had said and done, she replied: 'All my words and deeds are in the hand of God and I wait on Him in this. And I promise you that I do not wish to do or to say anything against the Christian faith; and if I had said or done anything, or if anything were on my body that the clerks might say was against the Christian faith that the Lord has established, I would not wish to persist in it but would reject it.'

Asked if she would agree to submit herself to the ordinance of the Church on this matter, she replied: 'I will not give you any more answers now; but on Saturday send me a priest if you do not wish to come, and I will give him an answer, with God's help, and this may be put in writing.'

Asked if, when her voices came, she paid reverence to them absolutely, as to a saint, she answered yes, and that if ever she did not do this she asked their pardon later. And also, she did not know how to make such a great reverence as was due to them, because she firmly believed that these were Sts Katherine and Margaret. And she said the same about St Michael.

Asked if, since candles were commonly offered to the saints of heaven, she did not offer, in church or elsewhere, lighted candles or other things to these saints who came to her, or had masses said, she replied no, unless this was during the offering of mass by the hand of the priest, in honour of St Katherine. And she believed that she was one of those who appeared to her, and she had not lit as many candles as she would gladly do for Sts Katherine and Margaret who were in heaven, whom she firmly believed to be those who come to her.

Asked if when she put candles before the image of St Katherine, she did it in honour of the one who appeared to her, she answered: 'I do it in honour of God, Blessed Mary, St Katherine who is in heaven, and of the one who reveals herself to me.'

110 According to the *Minute française*, Joan also asked for a woman's hood.

Asked if she always did or accomplished what her voices asked of her, she replied that she accomplished the command of God made to her through her voices with all her power, as far as she could understand it. And the voices did not command anything of her without God's good will.

Asked if in the matter of war she did anything without the counsel of her voices, she answered: 'You have my answer to this; read your book carefully and you will find it.'[111] Nevertheless she said that, at the request of the men-at-arms, a courageous attack was launched upon Paris, and also upon La Charité, at the request of her King. And this was neither against nor by the command of her voices.

Asked if ever she did anything against the will and command of the voices, she replied that she accomplished what she could and knew how to do according to her power. And as for the leap from the tower of Beaurevoir that she made against their command, she could not stop herself; and when the voices saw her need, and that she did not know how to stop herself, they protected her life and stopped her from killing herself. She also said that the voices had always helped her, whatever she had ever done in these great matters; and this was a sign that they were good spirits.

Asked if she had any other sign that these voices were good spirits, she answered that St Michael certified this for her before these voices came.

Asked how she knew it was St Michael himself, she replied that this was by his speech and by the language of angels; and she firmly believed that these were angels.

Asked how she knew that these were angels,[112] she answered that she very soon believed it and that she had wished to believe it. And she also said that St Michael, when he came to her, told her that Sts Katherine and Margaret would come to her, and that she should follow their counsel; they had been instructed to lead her and to advise her what to do, and she should believe what they said to her, and this was by the command of God.

Asked how she could tell that it was a good or a bad angel if the devil took upon himself the form or figure of a good angel, she replied that

111 This is presumably a reference to the record of her testimony being compiled by the notaries, the *Minute française*.

112 According to the *Minute française*, Joan was asked how she knew that this was the language of angels.

she would certainly know if it was St Michael or some other counter-feit in his likeness. Item, she said that on the first occasion, she had grave doubts whether this was St Michael who was coming to her and on this first occasion, she was very afraid; and she saw him many times before she was sure that this was St Michael.

Asked why she knew it was St Michael when she [finally] believed that it was him, when she had not known him the first time that he appeared to her, she answered that on the first occasion she was a young child and was afraid, and since then St Michael had taught her and showed her so many things that she firmly believed that this was him.

Asked what doctrine he taught her, she replied that above all he told her that she was a good child, and that God would help her; and among other things he told her that she should go to the aid of the King of France. And a great part of what the angel taught her is in this book;[113] and the angel recounted to her the hardship that had befallen the kingdom of France.

Asked about the height and stature of this angel, she answered that she would answer on the following Saturday, along with the other matter upon which she yet had to answer, namely what pleased God.

Asked if she did not believe that it was a great sin to offend Sts Katherine and Margaret who appeared to her and to act against their command, she answered yes, but that she knew she must improve and that the most that she had ever offended them was in the leap from Beaurevoir, for which she had asked their pardon and for other offences that she might have committed towards them.

Asked if Sts Katherine and Margaret would not take bodily vengeance for this offence, she replied that she did not know and she had not asked them.

Asked if she knew of any crime or fault for which she could or should die, since she had recently said that sometimes a person was hanged for telling the truth, she answered no.[114]

---

113 It is unclear whether this is a reference to the records of the Poitiers trial or to the minutes of the trial at Rouen.

114 Joan had made this comment during her testimony in the third public examination [36].

47. Eighth private examination (Saturday 17 March 1431)

Source: Tisset (ed.), *Procès de condamnation*, I, pp. 165–71.

Language: Latin

Joan was questioned in her prison cell by Jean de La Fontaine with the assistance of Nicolas Midi, Gérard Feuillet, Isembart de La Pierre and Jean Massieu.

Asked then in what form, size, appearance and clothing St Michael came to her, she answered that he was in the form of a very true and upright man, and that she would not say anything more about his clothing or other things. As for the angels, she saw them with her eyes and they would not have anything more from her on that. Item, she said that she believed just as firmly in the words and deeds of St Michael who appeared to her, as she believed that Our Lord Jesus Christ suffered His death and passion for us. And what moved her to believe this was the good counsel, good comfort and good teaching that he brought and gave to her.

Asked if she wished to submit to the verdict of the holy mother Church for all that she had done, whether good or bad, she replied that as for the Church, she loved it and wished to support it with all her power for our Christian faith; and it was not she who should be prevented from going to church or from hearing mass. And as for the good works that she had done and her coming, she must rely upon the King of Heaven who sent her to the son of Charles [VI] King of France, Charles [VII], who was King of France.[115] 'And you will see,' she said, 'that the French will soon accomplish a great task that God sends them, and in this he will shake the whole kingdom of France'. And she said this so that when it happened, it would be remembered that she had said it.

Required to tell the date within which this would happen, she answered: 'I wait on the Lord for this'.

Asked if she would submit her words and deeds to the verdict of the Church, she replied: 'I submit myself to God who sent me, to the Blessed Mary and to all the saints of heaven. And it seems to me that God and the Church are one, and no difficulty should be made about this. Why do you make difficulties about this?'

Then she was told that there was the Church triumphant where there

115 The *Minute française* said 'who would be King of France'.

is God, the saints, the angels and the souls who are already saved; and there was also the Church militant in which is the pope as God's vicar on earth, the cardinals, the prelates of the Church, the clergy and all the good Christians and catholics. And certainly when gathered together, this Church could not err and was governed by the Holy Spirit. This is why she was asked if she wished to submit herself to the Church militant, namely the one on earth, which had been described in this way. She answered that she came to the King of France on behalf of God, the Blessed Virgin Mary, all the saints of heaven and the Church victorious on high, and at their command; and she submitted all her good deeds and everything that she had done or would do to that Church. And on the question of whether she would submit to the Church militant, she said that she would not answer anything more for now.

Asked about what she had said on the subject of a woman's clothing that was offered to her so that she could go to hear mass, she replied that as for the clothing of a woman, she still would not take it as long as God liked. And if it were the case that she should come to sentencing,[116] she relied upon the lords of the Church mercifully to allow her to wear a woman's chemise and a hat for her head. [She said that] she would rather die than turn back from what God had made her do; and she firmly believed that God would not allow it to happen that she be brought so low that she would not have prompt help, by a miracle.

Asked why she asked for a woman's chemise at death's door, since she had said that she wore her clothing by the command of God, she answered: 'It is enough for God that it is long.'

Asked if her godmother who saw the Fairy Ladies was held to be a wise woman, she replied that she was held and reputed an honest woman, and not a prophetess or sorceress.

Asked whether it would please God that she had said that she would take the clothing of a woman if they would allow her to go [free], she answered that if she were given permission to go in woman's dress she would immediately put on male clothing and do what was commanded of her by the Lord. And she had formerly answered this, and nothing whatsoever would induce her to take an oath not to arm

116 The Latin record omits the words 'and that it were necessary to undress her in that sentence' from the original *Minute française*, a reference to the possibility of physical coercion to force her to change her clothing.

herself or to wear male clothing, but she would accomplish the command of the Lord.

Asked about the age and the garments worn by Sts Katherine and Margaret, she replied: 'You already have all the answer that you will get from me and you will have nothing more. And I have answered you as certainly as I can.'

Asked if she did not believe before this day that the Fairy Ladies were evil spirits, she answered that she knew nothing of that.

Asked if she knew that Sts Katherine and Margaret hated the English, she replied: 'They love what God loves and they hate what God hates.'

Asked if God hated the English, she answered that she knew nothing of the love or hatred that God had for the English or of what he would do to their souls, but she was certain that they would be driven out of France, with the exception of those who died there, and that God would send victory to the French against the English.

Asked if God had been for the English when they were prospering in France, she replied that she did not know whether God hated the French, but she believed that he wished to allow them to be beaten for their sins, if they were in sin.[117]

Asked what warrant and what help she expected from the Lord because she wore male clothing, she answered that she awaited no other reward than the salvation of her soul both for the clothing and for the other things that she had done.

Asked what arms she offered in the church of Saint-Denis in France, she replied that she offered her whole suit of plate armour [*blanc harnoys*],[118] fitting for a man-at-arms, with a sword that she had won before Paris.

Asked why she offered these arms, she answered that this was out of devotion, according to the custom of men-at-arms when they were wounded; and because she had been wounded in front of Paris, she offered them to St Denis, because this was the [battle] cry of France.[119]

---

117 Military defeat was often explained as divine punishment for sin, particularly by preachers and other clerics. See for example, C. J. Liebman, 'Un sermon de Philippe de Vilette, abbé de Saint-Denis, pour la levée de l'oriflamme (1414)', *Romania*, LXVIII, 1944–45, pp. 444–70.

118 See Joan's testimony during the fourth public examination, **37**.

119 The battle cry 'Montjoie Saint Denis' was attributed to the armies of Charlemagne in the *Chanson de Roland*, and supposedly referred to the mound of stones

Asked if she did this so that the arms might be worshipped, she replied no.

Asked what was the significance of the five crosses on the sword that she found at Sainte-Catherine-de-Fierbois, she answered that she knew nothing of this.[120]

Asked who persuaded her to have angels with arms, feet, legs and robes painted on her standard, she replied: 'You have my reply to that.'

Asked if she had had those angels who came to her painted, she answered that she had them painted in the manner in which they were painted in churches.

Asked if ever she saw them in the manner in which they were painted in the churches, she replied: 'I will not tell you anything more.'

Asked why she did not have the light which came to her with the angel or voices painted, she answered that this was not commanded of her.

48. Ninth private examination (Saturday 17 March 1431)

Source: Tisset (ed.), *Procès de condamnation*, I, pp. 172–9.

Language: Latin

The interrogation continued that afternoon, led by Pierre Cauchon and Jean Le Maistre, accompanied by Jean de La Fontaine, Jean Beaupère, Jacques de Touraine, Nicolas Midi, Pierre Maurice, Gérard Feuillet, Thomas de Courcelles, Isembart de La Pierre and John Grey, her guard.

Joan was asked if the two angels painted on her standard represented St Michael and St Gabriel. She answered that they were only there for the honour of God, who was painted on the standard. And she said that she only had this representation made of the two angels for the honour of God, who was depicted there holding the world.

---

set up to mark the site of the saint's martyrdom. By the late middle ages, it was established as the most important battle cry for the French royal army, associated with the great war banner known as the oriflamme, usually kept at the abbey of Saint-Denis: P. Contamine, *L'oriflamme de Saint-Denis aux XIVe et XVe siècles*, Nancy, 1975, and A. Lombard-Jourdan, *Fleur de lis et oriflamme: signes célestes du royaume de France*, Paris, 1991.

120 This may simply have been the mark of the armourer, though the judges clearly believed that the crosses were carved in order to bring good luck. See **67**.

Asked if these two angels depicted on her standard were the two angels who guarded the world, and why there were not more, seeing that she was commanded by God to take this standard, she replied that the whole standard had been commanded by God through the voices of Sts Katherine and Margaret who said to her, 'Take the standard on behalf of the King of Heaven.' And because they told her 'Take the standard on behalf of the King of Heaven' she had this figure of God and of the angels put there and coloured. And she did everything by the command of God.

Asked if she questioned the two saints as to whether she would win all the battles that she undertook and would secure victories by virtue of this standard, she answered that they told her to take it boldly and that God would help her.

Asked if she helped the standard more than the standard helped her, she replied that whether the victory was achieved by her, Joan, or by her standard, it was all for the Lord.

Asked if the hope of victory was founded upon this standard or upon herself, she answered that it was founded on the Lord and on no one else.

Asked if another person would have had as much good fortune as Joan herself if they had carried this standard, she replied: 'I do not know anything of this, and I submit it to God.'

She was asked whether, if one of her party had given her his standard, she would have carried it and would have had as firm a hope in this as in her own standard that designed for her by God; and she was particularly questioned about the standard of her King, if she had had it, etc. She answered: 'I carried the one assigned to me by God the more willingly. And yet in all I rely upon God.'

Asked what was the purpose of the sign that she put on her letters, and the names 'Jhesus Maria', she replied that the clerks writing her letters put them there, and some said that it was proper to put these two words 'Jhesus Maria'.

Asked if it had not been revealed to her that she would no longer be fortunate, and her voices would no longer come to her if she lost her virginity, she answered that this had not been revealed to her.

Asked if she believed the voices would have come to her if she had been married, she replied: 'I do not know. And on this I submit myself to God.'

Asked if she thought and firmly believed that her King did well to kill my lord the Duke of Burgundy,[121] she answered that this was a great injury to the kingdom of France; and whatever had befallen between these two princes, God had sent her to the aid of the King of France.

Joan was asked about her reply to us, the Bishop [Cauchon], that she would answer us and the men appointed by us just as she would do to our very holy lord, the pope.[122] Yet there were many questions to which she did not wish to reply: would she not answer more fully before the pope than she did before us? She replied that she had answered everything as honestly as she could; and if she knew anything, and she remembered that she had not said it, she would willingly tell it.[123]

Asked if it did not seem to her that she was bound to answer truthfully to our lord the pope, the vicar of God, on all that she might be asked regarding the faith and the matter of her conscience more fully than she had replied to us, she answered that she demanded to be led before our lord the pope, and then she would answer before him all that she should answer.

Asked about the material of one of her rings on which the names 'Jhesus Maria' were written, she replied that she was not sure about this, and if it was of gold, it was not fine gold; and she did not know whether it was gold or brass; she thought that there were three crosses on it, and no other sign that she knew, except these names 'Jhesus Maria'.

Asked why she gladly looked at this ring when she was going to any military engagement, she answered that this was for pleasure, and in honour of her father and mother; and having the ring in her hand and on her finger, she touched St Katherine who appeared to her in a visible form.

Asked what part of St Katherine she touched, she replied: 'You will not have another thing on this.'

Asked if she ever kissed or embraced Sts Katherine or Margaret, she answered that she had embraced them both.

121 The *Minute français* said: 'to kill or to have killed the Duke of Burgundy'. This was a reference to the assassination of John the Fearless, Duke of Burgundy, at Montereau on 10 September 1419.

122 The beginning of the fifth public examination.

123 The *Minute français* includes the following incomplete paragraph immediately after this one: 'Asked about the age, grandeur and clothing [of] the angel who brought the sign to her King'.

Asked if they had a pleasant odour, she replied that one should be certain that they had a pleasant smell.

Asked if she felt heat or anything else when embracing them, she answered that she could not embrace them without feeling and touching them.

Asked on what part of the body she embraced them, whether high up or low down, she replied that it was more fitting to embrace them low down than high up.

Asked if she had not given to these saints any garlands or chaplets [wreaths of flowers], she answered that she had given garlands many times in their honour to their images or representations in the churches; and she did not remember giving them to those who appeared to her.

Asked if, when she put garlands on the tree which had been spoken of before, she hung them in honour of those who appeared to her, she replied no.

Asked if she paid reverence to the saints by kneeling or bowing when they came to her, she answered yes; and she paid as much reverence to them as she could because she certainly knew that they were in the kingdom of heaven.

Asked if she knew anything of those who consorted with the fairies, she replied that she had never done this, and did not know anything about it, but she had certainly heard it said that they went there on Thursdays. But she did not believe in it and thought that this was just witchcraft.

Asked if anyone had hung her standard around the head of the King when he was crowned at Reims, she answered no, so far as she knew.

Asked why this standard was carried into the church at Reims at the consecration of her King, rather than those of the other captains, she replied that this standard had been involved in the [war] effort and this was a good reason for it to be honoured.

49. The interrogations are read in Joan's presence (Saturday 24 March 1431)

Source: Tisset (ed.), *Procès de condamnation*, I, pp. 181–2.

Language: Latin

On 18 and 22 March, the judges reviewed the records of the interrogations and certain reports written by theologians and lawyers, before calling for a series of articles to be drawn up against Joan. Two days later, Cauchon and Le Maistre visited her prison cell with a group of clerics so that Guillaume Manchon could read out the *Minute française* to the prisoner.

Then while these writings were being read to her, she said that she was surnamed 'd'Arc' or 'Rommée' and that in her region girls bore the surname of their mother. She then said that the questions and her replies should be read to her and that if she did not contradict what was being read, she held it to be true and confessed it.

On the article concerning her resumption of the clothing of a woman, she added these words: 'Give me a woman's dress to go to my mother's house and I will take it.' And this was in order to leave prison; and once she was outside the prison she would take counsel on what she should do.

Finally, after reading the contents of the register, Joan admitted that she believed that she had said what was written in the register and as it had been read to her, and she did not contradict anything contained in this register.

50. Joan asks permission to hear mass (Palm Sunday, 25 March 1431)

Source: Tisset (ed.), *Procès de condamnation*, I, pp. 182–3.

Language: Latin

The following day, Cauchon again visited Joan in order to persuade her to abandon her male clothing so as to be allowed to hear mass that Palm Sunday.

Joan replied to this by requesting that she be allowed to hear mass in the male clothing that she was wearing, and that she might also receive the sacrament of the Eucharist on the feast of Easter.

Then we told her to reply to what she had been asked, that is to say whether she was willing to abandon the clothing of a man if this had been granted to her.

But she answered that she had not had taken counsel on this and could not yet resume female clothing.

And we asked her if she wished to have counsel with the saints about whether she might take female clothing, to which she replied that she could be permitted to hear mass in that state, which she desired to the highest degree; but she could not change her outfit, and also the decision was not in her power.

After this the masters exhorted her to agree to resume an outfit appropriate to her sex, out of the great goodness and devotion that she seemed to have.

And Joan again answered that it was not in her [power] to do this, and if it were in her, this would be done very quickly.

She was then told that she should speak with her voices to find out if she could resume woman's clothing in order to receive the Eucharist [*viaticum*] at Easter.[124]

Joan replied to this that as far as this depended upon her, she would not receive the Eucharist [*viaticum*] by changing her costume for that of a woman; and she begged to be allowed to hear mass in the clothing of a man, saying that this outfit would not charge her soul, and that to wear it was not against the Church.

51. Joan is interrogated in prison (Easter Saturday, 31 March 1431)

Source: Tisset (ed.), *Procès de condamnation*, I, pp. 286–9.

Language: Latin

Having completed the Preparatory trial, the Ordinary trial of Joan of Arc began on Monday 26 March 1431.[125] Over the following days, the Promoter, Jean d'Estivet, presented Seventy Articles against Joan based solely upon the

---

124 The Latin term 'viaticum' usually referred to the last communion given to those about to die. This was and remains the form of communion offered on Holy Saturday, the day before Easter, when the Catholic Church abstains from the celebration of the sacrifice of the mass.

125 The Ordinary trial, or 'processus ordinarius', was the main stage of the trial during which the promoter (prosecutor) presented charges against the accused, who was then allowed to present their response.

testimony that she herself had provided during the Preparatory trial, rather than the evidence of any witnesses. Then on Saturday 31 March the judges and nine clerics questioned Joan in her prison cell, hoping that she would now answer the questions that she had evaded by asking for a delay [for example, at the end of document 41].

And first she was asked if she wished to submit to the judgement of the Church on earth for all that she said or did, whether it was good or evil, and especially for the matters, crimes and offences that had been attributed to her, and above all for what concerned the trial. She answered that she submitted to the Church militant regarding that which was sought from her, provided that it did not command her to do anything impossible. And she held it [to be] impossible that she revoke what she had done or said, as declared to the trial, on the subject of her visions and the revelations that she said that she had had from God; and she would not revoke them for anything. She would not stop doing what God made, commanded and would command her to do for any man alive. And it would be impossible for her to revoke these [visions and revelations]; and if the Church wished to make her do anything else contrary to the command that she said had been given by God, she would not do it for anything.

Asked if she would submit to the Church, if the Church militant told her that her revelations were illusions or diabolical things, she replied that she would always submit to God whose command she would always obey; and she certainly knew that what was written in her trial came from the command of God, and it would have been impossible for her to do contrary to what she claimed at the trial to have done at the command of God. And if the Church commanded her to do the contrary, she would not rely upon any man in the world except God, and she would always carry out the just command of God himself.

Asked if she believed herself subject to the Church of God on earth, namely to our lord the pope, the cardinals, archbishops, bishops and other prelates of the Church, she answered yes, God being served first.

Asked if she had a command from her voices not to submit herself to the Church militant on earth, nor to its judgements, she answered that she did not say anything that she found in her own head, but that her replies were by the command of her voices; they did not command her not to obey the Church, God being served first.

Asked if she had files [i.e. tools] at the castle of Beaurevoir, at Arras

or elsewhere, she answered: 'If any were found on me, I have nothing
more to say to you.'

52. The Twelve Articles of Accusation (5 April 1431)

Source: Tisset (ed.), *Procès de condamnation*, I, pp. 290–7.

Language: Latin

Between 2 and 5 April, the judges and their advisers whittled down the list of
Seventy Articles drawn up by the Promoter, Jean d'Estivet, to a list of
Twelve Articles which were disseminated for comment to the clerics
attending the trial, as well as to the University of Paris.

Article 1: And firstly, a certain woman says and affirms that, since
she was about thirteen years old, with the eyes of her body, she saw
appear in corporeal form St Michael, who would console her, and
sometimes St Gabriel. At times she also saw a great multitude of
angels; and since then, Sts Katherine and Margaret have appeared to
this woman so that she might see them corporeally. She sees them
every day, hears their voices and she has sometimes embraced and
kissed them, touching them materially and corporeally. And she has
seen the heads of these angels and saints, but she did not want to say
anything about the other parts of their bodies or their garments. And
[she claims] that the said Sts Katherine and Margaret spoke to her at
times by a certain spring, near to a great tree commonly called 'The
Tree of the Fairies'; and regarding this spring and this tree, the
common report says that the Fairy Ladies frequent them and that
many sick with the fever come to this spring and to this tree to
recover their health, although they may be located in a profane place.
And there and elsewhere she has adored them and paid reverence to
them on many occasions.

She also says that these Sts Katherine and Margaret appeared and
showed themselves to her crowned with very beautiful and precious
crowns; and from that moment, and on many subsequent occasions,
they told this woman by God's command that she must go to find a
prince of the world and promise him that, by the help and labours of
this woman, the prince would recover by force of arms a great
temporal domain and worldly honour, and that he would win victory
over his enemies; and also that this prince would receive this woman,
and assign to her both arms and an army of men-at-arms to execute
what was going to happen.

Moreover [she says that] the said Sts Katherine and Margaret commanded this woman, by God's command, to take and to wear the clothing of a man, which she has worn and still wears, obeying this command with such obstinacy that she said that she would rather die than abandon this outfit, sometimes saying this simply and at times [adding]: unless it was God's command. She has even chosen not to be present at the office of mass and to be deprived of the sacred communion of the Eucharist at the times ordained by the Church for the faithful to receive this sacrament, rather than resume the clothing of a woman and abandon the clothing of a man. These saints have also influenced this woman in this [matter] so much that, without the knowledge and against the will of her parents, even though she was seventeen years of age or thereabouts, she left her father's house and joined with a large group of men-at-arms, living with them night and day, and never, or rarely, having another woman with her.

And these saints told this woman and commanded her to do many other things, because of which she claimed to have been sent by God in heaven and the Church triumphant of the saints already in bliss, to whom she submits all that she has done which is good. But she prevaricates and refuses to submit herself, her actions and her words, to the Church militant, [even though she had been] asked and [charitably] admonished many times; she says that it is impossible for her to act contrary to what, during the trial, she has claimed to have done by the command of God. And on that point, she will not rely upon the decision or judgement of any living man but only upon the judgement of God. [She claims] that [these saints] revealed to her that she would be saved in the glory of the blessed, and that her soul would be saved if she preserved the virginity that she had vowed to them the first time that she saw and heard them. At the time of this revelation, she claimed to be as certain of her salvation as if she were then actually present in the kingdom of heaven.[126]

Article 2: Item, this woman says that the sign that led the prince to whom she had been sent to believe her on the subject of her revelations, to receive her and to let her take command in the wars,

---

126 In the revised version of the Twelve Articles that was read to Joan on 23 May 1431, this first article was greatly abridged: 'Firstly, Joan, you have said that, from the age of thirteen years or thereabouts, you have had revelations and apparitions of angels and of Sts Katherine and Margaret whom you have frequently seen with the eyes of your body; they have spoken with you; they often tell you and have told you many things set out in greater detail in the trial.'

was that St Michael came to this prince, accompanied by a multitude of angels of whom some had crowns and others had wings; with them were Sts Katherine and Margaret. And this angel and this woman walked together across the ground, via a road, stairs and the room, travelling far; the other angels and the said saints accompanied them. And one angel gave to the prince a very precious crown of pure gold and bowed down before the prince, paying reverence to him. And on one occasion she said that, when her prince received the sign, she thought that he was then alone, although many had been nearby; and on another occasion, so she believed, an archbishop received the sign of the crown and gave it to the prince, in the presence and in sight of several temporal lords.[127]

Article 3: Item, this woman knows and is certain that the one who visits her is St Michael, because of the good counsel, comfort and the wise instruction that this St Michael gave and showed her, and because he named himself, saying that he was Michael. And similarly she recognises Sts Katherine and Margaret, distinguishing one from the another, because they name themselves and greet her. This is why she believes that the St Michael who appears to her is truly St Michael, and that his words and deeds are true and good, just as firmly as she believes that Our Lord Jesus suffered and died for our redemption.

Article 4: Item, this woman says and affirms that she is as certain that some purely contingent future events will happen, as about what she really sees in front of her; and she boasts about having, and of having had, knowledge of certain hidden things through the revelations made to her verbally by the voices of Sts Katherine and Margaret: for example that she will be delivered from prison and that the French will achieve a more glorious deed in her company than any deed in the history of Christianity. [She boasts] too that without anyone showing them to her, she has recognised certain men whom she had never seen before, so she says, through revelations; and that she has revealed and discovered a sword hidden in the ground.

Article 5: Item, this woman says and affirms that, by the command of God and at His will, she has taken, worn, continually wears and dresses in an outfit customary for a man. And she then says that, as she had God's command to wear male clothing, she must have a short

127 The article is clearly highlighting the contradictions in Joan's earlier testimony.

tunic, hood, doublet, breeches and hose with multiple aiguillettes
[laces], the hair on her head cut in a circle above her ears, without
keeping anything on her body that proves or indicates the female sex,
excepting that which nature has given her as the distinctive mark of
her sex. And she has frequently received the Eucharist in this garb.
And she did not want, nor does she wish, to resume the clothing of a
woman, although she has been required and [charitably] admonished
on this point on many occasions, saying that she would rather die
than abandon the clothing of a man, sometimes saying this simply and
occasionally [adding]: unless this was at God's command. [She has
affirmed that] if she found herself in male clothing among those men
of her party for whom she recently bore arms, and if she could do as
she did before her capture and detention, this would be one of the
greatest blessings possible for the whole kingdom of France, adding
that she would not take an oath not to wear male clothing or to bear
arms, for anything in the world. And in all of this, she says that what
she did and does is right, obeying God and His commands.

Article 6: Item, this woman confesses and affirms that she had numerous letters written, at the top of which were put the names, 'Jhesus
Maria', with the sign of the cross. And sometimes she put a cross
[signifying that] she did not wish anyone to do what she had ordered
to be carried out in these letters. On others she had written that she
would have anybody who would not obey her letters or warnings killed,
and that the one who has greater right from God in heaven will be
revealed by this exchange of blows.[128] And she frequently says that
she has done nothing except by the revelation and command of God.

Article 7: Item, this woman says and confesses that at the age of
seventeen or thereabouts, spontaneously and through revelation, she
says, she went to find a certain esquire whom she had never seen
before, leaving her father's house against her wishes of her parents;
they became almost mad after they learned of her departure.[129] And
this woman asked the esquire to guide her or have her taken to the
prince who was mentioned before [Charles VII]. Then this esquire, a
captain, gave to this woman a man's outfit with a sword, at her
request, and he appointed and ordered a knight, a squire and four
servants to escort her. When they had reached the prince, this woman

128 This is a direct quotation from Joan's first letter to the English [4].
129 The esquire [*scutifer, armiger*] was Robert de Baudricourt.

said to him that she wished to conduct the war against his enemies, promising him that she would secure a great dominion for him, that she would defeat his enemies and that she had been sent for this purpose by God in heaven. She says that in what has just been described she acted properly, by the command of God and through revelation.

Article 8: Item, this woman says and confesses that, without being forced or impelled by anyone, she threw herself from a very high tower, preferring to die than to be delivered into the hands of her enemies and to survive the destruction of the town of Compiègne. She also says that she could not stop herself from throwing herself down in this fashion, although Sts Katherine and Margaret had forbidden her from leaping down. To offend them, she says, is a great sin, but she certainly knows that this sin was forgiven once she had confessed it. And she says that she has had a revelation about this.

Article 9: Item, this woman says and confesses that Sts Katherine and Margaret promised to lead her into heaven, if she carefully guarded the virginity of her body and her soul as she vowed to them. And she claims to be as certain of this, as if she was already in the glory of the blessed. And she thinks that she has not committed mortal sin because, so it seems to her, these Sts Katherine and Margaret would not visit her if she were in a state of mortal sin, as they do every day.

Article 10: Item, this woman says and affirms that God loves certain chosen and named people, while still pilgrims in this world [i.e. God has made His decision before their deaths], and that He does not love them more than He does this woman. And she knows this through the revelation of Sts Katherine and Margaret, who often speak to her in French and not English, since they are not on their side. And since she has known by revelation that the voices supported the prince mentioned above, she has disliked the Burgundians.

Article 11: Item, this woman says and confesses that she has paid reverence to these voices and spirits that she calls Michael, Gabriel, Katherine and Margaret, on many occasions, uncovering her head, bending her knees, kissing the ground upon which they walked and vowing her virginity to them, sometimes embracing and kissing Katherine and Margaret. She has touched them corporeally and materially, and asked for counsel and aid from them, sometimes calling them, although they often visit her without being summoned; she assents to, and obeys, their counsels and commands, and she has assented from the outset without asking counsel of anyone, such as her father or mother, a priest or prelate, or any other churchman. And, nevertheless, she firmly believes that the voices and revelations that she has had through these male and female saints come from God and at His command; and she believes this as firmly as she believes in the Christian faith and that Our Lord Jesus Christ suffered death for us. She adds that if an evil spirit were to appear to her, pretending to be St Michael, she would certainly be able to tell if this was St Michael or not. This woman also says that, of her own free will, without being forced or asked, she swore to the Sts Katherine and Margaret who appeared to her that she would not reveal the sign of the crown that she had to give to the prince to whom she was sent; and at the end she added: unless she had permission to reveal it.

Article 12: Item, this woman says and confesses that if the Church wanted her to do anything contrary to the command that she says God gave her, she would not do it for any reason whatsoever, affirming that she knows well that what is contained in the trial record accords with the command of God, and that it would be impossible for her to do the contrary. And she does not wish to submit to the decision of the Church militant on these matters, nor that of any man in the world, but only Our Lord God whose commands she will always follow, above all in the matter of revelations and on what she says that she has done because of the revelations. And she says that she did not make this reply, and the other replies, of her own accord, but that she made and gave them at the command of the voices and the revelations made to her, even though the judges and the others present in this place had frequently explained the article of faith 'one holy, catholic Church' [*unam sanctam ecclesiam catholicam*],[130] explaining to her that every faithful pilgrim in this world is bound to obey and to submit their actions and words to the Church militant, especially in the matter of faith and what concerns holy doctrine and Church laws.

---

130 This was a reference to the Nicene Creed. See footnote 133 below.

53. The opinions of the University of Paris
(Saturday 19 May 1431)

Source: Tisset (ed.), *Procès de condamnation*, I, pp. 361–4.

Language: Latin

The official Latin trial presents the opinions of a range of theologians and lawyers on the Twelve Articles, including the chapter of Rouen cathedral, eleven advocates of the ecclesiastical court at Rouen and over twenty-five other named individuals who had been present during the trial. In addition, Jean Beaupère, Jacques de Touraine and Nicolas Midi presented the Twelve Articles to the University of Paris, and the Faculties of Theology and Canon Law debated them on 29 April. The two Faculties adopted different approaches: the theologians analysed each article in turn whereas the canon lawyers presented a synthesis which also labelled the crimes and provided a clear conclusion. Their written comments were sent to Cauchon on 14 May and five days later were read out at Rouen.

(a) The conclusions of the Faculty of Theology

And firstly, as for the first article, the Faculty says, doctrinally,[131] after having considered the purpose, the manner and the content of the revelations, the quality of the person and the place, and the other circumstances, that either these are imagined, corrupting and pernicious lies, or that these apparitions and revelations are superstitious, from malign and diabolical spirits such as Belial, Satan and Behemoth.

Item, as for the second article, what it contains does not seem true and it is rather a presumptuous, corrupting, pernicious and fictitious lie, harmful to the angelic dignity.

Item, as for the third article, the signs indicated by her are not sufficient and this women believes lightly and affirms rashly. Moreover, in the comparison that she makes, her belief is evil and she strays from the faith.

Item, as for the fourth article, it contains superstition, divination, a presumptuous assertion and vain conceit.

Item, as for fifth article, the said woman is a blasphemer of God, and a despiser of God in His sacraments, setting aside divine law, sacred doctrine and the laws of the Church; she thinks evilly and strays from the faith, all the while boasting vainly. She must be held to be suspect

---

131 The Faculty emphasised that their opinion was 'doctrinal' because they were not making a direct judgement upon the concrete case of Joan of Arc, but rather commenting on the theological issues surrounding the case.

of idolatry and of the consecration of herself and of her garments to demons, imitating the rites of pagans.

Item, as for the sixth article, the said woman is a traitress, deceitful, cruel and thirsty for the shedding of human blood, seditious and an inciter of tyranny, blaspheming God in her commands and revelations.

Item, as for the seventh article, the said woman is impious towards her parents, she transgresses the commandment on the respect due to parents; she is outrageous, a blasphemer towards God; she strays from the faith and has made a rash and presumptuous promise.

Item, as for the eighth article, one finds a faintheartedness turning to desperation and implicitly to suicide, [along with] a presumptuous and rash assertion concerning the remission of an error; and the woman holds a reprehensible view regarding human free will.

Item, as for the ninth article, there is a presumptuous and rash assertion, a pernicious lie. This woman contradicts her [position] in the preceding article, and she misunderstands with regard to faith.

Item, as for the tenth article, there is a presumptuous and rash assertion, superstitious divination, a blasphemy towards Sts Katherine and Margaret, and a transgression of the commandment to love a neighbour.

Item, as for the eleventh article, this woman, in supposing that she has had, under the circumstances described in the first article, the revelations and apparitions of which she boasts, is an idolater, an invoker of demons, and a wanderer from the faith; she utters rash assertions and has made an unlawful oath.

Item, as for the twelfth article, the said woman is schismatic, holding a reprehensible view on the unity and the authority of the Church, an apostate, and until now strays stubbornly from the faith.

(b) The conclusions of the Faculty of Canon Law

Firstly that the said woman is schismatic, schism being an unlawful separation, due to disobedience, from the unity of the Church, and that this woman separates herself from the obedience of the Church militant, following what she has said, etc.[132]

Item, that this woman strays from the faith; she contradicts the article

132 A schismatic differed from a heretic in that they refused to accept the authority of the legitimate ministers of the Church without upholding doctrines that were condemned by the Church.

of the faith which is found in the minor Creed: 'one, holy, catholic and apostolic Church' [*Unam sanctam Ecclesiam catholicam*].[133] And, as the Blessed Jerome says, anyone who contradicts this article reveals themselves as not only ignorant, ill-intentioned and not catholic, but heretical.[134]

Item, that this woman is also apostate, both because she has had the hair that God gave her for a veil cut off for an evil purpose,[135] and also because, to the same end, she has abandoned the clothing of a woman and is dressed like a man.

Item, that this woman is a liar and soothsayer when she says that she is sent from God and that she speaks to angels and to saints, whereas she does not demonstrate this by the operation of a miracle or by testimony of the scriptures. When the Lord wished to send Moses into Egypt to the sons of Israel, he gave them a sign so that they would believe that he was sent from God: he changed a staff into a snake and a snake into a staff.[136] Likewise, so that John the Baptist could bring about his reform, he cited the special testimony of his mission found in the Scriptures, saying: 'I am the voice of the one who cries in the wilderness: prepare the way of the Lord',[137] as Isaiah had foretold (Isaiah 40: 3).

Item, that this woman, through presumption of and before the law, strays from the faith, firstly because she has remained in this state for a long time, which is an anathema by the authority of canon law;[138] secondly because she says that she would prefer not to receive the body of Christ, or to confess herself at the time ordained by the Church, rather than to resume woman's clothing after giving up the garb of a man. She is also vehemently suspected of heresy and should be diligently examined on the articles of the faith.[139]

Item, this woman also strays in that she claims to be certain of being taken into heaven, just as if she were already in the glory of the

---

133 The Nicene Creed was referred to as 'minor' because it originated in a Church Council and was therefore of less authority than that of the Apostles. It had originally been cited in the twelfth of the Twelve Articles of Accusation [**52**].

134 *Commentarii in Epist. ad Titum*, c. III.

135 The reference to a woman's hair is an allusion to I Corinthians 11: 15.

136 Exodus 7: 9.

137 Matthew 3: 3; Mark 1: 3; Luke 3: 4; John 1: 23.

138 An anathema was the most severe form of excommunication.

139 There were three levels of suspected heresy, slight, vehement and very great.

blessed, since in that journey, no one knows whether the traveller is worthy of glory or of punishment except the supreme Judge.

This is why, if this woman is charitably exhorted and duly warned by the competent judge, and she chooses not to return of her own accord to the unity of the catholic faith, to abjure publicly her error according to the decision of the judge, and to make appropriate reparation, she must be abandoned to the decision of the secular judge on whether she receives the punishment appropriate to the quality of her crime.

54. The abjuration and sentence (Thursday 24 May 1431)

(a) The official account

Source: Tisset (ed.), *Procès de condamnation*, I, pp. 386–93.

Language: Latin and French

Joan received a preview of the major points raised in the Twelve Articles when she was charitably admonished regarding her errors by the judges on 2 May, but it was not until 23 May that they were read out to her in French by Pierre Maurice in a slightly revised version, incorporating comments from the University of Paris. The following day, Joan appeared before the judges and clerics to hear the final sentence. She was placed on a public platform in the cemetery of the abbey of Saint-Ouen at Rouen. The proceedings began with Master Guillaume Érard delivering a sermon.

The said doctor began his sermon, taking for a theme the word of God written in chapter fifteen of John: 'The branch cannot bear fruit by itself, if it does not remain attached to the vine' (John 15: 4). Then he solemnly elaborated how all catholics must remain on the true vine of our holy mother the Church, planted by the right hand of Christ. He showed that Joan had been separated from the unity of our holy mother Church by numerous errors and grave crimes, and that she frequently scandalised Christian people. He [charitably] admonished and exhorted her, and all those present, [to adhere] to salutary doctrines.

When the sermon was over, this doctor spoke to Joan in these terms: 'Here are my lords the judges, who have repeatedly summoned and required you to submit all your words and deeds to our holy mother the Church, explaining and showing you that in your words and deeds are many that are evilly said and erroneous, in the opinion of the clerics.'

To which Joan replied: 'I will answer you. Regarding the submission to the Church, I have answered them on this point: let everything that

I have said and done be sent to Rome, to our holy lord the pope, upon whom I rely after God. As for my words and deeds, I have done them for God.'

Item, she said that she charged no one with her deeds and words, neither her King nor anyone else; and if there were any fault, it was hers alone.

Asked if she wished to revoke all her words and deeds which had been condemned by the clerks, she answered: 'I rely upon God and our lord the pope.'

And she was told that this would not do, and that it was not possible to go in search of our lord the pope so far away: also that the ordinaries were judges, each in their own diocese.[140] Therefore it was necessary for her to rely upon our holy mother the Church, and to adhere to what the clergy and the men who understood these things said, and what they had decided about her words and deeds.

And she was [charitably] admonished on this by us three times.

Then, as this woman did not wish to say any more, we, the said Bishop [Cauchon], began to pronounce our final sentence.[141] When we had read the greater part of it,[142] the said Joan began to speak and said that she wished to abide by all that the Church ordained and that we, the judges, wished to say and decree, saying that she would obey our ruling in all things. And she said repeatedly that since the churchmen said that the apparitions and revelations that she said she had seen[143] were not to be upheld or believed, she did not wish to maintain them; but in all things she would rely upon our holy mother the Church and us, the judges.

Then, too, in the presence of the aforenamed and in sight of a great crowd of clergy and people, she made and pronounced her revocation and abjuration, according to the contents of a schedule drawn up in French which was then read to her and which she herself repeated; and she signed the schedule with her own hand in the terms that follow:[144]

140 That is to say the bishops.

141 This final sentence was eventually given at the very end of the trial on 30 May 1431.

142 It is not clear at exactly what moment Joan spoke up during the final sentence. Two of the manuscripts of the official Latin record indicate that Joan's interruption came when she was 'fearing the fire.'

143 The phrase 'that she said she had seen' did not appear in the *Minute française*.

144 See the testimony of Aimon, lord of Macy [97].

[The abjuration of Joan] [145]

'Everyone who has erred and made a mistake in the Christian faith
and who later, through the grace of God, returns to the light of truth
and to the union of our holy mother Church, should very carefully
guard that the enemy from hell does not encourage them and make
them fall back into error and damnation.

For this reason, I, Joan, commonly called the Pucelle, a miserable
sinner who has recognised the snares of error in which I was bound
and returned to our holy mother the Church, by the grace of God, in
order to show that I am not pretending to return to her, but [doing
so] with a good heart and will, confess that I have sinned very
grievously in falsely pretending to have had revelations and apparitions from God, His angels, St Katherine and St Margaret; in leading
others astray; in believing madly and too lightly; in making superstitious divinations; in blaspheming God and His saints; in contravening
divine law, holy scripture and canon law; in wearing a dissolute,
shameful and immodest outfit, against natural decency, and hair cut in
a circle in a masculine fashion, against all decency of womankind; also
in bearing arms most presumptuously; in cruelly desiring the
shedding of human blood; in saying that I did all these things at the
command of God, His angels and the saints named before, and that I
acted properly in these matters and did not err; in despising God and
His sacraments, encouraging insurrections and practising idolatry by
adorating and invoking evil spirits. I also confess that I have been
schismatic and that I have strayed from the faith in many ways. With
a good will and without pretence, after having been returned to the
path of truth, thanks to the grace of God, by the holy doctrine and
good counsel of you, and the doctors and masters that you have sent
to me, I abjure, hate and renounce these crimes and errors, and
absolutely abandon and cut myself off from them. And on all of these
matters, I submit to the correction, disposition, amendment and
complete determination of our holy mother the Church and to your
good justice.

I also vow, swear and promise to my lord St Peter, prince of the
apostles, to our holy father the pope in Rome, his vicar, and to his
successors and to you, my lords, the reverend father in God my lord
Bishop of Beauvais and the religious brother Jean Le Maistre, vicar of
my lord the Inquisitor of the faith, as my judges, that I will never

145 The abjuration was presented in both French and Latin in the official record.

through any exhortation or other means return to these errors from which it has pleased Our Lord to deliver and remove me; but I will always remain in union with our holy mother the Church, and under the obedience of our holy father the pope in Rome.

And this I say, affirm and swear by God Almighty and by the holy gospels.

And in witness to this, I have signed this schedule with my signature.

Signed in this way: Jehanne +.

[In the light of Joan's abjuration, the judges accepted her back into the Church but condemned her to solitary penance in prison, so that she might never commit any further crime but also so that she might weep for her crimes, 'with the bread of grief and the water of sorrow'.]

(b) An alternative version of the abjuration

Source: Doncoeur (ed.), *La minute française*, p. 271.

Language: French

The Orléans manuscript of the *Minute française* includes the following version of the abjuration. Some historians believe that this is the actual document that Joan signed at Rouen, as Jean Massieu and others claimed at the Nullification trial [99]. Others are more suspicious: the document is described as giving 'the tenor of the schedule' which the judges had asked Joan to sign; the use of 'etc.' is extremely unusual in such an important document and suggests that material has been omitted; there is no oath such as would necessarily accompany such a document and such as appears in the version contained in the Latin record.

I, Joan, called the Pucelle, a miserable sinner, after I recognised the snare of error in which I was held, and now that I have, by God's grace, returned to our holy mother the Church, in order that it may be seen that I have not returned to her falsely, but with good heart and will, confess that I have grievously sinned in falsely pretending to have had revelations from God and His angels, St Katherine and St Margaret, etc.

And all my words and deeds which are contrary to the Church, I revoke; and I wish to remain in union with the Church, without ever departing.

In witness, my sign manual,

signed Jhenne +

55. The opening of the trial for relapse (Monday 28 May 1431)

Source: Tisset (ed.), *Procès de condamnation*, I, pp. 395–9.

Language: Latin

On the afternoon of 24 May, Joan agreed to resume wearing female clothing and allowed her hair to be shaved off completely. The judges returned to Joan's prison cell four days later with seven clerics and her guard, John Grey.

And because Joan had put on the clothing of a man, that is to say a tunic, hood and doublet with other garments used by men, though she had recently abandoned this outfit at our order and taken the clothing of a woman, we questioned her: when, and for what reason, had she taken male clothing again?

And Joan replied that she had taken this male clothing just recently and set aside that of a woman.

Asked why she had taken this male clothing, and who had induced her to wear it, she answered that she had taken it of her own free will, and that she preferred this male clothing to that of a woman.

She was then told that she had promised and sworn not to resume male clothing, but she replied that she never understood that she had made an oath not to resume this male clothing.

Asked once again for what reason she had taken it, she answered that she had done it because it was more lawful and convenient to wear male clothing when she was among men, than to wear the clothing of a woman. Item, she said that she had resumed it because what had been promised to her had not been kept, that is to say that she might go to mass and receive the body of Christ, and that she might be freed from her iron chains.

Asked if she had abjured before, and in particular sworn not to resume this male clothing, she replied that she would rather die than be in iron chains; but if she were allowed to go to mass, released from her chains and given a gracious prison,[146] she would be good and do what the Church wanted.

Item, because we, her judges, had heard it said by some people that she had still not abandoned the illusions of her pretended revelations

---

146 The term 'gracious' presumably means suitable and tolerable, though it does not appear commonly in the fifteenth century. The Latin record omits the words 'and if she had a woman servant' that appear in the Urfé manuscript of the *Minute française*.

which she had previously renounced, we asked her if she had heard the voices of Sts Katherine and Margaret since Thursday [the day of the abjuration]. She answered yes.[147]

Asked about what they told her, she replied that God told her through Sts Katherine and Margaret of the great pity of this treason to which she, Joan, had consented in making the abjuration and retraction in order to save her life, and that she had damned herself to save her life. Item, she said that before Thursday her voices told her what to do that day, and she then did it. She also said that her voices told her, when she was on the scaffold or platform in front of the people, that she should boldly answer the preacher who was speaking then. And Joan said that this was a false preacher, and that he had said that she had done many things that she had not done.[148] Item, she said that, if she declared that God had not sent her, she would damn herself and that in truth God had sent her. Item, she said that her voices told her, since Thursday, that she had done a great wrong in confessing that she had certainly not done that which she had done. Item, she said that what she had stated and recanted on Thursday, she only did and said out of fear of the fire.

Asked if she believed that the voices that appeared to her were Sts Katherine and Margaret, she answered yes, and that they came from God.

Asked to speak truthfully about that crown which was mentioned above, she replied: 'I have told you the truth about everything during the trial, as well as I knew how.'

Then she was told that she had said on the scaffold or platform in front of us, the judges, others and the people, when she made the abjuration that she had falsely boasted that the voices were Sts Katherine and Margaret. She answered that she had not understood it, to act or to speak in this manner.

Item, she said that she had not said or understood to dismiss her apparitions, that is to say that they were Sts Katherine and Margaret; and all that she did, she did out of fear of the fire, and she did not

147 A marginal note next to these words in three of the manuscripts of the Latin trial record says 'Responsio mortifera' – 'The fatal reply'.

148 This statement would seem to imply that the preacher, Guillaume Érard, had said far more in his sermon on 24 May than the French and Latin record implied. This would accord with the testimony of many witnesses during the Nullification trial who reported that he had attacked Charles VII for supporting a heretic and schismatic.

revoke anything except that which was against the truth. Item, she said that she would rather do penance on one occasion, that is to say to die, than to endure her pain in prison any longer.

Item, she said that she had never done anything against God or the faith, whatever they had ordered her to revoke, and she did not understand what was in the schedule of abjuration. Item, she said that she did not intend to revoke anything unless it pleased God.[149] Item, she said that if the judges wished, she would resume female clothing; and for the rest, she would not do anything more.

After hearing this, we left her to proceed further, according to law and to reason.

56. The final sentence of Joan (Wednesday 30 May 1431)

Source: Tisset (ed.), *Procès de condamnation*, I, pp. 410–14.

Language: Latin

On Tuesday 29 May, the judges met with over forty clerics, all of whom supported the decision to proceed against Joan for relapse. The following day she was summoned to appear at the Old Market of Rouen, near the church of St Sauveur, where the proceedings began with Master Nicolas Midi delivering a sermon on St Paul's first Epistle to the Corinthians: 'Where one member suffers, all the members suffer with it' (I Corinthians 12: 26). The judges then passed final sentence on Joan.

The author of schism and of heresy, the assailant of your heart, has seduced you, and you have again fallen – O, sorrow! – into these same errors and crimes already stated, just as the dog returns to his vomit, as is sufficiently and clearly established by your spontaneous confessions and assertions; and we have recognised by the most clear judgements that previously it was with words alone, and certainly more a lying heart than a sincere and faithful soul, that you had renounced your deceitful inventions. Therefore it follows that, declaring you to have fallen again into the sentence of excommunication that you had originally incurred, and into your previous errors, we call you a relapse

149 In the original *Minute française*, Joan is actually reported as saying: 'Item, she said that she had said *at that time* that she did not mean to revoke anything unless it pleased God.' In other words, she did not intended to disavow anything regarding her life and her acts at the moment of the abjuration. Translating this into Latin, Courcelles left out the words 'at that time' and thereby transformed the meaning of the statement.

and heretic, and by our present sentence that we deliver in writing and read aloud, while sitting in this tribunal, that we judge that you are a rotten limb that, so you do not equally infect the other limbs, must be cast out from the unity of the Church, cut off from her body and given up to the secular power:[150] we cast you off, separate and abandon you, calling upon this same secular power to limit its judgement of you this side of death and the mutilation of your limbs and, if true signs of repentance appear in you, to permit the sacrament of penance to be administered to you.

[The judges then repeated the original sentence that they had not finished delivering on 24 May, summarising the objectives and structures of the trial, but adding at the end of that document:]

You have falsely imagined revelations and divine apparitions; and you are a pernicious seductress, presumptuous, believing too lightly, rash, superstitious, a soothsayer, a blasphemer towards God and His saints and a despiser of God Himself in His sacraments; and you have transgressed against divine, sacred and ecclesiastical laws; and you are seditious, cruel, apostate and schismatic, and you err on numerous points of our faith; and that by what has gone before and in this manner, you have rashly offended against God and the holy Church. Moreover, although you have duly and sufficiently, frequently and very often been [charitably] admonished, not only by us, but also by expert and learned doctors and masters seeking the salvation of your soul, to seek to amend and correct yourself, you did not wish to submit to the arrangement, decision and correction of the holy mother the Church and refused to accept the cure. Moreover, with a hardened, obstinate and opiniated soul you have positively denied and have even expressly and on many occasions refused to submit yourself to our holy father the pope and to the holy General Council. Therefore it follows that, as [you are] obstinate and stubborn in the crimes, faults and errors above,[151] we declare you excommunicate by law and a heretic, and since your errors have been condemned in a public sermon, we judge that, as a limb of Satan cut from the Church, infected with the leprosy of heresy, so that you may not equally infect the other limbs of Christ, you must be abandoned to the secular power

150 The notion of the heretic as a rotten limb echoed the theme of sermon that had just been delivered by Nicolas Midi on the subject of Saint Paul's letter to the Corinthians.

151 It was not error in itself that characterised heresy, but the obstinate persistence in error and the refusal to listen to superiors.

and so we abandon you, beseeching this same power to limit its judgement of you this side of death and the mutilation of your limbs and, if true signs of repentance appear in you, to permit the sacrament of penance to be administered to you.

[The trial record then concluded without any account of the execution of Joan. The punishment of heretics was carried out by secular authorities and therefore was never detailed in inquisitorial records.]

III: DEBATING JOAN OF ARC (1431–1455)

57. Letter from Henry VI to the prelates of France (28 June 1431)

Source: Tisset (ed.), *Procès de condamnation*, I, pp. 426–30.

Language: French

Following the execution of Joan, letters were sent on behalf of Henry VI to the pope and to the cardinals, as well as to the Emperor Sigismund and other kings, princes and dukes outside France.[1] An additional letter was written in French to the bishops of France, and copied to other nobles, including the Duke of Burgundy, and to major cities and towns; this document was subsequently transcribed by a number of chroniclers, including Enguerrand de Monstrelet and Jean de Wavrin.

Reverend father in God, it is commonly enough known, having been spread everywhere already, that this woman who called herself Joan the Pucelle, a false prophetess, had dressed in the clothing of a man for two years or more, against divine law and the estate of her feminine sex, a thing abominable to God, and in this state went before our chief enemy. She frequently led him and those of his party, churchmen, nobles and ordinary people, to understand that she had been sent by God, presumptuously boasting that she often had personal and visible communication with St Michael and a great host of angels and saints of heaven, such as St Katherine and St Margaret. By these deceits that she was given to believe and by the hope that she created of future victories, she turned the hearts of many men and women from the path of truth, and won them over by fables and lies. She also dressed herself in arms made for knights and squires, raised a standard and, in a very great insult, arrogance and presumption, she asked to have and to bear the most noble and excellent arms of France, which she obtained in part [i.e. as element of her coat of arms], and wore in many battles and assaults, as did her brothers, so it is said: that is a shield *azure* [a blue background] with two fleurs-de-lys *or* [in gold] and a sword with the point upright, supporting a

---

1 Tisset (ed.), *Procès de condamnation*, I, pp. 423–6, 433–6.

crown.[2] In such a state, she set out to lead men-at-arms, and to command armies and great companies, in order to commit and to carry out inhuman cruelties, shedding human blood, stirring up sedition and unrest among the people, inciting them to perjuries and dangerous rebellions,[3] superstitions and false beliefs, disturbing all true peace and renewing mortal war. [She did this while] allowing herself to be worshipped and revered by many as a holy woman, and otherwise acting damnably in many other ways too long to list, which have nonetheless been well enough known in many places, at which almost all Christendom has been greatly scandalised.

But the divine power, taking pity on His loyal people, has not left them long in danger or suffered them to remain in these vain, dangerous and new beliefs with which they engaged so lightly; out of great pity and mercy, He chose to allow this woman to be captured before Compiègne and delivered into our jurisdiction and power. And the Bishop of the diocese in which she had been taken summoned us to deliver this woman, noted and defamed for the crimes of treason against God [*lese majesté divine*], to him as her ordinary ecclesiastical judge; [therefore] both out of respect for our holy mother the Church whose holy ordinances we wish to prefer to our own acts and desires, as is reasonable, as well as for the honour and the exaltation of our holy faith, we had the said Joan delivered to him to put on trial, without chosing that the men and officers of our secular law should take any vengeance or punishment, as it would have been reasonable and lawful to do, given the great injuries and sufferings, the horrible murders and detestable cruelties, and the other countless ills that she had committed against our lordship and our loyal and obedient people. This Bishop, together with the vicar of the Inquisitor of errors and heresies, having summoned a great and notable number of solemn masters and doctors of theology and canon law, began the trial against this Joan with all formality and due gravity.

[The letter then offered a brief but relatively accurate summary of the trial, as reported in the official records; it cited the judges' conclusions that Joan was 'superstitious, a witch, idolatrous, a caller up of demons, blasphemous towards God and His saints, schismatic and greatly erring in the faith of Jesus Christ', along with Joan's abjuration.]

---

2 This is an accurate description of the coat of arms given to Joan of Arc and her family by Charles VII.

3 Rebellion against Henry VI was also perjury if the individual had taken an oath in support of the Treaty of Troyes and the Dual Monarchy.

But it was scarcely any time after this that the fire of her pride, which had seemed to be extinguished in her, burst into poisonous flames again [fanned] by the breath of the Enemy; and soon this wretched woman fell back into the errors and wild folly that she had formerly professed and since recanted and abjured, as has been said. Therefore, following what the judgements and the institutions of the holy Church ordain, in order to prevent her from contaminating the other limbs of Jesus Christ, she was again [charitably] admonished in public, and, as she had fallen again into her accustomed crimes and faults, she was handed over to secular justice which immediately condemned her to be burned. And seeing her end approaching, she fully recognised and confessed that the spirits, which she said had so often appeared to her, were evil and false, and that the promises which these spirits had made to her, to have her freed, were untrue; and so she confessed that she had been mocked and deceived by these spirits.[4]

Such is the result of her works, such is the fate of this woman, and we are now making them known to you, reverend father in God, in order to inform you truthfully about this matter, so that throughout the parts of your diocese that seem fit to you, you may make these things known by public sermons or other means for the good and praise of our holy faith, and the edification of the Christian people who have been deceived and abused for a long time by the works of this woman.[5] [We also do this] so that you can, as belongs to your dignity, ensure that no one among the people entrusted to you may presume to believe lightly in such errors and dangerous superstitions, especially at this present time when we see many false prophets and trouble-makers [holding] damnable errors and mad belief who, rising against our holy mother Church in mad audacity and outrageous presumption, could perhaps infect the Christian people with the perilous venom of false belief, if Jesus Christ, in His mercy, did not provide [some remedy], and you and his ministers to which it pertains did not

---

4 This claim is almost certainly untrue, as demonstrated by both the official trial record and multiple statements at the Nullification trial. It appears to have originated in a posthumous inquiry that Cauchon held on 7 July 1431, at which Nicolas de Vendères, Martin Ladvenu, Pierre Maurice, Jean Toutmouillé, Jacques Le Camus, Thomas de Courcelles and Nicolas Loiseleur all reported that Joan had denounced her voices at the very end: Tisset (ed.), *Procès de condamnation*, I, pp. 416–22. The claim was apparently repeated by Jean Graverent in his sermon in Paris [59].

5 One example of such a sermon was that given by the Inquisitor of France, Jean Graverent, in Paris on 4 July 1431, as recorded by the Bourgeois of Paris [59].

diligently endeavour to repulse and punish the intentions and mad audacity of these blameworthy men.

Given in our town of Rouen, the 28th day of June [1431].

58. The *Journal* of Clément de Fauquembergue (June 1431)

Source: Clément de Fauquembergue, *Journal de Clément de Fauquembergue, greffier du Parlement du Paris, 1417–1435*, ed. A. Tuetey and H. Lacaille, 3 vols, Paris, 1903–15, III, pp. 13–14.

Language: French

On the 30th day of May 1431, by trial of the Church, Joan, who called herself the Pucelle and had been captured during a sally from the town of Compiègne by the men of my lord Jean de Luxembourg, along with others at the siege of the said town ... was set fire to and burned in the city of Rouen. And on the mitre which she had upon her head was written the following words: 'heretic, relapse, apostate, idolater'. And on a placard in front of the fire in which she was placed were written these words: 'Joan who had herself named the Pucelle, liar, pernicious person, abuser of people, soothsayer, superstitious woman, blasphemer of God, presumptuous, unbeliever in the faith of Jesus Christ, boaster, idolater, cruel, dissolute, invoker of devils, apostate, schismatic and heretic'. And the sentence was pronounced by my lord Pierre Cauchon, Bishop of Beauvais, the diocese where Joan had been captured, as has been said. And he called many notable churchmen from the duchy of Normandy, graduates in learned subjects, and many theologians and lawyers of the University of Paris, to hold this trial, as may be seen more fully in the trial record.

59. The Journal of a Bourgeois of Paris (c. 1431?)

Source: A. Tuetey (ed.), *Journal d'un Bourgeois de Paris, 1405–1449*, Paris, 1881, pp. 236–7, 244–6, 266–72.

Language: French

The journal of the so-called Bourgeois [burgher] of Paris was written by a cleric who was an eyewitness to events within the city during the dramatic period from 1405 to 1449. The author did not write his account on a day to day basis, but the fact that he poured scorn on the rumour of the impending arrival of Henry VI in the entry for April 1430, even though this actually happened in November 1431, would suggest that the author was composing this section, at least, very soon after the events in question. For the majority of the text, the author was a strong supporter of the Burgundians, though he appears to have reversed his allegiance by the time of the Valois recapture of Paris in 1436. Certainly his view of Joan after her death is somewhat more complicated than his initial reactions to her at the time of her attack on Paris in September 1429.

(a) The arrival of the Pucelle

Item, there was at this time a Pucelle, as they called her, alongside the Loire river, who called herself a prophet, and said: 'Such and such a thing will certainly happen.' And she was completely opposed to the Regent of France [the Duke of Bedford] and to his supporters. And it was said that, despite all the men who were laying siege before Orléans, she entered the city with a very great number of Armagnacs and a good quantity of provisions ... And many other things were said about her by those who loved the Armagnacs better than the Burgundians, or the Regent of France. They claimed that, when she was very small, and she was watching over the sheep, the birds from the woods and fields would come when she called them, and they would eat her bread in her lap, as if they were tame. The answer lies in the truth [*In veritate appocrisium est*].[6]

(b) The attack upon Paris[7]

Item, on the eve of the Nativity of Our Lady in September [7 September 1429], the Armagnacs mounted an attack upon the walls of Paris and they hoped to take it by assault. But they gained little there except for grief, shame and calamity, because many who had been in full health before the attack, were injured for life; but the fool never believes until he tries. For I say that these men were so full of great error and foolish trust that on the advice of a creature with them, who was in the shape of a woman, named the Pucelle – who this was, God knows [*qui c'estoit, Dieu le scet*][8] – that they unanimously

6 The Greek verb 'apokrino' means to separate or to answer.

7 The anonymous author had previously described the Armagnac victory at Orléans, recounting the story of an English commander who shouted abuse at Joan but was subsequently killed, presumably referring to William Glasdale: Tuetey (ed.), *Journal d'un Bourgeois de Paris, 1405–1449*, p. 237.

8 The French phrase 'qui c'estoit' has attracted much attention by recent scholars but is somewhat ambiguous. It can either be translated as 'who this was' (and hence questioning the identity of the Pucelle) or 'what this was' (referring to the undetermined sex of the 'creature'). Either way, the author is not clearly denying that the Pucelle was human.

conspired to attack Paris on the day of the Holy Nativity of Our Lady [8 September 1429]. Easily twelve thousand or more gathered, and came at around the time of high mass, between eleven and twelve, their Pucelle with them and very large number of wagons, carts and horses, all loaded with bundles of sticks [tied] by three ropes to fill up the moats of Paris. They began to attack between the Saint-Honoré gate and the Saint-Denis gate, and the assault was very savage; while attacking, they shouted many vile words at the people of Paris. And their Pucelle was there with her standard on the bank above the moats, and she said to the Parisians: 'Surrender yourselves, by Jesus, because if you do not surrender before it is night we will enter by force, whether you like it or not, and you will all be put to death without mercy.'[9] 'See here, you whore, you slut [*paillarde, ribaulde*]!' said one, and he shot his crossbow straight at her, and [the bolt] went right through her leg, and she fled. Another pierced right through the foot of man who carried her standard and when he felt himself to be wounded, he lifted his visor to see to draw the bolt from his foot and another man shot at him and hit him between the eyes and mortally wounded him; the Pucelle and the Duke of Alençon later swore that they would rather have lost forty of their best men-at-arms of their company than him. The fight was very fierce on both sides and went on until at least four in the afternoon, without anyone knowing who was getting the better of it. Shortly after four o'clock, the Parisians took heart and turned them back with their cannons and other artillery so much that they [the Armagnacs] were forced to retreat, to abandon their assault and to flee. The happiest were those who were best able to flee, because the Parisians had great cannons which fired from the Saint-Denis gate to well beyond Saint-Lazare, and which fired at their backs, at which they were very terrified. Thus they were put to flight, but no one left Paris to follow them, for fear of their ambushes. As they retreated, they set fire to the barn of the Mathurins near Les Porcherons, and they put into this fire, in great numbers, the men who had died in the assault and whom they had tied on to their horses, as the pagans used to do long ago in Rome. They cursed their Pucelle, who had promised them that they would certainly succeed in this assault on Paris, that she would sleep there that night and so would they all, that they would all be made rich by the wealth of the city, and that all who put up any defence there

9 At the end of the fourth private examination on Tuesday 13 March 1431, Joan denied that she had called upon the Parisians to surrender in the name of Jesus, but rather that of the King of France [43].

would be put to the sword or burned in their homes. But God, who through a woman called Judith thwarted the great enterprise of Holofernes, in His mercy ordained other than they thought ... Good should not come to those who wish to cause such slaughter on the day of the Holy Nativity of Our Lady.[10]

(c) The death of the Pucelle

Item, on the eve of the feast of Corpus Christi in this year, which was 30 May in the year 1431, my lady Joan, who had been captured before Compiègne and who was known as the Pucelle, was preached to in Rouen.[11] She was on a platform and everyone could see her clearly, dressed in male clothing. There she was shown what very great distress had fallen upon Christendom through her, especially upon the kingdom of France, as everyone knows: how she had come to attack Paris with fire and blood on the day of the Holy Nativity of Our Lady; the many great and terrible sins that she had done and caused to be done; how at Senlis and elsewhere she had caused simple people to commit idolatry, since through her false hypocrisy they followed her as if she were a holy Pucelle, because she gave them to understand that the glorious archangel St Michael, St Katherine, St Margaret and many other saints frequently appeared to her and spoke to her as one friend to another, and not by revelation as God has sometimes spoken to His friends, but bodily, mouth to mouth, as one friend speaks to another.

Item, it is true that she said that aged around seventeen, without feeling any shame and despite her father, mother, relations and friends, she often went to a beautiful spring in the region of Lorraine, which she called the 'Good Spring of the Fairies [of] Our Lord'. All those of that region used to go to this place, to recover their health

---

10 Nicolas Sellier, the *greffier* of the cathedral chapter of Notre-Dame, provided a little-known account of the attack upon Paris, in which he commented that the enemies were driven back by the obstinate resistance of the Parisians, fortified by 'their faith in God and in the glorious Virgin whose feast was celebrated in that city of Paris with honour'; a marginal note to his account also pointed out that Joan was subsequently captured at Compiègne and burned at Rouen: Tuetey (ed.), *Journal d'un Bourgeois de Paris, 1405–1449*, p. 244n.

11 It is not clear how the author had acquired such detailed knowledge of the trial. He must have spoken with witnesses, or seen the complete trial record: the *Instrumentum sententiae*, an official Latin document issued immediately after the execution of Joan, only included a summary of the acts of the trial and her abjuration, as well as the texts of the two sentences issued on 24 and 30 May 1431: Doncoeur (ed.), *Instrument public des sentences.*

when they had fevers. This Joan the Pucelle often went there underneath a big tree that shaded the spring, and St Katherine and St Margaret appeared to her and told her that she was to go to a captain whom they named. She went there without receiving permission from her father or her mother, and this captain dressed her in the manner of a man, gave her a sword, an esquire and four servants, and then mounted her on a good horse. At that point, she went to the King of France and said to him that she had come to him by the command of God, that she would make him the greatest lord in the world, and that it had been ordained that all those who disobeyed her would be killed without mercy; [she added that] St Michael and many angels had given her a very sumptuous crown for him, and there was also a sword in the ground for him, but she would not give it to him until the war had ended. With a great number of men-at-arms, but no women, she rode every day with the King, attired, dressed and armed in the manner of a man, a great staff in her hand. When any of her men made a mistake, she struck them very hard with this staff, like a very cruel woman.

Item, she says that she is certain to be in heaven at the end of her days.

Item, she says that she is absolutely sure that it is St Michael, St Katherine and St Margaret who speak to her often, whenever she wishes, and that she has frequently seen them with crowns of gold on their heads, and that everything that she does is at the command of God, and, what is more, she says that she knows a great deal about what is to come.

Item, many times she has received the precious sacrament of the altar while armed, dressed like a man, her hair cut round, in a hood with jagged edges, tunic, scarlet hose tied with a number of laces.[12] Some great lords and ladies said to her, reprimanding her for the mockery of her clothing, that this showed little respect to Our Lord to receive Him in such an outfit when she was a woman. She answered them at once that nothing would make her act otherwise and that she would prefer to die than to give up men's clothing, whatever the prohibition, and that if she wished, she would make thunder and other marvels if she liked, and that once someone had tried to harm her but she had jumped down from a high tower without hurting herself at all.

12 The use of laced hose may have been regarded as assertively masculine, given that women's stockings were usually held up by garters.

Item, in several places she had men and women killed, both in battle and in wilful revenge, because she had those who did not obey the letters sent by her killed immediately without pity whenever she could. She said and affirmed that she never did anything except by God's command transmitted frequently by the archangel St Michael, by St Katherine, and by St Margaret, who made her do this. [This was] not as Our Lord did to Moses on Mount Sinai, but they specifically told her secret things to come; they had ordered and prescribed everything that she did, be it concerning her clothing or otherwise.

This lady Joan held these false errors and worse, and they were all recounted in front of the people, who were appalled when they heard the story of these great errors that she had held against our faith, and which she still held. For, though her great evil spells and errors were shown to her, she was not horrified or shocked, but replied boldly to the articles put forward before her, just like one completely in league with the devil. This was very obvious, for she saw the clerks of the University of Paris who humbly begged her to repent and recant this evil error, so that all would be forgiven her through penance, or, if not, she would be burned before all the people and her soul damned to the depths of hell.[13] They showed her the edict, and the place where the fire would be built to burn her straightaway if she did not recant. When she saw that this was a certainty, she cried for mercy, and she recanted with words, and her gown was taken away, and she was dressed in the clothing of a woman.[14] But no sooner did she see herself like that than she fell again into her error just as before, calling for her male clothing. She was at once unanimously condemned to die and was tied to a stake which was on the platform (which was made of plaster) and the fire lit under her. She was soon dead and her clothes all burned. Then the fire was raked back, and her naked body was shown to all the people, with all the secrets that could or should belong to a woman, to remove any doubt from the people. When they had seen enough and looked as much as they liked at the dead body bound to the stake, the executioner started a great fire again round her poor carcass, which was almost all burned up, and flesh and bone

13 A reference to the session on 18 April 1431, at which the doctors and professors of theology from the University of Paris called upon Joan to renounce her errors and to submit to the Church.

14 The conflation of the events between the abjuration (24 May) and the final sentence (30 May) may undermine the credibility of the author's famous account of what occurred at Joan's execution.

were reduced to ashes. There were many people there, and elsewhere, who said that she had been martyred for her true lord. Others said that she was not, and that the one who had looked after her for so long had acted evilly.[15] Such things people said, but whatever evil or good she had done, she was burned that day …

Item, on the day of St Martin le Boullant [9 August 1431], a general procession was made to Saint-Martin-des-Champs where a friar of the Order of St Dominic [Jean Graverent] who was the Inquisitor of the faith and a master of theology, gave a sermon once again on everything that Joan the Pucelle had done.[16] He stated that she had said that she was the daughter of very poor people, that she had persisted in [wearing] the clothing of a man when she was about fourteen years old, and that from that time on, her father and mother would gladly have brought about her death if they could have done so without staining their consciences. So she had therefore left them, accompanied by the devil, and since then had killed Christian people, full of fire and blood, until at last she was burned. He also said that she had recanted and been assigned penance, that is four years in prison on bread and water, of which she did not do a single day, but was waited on in prison like a lady. And the devil appeared to her in three forms, that is St Michael, St Margaret and St Katherine, as she called them. He, that is to say this enemy or enemies in the form of these three saints, was very much afraid that he would lose her and he said to her: 'Miserable creature who has changed your dress for fear of death! Do not be afraid. We will protect you effectively from them all.' So she then immediately undressed and put on all the old clothes that she wore when riding, which she had pushed into the straw of her bed. She trusted this devil so much that she told him that she was sorry that she had ever agreed to give up her clothes. When the University, or those about her, saw this and that she had been so obstinate, she was handed over to the lay power to die. When she saw herself in this situation, she called on the enemies who appeared to her in the guise of saints, but after she was condemned not one of them appeared to her again despite her offering all the invocations that she knew. Then she realised, but it was too late. [The Inquisitor]

15 It is most likely that the author is referring to Charles VII, though the phrase is ambiguous and does not clarify which human or even diabolical ally is being cited.

16 The Dominican, Jean Graverent, was a professor of theology at the University of Paris and became Inquisitor of France in 1422. He had delegated his powers to Jean Le Maistre for the trial of Joan of Arc.

also said in his sermon that there were four of them, of whom three had been captured, that is to say this Pucelle, Pieronne and her companion,[17] as well as another called Catherine de La Rochelle who is with the Armagnacs;[18] the last said that when the precious body of Our Lord is consecrated, she sees the great and secret wonders of Our Lord God. All these four poor women, he said, had been under the direction of Brother Richard the Franciscan, to whose sermons at the Innocents and elsewhere all Paris had flocked, because he was their confessor. [The Inquisitor] also said that on Christmas day in the town of Jargeau, [Brother Richard] had given the body of Our Lord three times to this my lady Joan the Pucelle, for which he should be reprimanded, and he had given it two times to Pieronne that day, according to the evidence of their confession and of certain people who were present at the time when he gave them the precious sacrament.

60. Letter of remission regarding two inhabitants of Abbeville (6 July 1432)

Source: Tuetey (ed.), *Journal d'un Bourgeois de Paris, 1405–1449*, pp. 269–70n.
Language: French

This document is a pardon granted to two inhabitants of Abbeville by the English authorities which provides very rare evidence of public opinion regarding Joan of Arc.

After our enemy and opponents had entered our city of Paris with a woman in their company who was popularly known as the Pucelle, one particular day, the supplicants were in the company of a man named Colin Broyart in front of, and very near to, the home of a Marshal named Guillaume du Pont in our town of Abbeville, and they heard that some people were speaking about the case and excesses of the woman commonly known as the Pucelle, and especially a herald, to whom this Pucelle had said: 'Shit! Shit!' And the Pucelle did and said this, which was nothing other than improper. And likewise Colin

---

17 Pieronne the Breton was one of the penitents of the preacher, Brother Richard. She followed Joan of Arc at her sortie at Sully, was captured at Corbeil with an unidentified friend (who was subsequently released) by the English and Burgundian forces, and was burned at the stake for heresy on 3 September 1430. According to the Bourgeois, Pieronne had claimed that God often appeared to her in human form, dressed in a long white robe with a red tunic underneath.

18 The use of the present tense would suggest that this passage was written very soon after the events in question.

and others nearby said that no one should put faith in this woman and that those who gave credence to her were mad ...

61. *The Chronicle of the Cordeliers* (c.1432)

Source: S. Luce, *Jeanne d'Arc à Domremy: recherches critiques sur les origines de la mission de la Pucelle*, Paris, 1886, pp. 336–44.

Language: French

This anonymous chronicle stops on 25 July 1431, and was almost certainly written around 1432. The author was probably a Franciscan monk (who were known as Cordeliers in France because of the girdle of knotted cord that they wore), either from Picardy or Brabant Wallon. His report of military matters from the siege of Orléans to the capture of the Pucelle at Compiègne is often unreliable, but the work is interesting because it is the earliest 'Burgundian' account of Joan of Arc, and because the author was far less hostile towards her than later writers, such as Monstrelet, who certainly drew upon this source.

[1429] At this time there arrived before the dauphin a young girl born in Lorraine, the daughter of a poor farmer, who called herself Jeanette the Pucelle. She had guarded the sheep in the village in which she had been born. This Pucelle was very innocent in word and behaviour, or so it seemed, and she always let it be understood that through divine inspiration she had to take action to put the dauphin in possession of his kingdom of France and to have him obeyed throughout it. She insisted on this so much to her father and to her friends that she was taken before the dauphin by one of her brothers with others whom she found as her escort. And there, at her say so, the dauphin kept her at his court and set her up in great state, at which the majority of his supporters were greatly astonished because they regarded this Jeannette as foolish and naïve.

When she was retained by the dauphin and maintained in this high position, Jeanette asked to be mounted and armed as a man-at-arms, saying that she would do marvels. And this was done: she began by putting on arms and set out on the road. Shortly afterwards a great number of men-at-arms assembled to raise the siege of Orléans after the failure of the negotiations, as already described.[19] The Pucelle

___

19 The chronicle had described the failure of negotiations between messengers from Orléans and the Duke of Burgundy.

joined forces with this assembly, and raised a standard on which she had inscribed 'Jhesus', and claimed to have been sent by God to put the dauphin in possession of the kingdom of France.

[The chronicler reported the victories at Orléans, Beaugency, Jargeau and Patay.]

When the dauphin of Viennois had made preparations, and with the Pucelle always very close to him in arms as a captain with a great number of men under her, he began to conquer places and regions through the deeds and the fame of the Pucelle that began to spread everywhere. There was no fortress that did not opt to surrender at a simple word or invitation from her, thinking and believing because of her marvellous deeds that this was something divine, as she did astonishing feats of arms with her body and strength, and handled the shaft of a lance very effectively and was quick to make use of it, as was evident every day. In addition, she [charitably] admonished her troops in the name of Jesus and exhorted the people to return to Him and to obey the dauphin. In the end it happened that rumour ran as far as Rome that she had done miracles and that, when she came before a place, the people within, no matter what desire they might have had before to disobey the dauphin or her, were all transformed and overcome and had no power to defend themselves against her ...

[After the coronation of Charles VII at Reims on 17 July 1429] the Pucelle rode on horseback before the King, arrayed in plate armour and with her standard unfurled; when not in armour, she maintained the condition and dress of a knight, her shoes tied with laces to her feet, her hose and her doublet shapely and a hat on her head; she wore very handsome attire of cloth of gold and silk, nicely trimmed with fur.

[The author then provided an extremely neutral account of the subsequent events, even the attack upon Paris, in which he noted the encouragement that she gave to her troops, and Joan's capture at Compiègne.]

The capture of the Pucelle was very much celebrated everywhere, and those of the Burgundian side were very joyous indeed; but those of the other side were very mournful, because they had hopes [where] others had doubts about her actions. She was finally taken as a prisoner to Beaurevoir where she was for a long time, until she cunningly sought to escape through a window. But what she was using broke, so she fell from high up to the ground and almost broke her hips and back. After this injury she was sick for a long time and after she had recovered, she was handed over to the English through some mediations and financial agreements. She was taken to Rouen where her trial was held straight away and she was finally condemned, as will be said afterwards when there is a time and a place.[20]

On the penultimate day of May, Jeanette the Pucelle was burned at Rouen. She had been condemned to prison and reminded of her errors after the noble exhortation regarding her actions [i.e. the public sermon] that had been presented in that place, Rouen, in the presence of the Regent of France, of many high princes and prelates, both of France and of England, of the great council of King Henry, and of all those who wished to hear it. But when she saw that they wanted her to wear the clothing of a woman, she recanted, and said that she wished to die just as she had lived, and therefore she was condemned to die. The remains of her body were thrown in bags into the river so that they could never be used or employed for sorcery or any other evil.

62. The Duke of Bedford's memorandum (14/15 June 1434)

Source: N. H. Nicolas (ed.), *Proceedings and Ordinances of the Privy Council of England*, 7 vols, London, 1834–37, IV, pp. 222–5.

Language: English

John of Lancaster, Duke of Bedford, brother of Henry V, served as Regent for Henry VI in France from 1422 until shortly before his death in 1435. In June 1433, he crossed over to England to defend himself against accusations of mismanagement of the war, almost certainly emanating from his brother, Humphrey, Duke of Gloucester. Shortly before he returned to France in July 1434, he presented to the royal council a memorandum that provided an overview of the recent events in France, in order to make a case for the provision of additional funds for the continued defence of English lands. It is important to note that this oft-quoted document is the only source in which Bedford described Joan's impact on the war, apart from the public letter that he sent to Charles VII in August 1429 [24]; his normal silence on Joan is particularly important, given that the numerous letters, memoranda and even parliamentary speeches that Bedford made during the period from 1429 to

---

20 The author never discussed the trial, and so it is unclear whether he did genuinely intend to come back to this, and was unable to do so, or simply wished to avoid the matter altogether. In general, the Burgundian chroniclers avoided any direct discussion of the Rouen trial, preferring to quote Henry VI's subsequent letter [57].

1434, focused almost entirely upon the lack of adequate financial resources as an explanation for the losses suffered in France.[21]

And the truth is that after the death of my lord, your father [Henry V], on whose soul God have mercy, by the grace of God, and by the good labour and diligence of your loyal men and servants there, I being one of them, and wishing to do what good I could, various great and impressive victories were won there for you and in your cause against your foes, and the territories loyal to you were dramatically enlarged and increased, and a great part of Brie, Champagne, Auxerrois, Donzy, Nivernais, Mâconnais, Anjou and Maine were brought under your sway. And everything prospered there for you until the siege of Orléans, undertaken by God knows whose advice.[22] At which time, after the misfortune which befell the person of my cousin of Salisbury,[23] may God absolve him from sin, it seemed that there fell by the hand of God a great stroke upon your people assembled there, caused in great part, as I think, by lack of proper belief and by unlawful doubt aroused by a disciple and follower of the fiend called the Pucelle, who used false enchantment and sorcery ... [Her] strikes and complete victory not only greatly reduced the number of your people there but also drained the courage of the remnant in marvellous ways and encouraged your adversary's party and enemy to rally at once in great number ... [Many of] your great cities and towns such as Reims, Troyes, Châlons, Laon, Sens, Provins, Senlis, Lagny, Creil, Beauvais and the greater part of the counties of Champagne, Brie, Beauvoisin and also a part of Picardy surrendered without resistance or waiting for help.

---

21 This was an issue of great personal relevance to him because of the significant personal contribution that he had had to make to the war, particularly in 1429: J. Stratford (ed.), *The Bedford Inventories: the worldly goods of John, Duke of Bedford, Regent of France (1389–1435)*, London, 1993, pp. 14–20.

22 In May 1428, Bedford and the council in Paris had decided that the campaign should be directed against Angers and Mont-Saint-Michel, and it has recently been suggested that the decision to attack Orléans undermined Bedford's attempt to negotiate with Duke Charles of Orléans: M. K. Jones, "'Gardez mon corps, sauvez ma terre'. Immunity from war and the lands of a captive knight: the siege of Orléans (1428–1429) revisited', in M-J. Arn (ed.), *Charles d'Orléans in England (1415–1440)*, Cambridge, 2000, pp. 9–26. Yet it is important to note that Bedford himself had contributed at least 117,000 *livres tournois* to the siege of Orléans: Stratford, *Bedford Inventories*, p. 14.

23 Thomas Montagu, Earl of Salisbury, was in command of the siege of Orléans until he died as a result of a wound inflicted by a piece of shrapnel on 24 October 1428.

63. *Contra ducem Burgundie* by Jean de Rinel (1435)

Source: P. Chaplais (ed.), *English Medieval Diplomatic Practice, Part 1: documents and interpretations*, in 2 vols, London, 1982, II, pp. 648–52.

Language: French

Jean de Rinel was a notary and secretary of the king of France and nephew by marriage of Pierre Cauchon. He had worked for the English throughout the period of the Dual Monarchy, and became secretary to Henry VI in 1434. The following year, he wrote a tract in support of the English cause, demonstrating that the Treaty of Troyes (1420) was valid, and that Henry VI, rather than Charles VII, was the true king of France. This tract 'Against the Duke of Burgundy' was almost certainly written for the diplomats participating in the negotiations at the Congress of Arras in 1435.

It is well-known to all the world how great divisions and mortal wars arose in the realm of France between the princes and subjects of France and England over the right and title to the Crown of France, from which for one hundred years, by battles and other deeds, evils and irreparable damages have continually multiplied both by sea and on land. And after the now deceased King Henry [V] had recovered his region of Normandy, which belonged to him by law and by ancient heritage, recognising that it was impossible that this long and perilous war could be brought to an end by human judgement, because the Crown is not subject to any mortal man but only to God, [and that] because of the war the whole realm would fall into great ruin, he planned and attempted many times, and took great pains, trouble and effort to put an end to the war by a sweet and amicable agreement or treaty. [He did this] not only to end the ancient division between the two realms, but also, as a loving prince, to end the civil, internal and mortal division between the princes, nobles and communities of this realm and so that finally, among other things, the divided parties split by mortal hatred, might achieve union and concord under one head, and the poor people might live in peace and true justice. This desire of Henry's was not in vain, nor frustrated, because by the grace of Our Lord, within a short time, a sweet, reasonable and profitable peace acceptable to God and pleasing to all men of good will, was made and sealed with King Charles [VI] who has recently died, by the means of marriage, and with the agreement, consent and advice of the most excellent Queen of France, and the most high and powerful prince the Duke of Burgundy, whom, for many reasons that could be listed, reason moved to support, seek and achieve peace. This peace, both during the life of King Henry [V], father of our lord the present King, as well as since his death, has given and brought to the people of this realm very great fruit, because for a long time, the countryside of France, Picardy, Champagne, Brie, Burgundy and other regions, enjoyed such peace, justice and tranquillity that each person might work, travel and earn a living in safety, until the enemies and adversaries entered and put forward an uncontrolled woman, a sorcerer, idolater and heretic [Joan of Arc] who was justly burned for her horrible crimes. But the people, not recognising, and ungrateful for, the good and great blessings that God had given them, forgetting the efforts and great cost that the late King Henry and, since then, his son, our sovereign lord [Henry VI] had sustained for the safety and repose of these people, who had previously died of hunger, suddenly changed under the influence of the sorceress, so that they forgot the oaths that they had freely given to remain true and loyal subjects of the King our lord. As a result of their disobedience, peace has given way to war, repose to labour, wealth to poverty, joy to grief, hope to despair, concord to division, love to hate, and peaceful coexistence to a great hatred of neighbours and generally into greater war than before.

And though the peace was solemnly made, nevertheless some clerks are trying to argue that the peace should not be kept, principally for four reasons: the first, because it was made, so they say, through violence and fear; the second, because they wish to argue that King Charles who made it, swore to it and accepted it, was not in his right mind; the third, because the dauphin was not a party to it; the fourth, because it is lawful for the Duke of Burgundy to make peace [with Charles VII] without the consent of the King as, although the treaty states that neither the kings nor the lord of Burgundy might make any treaty or agreement with the dauphin without the consent of either of the two kings, who have since died, my lord the Duke of Burgundy is the only survivor and thus he can, so they say, make a treaty with the enemy.

[Rinel then proceeded to argue against these four points.]

64. *Audite celi* by Jean Juvénal des Ursins (1435)

Source: Jean Juvénal des Ursins, *Les écrits politiques de Jean Juvénal des Ursins*, ed. P. S. Lewis, 3 vols, Paris, 1978–93, I, pp. 196–7.

Language: French

In 1435, Jean Juvénal, a staunch supporter of Charles VII and successor to Pierre Cauchon as Bishop of Beauvais, composed an allegorical treatise entitled *Audite celi* ['Listen, O heavens']. This text set out the legal issues of the war for Valois diplomats attending the negotiations with the English and the Burgundians at the Congress of Arras in the summer 1435, together with a plea for a peaceful outcome to that diplomatic encounter. This source is significant because it demonstrates how the supporters of Charles VII removed Joan from their narratives by emphasising the wider story of God's support, but also because Jean Juvénal would later serve as one of the three judges in charge of the Nullification trial.[24]

[France is speaking to England in the presence of a third lady, the Church.] And because you say that the victories and conquests that the late Henry [V] achieved, such as in Normandy and other places, show that it is God's will that he might have the realm of France or at least the conquered territories, know that it could well be that the divine will was that this Henry should come into my land to chastise my children and those living here for the horrible sins that they committed, churchmen, nobles, merchants and labourers alike, and especially for the sedition and division that then flourished. And if there were great victories, such as Agincourt, and at many other notable towns like Rouen, Melun and others, this was only a divine execution to chastise my children, achieved through sedition and division. Because otherwise your Henry would not have dared to cause such harm in France; and it so happened that [sedition and division] had been well rooted and had been there for more than thirty years when this Henry came. And if he won the battles of Agincourt and of Verneuil,[25] this was only because of these sins; because commonly and often God punishes sinners by means of worse sinners than them, and the good especially are afflicted by the wicked.

24 His silence regarding Joan was equally conspicuous in a letter that he composed in 1433 for the Estates General, as well as a treatise that he composed in advance of a proposed meeting between Henry VI and Charles VII in 1446. His only brief reference to Joan appeared in a tract that he wrote in 1458 in support of the Duke of Alençon: Jean Juvénal des Ursins, *Les écrits politiques*, ed. Lewis, I, p. 81 and II, pp. 39–40, 420.

25 The battle of Verneuil took place on 17 August 1424, two years after the death of Henry V.

But this does not give you any right to the realm, or to the things which you say have been conquered by this Henry, because this Henry had no title or justification for this; and his act was violent and very vicious. And if you wish to know everything, God has better aided my master Charles, now King, and those who serve him. See how he was the saviour of Paris, and many notable householders, when his enemies, your allies, entered there [29 May 1418]; [also consider] the battle of Baugé [22 March 1421], of La Gravelle [26 September 1423] and many others; the death of the Duke of Clarence [at Baugé], and others of your nobles; the marvellous death, too, of King Henry. All these things clearly show that [Henry V] displeased God because he disturbed my land in this manner. Know too how the siege of Montargis was lifted [5 September 1427] and later that of Orléans [8 May 1429], and [know] the marvellous things that were done before the very noble, worthy and almost miraculous consecration of King Charles [VII] at Reims, the capture of the towns and cities on this campaign, the ways in which the sieges were raised that you and your allies had set before Compiègne [24 October 1430] and Lagny [10 August 1432] ...

65. *Formicarius* by Johannes Nider (c.1437)

Source: Quicherat (ed.), *Procès de condamnation*, IV, pp. 502–4.

Language: Latin

The German theologian Johannes Nider was born in the early 1380s and became a doctor of theology of the University of Vienna and prior of the Dominican convents at Nuremberg and then Basel. His most famous work was *Formicarius* ('The Ant Hill'), an educational treatise concerned with demonology and witchcraft, presented to the Council of Basel in 1439. Nider cited Joan as an example of a sorceress or witch, even though the Rouen trial had not condemned her on those grounds. Nevertheless the judges at Rouen had clearly associated Joan with witchcraft, and Nider echoed the sermon of the French Inquisitor, Jean Graverent, who had associated the Pucelle with other heretical women [59]. Moreover, he went on to recount the arrival of a 'false Joan' in Cologne in 1436, who fled after being challenged by the Inquisitor, Heinrich Kalt Eysen. He concluded that women had great potential for good, as seen in the examples of Deborah, Judith and Esther in the Old Testament, but that they risked falling into the depths of evil if they exceeded the limits of their condition and allowed themselves to be guided by evil spirits.

Moreover, within the last ten years, there was recently in France, a virgin [Pucelle?] named Joan of whom I have already spoken,[26] notorious for her prophetic spirit and for the power of her miracles, so it was thought. For she always wore male clothing, and she could not be softened by any persuasions of all the doctors to put aside these clothes and content herself with woman's garments, especially since she openly professed herself to be a virgin and a woman. She said: 'In this male clothing, as a sign of future victory, I have been sent by God to preach by word and by example, to help the true King of France, Charles, and to make him secure in his kingdom, from where the King of England and the Duke of Burgundy are striving to chase him.' For at that time those two men were together most grievously oppressing France with slaughter and arms.

Therefore, since Joan rode constantly like a knight with her lord, predicted many successes to come, was present at certain victorious battles and carried out other such wonders, not only France marvelled at these things, but every Christian kingdom was amazed. At last this Joan became so presumptuous that, before France had yet been attained, she already sent threats by letters to Bohemia, where there were then a multitude of heretics.[27] Then laymen and clerics, clerks and monks, were uncertain whether she was being ruled by a diabolical or divine spirit. Some very learned men wrote treatises about her in which they expressed not only diverse but also adverse opinions regarding the virgin [Pucelle]. But after she had helped King Charles greatly and had secured the kingdom for some years, until at last, by God's will, so it is believed, she was captured in arms by the English and imprisoned. Then a great number of masters were called and summoned, both canon and civil lawyers, and she was examined for many days. And, as I have heard from Master Nicole Amici, Licentiate of Theology, who was an ambassador for the University of Paris,[28] she at last confessed that she had a familiar angel of God, which was an evil spirit according to many interpretations and proofs. Because she been made a sorceress by this spirit,[29] they gave her up to be burnt by

26 He had only announced this in the preceding paragraph.

27 Presumably **30**.

28 Nicole Lami, rector of the University of Paris until 1429 and an ambassador to the Council of Basel. For the discussion of Joan at Basel, see M. D. Bailey and E. Peters, 'A Sabbat of demonologists: Basel, 1431–1440', *The Historian*, LXV, 2003, pp. 1375–95.

29 Nider used the term 'maga' rather than the standard 'malefica' (harmful sorceress), suggesting that he did not view her crime in this regard to be too serious: M. D.

public justice. And the King of England told the same story as in this account, in a letter to our Emperor, Sigismund.[30]

66. *Le champion des dames* by Martin Le Franc (1440–1442)

Source: Martin Le Franc, *Le champion des dames*, ed. R. Deschaux, 5 vols, Paris, 1999, IV, pp. 90–104.

Language: French

Martin Le Franc (c.1410–61) was taught by Thomas de Courcelles at the University of Paris, and then became a secretary to the Duke of Savoy, Amadeus VIII, uncle of the Duke of Burgundy. When Amadeus became Pope Felix V on 5 November 1439 at the Council of Basel, he named Le Franc as an apostolic protonotary. Shortly afterwards, Le Franc wrote *Le Champion des dames* (1440–42), a debate poem which presented a defence of women against the long traditions of medieval misogyny. In Book Four, he presented a list of women who were successful as leaders and as warriors, including the Amazons, Deborah, Judith and more contemporary figures such as the Countess of Montfort, Joan of Bavaria and Joan of Arc. This discussion of the Pucelle presumably drew upon his contact with individuals and documents in circulation at the Council of Basel, including *De mirabili victoria*. Many scholars have noted the remarkable decision to defend Joan of Arc in a book dedicated and presented to the Duke of Burgundy. Le Franc may have hoped that the court was more open to a reassessment of such matters in the aftermath of the rapprochement with Charles VII at Arras in 1435, but he also used this debate as a springboard for a lengthy statement of the need for the French princes to set aside their personal differences and recognise the need for unity and peace in France. Either way, his hopes were to be dashed: in a subsequent poem, Le Franc reported that *Le Champion des dames* had failed to find favour with the Duke because 'evil tongues' had advised the prince that either the poet or his poem should be burned.

[The **Champion** said:] 'What can the duchesses, the queens and the princesses do against their harmful enemies? What will those in the know think, when a Pucelle with few worldly possessions recently broke the most powerful men, and put them to death as swiftly as possible?

'I wish to talk about the Pucelle who delivered Orléans, where Salisbury lost an eye, and then was struck by evil death. It was she who

---

Bailey, *Battling Demons: witchcraft, heresy and reform in the late middle ages*, Philadelphia, 2003, p. 51n.

30 Tisset (ed.), *Procès de condamnation*, I, pp. 423–6.

recovered the honour of France and so she will rightfully enjoy perpetual renown.

'You know how she was taught to bear lances and armour, how the English were beaten by her great enterprise, how the King sallied out of Bourges, or of Blois, under [the influence of] her confidence, and went before Paris in France with a very great army of Frenchmen.

'You know very well from where she came, and why and how, so I will be silent about that. But whoever wishes to record her miracles in a book or a commentary, it should be said that it could not be the case that Joan did not have a divine spirit which inflamed and inspired her to complete such things.'

[The **Adversary** responded by citing Thomas Couette, who deceived the foolish mob into believing that he was a saint on earth, but was eventually burned in Rome.] 'Without speaking of the many ways in which the Pucelle took up arms, could not someone who loved Orléans have advised this saint, emboldened and inflamed her, and taught her what she should say? But, by God, I was told that it happened very differently.

'I was told that it was certain that she served as a page to a captain in her youth, from where the art of bearing armour came. And when youth overcame her [i.e. when she reached puberty] and wished to reveal her sex, she was counselled to dress in armour and bear a lance.

'Then, necessity [*force*] taught her the way in which she should come to Orléans and, as a simple shepherdess, question and answer, and how she should give signs to the King and to his Parlement, by which it would be understood that she came from God.

'It was also necessity [*force*] that instructed her to employ certain tactics. Many of the Englishmen believed that she used the art of necromancy, and in this way, their faith soon faltered and she abused their fantastic courage in diverse ways.

'Understand how this contrived farce was believed afterwards. As soon as fortune increased her deeds, there a cry was raised: "Now the war will be finished, if God and St Avoie aid us![31] Certainly the thing

---

31 The legendary St Avoie (or Avoye) was one of the companions of Saint Ursule who refused to marry a chieftain and lived alone in the Boulogne region. She was celebrated in the diocese of Paris.

is amply proven: God sends the Pucelle to France!'"

The **Champion** said boldly: 'She could not have provided the signs, if God had not been promoting her by His worthy powers. Also, she did in a moment what had not been done in twenty years before. Those to whom God gives courage always conquer and move forward.

'Also I believe in good faith that the angels accompanied her, because, as we see in Jerome, they love and embrace chastity.[32] And I hold for true that they helped her to win the outer boulevards, and at Patay blinded the English [who were] driven backwards.[33]

'For we must all assume that God, who is the author of peace, permits all those who reject it to be destroyed and consumed. But ought we to say that He never grants long life to those who, by word or by deed, do not wish peace to endure?

'Also, as I surmise, it was fitting that pride in high places was unseated by a little, humble creature.[34] Having preordained everything in this way, to bring down and confound the resolute pride of the English, God chose to send the Pucelle.

'A thousand reasons make apparent that the opinion held by myself and by others reveals the heavenly design. But the envious person does not know how to speak well because of righteous inclination, and puts an evil interpretation on the matter, only finding fault.

'People regarded it as scandalous that she dressed in the outfit of a man, for we read in Deuteronomy that Moses prohibited it [Deuteronomy 22: 5]. Do you not know what Gerson said about this? I am talking about Master Jean Gerson, who wrote a little treatise about her, more shrewd than we think.[35]

32 For an introduction to Jerome's views on chastity and virginity, see A. Blamires (ed.), *Woman Defamed and Woman Defended: an anthology of medieval texts*, Oxford, 1992, pp. 63–77.

33 This, along with the following five stanzas, do not appear in all of the nine surviving manuscripts and their removal presumably indicates an attempt to moderate Le Franc's defence of Joan of Arc, presumably in the context of the attack upon him by the 'evil tongues' at the Burgundian court. See the limited discussion in G. H. Merkle, 'Martin Le Franc's commentary on Jean Gerson's treatise on Joan of Arc', in *Fresh Verdicts on Joan of Arc*, pp. 177–88.

34 These comments echo the Magnificat, Luke 1: 46–55.

35 This is almost certainly a reference to *De mirabili victoria* [7], which was certainly in circulation at the Council of Basel, or perhaps *De quadam puella* [22]. Nevertheless the attribution of either of these works to Gerson remains problematic.

'The ancient law of Moses, to the extent that it is judicial, is not binding for Robin and Joanne [i.e. ordinary people] living under the sacramental [law of the New Testament], if such things that were then customary [and served] some special purpose, have not been reconfirmed by civil or canon law.[36]

'Do you not see that it was forbidden that anyone should eat an animal unless it had a cloven hoof and chewed its cud? No one dared to eat of hare, or of sow or piglet. But, nowadays, if someone offered you some, you would gobble them up!

'Also do not marvel, however unusual it is, if the Pucelle wore a doublet and short coat, for thus she was more feared, capable and nimble, and taken for a proud prince, not a simple little shepherdess.

'She wore a hat of felt, a hammered breastplate and short surcoat, I admit it. But her case was not that of most women. Long coats, you can have no doubt, are not good in warfare. Again, you very frequently hear that the habit does not make the monk.

'Bearing arms requires appropriate clothing; there is no one so foolish that he does not know this. Some things are suited for the town, and others for bearing a lance or battle-axe. When a falcon is released to hunt, his long jesses are removed. Also, the person who is hidden from his enemies does not need a long coat.

'Let them say what they wish about her: they may speak or remain silent. But praise for her is not necessary because of [any] lies they can offer. What more do I need to add? Through her virtue, through her courage, in spite of all opposition, the King of France was crowned.'

The **Adversary** with his deceitful appearance was very angry with Joan and said: 'I hold this language to be frivolous, because God never sent her. Ha! She was led astray too much by presumptuousness, whatever one might say. Also, reason sent her to burn at Rouen in Normandy.'

Free Will [who is the **Champion**] replied nimbly: 'That is mistaken, big head. How many saints do we celebrate who died shamefully!

---

36 The same argument had appeared in the first of the three truths in support of Joan's use of male clothing in *De mirabili victoria* [7].

Think of Jesus first, and then his blessed martyrs. So you must admit that you know nothing about this.

'Your arguments scarcely oppose the innocent Pucelle, nor may one reckon that the secret judgements of God on her were worse. And it is fitting that everyone agree to give her honour and glory for her very excellent valour, for her strength and for her victory.'

Then the **Adversary**, angry at hearing sermons about Joan, told him: 'You have preached too much on this; think of another woman to praise. You could not have presented a worse one to make your point, because it is enough to drive one crazy or to make one tear one's hair out.'

Free Will said: 'You are too much of a coward, and you show yourself to be too strongly opinionated, making it dangerous [for me] to praise those of our hearth [i.e. those of our side]. And if I have praised three or four foreigners, why would I remain silent about a female who wished to fight for France? Certainly, I will not do that!

'Especially when she did such virtuous things in such a short time, so that each person owes her immortal thanks, do I not have good cause to say any number of good things about her, as much as is possible? If you say that I am not right, you are biased.

'Because whatever one might say, she was led into battle grandly, fought valiantly and conducted herself wisely. So I have accounted her among the chivalrous women, because I seek to praise her among the women warriors.

'But may it please God that you barons, you princes, [and] you lords of France, in whom we still place hope of seeing our deliverance, have the courage and the endurance of this one woman, in order to overcome and destroy your enemies quickly.'

[Le Franc concluded the section with a long plea to these contemporary princes to learn from the example of the women, by overcoming hatred, discord and division, recognising the needs of the ordinary people, and restoring peace in both the Church and in France.]

67. *The Chronicle of Charles VII* by Jean Chartier (c.1445–1450)

Source: Jean Chartier, *Chronique de Charles VII*, ed. A. Vallet de Viriville, 3 vols, Paris, 1858, I, pp. 66–70, 87–9, 107–9.

Language: French and Latin

Jean Chartier (c.1385–1464) served as the royal historiographer from 18 November 1437, in which capacity he composed an official history of France in Latin, a continuation of the *Chronique du Religieux de Saint-Denys*, covering the years 1422 to 1450. Between 1445 and 1450, Chartier began to translate this material into French and, with regard to Joan of Arc, largely repeated his earlier testimony from the Latin chronicle. There is a clear, but as yet unexplained, textual relationship between Chartier's account of this period and those of other Valois chronicles such as the *Chronique de la Pucelle* and the Berry Herald.

[Chapter 36] At this time news came that there was a Pucelle near Vaucouleurs, in the marches of Barrois, who was twenty years of age or thereabouts, and said many times to a man named Robert de Baudricourt, captain of Vaucouleurs, and to many others, that they must take her before the King of France and that she would perform great services in his wars for him. She demanded this from them many times, but they only laughed and mocked her for this, and considered this Joan to be simple-minded, not taking any notice of her words. And finally this Joan acted so that she was taken before the King of France by a man named Ville Robert and by others in her company.

Having come before the King, she performed the bows and reverences customarily made before the King, just as if she had been brought up at the court. And in her submission and greeting, she said, addressing her words to the King: 'God grant you a good life, gentle King', even though she had not known him and had never seen him, and there were many lords who were more sumptuously and richly dressed than the King.[37] For this reason, he replied to Joan: 'I am not the one who is King, Joan', and pointing towards one of the lords, he said 'There is the King.' To which she replied: 'Ah, no, gentle prince, it is you and not the others.'

And then she was examined and questioned carefully by many wise clerks and other men of different status, to know who prompted her to come before the King. And she replied that she came to install the

37 In the earlier, Latin version of this chronicle, Chartier stated that Charles VII deliberately exchanged clothes with one of the courtiers: Jean Chartier, *La chronique latine de Jean Chartier (1422–1450)*, ed. C. Samaran, Paris, 1926, p. 59.

King in his lordship, and that God wished this, and that she would lift the English siege of the city of Orléans; and that after that she would take the King to be crowned at Reims, and that she wished to fight the English wherever she could find them. [She said that] the King needed to give her whatever force he could procure, because she did not have any doubt about lifting this siege, taking the King to be crowned at Reims, or about defeating and driving out the English, and she said many other amazing things. And she replied marvellously to the questions that were put to her. And with regard to the war, it seemed as if she was highly experienced. And many doctors, captains of war and others were astonished at her actions and the replies that she gave, both on spiritual matters and about the war.

[Chartier then recounted the raising of the army and their journey to Orléans, before returning to an earlier event.]

After she had been examined, the Pucelle asked the King if he would be willing to give her one of his armourers to go to Sainte-Catherine-de-Fierbois, to seek a sword that was in a certain place, having come there by the will of God, and which had five small crosses engraved on each side.[38] The King granted her wish, asking if she had ever been to this place, how she knew the sword was like this, and how it had been brought there. To which she replied that she had never been to, or entered, the church of Sainte-Catherine, but she knew for sure that this sword was there among many old scraps of metal, as she knew it by divine revelation, and that, by means of this sword, she should expel the enemies of the kingdom of France, and lead the King to be anointed and crowned in the city of Reims. After Joan had given this explanation, by the consent and commission of the King, one of his armourers went to that place and truly found the sword, and brought it to Joan, which was a most marvellous thing. With this, she campaigned and waged war on the enemies of the King in a very courageous fashion, and through her enterprise and this new beginning, she, and those named above, supplied this city, as has been said.

[Chapter 45] In the year 1429, at the beginning of the month of June, King Charles of France assembled a great army on the urging of Joan the Pucelle, who said that it was the will of God that King Charles should go to Reims to be consecrated and crowned. And whatever

---

38 Most of the manuscripts actually refer to 'five small swords' or 'five fleurs-de-lys', but these are undoubtedly copy errors judging by Joan's own testimony during the Rouen trial [**37, 47**].

reservations or doubts the King or his council had, it was decided, after the warnings of this Joan, that the King should order what men he could raise to travel to his coronation at Reims, since this town of Reims was then subject to the English ... [as was] generally all the region between the river Loire and the sea.

And the men-at-arms came from all parts to serve the king, and they each had high hopes that, with the help of this Joan the Pucelle, great good would come to the kingdom of France. They greatly desired to see her and desired to know her deeds, as a thing come from God. She always rode armed and in clothing of war, just like the other men-at-arms and captains. She also spoke cautiously about war as a captain would know how to do. And whenever it happened in the host that there was any cry to arms or alarm, she came, either on foot or on horse, as valiantly as the captain of the company should know to do, giving heart and courage to all the others, and urging them to act with good will and to guard the host, as was reasonable to do. In all other things, she was a very simple person, and lived a good and honest life, confessing very often and receiving the body of Our Lord nearly every week. She was always armed or otherwise in the clothing of a man. And it was said that it was a very strange thing to see a woman riding in such company, and for many other reasons, that there was no clerk or other person who would not marvel at everything she did.

[Chapter 59] Alençon and the other captains arrived with Joan and the army at Saint-Denis and the following day, the dukes and other French lords, in great company, went to the fields near to the gate of Saint-Honoré, upon a great hill that was called the Place aux Pourceaux, and brought up many cannons and culverins to fire into the city of Paris. And there were Englishmen parading along the wall of Paris, inside the city, with their lords among them carrying a large banner with a great red cross. Now it happened that the boulevard of this gate of Saint-Honoré were taken by assault ... And the French feared that the English and other men of Paris might sally out from the Saint-Denis gate, or somewhere else, to attack them. For this reason, the Duke of Alençon, the Duke of Bourbon, the Lord of Montmorency and others, with a great force [of men-at-arms] stayed behind this great hill in battle order. And there the Lord of Montmorency was made a knight, because he could come no nearer due to the cannons and the culverins that were firing without cease. And Joan the Pucelle said that she wished to assault the town of Paris, but she was not well informed about the deep water in the ditches. And nevertheless, she went with a very great force of men-at-arms, among whom was the Lord of Rais, Marshal of France, and descended into the outer ditch, where she remained for the whole day, along with this Marshal and a great company of men-at-arms. And there Joan was wounded by an arrow in the leg.

Nevertheless she did not wish to withdraw from this ditch, and did what she could to throw bundles of sticks and wood into the other ditch, to allow them to cross, which was impossible owing to the depth of the water that was there. And later, when it was night, the dukes of Alençon and of Bourbon sent for them, but she did not wish to retreat for anything, so that it was necessary for the Duke of Alençon to summon them and to pull them back. And so the whole company withdrew to La Chapelle, where they had lodged the night before. And the next day the dukes of Alençon and of Bourbon, Joan the Pucelle and the others returned to Saint-Denis, where the King of France was with his host. And there the arms of this Pucelle, which she offered out of great devotion, were displayed before the precious body of my lord St Denis and his companions.[39]

[Chapter 71. The English and the Burgundians laid siege to Compiègne.] And when this came to the attention of Joan the Pucelle, of whom mention has been made, she left Lagny to aid and assist those besieged in this town, into which Joan the Pucelle entered. And afterwards, great skirmishes started each day between the English and the Burgundians maintaining the siege, on the one hand, and the captains and men of this town on the other. And one day it happened that Joan the Pucelle was sallying out against this siege very valiantly and bravely, but the English and the Burgundians also charged very hard against her and her companions, so that it was necessary for Joan the Pucelle and the others to retreat. And some say that the gate was shut against them on their return, and others say that there was too great a press at that entrance. And finally, Joan the Pucelle was taken by these English and Burgundians and led away.

Many of those on the side of the King of the French were dismayed and angry at this capture. And she was held for a long time in prison by the Burgundians of the company of Luxembourg, who at last sold her to the English, by whom she was taken to Rouen, where she was

---

39 Jean Chartier later recounted how Joan's armour was seized by English and Burgundian troops on the order of Louis de Luxembourg, Bishop of Thérouanne, chancellor of Henry VI and brother of Joan's captor, Jean.

harshly treated.[40] And, after a great delay, without trial, but by their unwarranted will, they had her publicly burned in this town of Rouen, attributing to her many evil spells. And this was very inhumanely done, considering her life and the way that she lived. Because she confessed and received each week the body of Our Lord, as a good catholic. And there is no doubt that the sword that she sent to be found in the chapel of Sainte-Catherine-de-Fierbois, mentioned above, was found by a miracle, as everyone believes, especially seeing that by the means of this sword, at least before it was broken, she won the great conquests described above. And that is to say that after the battle of Patay, this Joan the Pucelle had had it proclaimed that no man of her company should keep any immoral woman or concubine. Nevertheless, she found some men breaking her command, so that she struck them with this sword, and it was broken. And when this came to the knowledge of the King, he ordered work to repair it, which could not be done; they could never repair it, which is a great proof that she had come by it divinely. And it is well known that after this sword was broken, Joan did not prosper in arms for the profit of the King or otherwise, as she had done before.

68. The *Chronicle* of Enguerrand de Monstrelet (1447?)

Source: Enguerran[d] de Monstrelet, *La chronique d'Enguerran[d] de Monstrelet en deux livres avec pièces justicatives (1400–44)*, ed. L. Douët d'Arcq, 6 vols, Paris, 1857–62, IV, pp. 314–15, 353–6, 386–9, 442–7.

Language: French

Enguerrand de Monstrelet (c.1390 or 1395–1453) was a nobleman, born in a village in Ponthieu. In 1430, he was the Bailly of Compiègne for his master Jean, Count of Luxembourg, and from 1436 to 1446, he held office in Cambrai. His chronicle covered the years from 1400 to 1444, and was presented as a sequel to the work of the most famous chronicler of chivalry, Jean Froissart. At the same time, his association with the Burgundians inevitably meant that Monstrelet was a hostile witness to Joan of Arc.

[Chapter 57] In this year [1429], a young girl, a Pucelle named Joan, aged around twenty years or thereabouts, who was dressed and presented as a man, came to King Charles at Chinon, where he was

---

40 In the equivalent chapter in the original, Latin version of this chronicle, Chartier had reported that Jean de Luxembourg committed suicide after this treachery, even though he actually died in 1440 at the castle of Guise: Jean Chartier, *La chronique latine*, ed. Samaran, pp. 30 and 62.

based for a great deal of the time. And she was born on the borders of Burgundy and Lorraine, in the town of Domremy, not far from Vaucouleurs. This Joan had for some time been a servant in an inn, and was bold in riding horses and leading them to water, and also in performing feats and other skills that young girls were not accustomed to do.[41] She was put on the right track and sent to the King by a knight named my lord Robert de Baudricourt, captain of Vaucouleurs, who gave her horses and four or six companions. She said that she was a Pucelle, inspired by the divine grace, and that she had been sent to the King in order to restore him to the possession of his kingdom, from where he had been banished and driven out unjustly, and which was now in such a deplorable state. She was in the household of the King for around two months, and she frequently urged him to give her men and support, and she would drive out his enemies, and exalt his lordship. During this time, neither the King nor his council put any great faith in her or what she said, and regarded her as a mad woman, out of her senses, because such words, or similar, were very dubious; [and it was dangerous] for great princes and other noble persons to believe [them], chiefly because of the anger of the Lord, and because of the blasphemy that might ensue in this world. Nevertheless, after she remained like this for a period of time, she received help, and men-at-arms and outfits of war were given to her. And she raised up a standard, on which she had painted the representation of our Creator. All her words were of the name of God, on which account the great majority of those who saw and heard her speak, sincerely believed that she had been inspired by God, as she declared herself to be. And she was examined many times by notable clerks and other wise men of great authority, in order to know more clearly her real intentions. But she always held to her purpose, saying that if the King was prepared to believe her, she would restore to him his kingdom. And after that time she did several acts which will be related in more detail below, that gained her great renown.

41 This was clearly a reference to the charge at Rouen that Joan had worked in a brothel at Neufchâteau [35]. Monstrelet's story was echoed by another Burgundian chronicler who had fought with Sir John Fastolf at the battle of Patay, Jean de Wavrin: 'This Joan had remained a long time at an inn and she was very bold in riding horses and leading them to water and also in performing other feats and exercises which young girls are not accustomed to do; and she was sent to the King of France by a knight named Sir Robert de Baudricourt, captain of the said place of Vaucouleurs appointed on behalf of the said King Charles': Jean de Wavrin, *Recueil des croniques et anciennes istoires de la Grant Bretaigne, a present nommé Engleterre*, ed. and trans. W. Hardy, 5 vols, London, 1864–91, V, p. 165.

[Monstrelet then offered a detailed account of Joan's military career within the wider story of the war, leading up the account of the attack on Paris:]

[Chapter 70] Item, while King Charles was at Compiègne, news was brought to him that the Regent, the Duke of Bedford, had gone with his whole army to Normandy, to fight the Constable [Richemont], who was despoiling the countryside around Evreux ... [And] in truth, had [Charles] come in full array to Saint-Quentin, Corbie, Amiens, Abbeville and to the many other strong towns and castles, the majority of the inhabitants there were fully prepared to receive him as their lord, and desired nothing more earnestly than to pay homage to him, and open their gates. Yet he was advised not to advance so far on the marches of the Duke of Burgundy, both because he was well supported by men-at-arms, and for the hope that he had that a firm treaty might be made between them

And after King Charles had stayed in Senlis for a few days, he departed and went with his army to Saint-Denis, which he found almost abandoned, because the men of this place had fled to Paris, that is to say the majority of the more powerful burghers and inhabitants of this city. His men were quartered at Aubervilliers, Montmartre, and in the villages around, close to Paris. Joan the Pucelle, who had a very high reputation, was then with him, and every day she pressed the King and his princes to launch an attack upon the city of Paris. It was determined that on Monday, the 12th day of September, the assault should be launched. After this decision was taken, all the soldiers were made ready. And on that Monday, King Charles joined battle between Montmartre and Paris, his princes with him. And this Pucelle, with banner unfurled, went to the Saint-Honoré gate with the very numerous men of the vanguard, carrying with them many scaling-ladders, bundles of sticks and other tools of war. In that place, she had many of her men enter the ditches, all on foot. And the assault began at ten o'clock, or thereabouts, [and it was] very hard, grim and cruel, and lasted without a break for four to five hours, or more. But the Parisians [the Burgundians and the English] ... defended themselves vigorously and with great courage. And, before the assault, they had each taken up favourable and suitable positions, on the orders of the captains. During the assault, many of the French were driven back and slaughtered, and there were a very great number killed and wounded by the cannons, culverins and other weapons that the Parisians shot at them. Among them, the Pucelle was very gravely wounded, and she remained the whole of the day in the ditches behind a small mound, until vespers, when Guichard de Chiembronne and others came to find her. And on the other side, there were many wounded among the defenders. At last, the French captains, seeing their men in such peril, recognising that it would be impossible to win the city by force, knowing that these Parisians were united in their defence without any divisions, suddenly sounded the retreat. They carried off the dead and wounded, and returned to their camp.

The following day, King Charles, sad and grieving at the loss of his men, went to Senlis, to have the wounded attended to and treated. And the Parisians were more unanimous than ever before, swearing that with all their power they would resist to the death this King Charles, who wanted to destroy them all, so they said. And it could well be that they shouted this, those who regarded themselves as greatly forfeit in his eyes for having driven him out of this city. And they had cruelly put to death his loyal servants, as has been described in another place.[42]

[From this point on, Monstrelet made almost no further reference to Joan, until he recounted the siege of Compiègne.]

[Chapter 86] Item, during the time that the Duke of Burgundy was quartered at Coudun, as has been said, and his men-at-arms in the villages between Coudun and Compiègne, it happened that at around five o'clock in the afternoon of the eve of the Ascension, Joan the Pucelle, Poton, and other French captains, together with four to five hundred combatants, all armed and on horse and on foot, sallied out of Compiègne by the gate of the bridge leading to Montdidier. And they intended to attack and to charge towards the camp of my lord Baudo de Noielle, which was at the end of the causeway of Margny. At this time, my lord Jean de Luxembourg, accompanied by the Lord of Crequi and eight or ten gentlemen, all on horseback, were camped not far from my lord Baudo. He was considering how this town of Compiègne might be besieged. And then these Frenchmen began to advance towards the camp at Margny in strength, as has been said, where most of the men were completely unarmed. Still, they assembled very quickly and a very great skirmish began, during which the alarm was cried in many places, both among the Burgundian and the

---

42 On 29 May 1418, the Duke of Burgundy and a group of partisan Parisians took over the city, forcing the Dauphin Charles to flee. On 12 July the Parisians murdered all their prisoners, including the Count of Armagnac and the Chancellor, fearing that they would be set free by the Count's partisans.

English parties. And the English entered the battle against the French
in the meadow outside Venette, where they were camped. And there
were around five thousand combatants. And on the other side, the
men of my lord Jean de Luxembourg, who were camped at Claroy,
learning of this fight, hastened to the relief of their lord and captain,
who was engaged in the skirmish, and around whom, for the most
part, the others rallied. In this encounter, the Lord of Crequi was
seriously wounded in the face. Finally, after this skirmish had lasted
for a long time, the French, seeing their enemies multiply in great
number, retreated towards their town, always with the Pucelle at
their rear, trying hard to keep her men together and to bring them
back without loss. But the Burgundians, knowing that reinforcements
were coming to them from all quarters, pursued them vigorously, and
charged them most aggressively. So it was at last, as I was told, that
the Pucelle was dragged from her horse by an archer – the Bastard of
Vendôme was nearby, to whom she surrendered and pledged her
faith. He lost no time in taking her as a prisoner to Margny, where he
put her under secure guard. Poton the Burgundian was taken with
her, and some others, but in no great number. And the French returned
to Compiègne, grieving and angry at their loss. And they were
especially displeased at the capture of this Pucelle, while, on the other
side, those of the Burgundian party and the English were overjoyed,
more pleased than if they had taken five hundred other combatants.
Because they did not fear or dread any captain or commander as much
as they had always feared this Pucelle until that day.

Shortly afterwards, the Duke of Burgundy came in full array from his
camp at Coudun where he had been based, to the meadow before
Compiègne. There the English, the Duke and those of other camps
assembled in great number, giving out great shouts and cheers for the
capture of the Pucelle. The Duke went to see her in the place where
she was held, and spoke some words to her, which I do not recall,
although I was present.[43] After this, the Duke and all his men returned
to their quarters, for that night and the Pucelle remained under the
guard and control of my lord Jean de Luxembourg, who a few days
later sent her, under a strong escort, to the castle of Beaulieu, and
from there to Beaurevoir, where she remained for a long time, as you
shall hear later.

43 This is the only time in the entire chronicle that Monstrelet referred directly to
   himself, making his failure to recall what was said at this famous meeting even
   more remarkable.

[Chapter 105] Here follows the condemnation that was enacted in the city of Rouen against Joan the Pucelle, as can be read in the letters sent by King Henry of England to the Duke of Burgundy, a copy of which follows.

[Monstrelet then transcribed the letter that Henry VI had sent to the clergy, nobles and towns of France after the execution of Joan [**57**].]

When this had been done, the King of England signified by his letters to the Duke of Burgundy that this just sentence should be posted by him and the other princes in many places, in order that their people and subjects should be assured and warned not to believe in errors like those of this Pucelle, or similar.

69. Letter of Charles VII to Guillaume Bouillé (15 February 1450)

Source: Doncoeur (ed.), *L'enquête ordonnée par Charles VII en 1450*, pp. 33–5.

Language: French

Guillaume Bouillé was Dean of the chapter at Noyon, a doctor of theology and a professor at the University of Paris, where he had served as Rector from 1437 to 1439. He was known to have been ashamed at the partisan actions of his own university against Joan, and of his own bishop at Noyon, Jean de Mailly, who had signed the letters that sent her to the scaffold. This may explain why Charles VII chose him to lead an inquiry into the faults and abuses committed by the judges and assessors at Rouen. On 4 and 5 March 1450, Bouillé questioned seven witnesses about the procedures that were followed at the original trial, and the dispositions of the judges.[44] Then the inquiry suddenly stopped, before Bouillé secured the documents that Charles had requested. It may be that the proceedings were interrupted by the war that still ravaged Normandy, or perhaps they were affected by the collapse of negotiations with the papal envoys over the Pragmatic Sanction of Bourges; this document had been issued by Charles VII and a national council of the Church on 7 July 1438, imposing severe restrictions upon the powers of the pope in France.

Charles, by the grace of God, King of France, to our friend and loyal counsellor, Master Guillaume Bouillé, doctor in theology, friendly greetings.

44 The witness statements were inadmissable in the subsequent Nullification trial because the investigation did not enjoy canonical authority. They were therefore not included in the official record of that trial, and are only edited in Doncoeur (ed.), *L'enquête ordonnée par Charles VII en 1450*.

A long time ago, Joan the Pucelle was taken and captured by our ancient enemy and adversaries, the English, and brought to the city of Rouen. They had her tried by certain persons who had been chosen and given this task by them, and during this trial they made and committed many errors and abuses, such that, by means of this trial and the great hatred that our enemy had against her, they had her put to death very cruelly, iniquitously and against reason. Because we wish to know the truth of this trial, and the manner in which it was carried out, we command, instruct and expressly charge you to inquire and diligently ask about this and what was said. And bring to us and the men of our great council the information that you find on this, or faithfully send it in a sealed letter. And in addition, compel all those who may know anyone who has any writings, documents or other things concerning this matter, by all due means and as you see fit, so that you may bring or send them to us, for examination as we see fit and as is reasonable. To do this, we give you power, commission, and special mandate in front of those present, and we order and command all our legal agents, officers and subjects to obey and listen carefully to you and to those acting for and deputed by you in this matter.

Given at Rouen, the 15th day of February, the year of grace 1450, and of our reign, the 28th.

70. Letter of Cardinal Guillaume d'Estouteville to Charles VII (22 May 1452)

Source: Doncoeur (ed.), *L'enquête du Cardinal d'Estouteville en 1452*, p. 28.

Language: French

During the preliminary inquiry into the Rouen trial of Joan of Arc in May 1452, the witness statements were recorded and authenticiated by the notaries, Compaing Vote and Dauvergne. The resulting dossier was sent by Cardinal Guillaume d'Estouteville to Charles VII, along with this letter that emphasised the direct relevance of the matter for the King.[45]

My sovereign lord,

I recommend myself most humbly to your good grace. And may it please you to know that the Inquisitor of the faith and Master

---

45 As the inquiry had canonical status, the witness statements were admissable at the trial in 1455–56, and so this dossier was inserted into the official Nullification trial record.

Guillaume Bouillé, Dean of Noyon, will shortly be coming to you, and they will reveal to you most clearly all that has been done in the trial of Joan the Pucelle. And because I know that this matter greatly touches your honour and estate, I have acted with all my power, and I will always work, as a good and loyal servant should do for his lord, so that you may be the more fully informed about these things. There is nothing more for the moment, my sovereign lord, save that you may always command me to accomplish your good desires. May it please God to keep you in good health and give you a good and long life.

Written at Paris on the 22nd day of May [1452]

Your very humble and obedient servant, the Cardinal d'Estouteville.

IV: THE NULLIFICATION TRIAL (1455–1456)

71. Letter from Pope Calixtus III (11 June 1455)

Source: Duparc (ed.), *Procès en nullité*, I, pp. 18–21.

Language: Latin

Between April and June 1455, the mother and brothers of Joan of Arc appealed to the new Pope, Calixtus III, to set up a commission to examine the Rouen trial of 1431. Calixtus III replied on 11 June, in a letter that was not presented in Paris until November. The document was a bull containing a response to the petition in a juridical form known as a 'rescript of justice' and is only known through its inclusion in the transcript of the start of the trial record. It was addressed to the three individuals who would serve as judges in the Nullification trial: Jean Juvénal des Ursins, Archbishop of Reims (d. 1473); Guillaume Chartier, Bishop of Paris (d. 1470); Richard Olivier de Longueil, Bishop of Coutances (d. 1470). Of the three, Jean Juvénal had the most curious relationship to Joan of Arc: firstly, he had been the immediate successor of Pierre Cauchon as Bishop of Beauvais in 1432, and therefore any attack upon Cauchon might threaten his own position, because of the doctrine of apostolic succession. Moreover he was a defender of the Pragmatic Sanction of Bourges, and hence opposed to any attempt by Calixtus III and Estouteville to interfere with the internal affairs of France. Certainly he was completely silent about Joan of Arc in his contemporary writings [**64**].

Bishop Calixtus, servant of the servants of God, to his brothers the Archbishop of Reims and the bishops of Paris and of Coutances, greetings and apostolic blessing.

We are willing to welcome the humble petitions of supplicants and to give them a favourable response whenever appropriate. A request has recently been presented to us on behalf of our dear lay children Pierre and Jean, called d'Arc, of the dear daughter in Christ, Isabelle, their mother, of their relatives and their neighbours in the diocese of Toul. [This] contains the following facts: although the deceased Joan of Arc, sister of Pierre and of Jean, and daughter of Isabelle, their mother, had detested all heresy during her life and did not hold any belief, [or make any] affirmation or declaration, that smacked of heresy or was contrary to the catholic faith and to the traditions of the holy Roman Church. Nevertheless the late Guillaume d'Estivet, or whoever was then Promoter of criminal matters of the episcopal court of Beauvais, having in all likelihood bribed certain enemies of Joan and of her brothers and mother, made a false report to Pierre, Bishop of Beauvais, of happy memory, and to the late Jean Le Maistre, of the [Dominican] Order of Preaching Friars, a professor, then alive, calling himself the delegate of the Inquisitor on heretical perversity in this region; and this Joan, who was then in the diocese of Beauvais, was accused of the crime of heresy and of having committed other crimes against the faith. Also this Bishop, by his authority as an ordinary, and Jean Le Maistre, claiming to have sufficient power in this case, thanks to the pretext of this false report, brought an inquiry [*inquisitionem*] against this Joan prosecuting this through a promoter. They also put her in prison under strong guard, although nothing called for it, neither the evidence of the case, nor vehement suspicion or public fame [*fame clamore*]. At last, although the inquiry had not been legitimately constituted and it could not establish that this Joan had fallen into heresy or other things contrary to the faith, or had committed abuses or crimes of this type, or had persisted in errors contrary to the faith, because this was neither notorious nor true, and although Joan had asked the Bishop and Jean Le Maistre that if they were claiming to accuse her of having said any words smacking of heresy or against the faith they should submit these questions to the examination of the holy apostolic see, whose judgement she would accept, they did not pay any attention: removing from Joan all means of defending her innocence and rejecting the rules of law, following their sole desire and their private will, proceeding in this matter of inquisition in a manner [that was] invalid and contrary to law, they brought an iniquitous and definitive sentence against Joan, judging her a heretic and guilty of other crimes and abuses of that type. On these grounds, Joan was then led cruelly to the last torture, to the peril of the souls of those who had condemned her; to the ignominy and disgrace, the pain and suffering of her mother, brothers and relatives.

As the petition indicates, the nullity of this trial of inquisition, as well as the innocence of this Joan, appears clearly in the acts and elsewhere; that she had been condemned maliciously, without having committed an error, emerges readily from the judicial documents. This is why the brothers, mother and relatives mentioned above, wishing to act above all to restore the honour of Joan and themselves, and to wipe out this mark of infamy suffered wrongfully, have humbly petitioned us to deign to have this lawsuit for the nullification of the false judgement and the justification of Joan opened again by some people chosen in that country to examine it and to determine it within a fixed period, and to delegate them to pursue the case of nullity and of justification, notwithstanding what has already been done. Therefore, we, moved by these petitions on this subject, command your brotherhood by apostolic mandate that [all three of] you, or two, or one of you, appoint a delegate for this purpose in the kingdom of France, such as the present Sub-Inquisitor for heresy and the Promoter of criminal affairs in the diocese of Beauvais, and all others that might be cited; having heard the statements made on all these points, decide what is just, ruling out all appeals, and have what you have decided observed with firmness, by ecclesiastical censure, notwithstanding the constitutions and apostolic ordinances and all matters to the contrary.

Given at Rome, at Saint Peter's, the year of the birth of Our Lord 1455, the 3rd day of the Ides of June, the first year of our pontificate.

72. The petition of Isabelle d'Arc (7 November 1455)

Source: Duparc (ed.), *Procès en nullité*, I, pp. 8–10.

Language: Latin

The proceedings opened in Paris when Isabelle d'Arc presented the following petition to Jean Juvénal des Ursins, Archbishop of Reims, Guillaume Chartier, Bishop of Paris, Richard Olivier de Longueil, Bishop of Coutances, and the Inquisitor, Jean Bréhal.

She had long ago given birth in lawful marriage to a daughter, and had raised her, duly marked with the sacrament of baptism and of confirmation, in the fear and the respect of God and in the traditions of the Church, so far as her age and her simple status allowed. As a result, growing up in the fields and the pastures, she went to the church often enough, received the sacrament of the Eucharist almost every month, even though of a tender age, after having been duly confessed, and gave herself over with devotion and fervour to fasts and prayers for the very great needs of the people at that time, with which she sympathised with all her heart. Nevertheless [there were] adversaries and people hostile to her, to her family, to those controlling public affairs, and to the people under whom this Joan and

her men served and worked; [these enemies] brought a case against
her faith, an insulting, outrageous and scornful action towards the
rulers and the people, although she had not undertaken anything
contrary to the faith. These opponents, without having been commissioned by any legitimate authority, despite the challenges and the tacit
and voiced appeals, after having taken away all means of defending
her innocence, condemned her in a baneful and iniquitous way, flouting
all the rules of procedure, charging her falsely and untruthfully of
many crimes, falsifying many articles that were turned around and
made contrary to her words, in order to secure the verdict. And after
she had received the sacrament of the Eucharist with the greatest
devotion, they had her burned most cruelly in a fire, to the damnation
of their souls, provoking tears from all and heaping opprobrium,
infamy and an irreparable wrong on this Isabelle and her [family].
Then the womb of this mother was moved for her daughter; all her
relatives were filled with sadness; but they contained their grief within
themselves, like many others who suffered in a similar way, until it
pleased the heavenly mercy to give calm after the storm, tranquillity
after the wars and light after the darkness, to return the city of Rouen
and also all Normandy to the natural sovereignty of France, and to
bring to a conclusion what had been started in the time of this Joan at
Orléans and at Reims. Then what has long been hidden may be
clearly revealed and become public, that is to say that this trial was
marred by fraud, by violence and equally by iniquity; and the nullity,
injustice and violence were discovered in many ways, both by the
examination of the trial record, and by public fame and the reports of
men worthy of belief.

[Isabelle went on to recount how she had petitioned the Pope to act on this
matter, leading to his agreement to set up a tribunal to investigate the
matter, as detailed in the previous document.]

73. Articles of interrogation for the Lorraine (20 December 1455)

Source: Duparc (ed.), *Procès en nullité*, I, pp. 250–1.

Language: Latin

The investigators sent to interview witnesses at Domremy, Vaucouleurs and
Toul in the Lorraine were provided with a list of questions to ask, condensed
down from a longer set of one hundred and one articles drafted by the

Procurator, on behalf of the d'Arc family, and the Promoter, on behalf of the judges. They necessarily shaped and limited the responses that the witnesses could offer.

[Article 1] Firstly, regarding her place of origin and the parish.

[Article 2] Item, who were her parents and what was their status? If they were good catholics and had a good reputation?

[Article 3] Item, who were her godfathers and godmothers?

[Article 4] Item, if in her early childhood, she was suitably brought up in the faith and good morals, in particular as much as is required for someone of her age and personal condition?

[Article 5] Item, regarding her regular dealings during her adolescence, from the age of seven until her departure from the paternal house.

[Article 6] Item, if she frequented the church and the holy places, and [did this] willingly?

[Article 7] Item, with what activities did she busy herself or was she at leisure during the period of her youth?

[Article 8] Item, if at that time she confessed freely and often?

[Article 9] Item, what was the common report regarding the tree called '[the Tree] of the Ladies', and whether it was common practice for young girls to dance there; and also with regard to the spring which is beside this tree, whether Joan frequented this with the other girls, and for what reason or on what occasion she went there?

[Article 10] Item, inquire about the manner in which she left that region and set off on the journey.

[Article 11] Item, if in that place of origin, any inquiries were made by the authority of the judges at the time of her capture before the town of Compiègne, and captivity by the English?

[Article 12] Item, if when Joan first fled her place of origin to go to Neufchâteau, because of the men-at-arms, she was always in the company of her father and mother?

Given and made at Rouen, the year of Our Lord 1455, the 20th day of the month of December.

74. Deposition of Jean Morel (28 January 1456)

Source: Duparc (ed.), *Procès en nullité*, I, pp. 252–5.

Language: Latin

Jean Morel was the first of twenty-one witnesses from Joan's home village of Domremy. He was described in the trial record as a labourer of around seventy years of age from Greux, near Domremy. His statement regarding Joan's childhood and religious practices were repeated by most of the other witness from the village.

[Responding to the 1st, 2nd and 3rd articles of document **73**] he declared upon oath that the Jeannette in question was born at Domremy and was baptised at the parish church of Saint-Rémy in that place. Her father was named Jacques d'Arc, her mother Isabelle, both labourers living together at Domremy as long as they lived. They were good and faithful catholics, good labourers, of good reputation, and of honest behaviour, as far as he saw or knew, because he often spoke with them. The same witness also said that he was one of Joan's godfathers, and her godmothers were the wife of Étienne Le Royer,[1] Béatrice, widow of Estellin, who lived at Domremy,[2] and also Jeannette, widow of Thiesselin of Vittel, who lived in the town of Neufchâteau.[3]

[On the 4th article] he declared upon oath that from her earliest childhood, Jeannette was well brought up in the faith as was appropriate, and instructed in good morals, as far as he knew, so that almost everyone in the village of Domremy loved her. Just like the other young girls she knew the *Credo*, the *Pater Noster* and the *Ave Maria*.

[On the 5th article] he declared that Jeannette was honest in her behaviour, just as any similar girl is, because her parents were not very rich. In her childhood, and right up to her departure from her family home, she followed the plough and sometimes minded the animals in the fields; she did the work of a woman, spinning and making other things.

[On the 6th article] he declared upon oath that, as he saw, this Jeannette often went to church willingly to the extent that sometimes

---

1 The wife of Étienne Le Royer, also known as Thévenin or Thouvenin Le Royer, testified on 29 January 1456, without adding to the statement of Jean Morel.

2 Beatrice, widow of Estellin, testified on 29 January 1456 [**75**].

3 Jeannette, widow of Thiesselin of Vittel, testified on 29 January 1456 [**76**].

she was mocked by the other young people. Also she sometimes went to the church or hermitage of Notre Dame de Bermont, near the village of Domremy, although her parents thought her in the fields, with the plough, or elsewhere. He also declared that when she heard the bell for mass, if she was still in the fields, she went to the village church to hear mass, as the witness certified that he had seen.

[On the 8th article] he declared that he saw Jeannette go to confession at Easter and at other solemn feasts. He saw her go to confess to my lord Guillaume Fronté [or Frontey], who was then priest of the parish church of Saint-Rémy of Domremy.

[On the 9th article] he declared upon oath that on the subject of the tree called 'of the Ladies', he once heard it said that women or supernatural persons – they were called fairies – came long ago to dance under that tree. But so it is said, since a reading of the gospel of St John, they did not come there any more. He also declared that in the present day, on the Sunday when the antiphon *Laetare Jerusalem* ['Rejoice, O Jerusalem'] was sung in church [the middle or fourth Sunday in Lent], commonly called in these parts the Sunday of 'the springs,' the young girls and lads of Domremy went under this tree to dance, and sometimes also in the spring and summer on feast days; sometimes they ate at that place.[4] On their return, they went to the spring of Thorns,[5] strolling and singing, and they drank from the water of this spring, and all around they had fun gathering flowers. He also declared that Joan the Pucelle went there sometimes with the other girls and did as they did; he never heard it said that she went alone to the tree or to the spring, which is nearer to the village than the tree, for any other reason than to walk about and to play just like the other young girls. And he has said nothing more.

[On the 10th article] he declared that when Jeannette left her father's house she went two or three times to Vaucouleurs to speak to the Bailly. He heard it said that Lord Charles, then Duke of Lorraine, wished to see her, and sent her a grey horse, so it was said. He did not know anything to add to his statement on this article, except that in the month of July [1429], he, the witness, went to Chalons-sur-

---

4 The fourth Sunday in Lent was known as 'Laetare Jerusalem', and continues to be regarded as a special day of joy as a break from the strain of the fast. From the early middle ages, popes used to carry a golden rose in their right hand when returning from the celebration of mass.

5 This is also called the 'Fontaine aux Groseilliers'; the Latin name is probably intended for *Rhamnus*, the buckthorn.

Marne when it was said that the King was going to Reims for his coronation, and there he saw Joan who gave him a red garment that she had worn.

[On the 12th article] he declared that when Joan went to Neufchâteau because of the armed bands, she was always in the company of her father and mother; they stayed at Neufchâteau for four days and then returned to the village of Domremy. And the witness knew this because he was with others from the village at Neufchâteau and at that time saw Jeannette and her father and mother.

75. Deposition of Béatrice, widow of Estellin (29 January 1456)

Source: Duparc (ed.), *Procès en nullité*, I, pp. 257–9.

Language: Latin

Béatrice was the third of the twenty-one witnesses from Domremy, and was described as being around forty-four years of age and the widow of a labourer from that village named Estellin.

[Responding to the 1st, 2nd and 3rd articles of document **73**] she declared upon oath that Jeannette was born in the village of Domremy to Jacques d'Arc and his wife Isabet, labourers, true and good catholics, honest and solid folk according to their abilities, but not very rich. Jeannette was baptised at the font of the church of Saint-Rémy in the village and her godfathers were Jean Morel of Greux, Jean de Laxart and the late Jean Rainguesson; her godmothers were Jeannette, widow of Thiesselin le Clerc, Jeannette, wife of Thévenin [Étienne] Le Royer, from the village, and herself, the witness who was testifying.

[On the 4th, 5th, 6th, 7th and 8th articles, Béatrice confirmed the previous statements that Joan was well brought up in the catholic faith and regularly attended church. She then added the following testimony].

After the village of Domremy was burned, Jeannette went every feast day to attend mass at Greux. She confessed willingly on the appropriate days, especially the very holy day of Easter, the resurrection of Our Lord Jesus Christ, and it did not appear to her that there was anyone better than her in the two villages. She took care of many chores in her father's house because sometimes she spun linen or wool, followed the plough, went to harvest when it was time, and sometimes watched over the village cattle and flocks when it was her father's turn. She did not know what else to say.

[On the 9th article] she declared that the tree in question was called 'the Tree of the Ladies'; and the witness once went with the lay lords of the village and their wives to stroll under this tree because of its beauty. She also declared that this tree was to be found beside the highway by which one travels to Neufchâteau. In the past she heard it said that the 'deadly ladies', in French the 'fées' [fairies], formerly went under that tree; but because of sins, so she said, they were not there anymore.

[Béatrice then echoed Jean Morel's account of the festivities surrounding the tree on the Sunday in the middle of Lent.]

She also declared that when the parish priest carried the cross over the fields on the eve of Ascension Day, he also went under this tree and sang the gospel there, and he also went to the spring at Thorns and to the other springs to sing the gospel, as she saw.

76. Deposition of Jeannette, widow of Thiesselin (29 January 1456)

Source: Duparc (ed.), *Procès en nullité*, I, pp. 263–5.

Language: Latin

Jeannette was the seventh of the twenty-one witnesses questioned at Domremy, and was described as being around sixty years of age and the widow of Thiesselin of Vittel, formerly a clerk at Neufchâteau. She repeated the usual statements about Joan's parents, godparents, religious upbringing and work for her father.

[Then responding to the 9th article of document 73,] she declared upon oath that the tree in question was called 'the Tree of the Ladies' because, it was said, in ancient days a Lord named lord Pierre Gravier, knight, Lord of Bourlémont,[6] went to meet a certain lady named 'Fée' [Fairy] under that tree and they spoke together. And she declared that she had heard this read in a romance. She also declared that the lords and ladies of the village of Domremy, that is to say Lady Béatrice, wife of Lord Pierre de Bourlémont, with her daughters, and this Lord Pierre, went sometimes, so it was said, for a stroll to this tree.

[Jeannette then repeated the account of events on the Sunday in the middle of Lent].

6 This is probably a reference to a fourteenth-century lord of Bourlémont.

77. Deposition of Jean de Nouillonpont (31 January 1456)

Source: Duparc (ed.), *Procès en nullité*, I, pp. 289–92.

Language: Latin

Jean de Nouillonpont, also known as Jean de Metz, was the first of six witnesses questioned at Vaucouleurs, and was described as being around fifty-seven years of age, and a nobleman of that town.[7]

[He was unable to offer any testimony in response to the first three articles of document 73, but with regard to articles four to ten] he declared upon oath that he knew what follows, namely that when this Joan the Pucelle came to the place and town of Vaucouleurs, in the diocese of Toul, the witness who was speaking saw her dressed in poor female attire, coloured red. And she stayed in the house of a certain Henri Le Royer of Vaucouleurs. The witness spoke to her, and said: 'My friend, what are you doing here. Will the King be driven from the kingdom and we be English?' The Pucelle replied to him: ' I am come here, to this chamber of the King,[8] to speak to Robert de Baudricourt so that he may take me, or have me taken, to the King. He does not care for me, or for what I am saying to him; nevertheless, before the middle of Lent, I must be with the King even if I have to lose my legs right up the knees.[9] Because no one in the world, neither kings, dukes, the daughter of the King of Scotland,[10] nor any others can recover the kingdom of France; there is no other help for him but me. Even so I would prefer to spin with my mother, that poor woman, because this is not my place. But it is necessary that I should go and do this, because my Lord wishes it.' And when the witness asked her who this Lord was, she told him that it was God. Then Jean, the witness, promised the Pucelle, touching her hand in a sign of faith, that he would take her to the King with God's help. He then asked her when she wished to leave, and she replied: 'Rather today than tomorrow, and tomorrow rather than later.' He also asked her if she wished to travel in those clothes; and she replied that she would like to have the

---

7 He had been ennobled by Charles VII in March 1448.

8 In both this statement and a number of other contemporary documents, Vaucouleurs is referred to as the 'chamber of the King' [*camera regis*], emphasising its connection with the Crown.

9 This was presumably a contemporary idiom, intended to suggest that Joan would carry out her mission even if she had to walk all the way.

10 Margaret, daughter of King James I of Scotland, was betrothed to the dauphin Louis, son and heir of Charles VII, on 30 October 1428.

clothes of a man. Then the witness gave her clothing and hose belonging to his servants to wear. Afterwards the inhabitants of the town of Vaucouleurs had the clothing, hose, garters and everything necessary made for her, and gave her a horse worth around sixteen francs.

Once dressed and provided with a horse, armed with a safe-conduct from the Lord Charles, Duke of Lorraine, the Pucelle left to speak with the Lord Duke, and the witness went with her as far as the city of Toul. When she returned to Vaucouleurs, around the Sunday 'des Bures'[11] – and it will be twenty-seven years ago at the next Sunday des Bures, if he is not mistaken – the witness and Bertrand de Poulengy,[12] together with two of their servants, Colet de Vienne, a royal messenger, and a certain Richard the Archer, conducted this Pucelle to the King, then residing at Chinon; this was at the cost and expense of the witness and of Bertrand de Poulengy.[13] Leaving the town of Vaucouleurs to take her to the King, they sometimes travelled at night for fear of the English and the Burgundians, who were to be found all along their route. They journeyed for eleven days, riding to the town of Chinon. While travelling with her, the witness asked her if she would do what she said. She replied to him that he should have no fear: she had received a command to do this, that her brothers in heaven told her what she had to do, and that four or five years ago her brothers in heaven and her Lord, that is to say God, told her that she must go to war to recover the kingdom of France.[14] He also declared that during this journey, he, the witness, and Bertrand slept every night by her, but Joan slept near to the witness with her doublet and hose done up; the witness believed in her so much that he would not have dared to make advances, and on oath he declared that he never had any desire or carnal feelings for her. During the journey she loved to hear mass and said to them: 'If we can hear the mass, we shall do well.' But, so that she was not recognised, they only heard mass twice on the road. The witness also declared that he believed the words of the Pucelle completely, and he was inspired by her words and by her

11 The 'Dimanche des Bures' was the first Sunday of Lent, that is to say 13 February 1429.

12 See **80** below.

13 According to the royal accounts, Jean de Nouillonpont received 100 *livres tournois* on 21 April 1429, as payment for the expenses that he and his companions had incurred, and he was granted a further 200 *livres tournois* 'for the expenses of the Pucelle'.

14 The brothers in heaven [*fratres de paradiso*] are presumably the voices that Joan heard, though it is curious that the witness describes them as being male.

love of God. He believed that she had been sent from God because she never swore, she loved to hear mass and when making an oath, she crossed herself with the sign of the cross. Thus they conducted her to the King at Chinon in the greatest possible secrecy. The witness also declared that this Pucelle loved to attend mass, as he saw, confessed often, and willingly gave alms; the witness frequently handed her money which she gave away out of love for God. The witness also declared that she was good, frank, pious, an excellent Christian, pleasant company and God-fearing.

78. Deposition of Durand Laxart (31 January 1456)

Source: Duparc (ed.), *Procès en nullité*, I, pp. 295–7.

Language: Latin

Durand Laxart was the fourth of the six witnesses questioned at Vaucouleurs, and was described in the record as being around sixty years of age and living at Burey-le-Petit (now known as Burey-en-Vaux). He was a cousin of Joan through his wife Jeanne le Vauseul, niece of Isabelle Romée or d'Arc.

[Responding to the 1st and 2nd articles of document 73] he declared upon oath that the Joan in question was related to his own wife Joan. He also knew Jacques d'Arc and his wife Isabet, the parents of Joan the Pucelle, good and faithful catholics with a sound reputation. He believed that Joan was born in the village of Domremy and that she was baptised at the font of Saint-Rémy in that place.

[On the 4th to 8th articles] he declared that Joan was of good disposition, pious, patient, and loved to go to the church to confess; she gave alms to the poor when she could, as he saw both in the village of Domremy and at Burey, because Joan stayed in his house for six weeks. She loved to work, she spun, followed the plough, watched over the animals and did all that was required of women.

[On the 10th article] he declared upon oath that he went to find Joan at her father's house and brought her to the house where he lived. She said to him, the witness, that she wished to go into France, to the dauphin, to have him crowned, declaring: 'Was it not once foretold that France would be devastated by a woman and then restored by a virgin?'[15] She told the witness that she wished to go to Robert de

15 See introduction, page 18 above.

Baudricourt who might have her taken to the place where the lord
dauphin was to be found. Robert often said to the witness that he
should take her back to her father's home and smack her. And when
the Pucelle saw that Robert did not want her to be taken to the place
where the dauphin was, she took clothes from the witness and said
that she wished to leave.[16] After she departed, the witness took her to
Vaucouleurs.[17] Then she was taken under safe-conduct to the lord
Charles, Duke of Lorraine. When the Duke saw her, he spoke with
her and gave her four francs, which Joan showed to the witness. After
the return of Joan to Vaucouleurs the inhabitants of the town bought
her a man's clothes, hose, garters and everything necessary. The
witness and Jacques Alain of Vaucouleurs bought a horse for her,
paying twelve francs which was later repaid to the witness by the lord
Robert de Baudricourt. This done, Jean de Metz, Bertrand de Poulengy,
Colet de Vienne and Richard the Archer, with two servants of Jean de
Metz and Bertrand, took Joan to the dauphin. And as the witness
says, he told all of this to the King. He does not know anything more
except that he saw Joan at Reims at the King's coronation.

79. Deposition of Catherine, wife of Henri Le Royer
   ### (31 January 1456)

Source: Duparc (ed.), *Procès en nullité*, I, pp. 297–9.

Language: Latin

Catherine was the fifth of the six witnesses who testified at Vaucouleurs. She
was described as being around fifty-four years of age, and the wife of Henry
Le Royer, who was questioned immediately after her but added nothing
significant to her testimony.

[Responding to the 1st to 8th articles of document **73**, Catherine
reported that Joan was a good and pious girl, and that she had met
her when Durand Laxart brought Joan to her house at Vaucouleurs.
With regard to the 10th article] she declared upon oath that when
Joan wished to withdraw, she was in Catherine's house for three weeks
[in total] at different times. And then [Joan] spoke to Lord Robert
de Baudricourt [asking] that he might have her taken to the place

16 Laxart's statement that he provided the clothes for Joan is contradicted by the
   testimony of Jean de Nouillonpont and Bertrand de Poulengy [**77, 80**].

17 This is a mistake and should either read that the witness took her from
   Vaucouleurs or that he led her to Saint-Nicolas-du-Port. See footnote 20 below.

where the dauphin was, but Lord Robert refused. She declared that
later she saw Robert de Baudricourt, then captain of the town of
Vaucouleurs, and my lord Jean Fournier, enter her house.[18] The priest
said to Joan that he had brought a stole [i.e. he was wearing mass
vestments] and he exorcised her in front of the captain, adding that if
she was a bad creature she should depart from them, and if she was a
good creature she should approach them. Then Joan drew near the
priest and threw herself on her knees before him. She said that the
priest had acted poorly because he had heard her confession. And
when she saw that Robert did not want to take her to the King, she
said, as the witness heard, that she needed to go to the place where
the dauphin was, adding: 'Have you not heard this prophecy, that
France will be destroyed by a woman, and restored by a virgin from
the marches of Lorraine?'[19] Then the witness remembered having
heard these words and was dumbfounded. The witness also declared
that Jeannette was very impatient and time weighed upon her like a
pregnant woman, because she was not taken to the dauphin. Then the
witness and many others had so much faith in her words that a certain
Jacques Alain and Durand Laxart wished to take and escort her to
Saint-Nicolas;[20] but they returned to Vaucouleurs because Joan, it was
said, declared that it was not honest for her to leave in this way. After
their return, some of the inhabitants of the town had tunic, hose,
garters, spurs and other similar things made for her. They bought a
horse for her, and Jean de Metz, Bertrand de Poulengy, Colet de
Vienne and three others took her to the place where the dauphin was.
She saw them mount their horses and ride away.

80. Deposition of Bertrand de Poulengy (6 February 1456)

Source: Duparc (ed.), *Procès en nullité*, I, pp. 304–7.

Language: Latin

Bertrand de Poulengy was the third of six witnesses to be questioned at Toul,
and was described as being around sixty-three years of age, and an esquire of
the household of the King of France.

18 Jean Fournier was the parish priest of Saint Laurent at Vaucouleurs.

19 See introduction, page 18 above.

20 Saint-Nicolas-du-Port – then a celebrated centre of pilgrimage – near Nancy. As
   both Poulengy and Laxart connect this pilgrimage with her visit to the Duke of
   Lorraine, whose residence was at Nancy, it is clear that Saint-Nicolas-du-Port is
   meant, and not the Chapel of Saint Nicolas near Vaucouleurs.

[Having made unremarkable comments in response to the first nine articles of document **73**, Poulengy was asked to respond to the 10th article. He] declared upon oath that Joan the Pucelle came to Vaucouleurs around Ascension day [13 May 1428], he thought. Then he saw her speaking to Robert de Baudricourt, the captain of the town; she said that she had come to Robert in the name of her Lord, so that he might tell the dauphin to hold firm and not to engage his enemy in battle, because the Lord would bring help before the middle of Lent. For Joan said that the kingdom did not belong to the dauphin but to her Lord, but the latter wanted the dauphin to become King and hold the kingdom in trust; she added that, despite his enemy, the dauphin would become King, and that she would lead him to be crowned. When Robert had asked who her Lord was, she replied, 'The King of Heaven'. After this, she returned to the house of her father with one of her uncles named Durand Laxart, from Burey-le-Petit.[21] Later, towards the beginning of Lent, Joan came back to Vaucouleurs, seeking a company to go to the lord dauphin. Seeing this, the witness and Jean de Metz together offered to take her to the King, then dauphin. After having gone on a pilgrimage to Saint-Nicolas and, thanks to a safe-conduct, having visited the Duke of Lorraine who wanted to see her, Joan returned to Vaucouleurs to the house of Henri Le Royer there. Then Bertrand, the witness who was speaking, and Jean de Metz, with the aid of others of Vaucouleurs, enabled her to exchange her female clothing, coloured red, for what they provided: a tunic and man's clothing, spurs, garters, sword and such like, as well as a horse. Then they set out with Joan to go to the dauphin, together with Julian, a servant of the witness, and Jean de Honnecourt, servant of Jean de Metz, Colet de Vienne and Richard the Archer. On setting out, the first day, they feared the bands of Burgundians and Englishmen, then all-powerful, and so they travelled during the night. The witness also declared that Joan the Pucelle said to him, to Jean de Metz and to the others travelling with them, that it would be well for them to hear mass, but they could not do it while they were in the war zone, lest they were recognised. Each night she slept with Jean de Metz and the witness, but fully dressed in her surcoat and her hose tied and closed. He also declared that at that time he was a young man but did not have the desire or any carnal longing to know a woman, and he would not have dared to proposition Joan because of the goodness that he saw in her. The

21 Laxart had testified at Vaucouleurs, a week before Poulengy [**78**].

witness added that they spent eleven days on the road before reaching the King, then the dauphin, and en route they had many anxieties. But Joan always told them that they had nothing to fear because once they arrived at the town of Chinon the noble dauphin would welcome them. She never swore, and the witness, so he said, was very inspired by her words, because it seemed to him that she had been sent by God. He never saw any evil in her, but she was always so good a girl that she deserved to be called a saint. Thus they travelled together without mishap to Chinon where the King, then the dauphin, was. When they had arrived they presented the Pucelle to the nobles and men of the King, to whom the witness referred regarding the actions of Joan [because this was his last encounter with her].

81. Deposition of the Count of Dunois (22 February 1456)

Source: Duparc (ed.), *Procès en nullité*, I, pp. 316–26.

Language: Latin

From 22 February to 16 March 1456, forty-one witnesses were questioned at Orléans, though the articles of interrogation for this phase of the investigation have not survived. The first witness was Jean, Count of Dunois and of Longueville (1402–68). He was also known as the Bastard of Orléans because he was the illegitimate son of Louis, Duke of Orléans (d. 1407). He was raised with Charles VII, whom he served loyally until his death. Soon after the capture of his half-brother Charles, Duke of Orléans, at the battle of Agincourt in 1415, Jean became the acting head of the house of Orléans.

[Dunois was] questioned by the Promoter on the 4th and 8th articles, and moreover on the 7th, concerning the subject of her arrival with the King, her conduct with the men-at-arms and her military talents, as well as her devotion, her charity, and her other virtues.[22]

Asked if he truly believed that Joan was sent by God to accomplish feats of arms, rather than by human skill, he replied that he believed that Joan was sent by God, and that her deeds of arms came from divine inspiration rather than human talent.

Asked what made him say this, he replied that it was for the following reasons. First when he was in the city of Orléans, then besieged by the English, news and rumours arrived – he asserted it – that a certain

22 This brief summary of the three of the articles of interrogation used at Orléans is our only evidence for the questions that were posed to the witnesses at this stage of the inquiry.

young girl, commonly called the Pucelle, had just passed through
Gien and claimed to be going to the noble dauphin in order to have
the siege of Orléans raised and to take the dauphin to Reims for his
coronation. As the witness had command over the city, because he
was the lieutenant-general in war, and he wished to know more about
this Pucelle, he sent the Lord of Villars, Seneschal of Beaucaire, and
Jamet de Tillay, later Bailly of Vermandois, to the king. On their
return these men reported to [Dunois], testifying publicly, in front of
all the people of Orléans who much desired to know the truth about
the arrival of this Pucelle, that they had seen her approach the King in
the town of Chinon. They also said that the King at first did not want
to receive her. The Pucelle waited for two days before she was allowed
to present herself to the King, though she continued to declare that
she had come to have the siege of Orléans lifted, and to take the noble
dauphin to Reims for his coronation, urgently asking for a troop of
men-at-arms, horses and weapons. A delay of three weeks or a month
ensued during which, on the King's order, the Pucelle was examined
about her words and deeds by clerks, prelates and doctors in theology,
to ensure that she might be accepted without risk. During this time
the King had a number of men-at-arms assembled to take supplies to
this city of Orléans. But after having heard the opinion of the prelates
and doctors, who had not found anything evil in this Pucelle, the King
sent her in the company of the Lord Archbishop of Reims, then
Chancellor of France,[23] and of the Lord of Gaucourt, then Grand
Master of the royal household,[24] to the city of Blois where the lords
had arrived who were to escort the supplies, that is to say the lords of
Rais and of Boussac,[25] Marshals of France, and with them was the
Lord of Culant,[26] the Admiral of France, La Hire,[27] and the Lord
Ambroise de Loré, later appointed Provost of Paris.[28] They all came
with Joan the Pucelle and the men-at-arms bringing the supplies in
good order through the Sologne directly to the bank of the Loire,
facing the church called Saint-Loup, in which were numerous brave

23 The archbishop was Regnault de Chartres (d. 1445), who had been appointed
   Chancellor in 1424.

24 Raoul de Gaucourt had been Bailly of Orléans at the time of the siege and testified
   after Dunois on 25 February 1456, largely repeating his testimony.

25 Gilles de Laval, Baron of Rais (d. 1440), and Jean de Brosse, lord of Boussac (d.
   1433).

26 Louis de Graville, lord of Culant (d. 1444).

27 Etienne de Vignolles, called La Hire (d. 1443).

28 Ambroisé de Loré died in 1446.

Englishmen.[29] It appeared to the lord giving evidence and to the other captains that the royal army accompanying the supplies was not big enough to confront [the English] and bring the supplies into the city. Above all, it seemed to them that the ships or boats (that were difficult to find) needed to fetch the supplies, had to cross against the current against the wind. Then Joan addressed the witness with these words: 'Are you the Bastard of Orléans?' He replied: 'Yes, I am he, and I am delighted at your arrival.' She countered: 'Is it you who advised me that I should come here on this side of the river and not go directly to where Talbot and the English are located?' He replied that he, and other even wiser men, had given this advice, believing it to be a better and safer course of action. Joan then replied in these words: 'In God's name, the counsels of God, my Lord, are safer and wiser than yours. You thought to deceive me, and you are the more deceived yourselves, because I bring you better help than has ever been given to any soldier or city, the help of the King of Heaven. But this does not come for the love of me; it comes from God, who, at the prayers of St Louis and of St Charlemagne,[30] has taken pity on the town of Orléans, and will not suffer his enemies to hold both the body of the Lord of Orléans and his town.'[31]

Moreover the witness said that straightaway, in an instant, the wind, which was blowing strongly against the boats loaded with supplies for Orléans, changed and became favourable. Then the sails were immediately raised and the witness climbed into a boat, accompanied by Brother Nicolas de Giresme, now Grand Prior of France, and they passed in front of the church of Saint-Loup in spite of the English. From that time the deponent had great confidence in Joan, more than before. He implored her to cross the river Loire and enter the town of Orléans, where there was a great longing for her. To do this was a problem for her because she said that she did not wish to leave behind her soldiers who were confessed, penitent and right-minded: for this reason, she refused to come. The deponent went to the captains in command of these men-at-arms; he begged them and asked them, for

29 The Sologne is the region to the south of the river Loire. Orléans is located on the north bank of the river.

30 Louis IX, King of France (d. 1270), was canonised by Pope Boniface VIII in 1297. Charlemagne (d. 814), King of the Franks and Emperor, was canonised by the anti-pope Pascal III and his cult was permitted at Aachen; but this was never ratified by the insertion of his feast into the Roman breviary or by the universal Church.

31 Charles, Duke of Orléans was then a prisoner in England, having been captured at the battle of Agincourt in 1415.

the need of the King, to accept that Joan might enter the city of Orléans, and for them to go to Blois with their troops, where they might cross the Loire in order to return to Orléans: there was no nearer place to cross. The captains agreed to this request and consented to go to Blois. Then Joan left with the witness [Dunois], having her standard in her hands, which was white with the image of Our Lord holding a fleur-de-lys. La Hire also crossed the river Loire with her and they entered the town of Orléans together. Because of this story, it seems to the lord deponent that Joan, in her conduct of the war, was led more by God than by human spirit, considering the change of the wind happened suddenly after her words giving hope of aid; the arrival of the supplies despite the English, [who were] much stronger than the royal army; and that this young girl claimed to have seen a vision of St Louis and Charlemagne praying to God for the safety of the King and of the city.

He also believed that she acted under the inspiration of God for another reason: because when the witness wished to go in search of the men-at-arms who were crossing at Blois to bring help to those of the city [of Orléans], Joan refused to wait or to give permission to the deponent to depart; on the contrary, she wanted to tell the English besieging the city to raise the siege and to leave for the kingdom of England, or else she would direct such a great assault against them that they would be forced to leave.[32] This letter was sent to Lord Talbot. Before then, the deponent says, around two hundred Englishmen could put to flight eight hundred or a thousand men of the royal army, but from that moment, four or five hundred men of the King fighting against almost all of the English forces, put pressure on the Englishmen at the siege to the point where they did not dare to leave their shelters and fortresses.

Item, he believed her to be acting on behalf of God for another reason: because on 27 May,[33] early in the morning, at the start of the assault against the enemy defending the boulevard of the bridge, Joan was wounded by an arrow which penetrated six inches into the flesh between the neck and shoulder. Nevertheless, despite this, she did not abandon the siege, nor did she seek any treatment for the wound. Meanwhile the assault lasted from morning until eight o'clock that

32 This may be a reference to the ultimatum that Joan sent to the English on 5 May 1429 [9].

33 This must, in fact, have been 7 May 1429.

evening, so that there seemed no hope of victory that day, and the witness had had enough and wanted the army to return to the town. Then the Pucelle came to him, asking him to wait a little longer; then, mounting her horse, she withdrew to a vineyard not far from the troops and remained in prayer in that vineyard for about seven or eight minutes. Then she returned, immediately took up her standard and placed it on the edge of the ditch; as soon as she was present, the English trembled and were seized by fear; the soldiers of the King recovered courage and began the ascent, delivering the boulevard by assault without meeting any resistance. The boulevard was thus taken and the English found there were put to flight and all killed. The witness says that among others, Glasdale and other principal English captains of this fortress, planning to retreat into the tower of the bridge of Orléans, fell into the river and drowned. This Glasdale had been the one who spoke most offensively, dishonourably and scornfully to the Pucelle. Once the fortress was taken, the witness and the Pucelle with the other Frenchmen returned to the city of Orléans where they were received with great joy and gratitude. Joan was taken to her house so that her wound could receive attention. After the treatment given by a surgeon, she had something to eat, taking four or five pieces of toast dipped in wine diluted with lots of water, and she did not take any other nourishment or drink that day. The next day, early in the morning, the English issued from their camp and lined up in battle order. At this sight the Pucelle got up from her bed and put on just a garment called in French a *jasseran* [a light coat of mail]; moreover she resolved that no one should attack the English or seek anything from them, but that they should be allowed to depart. And they did depart, without anyone pursuing them. From that moment the town was delivered from its enemies.

Item, the lord giving evidence also said that after the siege of Orléans the Pucelle, accompanied by the witness and other captains, went to the King at the castle of Loches to ask him to send men-at-arms to recapture the castles and towns situated on the Loire, that is to say Meung, Beaugency and Jargeau; this would allow [him] to move ahead more freely and safely to his coronation at Reims. She pressed the King on this subject very insistently and frequently, so that he might hurry up and not delay any further. Then the King acted with all possible diligence and sent the Duke of Alençon, the witness and the other captains with Joan to recapture the towns and castles. In fact they were returned to the royal obedience within a few days and when questioned and examined on this, the witness believed that it was thanks to the Pucelle.

Item, this lord declared, when questioned on this, that after the lifting of the siege of Orléans, the English reassembled a great army to defend the aforesaid towns and castles which they held. When the castle and bridge of Beaugency were besieged the English army went to the castle of Meung-sur-Loire, which was still under their control; but it could not help those besieged in the castle of Beaugency. When the English learned that the castle had been taken and placed under the obedience of the King, they gathered together into a single army, so large that the French believed that they were going to fix a day for battle. Thus the French arranged their army and lined up in battle formation, awaiting the English. Then, in the presence of the Constable,[34] the witness and of many others, the Lord Duke of Alençon asked Joan what should be done. She answered him in a loud voice: 'Do you all have good spurs?' At these words those present asked Joan: 'What are you saying?' Should we take to our heels?' Then Joan replied: 'No! It will be the English who will not defend themselves and will be beaten, and you will need spurs to rush upon them.' And this was the case: the English fled and more than four thousand were either dead or prisoners.

Item, this lord declared that he remembered, in all truth, that when the King was at the castle at Loches, the witness and the Pucelle went to see him after the lifting of the siege of Orléans. The King was in his private chamber, known in French as 'de retrait',[35] with the lord Christopher of Harcourt, Bishop of Castres, his confessor,[36] and the Lord of Trèves, formerly Chancellor of France.[37] Before entering this room, she knocked at the door and as soon as she had entered, she knelt down before the King and, embracing his legs, said these words, or something like them: 'Noble dauphin, do not continue to hold such long councils, but come quickly to Reims to take the deserved crown.' Then Christopher of Harcourt, speaking to her, asked her if she had

34 Arthur de Richemont, constable of France, d. 1458.

35 The *Chambre de retrait* was the second of three principal rooms used by the king during the daytime, located between the *Chambre à parer* and the innermost room, the *Chambre du roi*. They were separate from the rooms in which the king and the queen slept.

36 Gérard Machet was confessor of Charles VII while dauphin and king, but did not become Bishop of Castres until 1432, after the death of Joan of Arc.

37 Robert le Maçon, Lord of Tréves, had been chancellor from 1416 to 1422.

had this from her counsel, and Joan replied yes, she had been strongly urged in this regard. Christopher addressed Joan again: 'Do you not wish to say here, in the presence of the King, how your counsel appears when it speaks to you?' Blushing, she replied to him: 'I know enough of what you wish to know, and I will tell it to you willingly.' Then the King said to her: 'Joan, will it please you to make a statement on what he asks, here in the presence of those who are here?' She replied positively to the King, and expressed herself in these words or others similar: when she was at all unhappy because what she said on behalf of God was not believed, she went aside and prayed to God, complaining to Him that the people to whom she was speaking did not readily believe her; and as soon as the prayer to God was over, she heard a voice say to her, 'Daughter of God, go, go, go, I will be your aid', and when she heard this voice, she was thrilled and also wished to remain in that state forever. And, what is more, in repeating the words of her voice, she had surges of wonderful joy, raising her eyes to heaven.

Item, the witness declared, when questioned, that he recalled that after these victories the princes of the royal blood and the captains wanted the King to go to Normandy and not to Reims. But the Pucelle was always of the opinion that it was essential to go to Reims to have the King crowned; she gave as her reason that once the King had been crowned and consecrated, the power of his enemy would steadily decline, until in the end they would not be able to harm either the King or the kingdom. All accepted her advice. The first place where the King stopped and set up camp with his army was before the city of Troyes. There he took counsel with the princes of the blood and the other captains about whether they remain before this city, in order to besiege and capture it, or whether it would be better to pass it by, going straight to Reims and abandoning the city of Troyes. The council of the King was divided, hesitating about what would be most useful. Joan arrived, entered the council and said these words or something similar: 'Noble dauphin, order your troops to besiege the town of Troyes without indulging in longer deliberations, because in God's name within three days, I will bring you into this city, by love or by strength and force; and Burgundy, full of deceit, will be very amazed.' Then Joan immediately advanced with the royal army, pitched tents along the ditches, and took more admirable precautions than two or three more experienced or famous warlords would have done. She worked so hard that night, that the following day, the Bishop [Jean

Lesguisé⌉ and citizens of the city, frightened and trembling, placed themselves under royal obedience. As was later known, from the moment Joan gave her advice to the King not to give up the city, the citizens lost courage and only sought to flee and to take refuge in the churches. Once this city returned to the King's obedience, he left for Reims, where he received complete obedience and where he was consecrated and crowned.

Item, the witness declared, when questioned on the life and the morals of the Pucelle, that she was in the habit of repairing every day to a church at vespers or at twilight, and of having the bells there rung for half-an-hour; she collected together the mendicant friars who were following the royal army, and then went to pray and had an anthem in honour of the holy Mary, mother of God, sung by the mendicant friars.

Item, this witness said, when questioned on this, that when the King arrived at La Ferté and at Crépy-en-Valois, the people ran before him, full of elation and crying: 'Noël!' Then the Pucelle, who was then riding between the Archbishop of Reims and this witness, said these words: 'Here are a good people! I have never seen another people who rejoiced so much at the coming of so noble a King. How happy I would be if, at the end of my days, I were to be buried in this place!' Hearing this, the Lord Archbishop said: 'O Joan, in what place do you hope to die?' She replied: 'Where it will please God, for I know no more than you the time or the place. Would that it might please God, my creator, that I might retire, abandoning arms, and that I might go to serve my father and mother, looking after their sheep with my sister and my brothers, who would rejoice so much to see me.'

This lord also declared and attested, when asked about her life, virtues and the conduct of Joan in the midst of the men-at-arms, that she exceeded all other living people in temperance. He often heard the words of Lord Jean d'Aulon, knight, now Seneschal of Beaucaire, appointed and designated by the King to accompany the Pucelle and to protect her, because he was the wisest knight and a model of honesty. This knight said that he did not believe that a more chaste woman existed than her.[38] This witness also affirmed that neither he nor any others who were in the company of this Pucelle had any wish or desire to have commerce with a women or to associate with one; this appeared to the witness as almost miraculous.

38 See Jean d'Aulon's testimony [101].

Finally he said that fifteen days after he had taken prisoner the Earl of Suffolk at the surrender of Jargeau [12 June 1429], a scrap of paper was sent to this Count [of Dunois] containing four lines: they made mention of a young girl that would come from a 'Bois Chenu', riding on the back of the archers and against them.[39]

To conclude, the witness said among other things, questioned on this, that Joan did joke about deeds of arms and many military matters which perhaps had not occurred, in order to spur on the soldiers. Nevertheless when she spoke seriously about the war, her own actions and her vocation, she never claimed anything other than this: that she had been sent to raise the siege of Orléans, to help the oppressed people of that town and the neighbouring places, and to conduct the King to Reims so that he might be crowned.

82. Deposition of Master François Garivel (7 March 1456)

Source: Duparc (ed.), *Procès en nullité*, I, pp. 327–9.

Language: Latin

François Garivel was the third witness to testify at Orléans in 1456. In the trial record, he was described as a councillor-general to the King on taxation, and was said to be around forty years of age, which would have made him thirteen when Joan was questioned at Chinon and Poitiers.

Firstly regarding the articles, he declared that he recalled that when Joan the Pucelle arrived, the King sent her to Poitiers where she lodged in the house of the late Master Jean Rabateau, then royal advocate in the Parlement. By order of the king, famous doctors and masters were appointed in this city of Poitiers, namely Dom Pierre de Versailles, then Abbot of Talmond and later Bishop of Meaux, Jean Lambert, Guillaume Aimery of the Order of St Dominic, and Pierre Seguin of the Carmelite Order, all doctors in theology; Mathieu Menage and Guillaume Le Marié, bachelors in theology; and many other counsellors of the King, graduates in both laws.[40] They examined Joan repeatedly for almost three weeks, inspecting and considering her words and deeds. Finally, taking into consideration her attitude and

---

39 This appears to be a reference to a prophecy that was also cited by Mathieu Thomassin in the *Registre delphinal* in 1456, along with the poem *Virgo puellares* [6].

40 All these individuals are discussed in R. G. Little, *The Parlement of Poitiers: war, government and politics in France, 1418–1436*, London, 1984.

her answers, they said that this Pucelle was an honest girl: questioned by them, she had persisted in her answers, which is to say that she had been sent from the God of Heaven to help the noble dauphin, to restore him to his kingdom, to raise the siege of Orléans and to take the dauphin to Reims so that he might be crowned. But before this, it was necessary that she write to the English, urging them to leave because this was the will of God.

This witness also said when questioned that, when Joan was asked why she called the King 'dauphin' and not 'King', she replied that she would only call him King when he had been crowned and consecrated at Reims, the town to which she meant to take him. Moreover, the clerks asked her to show a sign to prove that she had been sent by God, but she told them that this sign, given to her by God, was the raising of the siege of Orléans; she had no doubt that this would happen if the King was willing to give her an army, even a small one.

The witness also said that this was a simple shepherdess who loved God very much because she confessed often and frequently received the sacrament of the Eucharist. Finally, according to the testimony of the witness, after a long examination carefully conducted by the clerks from various faculties, all were of the opinion that the King could lawfully receive her and that she could lead an armed troop to the siege of Orléans, because they found nothing in her that was not in accordance with faith and reason. He did not know anything more.

83. Deposition of Jean Luillier (16 March 1456)

Source: Duparc (ed.), *Procès en nullité*, I, pp. 330–2.

Language: Latin

On 16 March 1456, thirty-seven inhabitants of Orléans were questioned on the same day. The first witness was Jean Luillier the elder, who was described as being around fifty-six years of age and a burgher of Orléans. His statement was confirmed by all the subsequent witnesses, most of them fellow burghers and their wives, who occasionally added small glosses to his comments.

Questioned about the arrival of the Pucelle in the town of Orléans, he declared that she was very much wanted by all of the inhabitants of that city because of her fame, and the rumour that was then circulating. It was said that she had told the King that she had been sent by God to have the siege lifted from that town; and the citizens and all the inhabitants found themselves in such danger, because of the besieging enemy, that they did not know to whom to turn in order to be saved, except to God.

Item, asked if he was in the city when she entered, he replied in the affirmative, and he said that she was received with as much rejoicing and applause from all, men and women, young and old, as if she had been an angel of God, because they hoped to be delivered from their enemy thanks to her, which happened later.

Item, asked about what she had done in the town after her entrance, he declared that she exhorted them all to trust in God: if they had good hope and trust in God, they would be saved from their enemy. He also said that she wished to send a warning to the English before allowing an assault to be launched to drive them away. This was done because she herself warned the English in a letter telling them that they should withdraw from the siege and return to the kingdom of England, or else they would be made to go back by force and violence. He also said that from that moment on, the English were terrified and did not have the same power to resist as before; thus one could often see a small number of men from the town fighting against a great troop of Englishmen, pinning them back so that the English besiegers did not dare to leave their fortresses.

Item, asked about the lifting of the siege, he said that he certainly remembered that in the month of May, the 27th day of that month,[41] in the year of the Lord 1429, an assault was made against the enemy found in the boulevard of the bridge. It was said that during this attack she had been wounded by an arrow. This assault lasted from morning until evening, until those of the city wished to retreat into the town. Then Joan came, exhorting them not to retreat or to return into the city. Having spoken in this way, she seized her standard and placed it on the edge of the ditch, and immediately, in front of her, the English trembled and were frightened. The King's men took courage and began to climb in order to attack the boulevard, without meeting any resistance. The boulevard was then taken and the English, who were found there, fled, but all died. He also declared that Glasdale and other principal English captains of the fortress, thinking to retreat into the tower of the bridge, fell into the river and drowned there. Once the fortress was taken, all the supporters of the King re-entered the city of Orléans.

41 In actual fact 7 May 1429.

Asked furthermore about what happened afterwards, he declared that another day, that is to say on the following day, early in the morning, the English came out of their tents and formed up in battle order to fight, as it seemed. Having learned of and heard about this, the Pucelle rose from her bed and armed herself, but she did not wish the English to be attacked then or that anything be asked of them; on the contrary, she advised that they be allowed to depart. And in fact they did leave, without anyone pursuing them; and from then on the town was delivered from its enemies.

Item, asked whether the siege was lifted and the city delivered from the enemy by the service or means of this Pucelle, or rather by the strength of the men-at-arms, he replied that he, like everyone in the city, believed that if the Pucelle had not come on behalf of God to help them, all the inhabitants and the city would soon have fallen under the control and power of the besieging enemy. He did not believe that the inhabitants and the men-at-arms to be found in the city could have resisted the enemy forces, then so superior to them, for very long.

84. Deposition of Jacques L'Esbahy (16 March 1456)

Source: Duparc (ed.), *Procès en nullité*, I, p. 333.

Language: Latin

Jacques L'Esbahy, described as a fifty-year-old burgher of Orléans, confirmed the previous statement by Jean Luillier.

He added that he recalled that there were two heralds, one named Ambleville and the other Guienne, who were sent on the authority of the Pucelle to Saint-Laurent in order to inform Lord Talbot, the Earl of Suffolk and Lord Scales, that these English lords should leave in God's name and return to England; if not, they would come to harm. Then the English detained one of the heralds, named Guienne, and sent back the other, Ambleville, to say certain things to the Pucelle; Ambleville reported that the English had kept his comrade Guienne to burn him. Then Joan answered Ambleville, swearing in God's name that no harm would come to Guienne, but that he, Ambleville, should return boldly to the English: no harm would come to him and, on the contrary, he would bring back his comrade safe and sound. This is what happened.

He also added that he saw Joan at the moment of her entrance into the town of Orléans. She wished above all to go to the cathedral, to give homage to God, her creator. He did not know anything more.

85. Deposition of Jean de Champeaux (16 March 1456)

Source: Duparc (ed.), *Procès en nullité*, I, pp. 335–6.

Language: Latin

Jean de Champeaux confirmed the statement of Luillier.

He added that one Sunday he saw the men-at-arms of Orléans prepare for a great assault against the English, who were themselves drawing up in order of battle. Seeing this, Joan went out and approached the men-at-arms; she was asked if it was right to attack the English on that day, which was a Sunday; she answered that it was necessary to hear mass first. Then she sent to find a table [to serve as an altar], to bring the fittings of the church and to celebrate two masses which she and the whole army heard with great devotion. Once these masses had been celebrated, Joan said to look if the English were facing them; the reply was no, on the contrary, they had their faces turned towards Meung. When she heard this, she said: 'In the name of God, they are going; let them depart; and let us give thanks to God, without pursuing them, because it is the Lord's day.'[42]

86. Deposition of Charlotte, wife of Guillaume Havet (16 March 1456)

Source: Duparc (ed.), *Procès en nullité*, I, pp. 339–40.

Language: Latin

Charlotte was described as being around thirty-six years of age, and the daughter of Jacques Boucher, Treasurer of Orléans, at whose house Joan had lodged. She confirmed the previous statements.

She also added that at night she slept alone with Joan. She also declared that she never saw a glimpse of any sign of debauchery or lechery, either in her words or deeds, but only saw simplicity, humility and chastity. She also said that [Joan] was in the habit of often confessing her sins and that she heard mass every day.

42 This statement was confirmed by the four subsequent witnesses, Pierre Jougant, Pierre Hue, Jean Aubert and Guillaume Rouillart, as well as unnamed others.

She affirmed that Joan often said to the mother of the witness, in whose house she lodged, that she must put trust in God, and that God would help the town of Orléans and drive away the enemy.

What is more, she declared that she was accustomed, before making an assault, always to sort out her conscience [i.e. by making confession] and to receive the holy Eucharist after having heard mass.

87. Deposition of Master Jean Tiphaine (2 April 1456)

Source: Duparc (ed.), *Procès en nullité*, I, pp. 347–9.

Language: Latin

The next phase of the investigation took place at Paris between 2 April and 11 May 1456, though the articles of interrogation do not survive. Jean Tiphaine was the first of twenty witnesses to be questioned. He had studied and taught medicine at the University of Paris and served as a canon of the Sainte-Chapelle in Paris. He had also attended the Rouen trial, but claimed not to have given any opinion and said that he had only attended out of fear of the English. The Nullification trial record indicated that he was sixty years of age.

[Tiphaine provided unremarkable testimony in response to fourteen unidentified articles].

Questioned further about the illness that Joan had during the trial, he declared that he had been sent by the lord judges to visit her, and was brought to her by a man named Estivet. In the presence of this Estivet, of Master Guillaume de La Chambre, master in medicine, and several others, he took her pulse to know the cause of her malady, and he asked what [symptoms] she had and where she had pain. She replied that a carp had been sent to her by the Bishop of Beauvais which she had eaten, and she feared that this was the cause of her illness. Then this Estivet, always present, replied to her saying that she was speaking wrongly; he called her a whore [*paillardam*], declaring: 'You whore, you have eaten fish in brine and other things which are not suitable for you.' She replied that she had not done so, and this Joan and d'Estivet exchanged many rude words. Afterwards, however, the witness wished to know more about the malady of Joan, and learned from some people, also present there, that she had vomited a number of times.

The witness did not know anything more. Asked about this, he did not recall ever having given another opinion during the trial except on her illness.[43]

88. Deposition of Master Guillaume de La Chambre (2 April 1456)

Source: Duparc (ed.), *Procès en nullité*, I, pp. 349–52.

Language: Latin

Guillaume de La Chambre was the second of twenty witnesses to be questioned at Paris between 2 April and 11 May 1456. As a young graduate in medicine from the University of Paris he had treated Joan during the Rouen trial. He did not mention in his testimony that he had voted in favour of a sentence of relapse and heresy against Joan on 29 May 1431.

[La Chambre's comments on the first nine articles were limited].

On the contents of the 10th article, he declared that he had heard it said that Joan had been examined to know whether she was a virgin, and she was found to be [one]. The witness also knew, as he could certify according to medical science, that she was intact and a virgin, because he saw her almost naked when visiting her because of an illness; he felt her on the kidneys [*in renibus*] and as far as he could see, she was very narrow [*stricta*].

On the contents of the 11th, 12th, 13th and 14th [articles], he said and declared, in response to the questions, that he had seen the Lord Abbot of Fécamp cross-examining Joan on one occasion and Master Jean Beaupère interrupted with many other questions to which Joan did not then want to reply, so she said to them that they were doing her a great injustice in hounding her in this way, and that she had already replied to these questions.

As for her illness, which is mentioned in these articles, the witness declared that the Cardinal of England and the Earl of Warwick sent for him,[44] and he appeared before them, along with Guillaume Desjardins, master in medicine, and other doctors.[45] The Earl of Warwick

---

43 In reality, Jean Tiphaine had voted in support of the Abbot of Fécamp on 29 May 1431 during the trial of condemnation.

44 The Cardinal of England was Henry Beaufort (d. 1447), Bishop of Winchester and cardinal from 1426; he was the highest-ranking English clergyman at the trial of Joan of Arc. The Earl of Warwick was Richard Beauchamp (d. 1439).

45 Guillaume Desjardins had died in 1438, but another doctor who had treated Joan, Jean Tiphaine, testified immediately before La Chambre [87].

told them that he had been told that Joan had been ill, and he ordered them to investigate because the King certainly did not want her to die a natural death: for the King valued her, having paid dearly for her, and he did not wish her to die without having been judged and burned. The witness, Guillaume Desjardins and the others then went to see her. The witness and Desjardins pressed her on the right side, and found her feverish, so that they concluded that she needed to be bled and reported as much to the Earl of Warwick. He said to them: 'Be on your guard when bleeding her because she is cunning and could kill herself.' Nevertheless she was bled and soon recovered. After this recovery, a certain Master Jean d'Estivet arrived, who used abusive words against Joan, calling her a whore and a slut [*putanam, paillardam*]. She was so much inflamed by this that she had a fever again and fell ill. When this was brought to the knowledge of the Earl, he forbade this Estivet to abuse Joan any more.

89. Deposition of Master Thomas de Courcelles (2 April 1456)

Source: Duparc (ed.), *Procès en nullité*, I, pp. 355–9.

Language: Latin

Thomas de Courcelles was the fourth witness questioned at Paris. The fifty-six-year-old professor of sacred theology had served as Rector of the University of Paris from 1430 to 1432, and played a significant role in the trial of Joan of Arc. On 12 May 1431 he was one of just two individuals to vote in favour of torturing Joan and on 19 May he declared that she should be considered a heretic if she refused to obey the Church. Immediately after the trial he testified that Joan had renounced her voices on the morning of her execution, almost certainly a falsehood, and then translated the French record of the trial into Latin with the help of the notary, Guillaume Manchon, tactfully remaining silent about his own voting in the matter. Shortly afterwards he switched allegiances and not only represented Charles VII at the Congress of Arras but also delivered the funeral oration after the death of the King.

[Courcelles said that he did not know Joan before the trial, and, responding to the 5th and 6th articles, stated that he was summoned to attend the trial with Masters Nicolas Midi, Jacques de Touraine and Jean de Rouel]. Moreover, he did not know whether any preliminary inquiry had been made at Rouen or at Joan's birthplace, and he did not see any record of it. For at the start of the trial, and above all when the witness was present, the only question was the voices that she was said to have heard and which she insisted came from God.

And even though the trial record was shown to the witness, specifying that certain preliminary inquiries conducted at Rouen or in the place her birth were read in his presence [19 February 1431], he declared that he had no memory of ever hearing them being read out. Moreover he said that Master Jean Lohier then came to the town of Rouen, and it was commanded that the trial record be communicated to him. This Lohier, after he had seen the trial record, said to the witness that in his opinion Joan should not have been proceeded against in a matter of faith without a preliminary inquiry into her reputation and that such an inquiry was a legal requirement.[46] The witness [Courcelles] also said that he could clearly remember that when he was first consulted, he never argued that Joan was heretic, except in the circumstances or case that she obstinately refused to submit to the Church. When he was consulted on the third and final occasion, as far as he could testify in conscience before God, he believed that he had declared that Joan was the same as [she had been] before, and if she had been a heretic before, then she was still [a heretic]: but he never positively stated that she was a heretic. He also said that at the time of the first consultation, those giving opinions disagreed and argued vehemently about whether Joan should be declared a heretic. He also affirms that he never resolved that Joan should be tortured.

[Courcelles could not comment on the 8th article].

Item, questioned on the contents of the 9th article, he said and declared that Joan was imprisoned in the castle, guarded by Jean Gris and his servants, and that her feet were shackled in iron. But he did not know if she was always kept like this. Moreover he said that many of those present believed, and would certainly have preferred, that Joan should have been handed over to the Church and [put] into an ecclesiastical prison; but he did not remember that this had been discussed at the time of the consultations.

[Courcelles' responses to the remaining articles were generally unremarkable, until he was asked about the 26th, 27th and 28th articles]. He declared and attested that after the first sermon [on the day of the abjuration on 24 May 1431], news came that Joan had

---

46 Jean Lohier was a doctor of civil and canon law, whose concerns about the proceedings against Joan were also cited by Guillaume Manchon in March 1450 and May 1452, as well as in 1456 [**98**].

resumed male clothing. The Bishop accordingly returned to Joan's prison, in the company of the witness, and asked her why she had taken up these masculine clothes again. She replied that she had resumed this garment because it seemed preferable to wear it rather than a garment of a woman when surrounded by men.

90. Deposition of Louis de Coutes (3 April 1456)

Source: Duparc (ed.), *Procès en nullité*, I, pp. 361–7.

Language: Latin

Louis de Coutes was the sixth of the twenty witnesses at Paris, where he was described as around forty-two years of age and a squire and Lord of Nouvion and Rugles. He was the son of Jean de Coutes, a captain of Châteaudun and chamberlain to the Duke of Orléans.

Questioned first about the contents of the 1st, 2nd, 3rd and 4th articles, all the others being set aside because he knew nothing about them, he said and declared upon oath as follows: in the year that Joan came to the King at Chinon, he, the witness, was fourteen or fifteen years old. He was in the service of [Raoul,] Lord of Gaucourt, who was then captain of Chinon, and spent his time with him. At this time, Joan arrived at Chinon in the company of two men; she was taken to the king. The witness who is speaking saw her going to the King and returning many times. Joan was assigned quarters in a tower of the castle of Coudray. The witness stayed with Joan in that tower and throughout her stay he remained continually in her company during the day but at night she had women with her. He well recalled that at this time, when she was in the tower of Coudray, men of great estate frequently came to meet Joan, but he did not know what they did or said because the witness always withdrew when he saw these men arrive; he did not know who these men were.

He also said that during the time when he and Joan were in the tower he saw her often on her knees praying, as it seemed to him, but he could not catch what she was saying although she wept sometimes. Then Joan was taken to the town of Poitiers and then brought back to Tours, to the house of a woman called Lapau. There the Duke of Alençon gave Joan a horse, which the witness saw at the house of this Lapau. In this town of Tours, the witness was told and ordered to be a page of Joan, along with a certain individual named Raymond. From that time he was always with Joan, always going with her in his capacity as her page, serving her both at Blois and at Orléans, and until they reached the city of Paris.

He also said that while Joan was in the town of Tours she was given a suit of armour and also received a rank from the King. From Tours she went to Blois with a company of the King's men-at-arms and this company had great confidence in her from that time on. The witness did not remember for how long Joan stayed with the men-at-arms in that town. Then it was decided to leave Blois and to go to Orléans through the Sologne. Joan left fully armed, accompanied by the men-at-arms, whom she always urged to trust entirely in God and to confess their sins. And in this company the witness saw Joan receive the sacrament of the Eucharist.

He also said that, having arrived near Orléans, on the Sologne side of the river, Joan, the witness and many others were taken across the water to Orléans side and there entered the town. The witness added that Joan was very bruised on her arrival at Orléans because she had slept fully armed the night before leaving Blois for Orléans. At Orléans Joan was put up in the house of the Treasurer [Jacques Boucher] before the Bannier Gate, and in this house, as the witness saw, she received the sacrament of the Eucharist.

He also said that, on the day following her arrival at Orléans, Joan went to see the Lord Bastard of Orléans and met with him. On her return she was very irritated because, so she said, it had been decided not to stage an assault that day. Nevertheless she went to a boulevard that the King's men-at-arms were holding opposite the boulevard of the English. Joan spoke to the English who were in the other boulevard, telling them to withdraw in the name of Christ or she would drive them out. One named the Bastard of Granville then hurled abuse at Joan, asking her if she expected them to surrender to a woman, and calling the Frenchmen with Joan 'black-hearted pimps' [maquereaulx mescréans]. After this, Joan returned to her lodging and went up to her chamber, and the witness who is speaking thought that she was going to sleep. But shortly afterwards she came down and said these words to the witness: 'Ah! Blood-soaked boy, you did not tell me that the blood of France was being spilled!' And she ordered him to go and find her horse while she was armed by the lady of the house and her daughter. When the witness returned, having prepared her horse, he found Joan already armed; she then told the witness to go and find her standard which had been left upstairs, and the witness handed it to her through the window. Having taken her standard, Joan rushed off towards the Burgundy gate, and the lady of the house then told the witness to follow her, which he did. At that moment there was an attack or skirmish by Saint-Loup and in the course of this attack the boulevard was taken. Joan met some of the wounded Frenchmen which made her furious. The English were preparing the defence when Joan came against them in haste. As soon as the French saw Joan, they began to cheer and took possession of the bastille or fortress of Saint-Loup. He heard it said that certain churchmen, having put on their vestments, came before Joan and she received them hospitably, not allowing the least harm to be done to them, and had them taken to her lodging. But the other Englishmen were killed by the people of Orléans. That evening Joan dined at her lodging. She was very abstemious and often only ate a morsel of bread in a whole day and it was astonishing that she ate so little. When she was in her lodging, she only ate twice in a day.

He also declared that the next day, towards the third hour [nine o'clock], the soldiers of our King crossed the river in boats to attack the bastille, that is the fort of Saint-Jean-le-Blanc, which the French took along with the fortress of the Celestines [in fact the fortress of the Augustins]. Accompanied by the witness, Joan crossed the river Loire with these troops and then re-entered the town of Orléans where she went to sleep in her lodging with some women, as she was in the habit of doing; for every night she had a woman sleeping in her lodging with her, if she could find one, and if she could not find one during war and on campaign, then she slept fully dressed. From the following day, against the advice of many lords who reckoned that her decision was going to put the King's men in great danger, Joan had the Burgundy gate opened as well as a small [postern] gate near to the great tower: then she crossed the river with some men-at-arms to attack the bastille or fortress of the Bridge [the Tourelles], which the English were still holding. The King's men continued to attack the place from the first hour [six o'clock] until night. Joan was wounded and her armour was removed in order to treat her wound; as soon as it had been treated, she put on her armour again and went with the others to the attack and assault, which lasted from the first hour to the evening without a break. The boulevard was finally taken and Joan, remaining with the men-at-arms throughout the assault, exhorted them to have good courage and not to retreat because they would win the fortress before long. She was saying, it seems to him, that they would win the fortress when they saw the wind blowing her standard in its direction. However towards the evening, the King's men, seeing that nothing had happened and that night approached, despaired of taking possession of the fortress. Nevertheless Joan still persisted, promising them that they would win the fort that day without fail. Then the King's men prepared a new assault, and when the English saw it, they did not offer any defence but, terrified, were almost all drowned; and in the course of this last attack or final assault, the English offered no defence. The following day all the Englishmen who were surrounding the town departed for Beaugency and Meung. The King's army, including Joan, followed them and there, [the Englishmen] made an agreement either to fight or to hand over the town of Beaugency.[47] But when the day of the battle arrived, the English left Beaugency, pursued by the King's men and Joan. The vanguard was led by La Hire, which irritated Joan a great deal because she very much desired to have command of the vanguard. The King's men did so well that La Hire, who led this vanguard, fell on the English; the King's troops secured the victory and almost all the English were killed.

He also declared that Joan was very pious and felt great pity in the face of such killing, because on one occasion a Frenchman, who was escorting certain English prisoners, struck one of them on the head so hard that he left him for dead. Seeing this, Joan dismounted and [arranged for] the Englishman's confession to be heard, supporting his head herself and comforting him as far as she could. Afterwards she went in the company of the King's men to Jargeau, which was taken by assault and a number of Englishmen were taken prisoner there, among whom were Suffolk and de la Pole.[48] Then, after the lifting of the siege of Orléans and the victories that were won, Joan went with the troops to the King, then based in the town of Tours, and it was decided that the King should go to Reims to be crowned. The King left with the army, in which was Joan, and went to the town of Troyes, which submitted to the King, and from there to the town of Châlons, which also put itself into the hands of the King. He then went to Reims, where our lord the King was crowned and consecrated

47 Louis de Coutes is presumably indicating that the garrison made a conditional agreement or treaty [compositionem] to surrender the town if the English forces failed to meet the King's army in battle, thereby avoiding the worst consequences of an attack by storm.

48 John de la Pole, captain of Avranches, brother of William de la Pole, Earl of Suffolk.

in the presence of this witness because, as has been said, he was Joan's page and was always with her. And he stayed with her until Joan came before the city of Paris.

Moreover he declared that, as far as he could tell, Joan was a good and honest woman, living as a catholic; she heard mass with great pleasure and never missed this if possible. She was very angry when she heard men blaspheme the name of Our Lord and when she heard anyone swear, because he often heard her rebuke the Duke of Alençon when he swore or uttered some blasphemy in front of her. And in general no one in the army would have dared to swear or blaspheme in front of her, for fear of being reprimanded.

Moreover he declared that she did not want any women in the army. Indeed on one occasion, near Château-Thierry, seeing a woman on horseback, the mistress of one of the men-at-arms, Joan pursued her with a naked sword. But she did not strike this woman, and rather advised her gently and kindly not to be found again in the company of the men-at-arms, or she would be displeased with her.

The witness did not know anything more because, he said, he did not see her after Joan came before Paris.

91. Deposition of Gobert Thibaut (5 April 1456)

Source: Duparc (ed.), *Procès en nullité*, I, pp. 367–70.

Language: Latin

Gobert Thibaut was the seventh of the twenty witnesses to be questioned at Paris. He was described as around fifty years of age, and a squire and equerry of the King of France.

And questioned first on what he could testify or give in evidence regarding the contents of the 1st, 2nd, 3rd and 4th articles, he said and declared upon oath that he was in the town of Chinon when Joan arrived and approached the King who was also in that town of Chinon; but before that he did not have any great knowledge of this Joan. But henceforward he had much greater acquaintance with her because, when the King wished to go to Poitiers, Joan was also taken there and lodged in the house of Master Jean Rabateau. The witness also knows that Joan was questioned and examined in the town of Poitiers by the late Master Pierre de Versailles, professor of sacred theology, then Abbot of Talmont and later Bishop of Meaux until his death, and by Master Jean Érault, also professor of sacred theology; the witness went with them by the command of the late Bishop of Castres [Gérard Machet]. As he has said before, she was lodged in the house of Rabateau and there Versailles and Érault met Joan in the presence of the witness. And when they arrived at the house, Joan went to meet them; and she struck the witness on the shoulder, saying to him that she would be glad to have many men like him. Then Versailles told Joan that they had been sent to her from the King. She replied: 'I well believe that you have been sent to question me', adding: 'I do not know either A or B.' They then asked her why she had come. She replied: 'I come from the King of Heaven to raise the siege of Orléans and to lead the King to Reims so that he may be crowned and consecrated'. She asked them if they had paper and ink, and said to Master Jean Érault: 'Write what I say to you: You, Suffolk, Glasdale and La Pole, I call upon you to return to England, in the name of the King of Heaven.'[49] And on that occasion Versailles and Érault did nothing more that he remembered; and Joan remained in the town of Poitiers as long as the King. She also said that her counsel had told her that she should have gone more quickly to the King. The witness saw those who brought her to the King, that is to say Jean de Metz, Jean Coulon, and Bertrand Pollichon [Poulengy], with whom she was very familiar and friendly. Once, in his presence, these men who had brought Joan declared to [Gérard Machet,] late Lord [Bishop] of Castres, then the King's confessor, that they had come through Burgundy, crossing places occupied by the enemy, yet they had always passed without the least hindrance, at which they marvelled greatly.

He also declared that he had heard the deceased lord confessor say that he had seen it written that a certain Pucelle would come to the aid of the King of France. The witness had not seen and did not know whether Joan was questioned more than he said in his testimony. Nevertheless he heard the lord confessor and the other doctors say that they believed that Joan had been sent by God, and that they believed she was the one spoken of in the prophecy; also, given her attitude, her simplicity and her conduct, the King could rely on her because only good could be found or perceived in her, and nothing contrary to the catholic faith had been seen in her.

[Thibaut continued his testimony but, as he admitted, he was not an eyewitness to the events that he described].

49 Joan's letter to the English, dated 22 March 1429 [4].

92. Deposition of Simon Beaucroix (20 April 1456)

Source: Duparc (ed.), *Procès en nullité*, I, pp. 370–4.

Language: Latin

Simon Beaucroix was the eighth witness questioned at Paris. He was described as being around fifty years of age, and a squire and married clerk, living at Paris in the Hôtel-Neuf.

And questioned first on what he could give in evidence and testify regarding the contents of the 1st, 2nd, 3rd and 4th articles, he said and declared upon oath that he was in the town of Chinon, where our lord the King was present with the lord Jean d'Aulon, knight and Seneschal of Beaucaire,[50] when Joan came before the King. After speaking with the King and the others of the King's council, she was placed in the custody of this Aulon. Joan went in the company of Aulon from the town of Chinon to the town of Blois, and from the town of Blois along the Sologne to the town of Orléans. And he well remembered that Joan advised all the men-at-arms to make confession, to put themselves in a worthy state, assuring them that God would assist them and that, if they were in a worthy state, they would have the victory with God's help. It was then Joan's intention that the army should go directly to the fort or bastille of Saint-Jean-le-Blanc. This was not done, but they went instead to a place between Orléans and Jargeau to which the inhabitants of Orléans had sent boats to receive the supplies and take them into the town of Orléans. The supplies were put into the boats and brought to Orléans but because the men-at-arms could not cross the river Loire it was decided that they should go back and cross the river Loire at Blois because this was the nearest bridge within the King's obedience. Joan was very indignant at these words, fearing that they would retreat and leave the task unfinished. Joan did not want to go with the others to cross at Blois, but crossed the river by boat with about two hundred lances in her company; they all reached the other side of the river and entered the town of Orléans by land. The Lord Marshal of Boussac went that night to find the King's army which was near Blois. And the witness remembered that shortly before the arrival of the Lord Marshal of Boussac at Orléans, Joan said to Lord Jean d'Aulon that the Marshal of Boussac was en route and that she was sure that no harm would come to him.

50 See **101**.

And when Joan was in her lodging, moved by the spirit of God, so he said, she suddenly declared: 'In the name of God, our people have much to do!' She sent to find her horse, armed herself and went to the fort or bastille of Saint-Loup where there was an assault by the King's men against the English. After Joan had joined this attack the fort was taken. The next day the French in Joan's company went to seize the fort of Saint-Jean-le-Blanc. They approached an island and when the English saw that the King's men were crossing the water they abandoned the bastille of Saint-Jean-le-Blanc and retreated to another fort situated near the Augustins, where the witness saw the royal army in very great danger, and Joan saying: 'Let us advance bravely, in the name of God!' They came right up to the English, who found themselves in great peril, and who held three forts or bastilles. The fortress of the Augustins was immediately taken without much difficulty; then the captains were of the opinion that Joan should enter the town of Orléans, but she did not want to do so, declaring: 'Shall we leave our men?' And the next day the King's men came to attack the fort situated at the end of the bridge [the Tourelles], which was very strong and virtually impregnable; and the King's men had much to do because the attack lasted the whole day until the night. The witness saw the Seneschal of Beaucaire destroy the bridge with a bombard. It was already evening and they almost despaired of taking the fort or bastille of the bridge. Then the standard of Joan was called for and, when this was done, the King's men resumed the attack on the fort; straight away, without much difficulty, they entered with this standard. The English began to flee and when they reached the end of the bridge it collapsed and many of the English were drowned. The next day the King's men made a new sortie to fight the English. When they saw the French they fled and as Joan watched them run away pursued by the French, she said to them: 'Let the English go, do not kill them. They are going. Their flight is enough for me.' The same day the King's men left the town of Orléans and returned to Blois, arriving within the day. Joan stayed there for two or three days and then returned to Tours and to Loches, where the King's men were preparing to attack the town of Jargeau; and they went there and took the town by assault.

[Beaucroix then made general remarks regarding Joan's piety].

He also declared that Joan always slept with young girls, and did not wish to sleep next to old women. She strongly detested swearers and blasphemers, and scolded those who swore or blasphemed. On campaign, she never allowed any of her company to pillage because she never wanted food that she knew was stolen. On one occasion a Scotsman told her that she had eaten stolen calf, and she was very angry and wanted to strike the Scot for this.

He also declared that she never wanted to see women of ill repute riding in the army with the troops. Thus none of them dared to be around Joan and if she recognised any of them, she forced them to leave unless the men-at-arms were willing to marry them.

Finally the witness believed that she was a true catholic, believing in God and keeping His commandments, and also obeying as far as possible the instructions of the Church. [She was] also charitable, not only to the French, but also towards the enemy. All this the witness knew because he was in her company for a long time, and often helped her to arm herself.

He also declared that Joan was pained and displeased when honest women came to her, wishing to pay reverence: it seemed to her that this was a sort of devotion, which irritated her. He did not know anything more.

93. Deposition of Master Jean Barbin (30 April 1456)

Source: Duparc (ed.), *Procès en nullité*, I, pp. 374–6.

Language: Latin

The ninth witness to testify at Paris was Jean Barbin, described as being around fifty years of age and a royal advocate in the Parlement of Poitiers and then Paris.

And questioned first on the contents of the 1st, 2nd, 3rd and 4th articles presented in this case, the others having been omitted because he did not know anything to say in his statement, he said and declared upon oath that when Joan came to the King in the town of Chinon, he was in the town of Poitiers. He heard it said that the King did not wish to trust this Joan at first glance, but wished that first she might be examined by the clerks, and also, as he heard, the King sent to Joan's birthplace, in order to know from where she came. He sent Joan to be examined in the town of Poitiers where the witness then was, and where he met Joan for the first time. When she arrived at the town she was lodged in the house of Master Jean Rabateau; and while she was lodging there, he heard the wife of Rabateau say that

Joan was every day after dinner on her knees for a long time, and also at night; she frequently went into a small chapel in the house and there prayed for a long time. Many clergy visited her, that is to say Master Pierre de Versailles, professor of sacred theology and Bishop of Meaux when he died, and Master Guillaume Aimery, also a professor of sacred theology, along with other graduates in theology whose names he had forgotten; they questioned her about whatever they pleased. The witness then heard the doctors who had examined her and posed many questions to her, relate that she had replied with much wisdom, as if she had been a good clerk, so that they marvelled at her answers, and believed that this was divine inspiration, considering her life and conversation and behaviour. Finally the clerks, after having carried out these questions and cross-examinations, concluded that there was nothing bad in her and nothing that was contrary to the catholic faith; also, in light of the necessity in which the King and realm found themselves, since the King and his subjects were then in a desperate situation and without hope of any aid unless by an intervention from God, they also concluded that the King could turn to her. In the course of these deliberations, Master Jean Érault, professor of sacred theology, reported what he had once heard it said by a certain Marie d'Avignon who had formerly come to the King: she had told him that the kingdom of France had much to suffer and would have to endure a number of calamities, adding that she had had many visions regarding the desolation of the kingdom of France, and in particular she saw a quantity of armour which had been presented to her; she was terror-stricken by this, fearing that she would be forced to accept these suits of armour; then she was told not to be afraid, that she would not have to bear these arms; but that after her, a Pucelle [*Puella*] would come who would bear these arms and deliver the kingdom of France from the enemy. And this Érault believed firmly that Joan was the one of whom Marie d'Avignon had spoken.[51]

He also declared that the men-at-arms regarded her as a saint, because she bore herself so well in the army, in words and in deeds, following God, so that no one could reproach her.

He also declared that he heard Master Pierre de Versailles, who was once in the town of Loches in the company of Joan, say that the people threw themselves before the feet of her horse to kiss her hands

51 This prophecy does not appear amongst the surviving revelations and visions of Marie Robine, or Marie the Gascon. See page 18 above.

and feet. Then the Master said to Joan that she did wrong in allowing such things which were not suitable for her and that she ought to distrust such practices because she made men into idolaters. Joan replied: 'In truth, I would not know how to protect myself from such things, if God does not protect me.'

94. Deposition of the Duke of Alençon (3 May 1456)

Source: Duparc (ed.), *Procès en nullité*, I, pp. 380–8.

Language: Latin

Jean, Duke of Alençon (1407–76), was the twelfth witness to be questioned at Paris. Alençon had been a loyal servant of Charles VII in the aftermath of the Treaty of Troyes: he was captured by the English at the battle of Verneuil in 1424 and spent three years as a prisoner in Crotoy, before returning to lead Charles' army from the Loire campaign to the attack on Paris in September 1429. In the decade following the death of Joan of Arc, relations between Alençon and the King deteriorated, and he not only took part in the plot against Charles VII known as the Praguerie in 1440, but also negotiated with the English to assist their return to Normandy in 1455. The following year, he was arrested by Dunois four weeks after testifying at the Nullification trial; he was condemned to death by the peers of France in 1458 on a charge of *lèse-majesté* (treason), despite the pleading of one of the Nullification trial judges, Jean Juvénal des Ursins, who cited the Duke's service in 1429. Nevertheless, Alençon was pardoned and freed upon the accession to the throne of his godson, Louis XI, in 1461, but was again condemned to death in 1474; this time, too, he was set free, but died in 1476.[52]

Questioned first on what he could testify on the contents of the 1st, 2nd, 3rd and 4th articles, he said and declared upon oath that when Joan came before the King, who was in the town of Chinon, the witness was then in the town of Saint-Florent. While walking to hunt quails, one of his beaters came to inform him of the arrival with the King of a Pucelle, who said that she had been sent by God to put the English to flight, and to raise the siege established by them around the town of Orléans. So the following day, the witness went to the King at Chinon and he found this Joan there, who was meeting the King. At the arrival of the witness, Joan asked who he was and the King replied that this was the Duke of Alençon. Then Joan declared: 'You are very welcome indeed! The more that come together of the

---

52 S. H. Cuttler, *The Law of Treason and Treason Trials in Later Medieval France*, Cambridge, 1981, pp. 195–212.

royal blood of France, the better it will be.' The next day Joan went in response to the summons of the King, and when she saw the King, she bowed. The King took her into a room along with the witness and the lord of La Trémouïlle, whom the King held back, ordering the others to withdraw. Then Joan made many requests of the King, and among others that he might give his kingdom to the King of Heaven; after this donation, the King of Heaven would act as he had done for his predecessors, and restore him to his previous state. There were many other things that the witness does not recall, but which were discussed until dinner. After dinner the King went for a walk nearby and Joan rode before him with the lance. When the witness saw how she performed holding the lance and riding with the lance, he gave her a horse.

But then the King decided that Joan would be examined by the churchmen, and to this end were delegated [Gérard Machet,] Bishop of Castres, the King's confessor; the bishops of Senlis, Maguelonne and Poitiers [Jean Raffanel, Robert Alleman and Hugues de Combarel]; Master Pierre de Versailles, later Bishop of Meaux; Master Jordan Morin; and many others whose names he did not recall. They asked Joan, in the presence of the witness, why she had come and who had sent her to the King. She replied that she had come from the King of Heaven, that she had voices and a counsel who told her what she was to do; but the witness did not remember what this was. But later Joan, who was dining with the witness, confided in him that she had been questioned at length but that she did not know and could not do more than she had said to those who were questioning her. But when the King had heard the report of those commissioners charged with questioning her, he decided that Joan should go to Poitiers, where she would be examined again. The witness did not assist at this examination carried out at Poitiers, but he knew that later, at the King's council, what those who had examined her had said was reported: they had found nothing in her contrary to the catholic faith and, given the state of necessity, the King could turn to her. After this report, the King sent the witness to the Queen of Sicily to prepare the supplies for the army which was to be sent to Orléans;[53] he then met with the Lord Ambroise de Loré and a Lord Louis, whose name he does not recall, who prepared the supplies. But money was needed for this and, in order to obtain it, the witness returned to the King,

53 The Queen of Sicily was Yolande of Aragon, widow of Louis, Duke of Anjou and titular King of Sicily. She was the mother of Charles VII's wife Marie.

announced that the supplies were ready and that the only thing missing was the money for the food and the men-at-arms. The King then sent some people to deliver the necessary money to accomplish this enterprise; so the men-at-arms with the supplies were ready to leave for the town of Orléans, in order to try, if possible, to raise the siege. Joan was sent with these men-at-arms, and the King had a suit of armour made for her. Thus the men-at-arms and Joan departed, but the witness knew nothing about what happened en route and in the town of Orléans, except by hearsay, because he was not present and did not go with the men-at-arms. Nevertheless he subsequently saw the forts established around the town of Orléans and he noted their strength; he believed that they were taken more by a miracle than by strength of arms, especially the fort of the Tourelles at the end of the bridge, and the fort of the Augustins; if the witness had been in them with a small troop, he could certainly have hoped to resist the whole power of the enemy for six or seven days, and it seemed to him that they would not have been able to seize it. And he heard it reported by the men-at-arms and captains who were there, that they attributed almost all the events at Orléans to a miracle of God coming from on high, and not to the work of men; he heard this said many times by Lord Ambroise de Loré, recently Provost of Paris. The witness did not see Joan any more after she had left the King until the raising of the siege of Orléans. He returned to Selles-en-Berry from where he rejoined Joan and the other men-at-arms who were near Orléans. And they succeeded in assembling up to six hundred lances of royal soldiers with the intention of going to Jargeau, a town which the English occupied. That night they slept in a wood and the following morning other men-at-arms came, led by the Lord Bastard of Orléans, the lord Florent d'Illiers and other captains. When they were all assembled, there were around twelve hundred lances. There was then a discussion among the captains, because some were minded to attack the town and the others were opposed to this, asserting that the English had great strength and numbers. Joan, seeing these discussions between them, told them not to fear the numbers or to hesitate about attacking the English, because God would lead their enterprise; she added that if she had not been sure that God was guiding things, she would rather have watched over sheep than exposed herself to such dangers. At these words they set out towards the town of Jargeau, believing that they would seize the suburbs and pass through that night. But spotting them, the English came to meet them and at first drove them back. Seeing this Joan took her standard and set off to the attack, exhorting the men-at-arms to have good courage, and they achieved so much that the army of the King was installed in the suburbs of Jargeau that night. The witness believed that God led the affair because during the night there was almost no guard and if the English had come out of the town, the army of the King would have been in very great peril. The King's men were preparing the artillery, directing the bombards and engines towards the town in the morning; after some days they held council about what should be done against the English who were in Jargeau. During the council, it was reported that La Hire was in negotiations with the Lord of Suffolk and at this, the witness and the other captains were annoyed with La Hire and he was asked to return. After this incident, it was decided to launch the attack against the town, and the heralds cried: 'To the assault!' Then Joan said to the witness who was testifying: 'Forward, gentle Duke, to the assault!' And when it appeared to the witness that they were acting prematurely in joining so quickly in the attack, Joan said to him: 'Do not hesitate! This is the hour that pleases God.' She added that it was necessary to work when God wished it: 'Help yourself and God will help you.' Later she said to the witness: 'Ah! gentle Duke, are you afraid? Do you not know that I promised your wife to bring you back, safe and sound?'[54] This was in fact true: when he left his wife to join the army, she said to Joan that she feared greatly for her husband and that he had already been a prisoner [after the battle of Verneuil] and large sums had been spent to ransom him; she would gladly have asked him to stay. Joan replied: 'Lady, have no fear! I will give him back to you safe, in the state that he is or even better.'

He also declared that during the assault on the town of Jargeau, Joan told the witness who was in one place, to leave that spot because if he did not go, 'that engine [presumably a cannon] will kill you', she said, while pointing to an engine installed in the town. The witness moved and shortly afterwards, in the same spot that he had left, a certain Lord of Lude was killed by that engine.[55] The witness became very frightened, and after this marvelled at the words of Joan. Afterwards Joan joined the attack, and the witness was with her. During the advance of the assailants, the Earl of Suffolk had it shouted that he wished to speak with the witness who was testifying, but no one heard and the attack continued. Joan was on a ladder, holding her standard in her hand, when it was struck and she herself was hit on the head by

54 Alençon was married to Joan, daughter of Charles Duke of Orléans.
55 He was referring to Gilles de Daillon, Lord of Lude.

a stone which broke her helmet. But she was thrown to the ground and raising herself, said to the men-at-arms: 'Friends, friends! Come on! Come on! Our Lord has condemned the English! Now they are ours; have good courage!' In an instant the town of Jargeau was taken and the English retreated towards the bridges chased by the French; in the pursuit, more than eleven hundred were killed.

Once the town was taken [on 11 June 1429], the witness, Joan and the men-at-arms went to Orléans, then from Orléans to Meung, the town where the English were, that is to say the 'child of Warwick' and Scales.[56] The witness spent the night with a few troops in a church near to Meung where he was in great danger. The following day they went to Beaugency, where they met nearby with other royal troops and led an attack against the English who were in the town. After this attack, the English abandoned the town and took shelter in the castle; guards were then placed around the castle to prevent the English from leaving. When they were in front of the castle in this way, the witness and Joan learned that the Constable was arriving with some troops;[57] they, and the others of the army, were annoyed at this and wished to return to the town because they had an order not to receive the Lord Constable into their company. In the words of the witness, Joan declared that if the Constable came, she would leave. But the next day, before the arrival of the Lord Constable, they learned that the English were coming in great number and with them Lord Talbot. The troops shouted 'To arms' and then Joan said to the witness, who wanted to go because of the arrival of the Lord Constable, that it was necessary to help one another. But the English of the castle surrendered by agreement and left under a safe conduct delivered by the witness, who was at that time lieutenant of the King for this army. When the English were retreating, a man of the company of La Hire came to announce to the witness and to the King's captains that the English were approaching, that they would soon be in sight, and that they numbered around one thousand men-at-arms. At the noise, Joan asked what this man was saying, and having learned it, she declared to the Lord Constable: 'Ah! My good Constable, you have not come by my will, but now that you are here, you are welcome.' Many of the King's men were then frightened, saying that it would be good to

56 The garrison was commanded by John Talbot and Thomas Scales.

57 Arthur, Count of Richemont, Constable of France and brother of the Duke of Brittany. Although friendly to the French cause, he was distrusted by Charles, and, at this time, was in disgrace.

order horses [to flee]. Then Joan declared: 'In the name of God, we must fight them! [Even] if they were hanging from the clouds, we would have them, because God sends us to punish them', affirming that she was certain of the victory, adding the following words: 'The gentle King shall today have the greatest victory that he has ever received. And my counsel has said to me that they are all ours'. And the witness knew that the English were defeated and killed without great difficulty, and among them Talbot was captured. There was a great massacre of the English and then the King's men came to the town of Patay in Beauce; in that town, Talbot was brought before the witness and the Lord Constable in the presence of Joan. The witness declared to Talbot that he would not have believed in the morning that it would be this way; whereupon Talbot replied that it was the fortune of war. Afterwards they returned to the King who decided to go to the town of Reims for his coronation and consecration.

Occasionally he heard Joan say to the King that she would last for one year and no more, and that he should consider how best to employ her for that year; because she claimed to have four tasks, that is say to expel the English; to have the King crowned and consecrated at Reims; to free the Duke of Orléans from the hands of the English; and to raise the siege established by the English around the town of Orléans.

He also said that Joan was chaste and very much detested the women who follow the armies. The witness saw her once at Saint-Denis on the return from the coronation of the King, pursuing with a naked sword a girl living with the men-at-arms and in the pursuit she broke her sword. She was also very irritated when she heard the men-at-arms swear; she reprimanded them vehemently, and above all the witness who sometimes swore; and when he saw her, he refrained from swearing.

He also said that sometimes on campaign, he slept near Joan and the men-at-arms on straw; he sometimes saw Joan dressing, and sometimes he saw her breasts which were beautiful. But the witness never felt any carnal desire towards her.

He also said that, as far as he could judge, he had always held her to be an excellent catholic and an honest woman because he saw her receive the body of Christ many times and when she looked at the body of Christ, she very often shed many tears. She received the holy Eucharist twice a week and confessed often.

He also said that Joan, outside the sphere of warfare, was pure and youthful. But she was very skilful in war, both in carrying the lance and in deploying the army, organizing combat and preparing artillery. Everyone was full of admiration for the fact that she could bear herself so skilfully and prudently in military actions, as if she had been a captain fighting for twenty or thirty years, and above all with regard to the preparation of the artillery, in which she excelled.

Asked about this, he did not know anything more.

95. Deposition of Brother Jean Pasquerel (4 May 1456)

Source: Duparc (ed.), *Procès en nullité*, I, pp. 388–97.

Language: Latin

Jean Pasquerel was the thirteenth witness to testify at Paris, having failed to appear in 1452 after he was called to the inquiry chaired by Guillaume d'Estouteville. He was described in the trial record as an Augustinian friar from Bayeux.

Questioned first on the contents of the 1st, 2nd, 3rd and 4th articles read to him, he said and declared upon oath that he first had news of Joan, and knew that she had come to the King, when he was in the town [of Puy-en-Valais]. The mother of Joan was in this town and some of those who had accompanied her to the King, and because they knew the witness a little, they said to him that he must come with them to see this Joan, and that they would not leave him before having taken him to her. The witness then came with them to the town of Chinon, and from there to Tours, where he was a lector in a convent of the town.[58] In that town of Tours, Joan was lodged in the house of a burgher, Jean Dupuy.[59] There they found Joan, and those who had brought the witness addressed her in these terms: 'Joan, we bring you this good father; when you know him well, you will love him greatly.' Joan replied that she was very glad to see the witness, that she had already heard talk about him, and that she wished to confess to him the following day. He heard her confession the following day and said mass in her presence. From that day onward, the witness

---

58 The lector read the books in church; this prestigious office usually served a stepping stone to major orders.

59 Jean Dupuy may have been the husband of the woman named Lapau, mentioned by Louis de Coutes [90].

always followed and accompanied her until she was captured at the town of Compiègne.

He heard it said that Joan, when she came before the King, was inspected twice by women to establish whether she was a man or a woman; she was found to be a woman, but a young girl and a virgin. The lady of Gaucourt and the lady of Trèves inspected her, so he heard.[60] Afterwards, she was taken to Poitiers to be examined there by the clerks of the university who were present in order to decide what was to be done about her. Then Master Jordan Morin, Master Pierre de Versailles, the Bishop of Meaux now deceased, and many others examined her and after this investigation, concluded that, in view of the pressing necessity in which all the kingdom found itself, the King might turn to her, and that they had found nothing in her contrary to the catholic faith. When this was done, she was taken back to Chinon, and thought that she could speak with the King which she could not [do] at that time. But after a debate by the King's council, she was able to speak with him. That day, a man who was on horseback said these words: 'Is that there the Pucelle?', swearing to God that if he spent a night with her, she would not leave as a Pucelle. Joan the replied to this man: 'Oh! In the name of God, you blaspheme God and you are so near to your death!' Then this man, within the hour, fell into the water and drowned. This he heard from the mouth of Joan and many others who had been present.

The Lord Count of Vendôme brought Joan to the King and had her enter the royal chamber.[61] When he saw her, the King asked Joan for her name. She replied: 'Gentle dauphin, I am called Joan the Pucelle, and the King of Heaven commands through me that you will be consecrated and crowned in the town of Reims, and that you will be the lieutenant of the King of Heaven, who is the King of France.' After the King had posed many questions, Joan again said: 'On behalf of my Lord, I say to you that you are the true heir of France and son of the King; and he sends me to you to lead you to Reims, where you will receive the crown and consecration, if you wish.'[62] Having heard this,

---

60 The lady of Gaucourt was Jeanne de Preuilly and the lady of Trèves was Jeanne de Mortemer.

61 The Count of Vendôme was Louis de Bourbon, who had been taken prisoner by the English at Agincourt and freed in 1426.

62 The words 'and son of the King' are undoubtedly a reference to the rumours that Charles was in fact the illegitimate son of Louis, Duke of Orléans. Is it likely that Joan, or Charles VII, would have worried about such claims in 1429? More

the King declared to those present that Joan had told him certain secrets which no one knew, and could not know, except for God, and so he had great confidence in her. All these things the witness heard from Joan herself, because he was not then present.

He also learned from her that she was not happy at many of the questions which prevented her from carrying out the work entrusted to her, and that it was necessary and it was time to go to work. She also said that she had asked the messengers of her Lord, that is to say God, who appeared to her, what she ought to do, and they told her to take the standard of her Lord. For this Joan had her standard made on which was painted the image of Our Saviour sitting in judgement on the clouds of heaven; and there was also an angel painted holding in his hands a fleur-de-lys which the image of Christ was blessing. The witness arrived at Tours at the moment when this standard was being painted.

Shortly afterwards, Joan departed with the other men-at-arms to raise the siege before Orléans and the witness remained in her company and did not leave her until she had been captured before Compiègne. He served as her chaplain, hearing her confession and saying mass.

The witness also declared that Joan was very pious towards God and the holy Virgin, confessing nearly every day and receiving communion frequently. When she was in a place where there was a convent of mendicant friars, she asked the witness to remind her of the days on which the younger mendicants received the sacrament of the Eucharist, so as to receive it with them; and she asked this often in order to receive the sacrament with the young ones. He also declared that when she confessed, she wept.

The witness also said that at her departure from Tours to go to Orléans, Joan asked him not to leave her but to remain with her always as her confessor; this he promised to do. They stayed in the town of Blois for about two or three days, waiting for the supplies to be loaded on to the boats. She then told the witness to have a standard made to muster the priests, on which he should have painted an image of Our Lord being crucified; he did this. Then on two occasions each day, that is to say the morning and evening, she had all the priests called together by the witness and once gathered, they sang antiphons

---

importantly, did Pasquerel make such a controversial reference in 1456? They do not appear in perhaps the most important manuscript of the Nullification trial, British Library MS Stowe 84, and so may be a later addition to the text.

and hymns to the Blessed Mary, and Joan was with them. She did not allow the men-at-arms to be present among these priests unless they had confessed that day, exhorting them all to confess in order to come to these gatherings. All the priests at these gatherings were ready to hear the confession of all those who wished it.

When Joan left the town of Blois for Orléans, Joan made all the priests assemble around this standard and they walked ahead of the men-at-arms. Gathered like this, they travelled alongside the Sologne [south bank of the river], singing the *Veni creator Spiritus* and many antiphons; they camped that day in the fields and also the following day. The third day, they approached Orléans where the English had laid siege along the river Loire. The royal army came so close to the English that the Englishmen and the Frenchmen could watch one another while the troops of the King were bringing the supplies. The river was then so low that the boats could not return or go to the bank where the English were, but all of a sudden the water rose so that the boats could come in to the place where the royal troops were. Joan climbed into these boats with some men-at-arms, and entered Orléans. The witness returned with the priests and the standards to Blois, by Joan's command, and then, a few days after, he came without any difficulty to the city of Orléans by way of the Beauce, with many men-at-arms, the standard and the priests. When Joan learned of their arrival, she went to meet them and all together they entered Orléans without obstacle, and brought in the provisions in sight of the English. This was surprising because all these Englishmen, in great number and strength, armed and ready to fight, were watching the King's men-at-arms pass by, a weak force compared to them. They also saw and heard the priests who were singing, among whom was found the witness carrying the standard. Nevertheless, no Englishman attacked these men-at-arms and priests.

After this entry into Orléans, the King's men sallied out again from the town, at the request of Joan, to go against the English and to attack those who were in the fort or bastille of Saint-Loup. As for the witness, he went with the other priests after dinner to Joan's lodging; when they arrived there, she was calling out: 'Where are those who should arm me? The blood of our people is being spilt on the ground!' And, as soon as she was armed, she quickly sallied out of town and went to the fort of Saint-Loup where the attack and assault was taking place. On the road she met many of the wounded, and was very much distressed at this. She left with the others for the assault, so that, by force and violence, the fort was at last taken and the English who were there were taken prisoner. This was the eve of the Ascension of the Lord [4 May], the witness recalled, and there were many Englishmen killed. Joan was very distressed because she said that they had died unshriven, and she pitied them greatly, and she immediately confessed to the witness. She also asked him to exhort all the men-at-arms to confess their sins and to give thanks to God for the victory they had gained, or else she would not stay with them but would abandon their company. She added, on this eve of the Ascension of the Lord, that within five days the siege established before Orléans would be raised, and that no Englishman would remain before the town: and so it was because, as the witness has already said, the fortress or bastille of Saint-Loup, where there were monks, was taken on this Wednesday.[63] In that fortress there were more than one hundred chosen and well-armed men, of whom there was none who was not taken prisoner or killed. The same day, in the evening, Joan was in her lodging and declared to the witness that the following day was the Ascension of Our Saviour and that there would be no combat and that she would not put on her armour, out of respect for this feast, but that she wished that day to confess and to receive the sacrament of the Eucharist; this was done. She ordered that no one presume to launch an attack or assault, at least without confessing beforehand, and that watch also be kept so that loose-living women did not follow her, because God would then allow the war to be lost on account of the sins. And it was done as Joan had ordered.

The witness also said that on this feast of the Ascension, Joan wrote to the English in the forts and bastilles in these terms. [Pasquerel then cited Joan's third letter to the English, dated 5 May 1429, document **9**.]

Then Joan took an arrow, attached the letter to the end of the arrow with a thread, and ordered an archer to shoot it at the English, crying: 'Read this. Here is news.' The English received the arrow with this letter, read it and then began to exclaim loudly, shouting: 'Here is the news about the whore of the Armagnacs!' Hearing these words, Joan began to sigh and to weep copiously, invoking the help of the God of Heaven. Then she was consoled, so she said, because she had had news from her Lord. That evening, after supper, she asked the witness to get up earlier the following morning than he had done on

63 Established on the site of a convent in the previous December.

Ascension Day, in order to confess her early in the morning: and this he did.

The next day, a Friday [6 May], the day following the feast of the Ascension, the witness rose very early, heard Joan in confession and said mass in front of her and her men in the town of Orléans. Then they went to the attack which lasted from morning until evening. On this day the fortress of the Augustins was taken after a great assault. Joan, who was accustomed to fast every Friday, could not fast on that day because she was too tired and she ate. After this meal, a brave and famous captain came, whose name the witness does not remember. He said to Joan that the captains and the King's men had met to take counsel; it seemed to them that there were too few men-at-arms in comparison with the English, and God had already shown them great grace in the success already obtained, adding: 'Considering that the town is full of supplies, we could certainly hold it while awaiting help from the King; it does not seem expedient to the council that the troops should go out tomorrow.' Joan replied to them: 'You have been to your council, and I to mine; and believe that the counsel of God will be accomplished and done, but the other will perish', adding to the witness who was then near her: 'Get up even earlier than today, and do the best you can. Always stay near me because tomorrow I will have much to do, more than I have ever done, and tomorrow the blood will flow from my body on to my breast.'

When Saturday [7 May] came, the witness got up early and celebrated mass, and Joan went to the assault on the fortress of the bridge [the Tourelles] where there was the Englishman, Glasdale. The attack lasted from morning to sunset without interruption. In this assault, after dinner, Joan was struck by an arrow above her breast as she had predicted. When she felt herself wounded, she was afraid and wept, but then she was comforted, as she said. Some of the men-at-arms saw her wounded in this way and wished to treat her by an incantation, to 'charm' her, but she refused, saying: 'I would prefer to die rather than to do a thing which I know to be a sin, or to be against the will of God', adding that she certainly knew that she would have to die but did not know when, where and how, or at what time; nevertheless if a remedy could be used on her wound without sin, she would accept treatment. Then olive oil and lard were applied to the wound, and after this dressing, Joan confessed to the witness, weeping and lamenting. Then she returned again to the attack and the assault, saying and crying: 'Glasdale! Glasdale! Yield, yield to the King of

Heaven! You called me a whore but I have great pity for your soul and for those of your men.' Then Glasdale, armed from head to foot, fell into the river Loire and drowned. At this, Joan, moved by pity, began to weep copiously for the soul of Glasdale and for the others who drowned there in great number. On this day all the English who were on the other side of the bridge were taken prisoner or killed.

Then that Sunday [8 May], before dawn, all the Englishmen who remained in the fields around Orléans mustered, came to the ditches around the town of Orléans, and then left for the town of Meung-sur-Loire, where they remained for several days. On this Sunday there was also a solemn procession and sermon in the town of Orléans. It was then decided to return to the King and Joan set out. The English assembled and went to Jargeau which was taken by assault. Then the English were defeated and beaten near the town of Patay.

As she had said, Joan still wished to travel to the coronation of the King and so she went to Troyes in Champagne, from Troyes to Châlons, and from Châlons to Reims, where the King was miraculously crowned and consecrated, just as Joan had predicted from her arrival. The witness often heard Joan say that it was her job to do this, and when it was said to her that: 'Never have such things been seen as those of yours. In no book can one read of such things', she answered: 'My Lord has a book from which no clerk has ever read, however perfect he may be in clerkship.'

The witness also said that each time that she had ridden on campaign and approached a stronghold, she always lodged separately with women. He saw her many times at night, kneeling on the ground, praying to God for the prosperity of the King and for the accomplishment of the mission that God had entrusted to her.

He also declared that, in the army on campaign, sometimes the necessary supplies were not to be found, but she never wished to eat provisions taken by pillage. The witness firmly believed that she had been sent by God because she did good deeds and was full of all the virtues. She had great pity for the poor men-at-arms, even if they were from the English side, and when she saw them dying or wounded she had them confessed. She feared God very much because for nothing in the world would she ever wish to do anything that might displease God. When she was wounded in the shoulder by a crossbow bolt so that the bolt went through from one side to the other, some wished to treat her by an incantation, promising that she would be immediately cured. But she replied that this was a sin and that she would prefer to die rather than to offend Our Lord by such incantations.

[Pasquerel denounced the judgement of the trial at Rouen as unjust].

Our lord the King and the Duke of Alençon had full knowledge of her actions and deeds, and they were also well-informed about certain secret matters which they could reveal if they chose. The witness does not know anything more, except what Joan said to him many times, that is to say that if she were to die, our lord the King would build chapels to pray to God for the souls of all those who had died in the war, for the defence of the realm.

96. Deposition of Simon Charles (7 May 1456)

Source: Duparc (ed.), *Procès en nullité*, I, pp. 399–402.

Language: Latin

Simon Charles was the fifteenth witness to appear at Paris. He was described as being around sixty years of age, and the President of the Chambre des Comptes (chief audit court) of the King.

Questioned first on what he could depose and testify with regard to the contents of the 1st, 2nd, 3rd and 4th articles produced in this case, he said and declared upon oath that he only knew what follows: that is to say that in the year when Joan came to the King, the witness had been sent by the King on a mission to Venice and he returned around the month of March. He then heard from Jean de Metz, who had brought this Joan to the King, that she was with the King. He also knew that when Joan arrived at the town of Chinon, the council discussed whether the King should hear her or not. She was first asked why she had come and what she wanted. Although she did not wish to say anything except to the King, she was nevertheless forced on behalf of the King to reveal the purpose of her mission. She said that she had two commands from the King of Heaven, that is to say one to raise the siege of Orléans, and the other to conduct the King to Reims for his coronation and consecration. Having heard this, some among the King's councillors said that the King should not have any faith in this Joan, and the others said that, since she declared that she had been sent by God and that she had certain things to say to the King, the King should at least hear her. But the King decided that she should first be examined by the clerks and churchmen, which was done. Finally, and not without difficulty, it was decided that the King would hear her. Then she entered the castle at Chinon to come before the King, who was still hesitating to meet her, following the opinion of senior members of his court. But then it was announced to the King that Robert de Baudricourt had written to him, that he had sent this woman, that she had passed through the territories of the King's enemies, that she had forded many rivers, almost miraculously, in order to reach the King. For this reason, the King was urged to hear her and he gave an audience to Joan. When the King knew that she was coming, he withdrew to one side, stepping back from the others. But Joan clearly recognised him and bowed to him; she had a long meeting with him. After he had heard her, the King appeared joyful. Then the King, not wishing to do anything without the advice of the ecclesiastics, sent Joan to the town of Poitiers so that she might be examined by the clerks of the university. After the King learned that she had been investigated and nothing had been found in her except good, he had her armed and gave men to her; she also received control over military affairs.

The witness said that Joan was very simple in all her actions except for war, where she was very experienced. The witness heard from the mouth of the King many good words about Joan, and this was at Saint-Benoît-sur-Loire; in that place the King took pity on her, for the pain that she was coping with, and he ordered her to rest. Then, in tears, Joan said to the King that he should have no doubt, and that he would recover the whole of his kingdom and would be crowned quickly. The witness also said that she severely reprimanded the men-at-arms when she saw them doing anything that it seemed to her they should not do.

He knew nothing about what happened at Orléans, except by hearsay, because he was not present. But he heard the following from the Lord of Gaucourt.[64] When she was at Orléans, the men who had command of the royal troops decided that it did not seem a good idea to stage an attack or assault on the day when the fortress of the Augustins was taken; and this Lord of Gaucourt was commissioned to guard the gates to prevent a sortie being made. Nevertheless Joan was not happy, but was of the opinion that the men-at-arms should make a sortie with

---

64 This story did not appear in Gaucourt's testimony to the Nullification trial on 25 February 1456: Duparc (ed.), *Procès en nullité*, I, pp. 326–7.

townspeople to attack the bastille, and many of the men-at-arms and townspeople were of the same view. Then Joan told the Lord of Gaucourt that he was a bad man, adding: 'Whether you wish it or not, the men-at-arms will come, and they will win as they have won before.' The men-at-arms holding the town left against the will of the Lord of Gaucourt, and went to the assault and capture of the bastille of the Augustins, which they took by force and violence. And he heard my lord of Gaucourt say that he himself was in great danger.

The witness also declared that Joan went with the King to the town of Troyes, which the King wished to pass through in order to go to Reims for his coronation. But once the King arrived before Troyes, the troops saw that they were without supplies and were in despair, and almost all were ready to retreat. Then Joan told the King not to hesitate and the following day they would seize the town. Joan then took her standard, followed by many men on foot, and she ordered that each gather a bundle of sticks to fill the ditches. They took many and the following day, Joan cried: 'To the assault', pretending to place the bundles of sticks in the ditches. Seeing this, the citizens of Troyes, fearing the assault, sent someone to negotiate a surrender with the King. An agreement was then concluded with the citizens and the King entered the town of Troyes in great array, Joan carrying her standard near to the King.

The witness declares that shortly afterwards, the King left Troyes with his army and went towards Châlons, and then Reims. But as the King feared that he might meet resistance at Reims, Joan said to him: 'Do not fear anything because the burghers of the town of Reims will come to meet you'; and before the troops had neared the town the burghers met them. The King had feared the resistance of the people of Reims because if they had rebelled, he had no artillery or engines for the siege. And Joan told the King to proceed boldly and not to fear anything, because if he would go forward courageously he would recover all his kingdom.

97. Deposition of Aimon, Lord of Macy (7 May 1456)

Source: Duparc (ed.), *Procès en nullité*, I, pp. 404–6.

Language: Latin

The seventeenth witness, Aimon, Lord of Macy, was described as being around fifty-six years of age and a knight.

Asked about the contents of the 1st, 2nd, 3rd and 4th articles produced in this case, he said and declared upon oath that he first met Joan when he saw her detained in the prison cells in the castle of Beaurevoir, for and in the name of the Count of Ligny;[65] he saw her many times in prison and spoke with her often. Many times too, in sport, he tried to touch her breasts, trying hard to put his hands on her bosom; but Joan was not prepared to put up with this, and pushed away the witness as hard as she could, because this Joan was of honest behaviour in words and deeds.

He also said that Joan was taken to the castle of Crotoy, where a very important prisoner was then being held, named Master Nicolas d'Ecqueville, Chancellor of the church of Amiens, doctor in both laws. He very often celebrated mass in the prison, which Joan also very often heard. Also the witness subsequently heard this Master Nicolas say that he had heard Joan's confession, and that this was a good and very pious, Christian girl; and he said many good things about her.

The witness also said that this Joan was taken to the castle of Rouen, and put into a prison looking towards the fields. While she was being held prisoner in that town, the Lord Count of Ligny arrived, in the company of whom was the witness. And one day the Count of Ligny wanted to see Joan, and came to her together with the counts [earls] of Warwick and of Stafford, and in the presence of the English chancellor, then Bishop of Thérouanne and the brother of the Count of Ligny,[66] and of the witness. The Count of Ligny addressed her, speaking to her in this way: 'Joan, I have come here to put you to ransom on condition that you promise never to bear arms against us.' She replied: 'In the name of God, you mock me! For I well know that you have neither the will nor the power.' And this she repeated many times because the Count repeated his words. She added: 'I well know that the English will put me to death, thinking to win the kingdom of France after my death. But even if they were a hundred thousand more than they are at present, these "godons" [blasphemers] would not have the kingdom.' The Earl of Stafford was indignant at these

---

65 The Count of Ligny was Jean de Luxembourg, whose vassal, Lionel, Bastard of Vendôme, had captured Joan of Arc during the siege of Compiègne.

66 Jean de Luxembourg's brother was Louis de Luxembourg, Bishop of Thérouanne and Chancellor of France on behalf of Henry VI. He had helped to negotiate the ransom of Joan of Arc and attended the trial on 23 May, as well as assisting in the abjuration and execution. He became Archbishop of Rouen in 1437 and a cardinal in 1439, four years before his death.

words, and half drew his dagger to strike her, but the Earl of Warwick prevented him. Some time afterwards, the witness was still in the town of Rouen when Joan was led to the square in front of Saint-Ouen, where a great sermon was preached by Master Nicolas Midi,[67] who said among other things, as the witness heard: 'Joan, we have so much pity for you; it is necessary that you retract what you have said, or we must certainly hand you over to the justice.' She replied that she had done nothing evil, and that she believed in the twelve articles of the faith and in the ten commandments, adding that she referred herself to the Roman curia and wished to believe everything that the holy Church believed. Despite this, she was strongly urged to recant, but she said: 'You work too hard to seduce me', and, to escape the danger, she said that she was prepared to do all that they required. Then a certain secretary of the King of England who was present there, named Laurent Calot, drew from his pocket a short written schedule which he handed Joan to sign;[68] but she replied that she did not know how to read or to write. Notwithstanding this Laurent Calot, the secretary, handed to Joan the schedule and a pen to sign it, and in mockery, Joan made a sort of round mark. Then Laurent Calot took the hand of Joan, holding the pen, and made her make a sort of signature, which the witness did not remember.

And he believed that she was in heaven.

98. Deposition of Master Guillaume Manchon (12 May 1456)

Source: Duparc (ed.), *Procès en nullité*, I, pp. 415–28.

Language: Latin

Guillaume Manchon (1396–1456) was the second of the nineteen witnesses, mostly connected with the original trial in 1431, who testified at Rouen. He had previously testified before the earlier inquiries in March 1450 and May 1452.

[Manchon began his testimony in 1456 by confirming that Joan had come from Rouen, that Pierre Cauchon was appointed as her judge because she had been captured in his diocese of Beauvais, and that he, Manchon, and Guillaume Colles had been appointed as notaries for the trial.]

---

67 The first sermon was actually given by Guillaume Érard.

68 Laurent Calot was a secretary of the King of England, who most notably signed the letter of guarantee given to the judges and assessors who took part in the Rouen trial.

Having been shown the trial record that he had been forced to submit, the witness affirmed that this was the true record drawn up during the course of the trial. He agreed that it had been signed by himself and his colleagues, that it contained the truth and that he had drawn up two further exemplars in this fashion: one had been given to the Lord Inquisitor, one to the King of England and another to the Lord Bishop of Beauvais. This trial record was drawn up from the *Minute française*, the same *Minute* that he said he had given to the lord judges and which had been written in his own hand. This record was later translated from French into Latin by Master Thomas de Courcelles and the witness; the form in which it now stood, long after the death and execution of Joan [in 1456], was just as good as possible, following the truth. The witness also said that this master Thomas played no part in the *Libellus* or the other [documents] prepared during the course of the trial, nor did he greatly interfere with this.[69]

Questioned about the French trial record, which was shown to the witness and in which the word '*Nota*' was found at the top of many articles, he replied as follows: in the course of the first cross-examinations of Joan, on the first day, there was a great tumult in the chapel of the castle at Rouen and Joan was interrupted at almost every word when she was speaking about her apparitions. There were two or three secretaries of the King of England there, who wrote down the words and the testimony of Joan as they pleased, leaving out her excuses and anything which served to exonerate her. The witness then protested, saying that if order was not established there, he would not continue to record events in this affair. As a result, the venue was changed on the following day and they met in a room of the castle near the great hall, with two Englishmen guarding the entrance. And sometimes, because there was a problem regarding the replies of Joan and her words, and because some were saying that she had not replied as the witness had written, where it appeared to him that there was a difficulty, the witness wrote '*Nota*' at the top.

The witness did not know whether Joan lived as a catholic, except that often, during the trial, he heard her ask to hear mass, that is to say on Palm Sunday and Easter Sunday, and also asking on Easter day to be confessed and to receive the body of the Lord. And never-

69 See **89**. This *Libellus* was presumably the document prepared by Jean d'Estivet, presenting the Seventy Articles against Joan, alongside quotations from the *Minute française* that supposedly supported each charge.

theless she was not allowed to make confession, unless to one Master
Nicolas Loiseleur, and she complained greatly about this refusal.[70]

On the contents of the 5th and 6th articles, he declared that the
judges claimed, as was contained in the trial record, that they had had
inquiries made [to justify their charges against Joan], but he did not
remember having seen or read them, and only knew that if they had
been produced they would have been inserted into the trial record. As
for whether the judges proceeded out of hatred or otherwise, he
referred it to their consciences. Nevertheless he knew and firmly
believed that, if he had been on the side of the English, he would not
have treated Joan in this way, and he would not have put her on trial
in this way. For she was led to the town of Rouen, and not to Paris,
because, so he believed, the King of England was present in Rouen,
with the leading men of his council.[71] And the witness was forced to
participate in this affair as a notary, and he did so against his will,
because he did not dare to go against an order of the lords of the
King's council. It was the English who wanted this trial, and it was
carried out at their expense. Nevertheless, he believed that neither the
Bishop of Beauvais nor the Promoter were compelled to lead this trial
against Joan, but both of them acted willingly. With regard to the
assessors and the other counsellors, he believed that they would not
have dared to refuse to come, and there was no one who was not afraid.
For at the start of the trial, there was a meeting in a certain house
near the castle, where the Lord Bishop of Beauvais, the Abbot of
Fécamp,[72] Master Nicolas Loiseleur and many others summoned the
witness [Manchon]. The Bishop told him that it was necessary that
he serve the King, and he intended to bring an excellent case against
Joan, and another notary would be designated to assist him; then
Boisguillaume [Guillaume Colles] was named.

The witness also declared that often before the start of the trial and
again during the trial, Joan asked to be taken to an episcopal or
ecclesiastical prison; nevertheless, on this point, she was not heard,
and her request was not granted, because, as the witness said and

70 See below, pages 326 to 327.

71 Henry VI was in Rouen from July 1430 until late November 1431.

72 The Abbot of Fécamp was Gilles de Duremort, a prominent councillor and
ambassador for the English administration in France at the time of Joan's trial.
Jean Massieu later claimed that he participated in the trial more out of hatred for
Joan and love of the English, than for justice [99]. But in 1452, Nicolas
Houppeville had claimed that, after criticising the trial, he was only freed from an
English jail in Rouen through the Abbot's intervention.

believed, the English would not surrender her and the Bishop would not have wanted her to be kept outside the castle.

He also said that no counsellor would have dared to say this, because each one feared displeasing the Bishop and the English. Because at the time of the trial, the late Master Jean Lohier came to Rouen; summoned by the Bishop, and [when] required to give his advice on the trial of Joan he gave some replies that [Manchon] did not know, because he was not present. But on the following day he went before this Lohier in the church and asked him if he had seen the trial. Lohier replied that he had seen it and that it was null and that it could not be upheld because the trial was being carried out in the castle, a place that was not safe for the judges, the counsellors and those taking part; and in addition, the trial concerned many people who had not been summoned; also because there was no advocate [assisting Joan], and for many other reasons. Finally, this Lohier said to the witness that he would not stay in this city of Rouen but would leave, and that it seemed to him that they intended to put [Joan] to death.[73] Then he left; and the witness was convinced that after this day he would not have dared to stay in this town and under the domination of the English. About two days after these events, the Lord Bishop, when asked by the doctors and counsellors whether he had spoken with this Lohier, replied in the affirmative, [adding] that Lohier had wanted an interlocutory judgement against the trial and wished to challenge it, and that he would do nothing for him.[74]

He also declared that a certain master, Jean de La Fontaine, had been sent to carry out the interrogation of Joan in place of the Lord Bishop of Beauvais.[75] For this reason, in holy week, with two monks of the Order of Preaching Friars, that is to say Isembart de La Pierre and Martin Ladvenu, he had gone to see Joan, and wanted to encourage her to submit herself to the Church. When this came to the knowledge of the Lord of Warwick and of the Lord Bishop of Beauvais they were annoyed, and, out of fear, this La Fontaine left this city and did

---

73 Manchon had offered the same story in his testimony in March 1450 and May 1452, and Thomas de Courcelles had mentioned Lohier in 1456 [**89**].

74 In canon law, an interlocutory sentence was pronounced during the course of a trial, before the final sentence, in order to settle some incidental point arising; they could be given without special formalities.

75 Jean de La Fontaine was appointed as an examiner of witnesses for the trial of Joan of Arc on 9 January, and was deputed to question Joan in prison from 9 to 17 March.

not return again;[76] and the two other brothers were also in great danger.

He also declared that a certain master, Nicolas de Houppeville, was summoned to take part in the trial, and because he declined to act he was in great danger.[77] He added that Master Jean Le Maistre, Vice-Inquisitor, avoided taking part there as much as possible, because he was strongly opposed to it.

He also declared that once, during the questioning of Joan, Master Jean de Châtillon, who favoured her in some way, said that perhaps she need not reply, or said something else that he does not recall.[78] This did not please the Lord Bishop of Beauvais and some of his supporters, and there was a great uproar at his words. Then the Bishop told him to be quiet and to let the judges speak.

He also declared that he certainly remembered that another man spoke to Joan during a session and tried to direct and warn her on the subject of her submission to the Church. The Bishop said: 'Be silent, in the devil's name!' But he did not remember the name of the person concerned.

He also declared that on one occasion, a man whose name escaped him said things regarding Joan that displeased the Lord of Stafford.[79] The latter then followed the speaker with his sword unsheathed to a certain place of sanctuary, and he would have struck him if he had not been told that the man was in a sacred place of immunity.

He also declared when questioned on this, that the men who seemed

76 The story that La Fontaine incurred the wrath of Cauchon for counselling Joan was originally presented by Manchon in March 1450 and May 1452, and was repeated in 1456 by Jean Massieu [**99**]. Martin Ladvenu never confirmed this account and, when Isembart de La Pierre told the same story in 1452, he did not mention that he himself had been involved in the incident.

77 In both 1452 and 1456, Nicolas de Houppeville testified that he had nearly been imprisoned for criticizing the trial, and this story was repeated by a number of his fellow clerics in 1452, including Isembart de La Pierre, Richard de Grouchet (1452), Martin Ladvenu, and by the witnesses in 1456, such as Guillaume Manchon and Guillaume de La Chambre.

78 Jean Hulot de Châtillon was a doctor in theology from the University of Paris and a friend of Cauchon and Beaupère. He was an extremely conscientious participant in the trial of Joan, culminating in his vote for her to be handed over to the secular authorities after her relapse and his direct assistance in the execution. Manchon's comments regarding Châtillon were repeated by Jean Massieu in 1452 and in his testimony in 1456 [**99**].

79 Humphrey Stafford (1402–60) accompanied Henry VI to France in 1430 and became lieutenant-general of Normandy where he stayed until 1432.

to have the most partisan spirit were [Jean de] Beaupère, [Nicolas] Midi and [Jacques] de Touraine.

Item, questioned on the contents of the 9th article, he replied that he knew on this subject that once the Bishop of Beauvais, the Earl of Warwick and he, the witness, entered the prison where Joan was, and there they found her in shackles of iron. He heard it said that at night her body was fastened by an iron chain, but he did not see her secured in this way.[80] There was no bed or anything to sleep on in that prison. But there were four or five guards of the lowest kind.

Item, questioned on the contents of the 10th article, he replied that he knew nothing.

On the contents of the 11th, 12th, 13th and 14th articles, he declared that, after the nomination of the witness and Boisguillaume as notaries to draw up the record of Joan's trial, the Lord of Warwick, the Bishop of Beauvais and Master Nicolas Loiseleur told the witness and the other notary what follows: Joan was speaking with wonder about her apparitions and so they decided, in order to know the truth about her more fully, that Master Nicolas should pretend to be from the region of Lorraine, like Joan, and under the obedience of the King of France.[81] He would enter the prison in the clothing of a layman, the guards would retire, and Joan and he would remain alone in the prison. In a room adjoining the dungeon, an opening was made specially, and the witness and his associate were ordered to go there in order to hear what Joan was saying; the Bishop and the Earl were also there and could not be seen by Joan. Then Loiseleur began to question Joan, pretending to give news about the state of the realm and about her revelations; Joan replied, believing that he was from her region and under the obedience of the King of France. But as the Bishop and the Earl had told the witness and his associate to write down her replies, the witness replied that he would not do it and that it was not honest

---

80 A succession of witnesses in 1450, 1452 and 1456 reported on the chains and shackles used to manacle Joan. On 3 May 1452, an inhabitant of Rouen named Pierre Cusquel testified that 'he was used to entering the castle thanks to his employer, Jean Son, a master of masonry. With the permission of the guards, he twice entered the prison of Joan and he saw her in shackles of iron and attached by a long chain fixed to a beam. And in the house of the witness was hung a cage of iron, in which, it was said, she was to be shut up. However he did not see her in that cage.' Also see Jean Massieu's testimony [99].

81 This story had originally been cited by both Manchon and Jean Massieu in their testimony to the inquiry in March 1450, and was repeated in 1456 by Guillaume Colles.

to begin the trial record in this way; but if she said the same things in open court they would write them down completely willingly. He added that afterwards Joan always had great confidence in this Loiseleur, so much so that he heard her confession many times after these deceptions and Joan was generally not brought into court without having spoken with Loiseleur beforehand.

He also declared that during the trial she was tired out by the numerous and varied questions. Almost every day there was an interrogation in the morning which lasted for around three or four hours; and sometimes they chose some difficult and subtle questions regarding Joan's testimony upon which to question her again for two or three hours after the meal. Frequently they passed from one question to another, changing the subject; and despite these changes, she replied with wisdom and kept a clear memory of [what she had said], because she very often said: 'I have already replied to you on this,' adding, 'I refer to the clerk', that is to say the present witness [Manchon].

[Manchon offered no comment on the 15th, 16th and 17th articles, and then responded to the 20th and 21st by claiming that he had not been involved in drafting the Twelve Articles and could offer little information, despite heavy prompting by the interrogators who showed him a note that he and the other notaries had apparently written on 4 April 1431, complaining that the Twelve Articles did not accord with Joan's testimony during the Trial].

On the contents of the 22nd article, he declared that at the start of the trial, when Joan was questioned, there were some notaries hidden in a window by curtains. Master Nicolas Loiseleur was hidden with them, he believed, keeping an eye on what these notaries were writing. And they wrote what they chose, leaving out the justifications of Joan. But he, the witness, was at the feet of the judges with Guillaume Colles and the clerk of Master Guillaume Beaupère,[82] and they were writing. But there was a great difference in their writings, so that there was a serious disagreement between them. For this reason, as he has said before, on the points where he saw a difference, he put a 'Nota', so that later Joan might be questioned again.

On the contents of the 23rd, 24th, 25th and 26th articles, he declared that when the proceedings were complete, consultations took place and there was a meeting on this matter. Then it was decided that Joan

---

82 The clerk of Jean Beaupère was Jean Monnet who had given testimony in Paris on 3 April 1456, without mentioning this story of hidden notaries: Duparc (ed.), *Procès en nullité*, I, pp. 359–61.

should be preached to; she was taken to a small gate with Master
Nicolas Loiseleur as her counsel, who accompanied her and said to
her: 'Joan, believe me, because you will be saved if you want. Take
your clothing [of a woman] and do whatever you are told; if not you
will be in danger of death. And if you do what I tell you, you will be
saved, and you will receive good [treatment] and no harm, and you
will be handed over to the Church.' Then she was taken to a scaffold
or platform. Two sentences had been prepared, one of abjuration and
the other of condemnation, that the Bishop had in front of him. While
the Bishop was pronouncing the sentence of condemnation and reading
the end of condemnation, Master Nicolas Loiseleur was telling Joan
to do what he had suggested and to resume female clothing. There
was then a short interruption and one of the Englishmen present said
to the Bishop that he was a traitor; the Bishop replied that he lied.[83]
After this interlude, Joan replied that she was ready to obey the
Church; then the abjuration was pronounced which was read to her.
But the witness did not know whether she repeated it after the reader
or whether she declared that she was in agreement after it had been
read; nevertheless she was smiling. The executioner was there with a
cart, waiting for her to be given to him for burning. The witness also
said that he did not see the letter of abjuration being written but it
was done after the conclusion of the [stage of the trial at which the
judges received] opinions [between 19 and 23 May 1431] and before
coming to that place. He had no recollection of this schedule of
abjuration ever being explained to Joan or given to her to take in or
to read before the moment that she made this abjuration. The first
sermon, the sentence and the abjuration were read the Thursday after
Pentecost [24 May 1431]; the sentence condemned her to perpetual
imprisonment.

Asked about what led the judges to condemn her to perpetual imprisonment, given that they had promised her that nothing bad would
happen to her, he declared that he believed that this happened because
of a clash of loyalties; and they feared that she would escape; but
whether they judged rightly or wrongly, the witness referred to law
and to the conscience of the judges.

83 The story that Cauchon was verbally attacked by an anonymous Englishman on
   the day of the abjuration for failing to take the opportunity to condemn Joan, was
   supported by two previous witnesses, Jean Beaupère (5 March 1450) and Jean de
   Mailly, Bishop of Noyon (2 April 1456): Doncoeur (ed.), *L'enquête ordonnée par
   Charles VII en 1450*, pp. 56–7, and Duparc (ed.), *Procès en nullité*, I, p. 354.

Then asked about the contents of the 26th and 27th articles, he declared that during the trial he had heard Joan complain to the Bishop and to the Earl of Warwick when she was asked why she did not put on the clothes of a woman, because it was not decent for a woman to have a tunic and hose of a man, attached with many tightly knotted laces. She replied that she did not dare take off the hose, or to keep them otherwise than tightly knotted, because as the Bishop and Earl well knew, her guards had tried many times to violate her; and once when she was crying, this Earl, hearing her cries for help, came to her and if he had not come her guards would have raped her.[84] She complained about this.

On the content of the other articles, beyond what he said in his deposition, the witness declared what follows. The Sunday following, on the feast of the Holy Trinity [27 May 1431], he was commanded by the Bishop and the Earl of Warwick to go to the castle of Rouen with the other notaries because Joan was said to have relapsed and to have resumed men's clothing. Commanded in this way, they came to the castle and when they arrived in the courtyard of the castle, some fifty or so armed Englishmen abused the witness and his colleague, telling them that they were traitors and that they had behaved badly during the trial. With great difficulty and fear they managed to escape from their hands. They were enraged, he believed, because Joan had not been burned after the first sermon and sentence.[85] Furthermore, on the Monday, at the command of the Bishop and the Earl, the witness returned to the castle, which he would not have dared to enter, because of the fright recently experienced by himself and his colleagues, if he had not had been under the protection of the Earl of Warwick, who led him into the prison. There he found the judges and a small number of other men. In the presence of the witness, Joan was asked why she had resumed this male clothing. She replied that she had done it to protect her chastity, because she was not safe in her female garments with guards who wished to molest her; she had complained many times about this to the Bishop and to the Earl, and

---

84 Similar stories of a threat to Joan appear in the testimony of Martin Ladvenu in 1450 and in 1456, Jean Toutmouillé in 1450, Isembart de La Pierre in 1452, in Doncoeur (ed.), *L'enquête ordonnée par Charles VII en 1450*, pp. 39–45 and Duparc (ed.), *Procès en nullité*, I, pp. 185–7 and 440–4.

85 Manchon had also told this story in 1450, but the only corroborating testimony was that of Jean Beaupère in 1450, who claimed that he and Nicolas Midi had been threatened by the English soldiers: the other notary, Guillaume Colles, did not mention any such problems.

the judges had promised her that she would be in the hands, and in the prison, of the Church, and that she would have a woman with her. She had added that if it pleased the lord judges to put her in a safe place, where she would have nothing to fear, then she was ready to resume female clothing, all of which, in the words of the witness, was contained in the trial record.[86] On the other things which it was claimed she had abjured, Joan declared that she had not understood anything of what was contained in the abjuration. And all that she had done, she had done out of fear of the fire, seeing the executioner ready with his cart. The witness also said that afterwards the lord judges deliberated with the counsellors on this point, until the Bishop pronounced another sentence on the following Wednesday, as was indicated more fully in the trial record.

Asked whether the sacrament of the Eucharist was administered to Joan, he replied in the affirmative, on the morning of this same Wednesday, before the sentence was pronounced against her.

Questioned as to how they granted the sacrament of the Eucharist to her, considering that they had declared her excommunicate and a heretic, and if they had absolved her according to the forms of the Church, he declared that the judges and the counsellors debated whether the sacrament should be given to her at her request, and if she should be absolved during the act of penitence. Nevertheless he did not see her being given another absolution.

He also declared that after the sentence declared by the Bishop, who handed her over and abandoned to the secular justice, the Bailly only said, without any other form of trial or sentence: 'Take her away! Take her away!'[87] At these words, Joan made such pious lamentations that almost all were moved to tears, even the judges.

The witness said that he had been so shaken that he remained terror-stricken for a month. He well knew that her end and her death were very catholic, in everyone's opinion; and she never wished to retract her revelations, but persisted on that subject until the end.

He also said that with the money he received for his pain and efforts,

---

86 The claim that Joan had resumed male clothing in order to protect herself against the guards was repeated by a number of clerics involved in the Rouen trial, including Thomas de Courcelles [89], as well as Isembart de La Pierre (1450), Jean Toutmouillé (1450) and Martin Ladvenu (1450 and 1456).

87 On the same day as Manchon testified, Laurent Guesdon, lieutenant of the Bailly in 1431, also claimed that Joan was executed without any lay sentence being passed.

in attending this trial, he bought a missal, in order to remember her and to pray to God for her.

He did not know anything more. As for the rest, he referred to the contents of the [Rouen] trial record and to his previous testimony [on 8 May 1452] before Master Philippe de Rose, Treasurer of Rouen, committed and delegated by the Lord Cardinal d'Estouteville, legate in France; this deposition had been read to him and he continued to maintain [what he had said].

99. Deposition of Master Jean Massieu (12 May 1456)

Source: Duparc (ed.), *Procès en nullité*, I, pp. 428–35.

Language: Latin

Jean Massieu (born c.1400) was the third witness to be questioned at Rouen in 1456. He had served as the usher at the trial of Joan of Arc 1431, and had testified before the previous inquiries in 1450 and 1452.

He said and declared upon oath that he knew only what follows on the content of the 2nd, 3rd and 4th articles of the petitioners and plaintiffs ... [In] the trial [of Joan], the witness, who was then a dean of Christianity at Rouen, was the executor of the mandates brought against her. He also had the responsibility of summoning the counsellors, of taking Joan before her judges and taking her back ... In his opinion, this was a good girl, simple and pious; because it happened once when he was taking her before her judges that she asked the witness if there was some chapel or church en route at which was the Corpus Christi [the Eucharist]. The witness replied in the affirmative, showing to her a chapel situated under the castle where the body of Christ was. Then with great insistence, Joan asked him to take her there so that she could pay respect to God there and pray. The witness did this willingly, and allowed Joan to pray on her knees before the chapel; she prayed there very devotedly, kneeling down. But the Lord Bishop was very angry at this and commanded the witness not to allow her to come there to pray in this way.

Item, regarding the contents of the 5th and 6th articles posed, he replied that he did not know if there was any [preliminary] inquiry into her, because he never saw anything. Nevertheless he knew that quite a number of people had great hatred for her, and especially the English, who feared her very much because, before her capture, they

would not have dared to come into a place where they believed her to
be present. He heard it said that the Bishop of Beauvais did everything at the instigation of the King of England and his council, then
based at Rouen; and he believed that this Bishop did not act not out of
a zeal for justice but at the will of these Englishmen, at this time
present in great numbers in the town of Rouen where the King of
England was found. And at that time there was a murmur among the
counsellors at the fact that Joan was in English hands. For they were
saying that Joan should have been delivered into the hands of the
Church; but the Bishop himself took no notice and delivered her
instead into the hands of the English. This Bishop was very attached
to the English party, and many of the councillors were very afraid and
were not free agents, such as Master Nicolas [de] Houppeville who,
when he realised this, did not chose to participate in the deliberations
and was banished with many others, whose names he did not recall.

He also said that Master Jean Le Fèvre, of the Augustinian Friars,
currently Bishop of Démétriade, recognised that Joan was extremely
worn down by being asked if she was in a state of grace; although in
his opinion she was offering satisfactory replies, nevertheless the
interrogators were pestering her on this point and so he announced
that they were persecuting her too much. Then the questioners told
him to be silent, but he [the witness] did not recall their names.[88]

[Massieu then repeated the claims of Manchon that the Abbot of Fécamp
was acting out of hatred for Joan and partiality towards the English, and that
Jean de Châtillon and Jean de La Fontaine criticised the proceedings].

He also knew that Master Jean Le Maistre, involved in the trial as
Inquisitor, frequently declined to act so as not to participate in the
proceedings, and did everything possible not to be present any more
at the trial; but he was told that he risked death if he did not take part.
He was compelled to come by the English, and the witness heard this
Le Maistre say to him many times: 'I see that if one does not do as the
English wish in this business, death is near.' And the witness himself
was in great danger, because in taking Joan on the journey there and
back, he met an Englishman, a cantor of the chapel of the King of
England, named Anquetil, who asked him what he thought about this
Joan.[89] When the witnesses had replied that he saw nothing but good

88 Le Fèvre confirmed this story in his testimony in May 1452 and on 12 May 1456.

89 Massieu was the only witness to refer to this individual throughout the course of
   the Nullification inquiries. He had identified him as Eustache Turquetil when
   recounting this story in March 1450 and May 1452.

in her, and that she seemed to him to be a good woman, the cantor reported this matter to the Earl of Warwick. The latter was very angry with the witness, and he had to do many things on account of this, but finally left after making his excuses.

Then questioned as to what he could attest or declare regarding the contents of the 7th article, he said and declared that, beyond what he had already said, he remembered that one day, near the beginning of the trial, Joan accused the Bishop of Beauvais of being her enemy. And the Bishop replied: 'The King has ordered me to carry out your trial, and I will do it.'

Item, questioned about what he could attest or declare about the contents of the 8th and 9th articles, he declared on the subject of the prison that he knew for sure that Joan was in the castle of Rouen in a room on the middle floor, reached by eight steps; there was a bed in which she slept and there was a great piece of wood to which was fastened a chain of iron with which Joan was shackled, and which was padlocked to the piece of wood. There were also five Englishmen of the most lowly status, *houssepailliers* in French [that is to say grooms], keeping guard, who much desired her death and very often derided her, and she reproached them.

He also declared that he had heard Étienne Castille, locksmith, say that he had constructed for her an iron cage in which she was held standing up, attached by the neck, the hands and the feet, and that she had been in this position from the time that she had first been brought to the town of Rouen until the start of the trial. But he did not see her in this position, for she was always out of irons when he fetched her or took her back.

Item, questioned about what he could declare or attest with regard to the contents of the 10th article, he said and declared that he certainly knew that she was examined to discover whether she was a virgin or not, by the matrons and midwives on the orders of the Duchess of Bedford, in particular by Anne Bavon and another matron whose name he did not remember. After this examination, they reported that she was a virgin and intact; and this he heard reported by this Anne. For this reason the Duchess of Bedford forbade the guards and others to commit violence against her.

Then asked about the contents of the 11th, 12th, 13th and 14th articles, he said and declared that, at the time of the interrogations of Joan, there were six assessors with the judges to question her; and sometimes, when one questioned her and she was replying to his question, another interrupted her reply, so that she often said these words to those who were interrogating her: 'Good lords, act one at a time' ...

On the contents of the 17th article, he declared that he had heard that Joan was asked if she was willing to submit herself to the Church triumphant or militant; she replied that she was prepared to submit herself to the judgement of the pope. He also declared that it was commonly recounted that a certain Master Nicolas Loiseleur pretended to be a prisoner and entered her prison, and that by this means, he influenced Joan to speak and act opposite to her instincts with regard to this [issue of] submission to the Church ...

Questioned next on what he could declare or attest with regard to the contents of the 22nd, 23rd, 24th and 25th articles, he declared as follows regarding the abjuration mentioned in these articles. At the time of the sermon given at Saint-Ouen by Master Guillaume Érard, the latter was holding a certain schedule of abjuration and said to Joan: 'You will abjure and sign this schedule!' The schedule was then given to the witness to read, and he read it in front of Joan. In this schedule, he well recalled, she was told that in future she must not bear arms again, or male attire, or short hair, with many other things which he no longer remembered. He well knew also that the schedule was of about eight lines and no more, and he knew with certainty that this was not the one mentioned in the trial record because the witness read a different one inserted in the trial record from that which Joan signed.

He also said that when Joan was made to sign this schedule, a great murmur arose among those present, so much so that he heard the Bishop say to someone:[90] 'You will apologise to me', assuring them that after receiving this affront, he would not continue the procedure unless he received an apology. During this time the witness warned Joan of the danger that she was in regard to the signature of the schedule, because he saw clearly that Joan did not understand the schedule, nor the danger which threatened her. Then Joan, pressed to sign the schedule, said: 'Let this schedule be examined by the Church and the clerks, into whose hands I should be placed. If they advise me to do this, I will do it willingly.' Straight away Master Guillaume

90 According to another witness, Jean Marcel, the culprit was Laurent Calot, secretary to Henry VI.

Érard declared: 'Do it now! If not, you will die by fire today.' Joan then replied that she would rather sign than be burned; at that moment, a great tumult arose among those present and many stones were thrown, but he did not know by whom. When the schedule was signed, Joan asked the Promoter whether she was going to be put into the hands of the Church and where she would be taken. The Promoter replied: to the castle of Rouen; she would be taken there dressed in female clothing.

Questioned then regarding the contents of the 26th article, he declared that, on the feast of the Holy Trinity [27 May 1431], Joan, accused of relapse, replied that while sleeping in her bed the guards removed her female clothing which was on the bed and put there the garments of a man; and, although she had asked the guards to return her female clothes, so that she could get up and purge her stomach, they refused to return them, saying that she was not having anything other than the clothing of a man. And, as she added, her guards should have been well aware that her judges had forbidden her to wear this outfit, but even so the guards refused to return to her the woman's clothing that they had removed. Nevertheless, driven by a natural need, she took the clothing of a man, and could not obtain any other outfit from these guards for the whole day, so that many people saw her in man's clothing, and for this she was judged a relapse; for this day of the Holy Trinity, many people were sent to see her in this state, to whom Joan set out her excuses. Among others, she saw Master André Marguerie, who was in great danger, because, having declared: 'We ought to know from her why she took up male clothing again', an Englishman then lifted his lance which he held and wanted to strike this Master André. And then this Master André and many others withdrew out of terror.[91]

Then questioned on the contents of the other articles, he declared that he did not know anything that he could add to his earlier testimony regarding the abjuration. As for the sentence and Joan's death, Brother Martin Ladvenu heard Joan in confession and afterwards sent the witness who is speaking to the Lord Bishop of Beauvais, to let him know how she had made her confession and that

---

91 Massieu had told this story of Joan being forced to wear male clothing, and the threats to Marguerie, in March 1450 and May 1452. Giving testimony on the same day, Marguerie confirmed that the English were furious when he asked why Joan had resumed male clothing.

she was asking to receive the sacrament of the Eucharist. The Bishop consulted some people on this subject and, after having deliberated, declared to the witness that he might inform Brother Martin to administer the sacrament of the Eucharist to her with all that she asked for. The witness then returned to the castle and reported this to Brother Martin. Brother Martin gave the sacrament of the Eucharist to Joan in the presence of the witness. Afterwards she was brought out in woman's clothing and led by the witness and Brother Martin to the place where she was burned. En route, Joan made such piteous lamentations that the witness and Brother Martin could not hold back their tears.

[Massieu repeated his account given on 5 March 1450 of how Joan was given a small cross by an Englishman, while he himself arranged for a cross to be brought from a local church.]

Also at that time, he heard Jean Fleury, clerk of the Bailly and *greffier* [clerk of the court], say that according to the executioner, once her body was burned and reduced to ashes, her heart remained intact and full of blood. And the executioner was charged with collecting her ashes and all that remained of her, and throwing them into the Seine, which he did. He did not know anything more.

100. Deposition of Brother Seguin Seguin (14 May 1456)

Source: Duparc (ed.), *Procès en nullité*, I, pp. 470–3.

Language: Latin

The Dominican Seguin Seguin was the last witness to be questioned at Rouen. He was described as being around seventy years of age and a professor of sacred theology, and dean of the faculty of theology at the University of Poitiers.

And questioned first on the contents of the 1st, 2nd, 3rd and 4th of the articles produced in this case, especially on the knowledge that he had regarding this Joan, he said and declared upon oath that which follows. It was clear that before he saw seen Joan he had heard talk about her from Master Pierre de Versailles, professor of sacred theology, at the time of his death Bishop of Meaux. The latter had heard it said by some men-at-arms that they had gone to meet Joan on her journey to the King and that they had set up an ambush to capture and rob her and her companions. But when they meant to do it, they could not move from the place where they were and in this way Joan went on with her companions, without harm.

He declared that he saw her for the first time in the town of Poitiers. The King's council was then assembled in the house of a certain woman, La Macée, in the town of Poitiers, and among the councillors was the Archbishop of Reims, then Chancellor of France. They summoned the witness along with Jean Lambert, professor of sacred theology at the University of Paris; Master Guillaume Le Marié, canon of Poitiers and bachelor in theology; Master Guillaume Aimery, professor of sacred theology, of the Order of St Dominic; Brother Pierre Turelure; Master Jacques Maledon; and many others whose names he no longer recalled. [The councillors] told [the experts] that they had been delegated by the King to question Joan, and to give their opinion of her to the council. [The councillors] sent them to the house of Master Jean Rabateau in the town of Poitiers where Joan was lodging to examine her. When they had arrived, they posed many questions to Joan. Among other questions Master Jean Lambert asked her why she had come, because the King wanted to understand what had induced her to come to see him. She replied in a grand manner that while watching the animals, a voice had come to her, and said to her that God had great pity for the people of France, and that it was necessary for her to go to France. Having heard this, she began to weep; the voice had then told her to go to Vaucouleurs where she would find a captain who would led her safely into France and to the King, and that she must not have any doubt. She had done this and had reached the King without any hindrance. Then Master Guillaume Aimery asked her: 'You have declared that the voice told you that the will of God is to deliver the people of France from the ordeal in which she now finds herself. If he wants to deliver them, he does not need to make use of men-at-arms.' Joan then replied: ' In the name of God, the men-at-arms will fight and God will give victory.' Master Guillaume was pleased with this reply.

The witness asked her what language the voice spoke to her; she replied that it was a better language than his, the witness speaking Limousin. He posed another question to her, that is to say whether she believed in God; she replied yes, and even more than the witness. Then the witness said to Joan that God did not want her to be believed, unless some reason was shown why they should give credence to her, and that they, the counsellors, would not recommend the King to entrust men-at-arms to her, and to put them into danger, on her word alone, unless she had anything else to offer in support. She replied: 'In the name of God, I am not come to Poitiers to show signs: but take me to Orléans and I will show you the signs proving by whom I have been sent'; she asked that men might be entrusted to her, as many as seemed appropriate, and she would go to Orléans. She then revealed to the witness and to the others present four events that were going to happen and which occurred shortly afterwards. Firstly that the English would be beaten, the siege before Orléans lifted and the town delivered from the English; but beforehand she would issue a summons to them [i.e. document 4]. Secondly she declared that the King would be crowned at Reims. Thirdly, the town of Paris would be restored to the obedience of the King; finally, the Duke of Orléans would return from England. The witness saw all these things come true. They reported all of this to the King's council and were of the opinion, considering the urgent necessity and the danger in which the town of Orléans stood, that the King could turn to Joan and send her to Orléans.

The witness and the others commissioned also investigated the life and morals of Joan, and found that she was a good Christian, that she was living as a catholic, and that she was never found idle. And also, in order to be better informed about her behaviour, women were placed with her who reported her actions and habits to the council. And the witness believed that this Joan was sent from God, given that the King, and the subjects in his obedience, did not have any more hope; on the contrary, they expected to be defeated. He well remembered, also, that Joan was asked why she had a standard; she replied that she did not wish to use her sword or to kill any one.

The witness also declared that Joan was very angry when she heard the name of God being taken in vain, and that she was horrified by those who swore in this way. For she told La Hire, who was accustomed to use many oaths and to use God's name in vain, that he should not swear any more: when he wanted to use God's name in vain, he should [swear] on his own staff. And afterwards, in the presence of Joan, La Hire was accustomed to swearing on his staff.

The witness did not know anything more.

101. Deposition at Lyon of Jean d'Aulon (28 May 1456)

Source: Duparc (ed.), *Procès en nullité*, I, pp. 475–87.

Language: French

Jean d'Aulon was described as a knight, councillor and master of the household of the King, and seneschal of Beaucaire. He was questioned at Lyon by the Vice-Inquisitor, Jean des Prés, and his testimony was recorded by two local notaries, Hugues Belièvre and Bartholomé Bellièvre, and then sent to Rouen.

And firstly, he said that twenty years ago or thereabouts, while our lord the King was at Poitiers, he was told that this Pucelle, who was from the Lorraine, had been brought to this lord by two gentlemen, one named Bertrand and the other Jean de Metz, saying that they were of the company of my lord Robert de Baudricourt, knight; they presented themselves there. [Jean d'Aulon] went to this place, Poitiers, to see her.

He said that after this presentation, this Pucelle spoke privately to our lord the King, and told him several secret things, though the witness did not knew what, except that shortly afterwards, [the King] sent to fetch some of his councillors, among whom was the witness [Aulon]. He then told them that the Pucelle had said to him that she had been sent by God to help him recover his kingdom, which at that time was for the most part occupied by the English, his ancient enemy.

He said that after the King had made this announcement to his councillors, it was thought advisable to investigate this Pucelle, who was then sixteen years of age or thereabouts, upon certain points concerning the faith.

He said that, to do this, the King sent for certain masters in theology, jurists and other expert people, who might examine her well and diligently on these points.

He said that he was present at the said council when these masters made their report on what they had discovered regarding the Pucelle; at which it was publicly said by one of them that they did not see, know, or recognise in this Pucelle anything other than what should be in a good Christian woman and a true catholic, and they held her as such; and it was their opinion that she was a very good person.

He also said that after the report had been made to their lord by these masters, this Pucelle was handed over to the Queen of Sicily, mother of our sovereign lady the Queen, and to certain ladies with her, by whom the Pucelle was seen, visited, and looked at secretly, and examined with regard to the private parts of her body; but after they had seen and looked at everything that might be looked at in this case, this lady said and related to the King that she and the other ladies certainly found that this was a true and complete virgin [*pucelle*], in whom there did not appear any corruption or violence.

He said that he was present when this lady made her report.

He said that when these things had been heard, considering the great goodness which there was in the Pucelle, and that she had said to him that she had been sent to him by God, the King concluded in his council that henceforward he would make use of her in his wars, given that she had been sent for this.

He said that it was then decided that she would be sent to the city of Orléans, which was then besieged by the ancient enemy.

He said that for this reason, people were given to attend on her and others to escort her.

He said that he who was speaking was appointed as her guard and escort by our lord the King.

He also said that that, for her physical protection, the King had armour made for this Pucelle, fit for her body, and, this done, appointed a number of men-at-arms for her and for those of her company, to lead and guide them safely to the city of Orléans.

He said that immediately afterwards he set out on the road with them to go there.

He said that as soon as it came to the knowledge of my lord of Dunois, then called the Bastard of Orléans, who was in this city in order to protect and guard it from the enemy, that the Pucelle was coming that way, he had a number of men of war assembled to meet her, such as La Hire and others. And in order to do this and to lead and guide her more safely into the city, this lord and his men went by boat and travelled to meet her by the river Loire, about a quarter of a league distant, and there they found her.

He said that the Pucelle and [Aulon] immediately entered the boat, while the remainder of the men of war returned toward Blois. And with my lord of Dunois and his men, they entered the city safely and securely; my lord of Dunois lodged her there well and decently in the house of one of the notable burghers of the city, who had married one of the leading women from there.

He said that, after my lord of Dunois, La Hire and certain other captains of the party of our lord the King had conferred with the Pucelle as to what was it was best to do for the custody, protection and defence of the city, and also by what means the enemy could be most effectively harmed, it was agreed and concluded between them that it was necessary for a number of men-at-arms of their party, who were then near Blois, to join them and so they had to go and find them. To effect this and to bring them into the city, my Lord of Dunois, the one who is speaking and certain other captains with their followers were appointed; they went to the area around Blois to bring them and make them come.

He said that as soon as they were ready to leave in search of those who were in the area around Blois, when this came to the notice of the Pucelle she immediately mounted her horse and, together with La Hire and some of her men, went out into the fields to keep the enemy from doing them injury. And, in order to do this, the Pucelle went with her men between the army of her enemy and the city of Orléans; and it happened that, notwithstanding the great power and number of men-at-arms in the host of the enemy, still, by the mercy of God, the Lord of Dunois and the one who is speaking passed through with all their followers and safely went on their way. And in the same way the Pucelle returned with her men to the city.

He also said that as soon as she knew of the approach of the aforesaid men, and that they were bringing with them the others they had gone to fetch to reinforce the city, immediately the Pucelle mounted her horse and, with a party of her men, went ahead of them in order to support and help them, if needed.

He said that in the sight and knowledge of the enemy, the Pucelle, Dunois, the Marshal [either Gilles de Laval, Baron of Rais, or Jean de Brosse, Lord of Boussac], La Hire, and the one who was speaking [Aulon], entered the city with their followers, without any opposition whatsoever.

Moreover [Aulon] said that on the same day, after dinner, my said Lord of Dunois came to the Pucelle's lodging, where she and [Aulon] had dined together. And, in conversation, the Lord of Dunois told her that he knew for certain from trustworthy people that an enemy captain named Fastolf would shortly join the [English forces] who were at the siege, not only to give them help and to reinforce them, but also to supply them, and that he was then at Vinville.[92] It seemed to [Aulon] that the Pucelle was delighted at these words and she said to my lord of Dunois something like this: 'Bastard! Bastard! In the name of God, I command you that as soon as you know of the coming of the said Fastolf, you will let me know. Because, if he passes without my knowledge, I promise you that I will have your head.' To which the Lord of Dunois replied that this did not worry him because he would certainly let her know.

He said that after these words, the one who was speaking, being tired and overdone, lay down on a couch in the room of the Pucelle to rest himself a little, and also the Pucelle lay down with her hostess on another bed to sleep and rest in the same way. But, as the one who was testifying began to fall asleep, suddenly this Pucelle arose from her bed and, making a great noise, woke him. And then the one who was speaking asked her what she wanted; to which she replied: 'In the name of God, my adviser has told me that I should attack the English; but I do not know whether I should go to their fortress or against Fastolf, who is to supply them.' At which the one who was testifying immediately got up and, as quickly as possible, he armed the Pucelle.

He said that as soon as he had armed her, they heard a great noise and cry made by the townspeople, saying that the enemy were doing much harm to the French. Then the one who was speaking also armed himself and while he was doing this, without his knowledge, the Pucelle left the room and went into the street where she found a page mounted on horseback, who at once got down from the horse. She immediately mounted it and, as straight and as speedily as she could, she went directly to the Burgundy Gate, where there was the greatest noise.

He said that he immediately followed the Pucelle; but, go as quickly as he might, she was already at the gate.

He said that when they came to the gate they saw one of the towns-people being carried away who was very badly wounded; and then the Pucelle asked those carrying him who this man was. They replied that he was a Frenchman. Then she said that she never saw French blood without her hair standing on end.

He said that, at that time, the Pucelle, the one who was speaking

92 Sir John Fastolf (d. 1459).

[Aulon] and many other men of war of their company, went out from the city to help the French and to harm the enemy as much as they could. But as soon as they were outside the city, [Aulon] was told that never had so many men-at-arms been seen on their side [presumably the English side] as were there then.

He said that from this place, they went towards a very strong fortress of the enemy, called the fortress of Saint-Loup, which was immediately attacked by the French, and, with very little loss to them, was taken by assault; and all the enemy within were killed or taken. The fortress remained in the hands of the French.

He said that after this was done the Pucelle and those of her company withdrew into the city of Orléans, where they refreshed themselves and rested for that day.

He said that on the following day the Pucelle and her men, seeing the great victory over the enemy obtained by them the day before, sallied out from the town in good order to attack another fortress before the city, called the fortress of Saint-Jean-le-Blanc. To do this, given that they could not get to this fortress by land because the enemy had built another very strong fort at the end of the bridge of the city [the Tourelles], making it impossible for them to cross there, they decided to cross over to a certain island in the river Loire, and assemble there to take the fortress of Saint-Jean-le-Blanc. To cross to the other arm of the river Loire, two boats were brought, from which they made a bridge to reach this fortress.

He said that after this was done, they went towards this fortress, which they found quite deserted because as soon as the English there perceived the coming of the French, they fled and retreated to another stronger and greater fortress, called the fortress of the Augustins.

He said that, seeing that the French were not powerful enough to take the fortress, it was decided that they should return without doing anything more.

He said that, in order to return and cross more safely, the most famous and courageous men of war of the French side were ordered to remain behind [as a rearguard], in order to keep watch in case the enemy could strike during the retreat. My lord of Gaucourt, my lord of Villars, then Seneschal of Beaucaire, and the one who is testifying [Aulon] were ordered to do this.

He said that as the Frenchmen were withdrawing from the fortress of

Saint-Jean-le-Blanc to the island, the Pucelle and La Hire crossed together, each with a horse, in a boat from the other side of the island; and they mounted on these horses as soon as they had crossed, each with their lance in their hand. And as soon as they saw that the enemy was sallying out of the fortress to rush upon their people, immediately the Pucelle and La Hire, who were always in front to protect them, couched their lances and were the first to begin to drive into the enemy; and then each man followed them and began to strike against the English in such a manner that they forced them to retreat into the fortress of the Augustins.

[Jean d'Aulon then described how he himself led the French forces who broke through the defences of this fortress.]

And in this way, the Pucelle and those who were with her obtained victory over the enemy that day. And a great battle was won and the lords and their men remained in front of this place all that night with the Pucelle.

He also said that the next day, in the morning, the Pucelle sent to fetch all the lords and captains who were before the captured fort, to consult about what was to be done. By their advice, it was concluded and resolved to attack that day a great boulevard that the English had made before the fortress of the Tourelles, and that it was necessary to take possession of it before doing anything else. In order to put this into execution, the Pucelle, the captains and their men went from place to place before the boulevard this day, very early in the morning, and they assaulted it from all sides and made every effort to take it, so that they were before the boulevard from morning until sunset without being able to take or win it. And the lords and captains who were with her, seeing that they could not well gain it this day, considering how late it was and also that they were all very tired and worn out, agreed among them to sound the retreat for the army. This was done, and, at the sound of the trumpet call, each one retreated for that day. During this retreat, [Aulon] who had been carrying the standard of the Pucelle and still holding it upright in front of the boulevard was fatigued and worn-out, and gave the standard to one named Le Basque, who was with the Lord of Villars. And because [Aulon] knew Le Basque to be a brave man, and he feared that harm would come from the retreat, and that the fortress and the boulevard would remain in the hands of the enemy, he had the idea that if the standard were pushed ahead, due to the great affection in which he knew it was held by the soldiers, they could by this means win the boulevard. And then [Aulon] asked Le Basque if he would follow him when he entered and went to the foot of the boulevard; he said and swore that he would do this. And then [Aulon] entered the ditch and went up to the base of the side of the boulevard, covering himself with his shield for fear of the stones, and left his companion on the other side, believing that he would follow him step by step. But when the Pucelle saw her standard in the hand of Le Basque, and because she believed that she had lost it, as [Aulon] who had been carrying it had gone into the trench, she came and took the standard by the end in such a way that he had to let it go, crying, 'Ha! My standard! My standard!' And she shook the standard in such a way that the one who is testifying imagined that others might think that she was making a sign to the others by doing this. And then he who was speaking cried: 'Ha, Basque! Is this what you promised me?' And then La Basque tugged at the standard that he dragged it from the hand of the Pucelle, and after this, he went to [Aulon] and brought the standard. Because of these things, all those in the army of the Pucelle gathered together and rallied again, and assailed this boulevard with such great fierceness that, a short time afterwards, the boulevard and the fortress were taken by them, and abandoned by the enemy, and the French entered into the city of Orléans by the bridge.

And he said that on this very day, he had heard the Pucelle say: 'In the name of God, the town shall be entered this night by the bridge.' This done, the Pucelle and her followers returned into the town of Orléans, in which the one who was speaking had her injury dressed because she had been wounded by an arrow at the assault.

He also said that on the next day all the English who still remained before the town on the other side of the fortress of the Tourelles raised their siege and left, all confused and defeated. And so in this way the city was delivered from the hands of the enemy by means of the help of Our Lord and of the Pucelle.

Moreover he said that, some time after the King's return from his coronation, he was advised by his council, who were then at Meung-sur-Yèvre, that it was very necessary to recover the town of La Charité which the enemy was holding. But it would be necessary first to take the town of Saint-Pierre-le-Moûtier, which was likewise held by the enemy.

He said that to do this and to assemble men, the Pucelle went to the town of Bourges in which she held her muster, and from there she went to besiege the town of Saint-Pierre-le-Moûtier with a number of men-at-arms led by Lord d'Albret.[93]

He said that after the Pucelle and her followers had laid siege to the town for some time, an assault was ordered upon the town. And so it was done and those who were there did their very best to take it, but because of the great number of men-at-arms in the town, its great strength and also the marvellous resistance that those inside put up, the Frenchmen were compelled and forced to retreat. And at this time, [Aulon] was wounded by a shot in the heel, so that he could not stand up or walk without crutches. He saw that the Pucelle was left accompanied by very few of her own men or others, and feared that trouble would follow. He mounted a horse and went immediately to her aid, asking her what she was doing there alone in this way and why she had not retreated like the others. After taking her helmet from her head, she replied that she was not alone and that she still had in her company fifty thousand of her men and that she would not leave until she had taken the town.

And he said that at that time, whatever she said, she did not have with her more than four or five men, and this he knows for sure, and many others who also saw her. For this reason, he told her again that she should leave that place and withdraw to the rear as the others were doing. And then she told him to bring bundles of sticks and wood to make a bridge across the ditches of the town, so that they could better approach it. And as she said these words to him, she cried out in a loud voice: 'Everyone to the faggots and hurdles, to make the bridge!' This was immediately done and carried out afterwards, at which the one who is testifying was very astonished, for immediately the town was taken by assault, without much resistance at that time.

He said that all the deeds of the Pucelle seemed to him to be more divine and miraculous than otherwise, and that it was impossible for so young a maiden [*pucelle*] to do such things without the will and guidance of Our Lord.

He also said that for the space of a whole year, by the command of our lord the King, he remained in the company of the Pucelle and during that time he neither saw nor knew of anything in her which should not be in a good Christian; and he has always seen and known her to

93 Charles II d'Albret (d. 1471).

be of very good life and modest conversation in all and every one of her actions.

He also said that he knew this Pucelle to be a very devout creature; she showed her intense devotion in hearing the divine service of Our Lord, which she wanted to hear constantly, that is to say high mass on solemn days with the hours following,[94] in whatever place she was, and on other days low mass. And she was used to hearing mass every day, if possible.

He also said that many times he saw and knew that she confessed, received communion and did all that belongs to a good Christian, and that he never heard her swear, blaspheme or perjure the name of Our Lord or the saints when he was talking with her, for whatever reason or cause that might befall.

Moreover he said that, not withstanding that she was a young girl, beautiful and shapely, and that many times while helping her put on armour and otherwise he had seen her breasts and sometimes her naked limbs while dressing her wounds, and that she was often near him and also that he was vigorous, young and in good health, still, whatever sight or contact he might have had with the Pucelle, he was not moved by her body to any carnal desire towards her and nor were any of the other men or squires, as [Aulon] heard them say and state many times.

And he said that, in his opinion, she was a very good Christian, and that she must have been inspired, because she loved everything that a good Christian man or woman ought to love, and she especially loved a good honest man whom she knew to be of chaste life.

Moreover, he said that he heard many women say that they saw this Pucelle naked many times and knew about her secrets, and she never had the secret illness of women [i.e. menstruation], and that no one could ever know or perceive anything by her clothes, or otherwise.[95]

He also said that when the Pucelle had anything to do concerning military matters, she said to [Aulon] that her adviser had told her that she ought to do it.

He said that he asked her who was this adviser and she replied to him that there were three counsellors, of whom one always remained with

94 In other words, Joan recited certain prayers from the Breviary that were required to be said at fixed hours of the day or night as part of the Divine Office.

95 See page 48 above.

her, another went away but often came and visited her, and the third was the one with whom the two others consulted. And it happened that, on one occasion, among others, when [Aulon] prayed and begged her to show him the adviser; she replied that he was not worthy or virtuous enough to see them. And [Aulon] desisted from speaking or asking her about this.

And he firmly believed, as he said above, that, considering the deeds, actions and outstanding conduct of the Pucelle, she was full of all the virtue which could or should be in a good Christian.

102. The Sentence of Nullification (7 July 1456)

Source: Duparc (ed.), *Procès en nullité*, II, pp. 605–10.

Language: Latin

On the 7 July, the three judges, Jean Juvénal des Ursins, Archbishop of Reims, Guillaume Chartier, Bishop of Paris, and Richard Olivier de Longueil, Bishop of Coutances, gathered in the archepiscopal palace at Rouen. The Archbishop then read out the final sentence of the Nullification trial.

.... [We] consider that the actions of the deceased [Joan] were more worthy of admiration than condemnation; we are amazed at the judgement brought against her, which condemned her, by reason of its form and its substance; and we say that it is very difficult to bring a sure judgement in such questions because as the Blessed St Paul declared with regard to his own revelations, we do not know whether she had [experienced] them in physical form or as spirits and so we rely on God in this matter.

We declare first, as justice demands, that we decree that these [Twelve Articles, document 52] beginning with 'A certain woman,' inserted in the record of the so-called trial and the instrument of the so-called sentences brought against the said deceased [Joan], were and are extracted from the so-called trial record and from the so-called declarations of the deceased in a malicious, deceitful, slanderous manner with fraud and spitefulness. The truth was passed over in silence, and false assertions were introduced at many essential points, so that the minds of those who were deliberating and judging could be drawn towards another opinion. Numerous aggravating circumstances not contained in the trial record and in the declarations cited above were also added, without due cause, and nothing was said about

some circumstances that exonerated and justified her on many points.
Finally the forms of words were modified, changing the substance.
This is why we quash, reject and annul these articles as false,
extracted by slander and deceit, different from the testimony. We
have had them extracted from the trial record and here we order in
justice that they be torn up ...

We say and pronounce that we judge that this trial record and
sentences that contain deceit, slander, contradiction and manifest error
of law and of fact, as well as the aforesaid abjuration, the execution
and all that then ensured, were and are null, invalid, without effect or
value.

And nevertheless, as is necessary and required by reason, we quash,
suppress and annul them, removing all of their strength. We declare
that this Joan and the plaintiffs, her relatives, have not suffered or
incurred any mark or stain of infamy because of what has been said,
and that she was innocent and that she was justified in all of this. And,
insofar as it is necessary, we justify her in this completely.

We order the immediate carrying out of the execution of our sentence
and its solemn publication in two places in this city: straight away in
one, that is to say the square of Saint-Ouen, with a general procession
to start and a public sermon; on the following day, in the other at the
Old Market, that is to say where Joan died in a cruel and horrible fire,
with a solemn sermon, and with the erection there of a worthy cross
in her perpetual memory and to implore the salvation of her and all
the other faithful departed. With regard to this matter, we reserve to
ourselves the further execution, publication and clear notification of
our sentence in the cities and important places of this kingdom, as we
may see fit for the memory of this in the future, and anything which
may yet remain to be done.

V: THE MEMORY OF JOAN OF ARC

103. *Commentarii rerum memorabilium* by Pope Pius II (1459?)

Source: Aeneas Silvius Piccolomini, *Commentarii rerum memorabilium que temporibus suis contingerunt*, ed. A. von Heck, 2 vols, Vatican, 1984, I, pp. 381–7.

Language: Latin

Aeneas Silvius Piccolomini (1405–64), who was elected as Pope Pius II in 1458, wrote the only medieval papal autobiography. He had travelled to France shortly after the death of Joan of Arc as a secretary of Cardinal Albergati, a papal mediator, but his comments on the Pucelle were composed after the Bishop of Arras, Jean Jouffroy, had attacked her in an eulogy for the Duke of Burgundy delivered to the Congress of Mantua in 1459: the Bishop claimed that Charles VII was stifling public debate about Joan, presumably referring to the Nullification trial, and argued that she had in fact been a puppet of one of the French nobles who intended to restore Valois morale and spirit.[1]

Meanwhile, when the cause of France was almost desperate, a girl of sixteen years of age named Joan, the daughter of a poor farmer, when she was watching pigs in the country near Toul, was inspired by the holy spirit, as her deeds proved.

[Joan persuaded Robert de Baudricourt to give her an escort and send her to Charles VII].

The virgin, dressed in the clothing of a man, passed unharmed through all difficulties and went to the dauphin who was then at Bourges. Disheartened by so many reverses, he was by now not so much concerned about holding on to his kingdom, as about finding a place where he could live in safety as a private individual. In Spain, the King of Castile and of Leon, who was bound to the dauphin by ties of blood and friendship, was regarded as the most powerful prince: he had decided to hand over the care of the kingdom of France and of the Crown, and to receive a little corner of the earth there in which he could hide safely.

---

1 Joseph Kervyn de Lettenhove (ed.), *Chroniques relatives à l'histoire de Belgique sous la domination des ducs de Bourgogne*, 3 vols, Brussels, 1876, III, pp. 117–206.

While he was contemplating this, the virgin [*virgo*] arrived and sought an audience, having handed over the letters of the prefect [presumably Robert de Baudricourt]. The dauphin, concerned that this strange occurrence might be a trick, sent the girl [*puella*] to be examined by his own confessor, the Bishop of Castres [Gérard Machet], a most eminent theologian, and put her in the charge of noble matrons. When Joan was questioned about her faith, she replied in conformity with the Christian religion. When examined as to her character, she was found to be chaste and very honest. The examination lasted for many days. They found no deceit, guile or evil intent in her. The only difficulty was her dress. When asked why she had worn the garments of men that were forbidden to women, she replied that she was a virgin, and either outfit was suitable for a virgin. She had been instructed by God to wear men's dress and to use the arms of men. Having been examined, she was again sent before the dauphin. 'I have come to you, son of kings,' she said, 'at the command of God, not by my own counsel. He commands you to follow me. If you obey, I will restore your throne to you, and very soon, I will place the crown on your head at Reims' ...

The matter was discussed in council for some time with various opinions. Some said the girl [*puella*] was crazy, others that she was bewitched, others thought that she was inspired by the Holy Ghost, and these last referred to the facts that Bethulia and other cities had once been saved by women,[2] and that the kingdom of France had often been aided by divine influence; it might be that now too it was to be defended by a virgin sent by God, and that the task had been committed to the weaker sex so that the French might not trust in their own virtue with pride, as was their habit; in any case a girl whose advice was so full of sense could not be regarded as mad.

This opinion prevailed and they entrusted the matter of Orléans to the girl [*puella*]. A woman was made the commander of the war. Arms were brought, horses led up. The girl mounted the most spirited one and then she made this horse leap, run, and turn in circles, gleaming in her armour and brandishing her spear, just as in the stories told about Camilla.[3] When the nobles saw this, no one could be found that scorned the leadership of a woman. The most

2 Bethulia was the city that Judith delivered from the siege of Holofernes, according to the Book of Judith.

3 See footnote 148, page 55.

noble took up arms and eagerly followed the virgin and, when all was
ready, she set out on the journey.

[Aeneas offered an uneven account of the Pucelle's role at Orléans, Reims,
Paris and Compiègne.]

It happened that the virgin [*virginem*] was captured in battle and sold
to the English for ten thousand pieces of gold, and taken to Rouen, in
which place she was carefully examined as to whether she had dealings
with soothsayers or the devil, and what she thought about heretical
beliefs. They found nothing worthy of correction except her dressing
as a man and they did not think this worthy of the ultimate penalty.
She was put back into prison, having been warned of this punishment
if she wore men's clothes any more. She, who had learned to bear
arms, and delighted in the exercise of the soldier, was tempted by her
guards, who personally offered her a military cloak at one time, and
then a cuirass or a breastplate, or some armour at another time; sometimes she would unthinkingly put on men's garments or arms, not
knowing that she was putting on death. It is possible that the English,
who had been vanquished by her in so many battles, never regarded
themselves as entirely safe with the virgin alive, even though she was
a prisoner, and that they feared that she might escape or work some
magic and therefore sought an excuse for her death. When the judges
learned that the girl had taken the clothing of a man, they condemned
her to be burned as a relapse. She bore the flames with unshakable
and undaunted spirit. Her ashes were thrown into the river Seine so
that they could never be honoured.

Thus died Joan, an astonishing and marvellous virgin, who restored
the kingdom of France when it had collapsed and was almost torn
asunder, who inflicted so many heavy defeats upon the English, who,
having been made a commander of men, kept her purity unstained
among companies of soldiers, about whom no breath of scandal was
ever heard. Whether she was a divine work or a human invention, I
would find it difficult to say. Some think that, when the English cause
was prospering and the French nobles were at variance among themselves and thought no one fit to be commander, one shrewder than
the rest evolved the cunning scheme of declaring that a virgin had
been sent by heaven, and of giving her the command that she asked
for, since there was no man alive who would refuse to have God for
his leader. And so it happened that the conduct of the war and the
high command were entrusted to a girl. Nor would this have been

difficult to manage for the French, who believe everything that they hear. Yet it is most evident that it was by the command of the Pucelle that the siege of Orléans was raised, that it was by her arms that whole country between Bourges and Paris was subdued, that it was by her advice that Reims was recovered and the coronation was celebrated there, that it was under her command that Talbot was routed and his army cut to pieces [at the battle of Patay], that it was by her daring that the gate of Paris was burned, and that it was by her quick wit and industry that the fortune of French cause was restored. It is a matter that should be recorded, although future generations are likely to regard it with more wonder than credulity.

104. The English *Brut* chronicle (c.1464–1470)

Source: F. W. D. Brie (ed.), *Brut, or the Chronicles of England*, Early English Text Society, original series, 136, London, 1908, pp. 500–1.

Language: Middle English

The only English fifteenth-century chronicle to offer anything more than a passing reference to Joan of Arc was one contination of the *Brut* chronicle, probably composed between 1464 and 1470.[4] This account was copied by William Caxton in his *Polychronicon*, and thereby influenced the overtly hostile English views of Joan in the sixteenth century.[5]

About this time and before, the realm being in great misery and tribulation, the dauphin, with his party, began to make war, to take certain places and to harry to the Englishmen by means of his captains, that is to say Le Hire, Potonde, Sayntralles and especially a maid which they named 'la Pucelle' of God. This maid rode like a man, and was a valiant captain among them, and took upon herself many great

4 An earlier account, Continuation D, written around the time of Joan's capture, merely reported the battle at Compiègne and stated: 'And at that same journey was taken the witch of France that was called the "Pucelle"; and she was taken all armed as a man of arms; and by her craft of sorcery, all the Frenchmen and her company trusted for her to have overcome all the English people. But God was lord and master of that victory and discomfiture, and so she was taken, and brought and kept in hold by the king and his council all times at his commandment and will.' (Brie (ed.), *Brut, or the Chronicles of England*, p. 439).

5 Ranulph Higden, *Polychronicon Ranulphi Higden monachi Cestrensis: together with the English translations of John Trevisa and an unknown writer of the fifteenth century*, ed. Joseph R. Lumby, 9 vols, Rolls series, 41, London, 1882, VIII, p. 561. Caxton also printed this story in his version of the *Brut*, the *Chronicles of England*, published in 1480.

enterprises, so much so that they believed that they would recover all their losses by her; notwithstanding, at the last, after many great feats, by the help and prowess of Sir John Luxembourg, which was a noble captain of the Dukes of Burgundy, and many Englishmen, Picards and Burgundians, who were of our party, before the town of Compiègne, the 23rd day of May, the aforesaid Pucelle was taken in the field, armed like a man, and many other captains with her, and were all brought to Rouen; and there she was put in prison and there she was judged by the law to be burnt. And then she said that she was with child, whereby she was respited a while; but in the end, it was found that she was not with child, and then she was burnt in Rouen, and the other captains were put to ransom, and treated as men of war were well accustomed.

105. Remembering Joan in Orléans

(a) Chronique de l'établissement de la fête du 8 mai (1452?)

Source: P. Charpentier and C. Cuissard (eds), *Journal du siège d'Orléans [et du voyage de Reims]* 1428–29, *augmenté de plusieurs documents, notamment des comptes de ville,* Orléans, 1896, pp. 152–5.

Language: French

This short chronicle provides an account of the deliverance of Orléans and was probably written by someone with religious training who had been an eye-witness to these events. It survives in a manuscript in the Vatican Library, immediately before a transcription of the indulgences granted in June 1452 by Cardinal Guillaume d'Estouteville for the celebration of the feast of the liberation of the city (a document that makes no reference to Joan of Arc). It is therefore probable that the chronicle was written around 1452 as part of the effort to establish this feast.

Item, considering [the victories of Joan], the Bishop of Orléans, with all of the clergy, and also by the ordinance of my Lord of Dunois, the Duke of Orléans' brother, with the agreement of the council and also of the burghers, the townsmen and the inhabitants of Orléans, ordered a great procession for the eighth of May. And everyone was to carry a light, and the procession would go as far as the Augustins and everywhere where there had been battles. At each site where the forces of the town had been located, proper respect, services and prayers would be given, and the twelve magistrates of the town would each hold a candle in their hands; [and then] four would remain at [the cathedral of] Sainte-Croix, four at [the church of] Saint-Euverte and four at [the church of] Saint-Aignan. And the next day, mass would be said for the dead, and there they would offer the bread and the wine, and each magistrate would give eight deniers as an offering. And they would bring the chalices from the churches, and in particular, those of my lord St Aignan and my lord St Euverte, who were the guardians of the town of Orléans. For in this time it was rumoured that while the English had held the siege, they had witnessed two prelates dressed in pontifical clothing who came and walked around the walls of the town of Orléans ...[6]

One can never give too much praise to God and the saints, for everything that was done, was done by the grace of God. Thus everyone should participate in this procession with great devotion, especially the people of this town of Orléans considering that the people of Bourges in Berry [take part in a feast] solemnly on the Sunday after the Ascension, because [the deliverance of Orléans fell on the Sunday after the Ascension]. And many other towns do the same, for if Orléans had fallen into the hands of the English, the rest of the realm would have been seriously harmed. And to recognise the grace of God, which he desired to demonstrate in the town of Orléans by keeping it from its enemies, the procession should be continued and not abandoned ungratefully, for through such actions comes great strife. Everyone must go to the procession and carry a burning light in their hand. They return around the town, that is to say [walking] in front of the church of Notre-Dame-de-Saint-Paul where they should give great praise to Our Lady, and from there to [the cathedral of] Sainte-Croix and hear the sermon there, and the mass afterwards, and also as before, the vigils at [the church of] Saint Aignan, and the next day, the mass for all the dead.

And each person should praise and give thanks to God, for it may by chance be that there are at present many young people who would have difficulty believing that all this had occurred. But all must believe that this was true and the very great grace of God. For during

6 Saint Euverte (d. 391) and Aignan (d. 453) had been bishops of Orléans, and Aignan was regarded as the patron saint of the city; they were credited with saving the city from pagans. In the mystery play that was presented at Orléans to celebrate the victory in 1429, the two saints appealed directly to God: 'It is for these people that I would pray in their great need, that you should grant them peace and tranquillity; men who are wrongfully in great adversity, for no cause or reason, at the hands of men full of iniquity, to whom our home does not belong': V. L. Hamblin (ed.), *Le mistere du siège d'Orléans*, Geneva, 2002, pp. 305–6.

the siege, there was never any dissension between the men-at-arms and those of the town, even though they had previously hated each other like cats and dogs. When the [men-at-arms] joined forces with the town, they were like brothers and those of the town did not leave them wanting for any need if it was within their power to help. And for such loyal service the townsmen and inhabitants of the said town of Orléans were and remain in the good grace of the King, which he has shown them, and continues to show them day by day, as is revealed by the maintenance of the great privileges that he has given to them.

(b) *Journal du siège d'Orléans* (1467)

Source: Charpentier and Cuissard (eds), *Journal du siège d'Orléans*, pp. 76–89.

Language: French

This anonymous chronicle covers events from the start of the siege of Orléans on 12 October 1428 to the end of September 1429 and was almost certainly completed by 1467 when Pierre Soudan, whose father had taken part in the siege, was commissioned by the municipal leaders to submit a copy to the city archives. It combines a diary or register of the events written by an inhabitant of the city at the time of the siege, with additional information derived from Valois chroniclers such as Jean Chartier and the Berry Herald, and witnesses at the Nullification trial such as Dunois. After providing standard accounts of Joan's origins, journey to Chinon and initial meetings with Charles VII, the *Journal* then reported that Joan was brought into the city of Orléans late in the evening of Friday 29 April 1429, riding fully armed on a white horse.

Entering Orléans in this way, she had the Bastard of Orléans on her left, very richly armed and mounted. Afterward came many other nobles and brave lords, squires, captains and men-at-arms, as well as some from the garrison, and also the citizens of Orléans, who had gone ahead of her. Moreover the other men-at-arms and citizens of Orléans came to receive her, carrying many torches and rejoicing as much as if they had seen God descend among them, and not without reason, because they had endured much worry, labour and pain, and what was worse, great fear of not being rescued and of losing their bodies and goods. But they all felt already comforted, as though freed of the siege by the divine virtue that they were told resided in that simple Pucelle, whom they regarded with great affection, men as much as women and little children. And there was an amazing crowd pressing to touch her, or the horse on which she rode, so much so that one of those who were bearing the torches came so close to her standard that the pennant caught fire. So she spurred her horse, turning him gently toward the pennant whose fire she extinguished, just as if she had extensive military expertise; the men-at-arms considered this a great marvel, as did the citizens of Orléans, who accompanied her throughout the city, rejoicing greatly ...

[A week later, early in the morning of Saturday 7 May] the French attacked the Tourelles and the boulevard, while the English were attempting to fortify it. And there was a spectacular assault during which many great feats of arms were performed, both by those attacking and by those defending it ... And among the others wounded there [was] the Pucelle, struck by an arrow between the shoulder and the throat so deeply that it passed right through. All the attackers were very distressed and incensed by this, and especially the Bastard of Orléans and the other captains who came before her and said to her that it would be much better to leave the assault until the following day. But she heartened them with many beautiful and bold words, exhorting them to keep up their courage. Not wishing to believe her, they abandoned the assault and went to the rear, planning to have their artillery withdrawn until the following day. She was very distressed by this and said to them: 'In the name of God, you will enter inside very shortly, do not have any doubt, and the English will have no more strength against you. So rest yourselves a little, drink and eat.' This they did because they obeyed her in the highest degree. And when they had drunk, she said to them: 'Return by God to the assault once again, because, make no mistake, the English will not have any more strength to defend themselves, and their Tourelles and their boulevards will be taken.'

And having said this, she left her standard and went on her horse to a place nearby to pray to Our Lord, and said to a gentleman who was close by there: 'Watch out for when the tip of my standard touches the boulevard.' Shortly afterwards, he said to her: 'Joan, the tip touches there!' And then she replied to him: 'All is yours; enter there!' These words were soon afterwards recognised as a prophecy because when the brave leaders and men-at-arms who were then remaining inside Orléans saw that they meant to attack again, some of them sallied out of the city across the bridge. Because many arches had been broken, they took a carpenter with them and they carried gutters and ladders, from which they made gangplanks. And seeing that these were not long enough to span the two ends of one of the broken arches, they joined a little piece of wood to one of the longest gutters and fixed it so that it held ... Those who had crossed over plunged into the assault with their other comrades. It lasted for a short time afterwards, because as soon as they had begun again, the English lost all their strength to resist any more and tried to enter the boulevard inside the Tourelles. Although a few of them were able to save themselves, the four or five hundred soldiers there were all killed or drowned, except for a some small number who were taken prisoner; none of these [were] great lords, given that Glasdale ... and many other knights, bannerets and noblemen of England were drowned, because while they were trying to save themselves, the bridge collapsed under them. This was a very great shock for the strength of the English and a great injury to the brave Frenchmen who would have been able to receive a great sum of money for their ransom. Nevertheless they celebrated greatly and praised Our Lord for this great victory that he had given to them. And were certainly right to do this because it was said that this assault, which lasted from the morning until sunset, was so strongly fought on both sides that it was one of the greatest feats of arms that had been done for a very long time. And it was also a miracle of Our Lord, done at the request of St Aignan and St Euvertre, formerly bishops and patrons of Orléans, as it clearly appeared according to the common opinion, and especially to those people who were that day brought inside the city. One of them attested that for him, and for the other Englishmen inside the Tourelles and the boulevards, it seemed that when they were attacked they saw an astonishing number of people, as if the whole world was assembled there. For this, all the clergy and the people of Orléans very devoutly sang *Te Deum laudamus* and had all the city bells rung, very humbly thanking Our Lord and the two saint confessors for this glorious divine comfort. They celebrated everywhere, giving wondrous praise to their valiant defenders, and especially and above all others to Joan the Pucelle. She spent that night in the fields with the lords, captains, and men-at-arms, both to guard the Tourelles that had been so valiantly conquered, and to learn if the English on the [northwestern side around the church] of Saint-Laurent would march out to aid or to avenge their comrades. But they did not attempt it.

[The following day, Sunday 8 May 1429, Joan held the French back from attacking the English, who soon decided to abandon the siege. The victory was marked by a solemn procession through the city.]

SELECT BIBLIOGRAPHY

Allmand, C. T. *The Hundred Years War: England and France at war, c.1300–c.1450*, revised edition, Cambridge, 2001.

Ankarloo, B. and Clark, S. (eds) *Witchcraft and Magic in Europe: the middle ages*, London, 2002.

Armstrong, C. A. J. *England, France and Burgundy in the Fifteenth Century*, London, 1983.

Astell, A. and Wheeler, B. (eds) *Joan of Arc and Spirituality*, Basingstoke, 2003.

Bailey, M. D. 'From sorcery to witchcraft: clerical conceptions of magic in the later middle ages', *Speculum*, LXXVI, 2001, pp. 960–90.

Bailey, M. D. *Battling Demons: witchcraft, heresy and reform in the late middle ages*, Philadelphia, 2003.

Bailey, M. D. and Peters, E. 'A Sabbat of demonologists: Basel, 1431–1440', *The Historian*, LXV, 2003, pp. 1375–95.

Beaune, C. *The Birth of an Ideology: myths and symbols of nationhood in later medieval France*, Berkeley, 1992.

Blockmans, W. and Prevenier, W. *Promised Lands: the Low Countries under Burgundian rule, 1369–1530*, Philadelphia, 1999.

Brown, C. J. 'Allegorical design and image-making in fifteenth-century France: Alain Chartier's Joan of Arc', *French Studies*, LIII, 1999, pp. 385–404.

Brown-Grant, R. '"Hee! Quel honneur au femenin sexe!" Female heroism in Christine de Pizan's *Ditié de Jehanne d'Arc*', *Journal of the Institute of Romance Studies*, V, 1997, pp. 123–33.

Contamine, P. *De Jeanne d'Arc aux guerres d'Italie. Figures, images et problèmes du XVe siècle*, Orléans, 1994.

Contamine, P. *Des pouvoirs en France, 1300–1500*, Paris, 1992.

Crane, S. 'Clothing and gender definition: Joan of Arc', *Journal of Medieval and Early Modern Studies*, XXVI, 1996, pp. 297–320 [reprinted in D. N. Baker, *Inscribing the Hundred Years' War in French and English Cultures*, Albany, 2000, pp. 195–219].

Crane, S. *The Performance of Self: ritual, clothing and identity during the Hundred Years War*, Philadelphia, 2002.

Curry, A. *The Hundred Years War, 1337–1452*, 2nd edition, Basingstoke, 2003.

Curry, A. 'The "coronation expedition" and Henry VI's court in France, 1430 to 1432', in J. Stratford (ed.), *The Lancastrian Court: proceedings of the 2001 Harlaxton Symposium*, Donington, 2003, pp. 29–52.

Cuttler, S. H. *The Law of Treason and Treason Trials in Later Medieval France*, Cambridge, 1981.

DeVries, K. *Joan of Arc: a military leader*, Stroud, 1999.

Elliott, D. 'Seeing double: Jean Gerson, the discernment of spirits, and Joan of Arc', *American Historical Review*, CVII, 2001, pp. 26–54.

Elliott, D. *Proving Woman: female spirituality and inquisitional culture in the later middle ages*, Princeton, 2004.

Famiglietti, R. C. *Royal Intrigue: crisis at the court of Charles VI, 1392–1420*, New York, 1986.

Fraioli, D. 'The literary image of Joan of Arc: prior influences', *Speculum*, LVI, 1981, pp. 811–30.

Fraioli, D. *Joan of Arc: the early debate*, Woodbridge, 2000.

Francq, H. G. 'Jean Gerson's theological treatise and other memoirs in defence of Joan of Arc', *Revue de l'Université d'Ottawa*, XLI, 1971, pp. 58–80.

Garber, M. B. *Vested Interests: cross-dressing and cultural anxiety*, New York, 1992.

Guenée, B. *Un meurtre, une société. L'assassinat du duc d'Orléans, 23 novembre 1407*, Paris, 1992.

Hanawalt, B. A. and Noakes, S. 'Trial transcript, romance propaganda: Joan of Arc and the French body politic', *Modern Language Quarterly*, LVII, 1996, pp. 605–31.

Hotchkiss, V. R. *Clothes Make the Man: female cross-dressing in medieval Europe*, New York, 1996.

Housley, N. *Religious Warfare in Europe, 1400–1536*, Oxford, 2002.

Jackson, R. A. *Vive le roi! A history of the French coronation from Charles V to Charles X*, Chapel Hill, 1984.

Jeanne d'Arc: une époque, un rayonnement. Colloque d'histoire médiévale, Orléans, Octobre, 1979, Paris, 1982.

Jones, M. K. '"Gardez mon corps, sauvez ma terre". Immunity from war and the lands of a captive knight: the siege of Orléans (1428–1429) revisited', in M-J. Arn (ed.), *Charles d'Orléans in England (1415–1440)*, Cambridge, 2000, pp. 9–26.

Kelly, H. A. *Inquisition and Other Trial Procedures in the Medieval West*, London, 2001.

Kennedy, A. J. 'La date du *Ditié de Jehanne d'Arc*: réponse à Anne D. Lutkus et Julia M. Walker', in E. Hicks (ed.), *Au champ des escriptures. IIIe colloque international sur Christine de Pizan*, Paris, 2000, pp. 759–70.

Lea, H. C. *The Inquisition of the Middle Ages: its organization and operation*, London, 1963.

Lewis, P. S. *Essays in Later Medieval French History*, London, 1985.

Lewis, P. S. *Later Medieval France: the polity*, London, 1968.

Lightbody, C. W. *The Judgements of Joan: Joan of Arc, a study in cultural history*, London, 1961.

Little, R. G. *The Parlement of Poitiers: war, government and politics in France, 1418–1436*, London, 1984.

Luce, S. *Jeanne d'Arc à Domremy: recherches critiques sur les origines de la mission de la Pucelle*, Paris, 1886.

McInerney, M. B. *Eloquent Virgins from Thecla to Joan of Arc: the rhetoric of virginity from Thecla to Joan of Arc*, Basingstoke, 2003.

Pernoud, R. and Clin, M-V. *Joan of Arc: her story*, revised and trans. J. Duquesnay Adams, New York, 1998.

Perroy, E. *The Hundred Years War*, trans. W.B. Wells, London, 1951.

Peyronnet, G. 'Gerson, Charles VII et Jeanne d'Arc: la propagande au service de la guerre', *Revue d'Histoire Ecclésiastique*, LXXXIV, 1989, pp. 334–70.

Pollard, A. J. *John Talbot and the War in France, 1427–1453*, London, 1983.

Potter, D. (ed.) *France in the Later Middle Ages*, Oxford, 2004.

Quicherat, J-E-J. *New Aspects of the Case History of Jeanne d'Arc*, trans. H. G. Francq, Brandon, 1971.

Schnerb, B. *Armagnacs et Bourguignons, la maudite guerre*, Paris, 1988.

Sullivan, K. *The Interrogation of Joan of Arc*, Minneapolis, 1999.

Thompson, G. L. *Paris and its People under English Rule. The Anglo-Burgundian regime, 1420–1436*, Oxford, 1991.

Vale, M. G. A. 'France at the end of the Hundred Years War (c.1420–1461)', in C. T. Allmand (ed.), *The New Cambridge Medieval History, VII: c.1415–c.1500*, Cambridge, 1998, pp. 392–407.

Vale, M. G. A. *Charles VII*, London, 1974.

Van Herwaarden, J. (ed.) *Joan of Arc: reality and myth*, Hilversum, 1994.

Vauchez, A. *Laity in the Middle Ages: religious beliefs and devotional practices*, ed. D. E. Bornstein and trans. M. J. Schneider, Notre Dame, 1993.

Vaughan, R. *Philip the Good: the apogée of the Burgundian state*, Harlow, 1970.

Verger, J. 'The University of Paris at the end of the Hundred Years War', in J. W. Baldwin and R. Goldthwaite (eds), *Universities in Politics: case studies from the late middle ages and early modern periods*, Baltimore, 1972, pp. 47–78.

Voaden, R. *God's Words, Women's Voices: the discernment of spirits in the writing of late-medieval visionaries*, Woodbridge, 1999.

Warner, M. 'The Anglo-French Dual Monarchy and the house of Burgundy, 1420–1435: the survival of an alliance', *French History*, XI, 1997, pp. 103–30.

Warner, M. *Joan of Arc: the image of female heroism*, London, 1981.

Waugh, W. T. 'Joan of Arc in English sources of the fifteenth century', in J. G. Edwards, V. H. Galbraith and E. F. Jacob (eds), *Historical Essays in Honour of James Tait*, Manchester, 1953, pp. 387–98.

Wayman, D. G. 'The Chancellor and Jeanne d'Arc', *Franciscan Studies*, XVII, 1957, pp. 273–305.

Wheeler, B. and Wood, C. T. (eds) *Fresh Verdicts on Joan of Arc*, New York, 1996.

Wood, C. T. *Joan of Arc and Richard III: sex, saints and government in the middle ages*, Oxford, 1988.

INDEX

INDEX